Harley  Plays: One

The Voysey Inheritance, Waste, The Secret Life, Rococo, Vote by Ballot

Harley Granville Barker (1877–1946) was the most brilliant British director of the first quarter of this century. His best known plays, including *Waste* (banned by the Lord Chamberlain), were written as contributions to his Company's repertoire of provocative modern drama for a national theatre. A major retrospective of his work in recent years includes the Royal National Theatre's production of the *The Voysey Inheritance* in 1989 and productions of *The Madras House*, *The Secret Life* and *Voysey* at the Lyceum Theatre for the Edinburgh Festival in 1992.

This is a companion to the forthcoming volume, *Granville Barker Plays: Two*, which will contain *The Marrying of Ann Leete*, *The Madras House*, *His Majesty* and *Farewell to the Theatre*.

Harley Granville Barker's plays include: *The Marrying of Ann Leete*, written 1899, first presented by Stage Society, 1902, first public production by the Royal Shakespeare Company at the Aldwych Theatre, London 1975; *The Voysey Inheritance*, written 1903–5, first produced at Court Theatre, 1905, revised version produced at Sadler's Wells Theatre, 1934; *Waste*, written 1906–7, first presented by Stage Society, 1907, second version written 1925–6, first produced at Westminster Theatre, 1936; *The Madras House*, written 1909–10, first produced 1910 at Duke of York's Theatre, revised 1925 for production at Ambassadors' Theatre; *The Secret Life*, written 1919–22, first professional production at the Orange Tree Theatre, Richmond, 1989; *His Majesty*, written 1923–28, first produced at the Edinburgh International Festival at St. Bride's Centre by Orange Tree Theatre Company in 1992.

in the same series

Aeschylus (two volumes)
Jean Anouilh
John Arden
Arden & D'Arcy
Aristophanes (two volumes)
Peter Barnes
Brendan Behan
Aphra Behn
Edward Bond (four volumes)
Bertolt Brecht (three volumes)
Howard Brenton (two volumes)
Büchner
Bulgakov
Calderón
Anton Chekhov
Caryl Churchill (two volumes)
Noël Coward (five volumes)
Sarah Daniels
Eduardo De Filippo
David Edgar (three volumes)
Euripides (three volumes)
Dario Fo
Michael Frayn (two volumes)
Max Frisch
Gorky
Harley Granville Barker
Henrik Ibsen (six volumes)
Lorca (three volumes)
Marivaux
Mustapha Matura
David Mercer
Arthur Miller (three volumes)
Anthony Minghella
Molière
Tom Murphy (two volumes)
Peter Nichols (two volumes)
Clifford Odets
Joe Orton
Louise Page
A. W. Pinero
Luigi Pirandello
Stephen Poliakoff
Terence Rattigan (two volumes)
Ntozake Shange
Sophocles (two volumes)
Wole Soyinka
David Storey
August Strindberg (three volumes)
J. M. Synge
Ramón del Valle-Inclán
Frank Wedekind
Oscar Wilde

HARLEY GRANVILLE BARKER

Plays: One

The Voysey Inheritance (1934 revision)
Waste (1926 revision)
The Secret Life
Rococo
Vote by Ballot

with an introduction by Margery Morgan

Methuen Drama

METHUEN WORLD CLASSICS

This edition first published in Great Britain 1993
by Methuen Drama
an imprint of Reed International Books Ltd
Michelin House, 81 Fulham Road, London SW3 6RB
and Auckland, Melbourne, Singapore and Toronto
and distributed in the United States of America by HEB Inc.,
361 Hanover Street, Portsmouth, New Hampshire NH 03801 3959.

Reprinted 1997

ISBN 0–413–67530–0

A CIP catalogue record for this book is available at the British Library

Front cover: *The Breakfast Table* (1884) by John Singer Sargent, oil on
canvas, 21¾ × 18¼ inches. Bequest of Grenville L Winthrop, courtesy
of Fogg Art Museum, Harvard University, Cambridge, Mass., USA.
(1943.150)

Typeset by Deltatype Ltd, Ellesmere Port, South Wirral, in 10/11 Plantin
Printed and bound in Great Britain by Cox & Wyman Ltd,
Reading, Berkshire

Contents

A Chronology

1877   Born, 25 November, in an apartment in Sheffield Terrace, Kensington, first child and only son of a young surveyor and his half-Italian, half-Scottish wife, who earned her living with drawing-room and platform recitations.

1882   Birth of his only sister, Grace.

1891   After years of reciting in his mother's programme, Granville Barker appeared with a company of juveniles in a dramatisation of Anstey's *Vice Versa* at Harrogate Spa Rooms, in May. Then embarked on six months' training for the stage with Sarah Thorne, lessee of the Theatre Royal, Margate.

1892   First London engagement, as Third Young Man in *The Poet and the Puppets*, a skit on Oscar Wilde, at the Comedy Theatre.

1894   Understudied during Florence Farr's season at the Royalty Theatre, when Shaw's *Arms and the Man* and Yeats's *Land of Heart's Desire* were first performed. Appeared in charity performance of *King Robert of Sicily*, at the Lyric Theatre in July. The cast included his mother and sister, Berte Thomas, Ben Webster (in the title role) and the young Clara Butt. (May have been his first production.)

1895–6   Toured with Ben Greet's Company, playing minor roles in Shakespeare plays. Wrote *The Family of the Oldroyds*, first of a series of unpublished plays, in collaboration with fellow-actor, Berte Thomas.

1897   July, played Hastings, in *She Stoops to Conquer*,
           to Gordon Craig's Young Marlow, at Kingston-
           on-Thames.

1899   Production of *The Weather-Hen* by Granville
           Barker and Berte Thomas at Terry's Theatre,
           then at the Comedy. Played lead in *Richard II*
           for William Poel's Elizabethan Stage Society.
           Joined committee working for a National
           Theatre, along with Gilbert Murray and William
           Archer.

1900   Involved with the newly-founded Stage Society,
           acting in plays by Ibsen, Hauptmann and Shaw
           (especially as Marchbanks in *Candida*), and
           directing short plays by Maeterlinck, Yeats and
           Fiona MacLeod.

1901   Joined the Fabian Society.

1902   Directed his own play, *The Marrying of Ann
           Leete*, for the Stage Society, and played Frank in
           the Society's presentation of Shaw's banned *Mrs
           Warren's Profession*. Played Osric in *Hamlet* for
           Forbes Robertson at the Lyric Theatre.

1903   10 August, took the lead in William Poel's
           production of Marlowe's *Edward II*.

1904   *Scheme and Estimates for a National Theatre*, by
           William Archer and Granville Barker, privately
           printed and distributed. Barker's productions of
           Shakespeare's *Two Gentlemen of Verona* and
           Euripides's *Hippolytus* (translated by Gilbert
           Murray) led to the first of the Vedrenne-Barker
           seasons at the Court Theatre, Sloane Square.
           First production of *Prunella* by Laurence
           Housman and Granville Barker in December.

1905   February, first production of *The Voysey
           Inheritance*.

1906   24 April, marriage of Granville Barker to Lillah

McCarthy, leading actress in the Court Theatre Company.

1907   Elected to Executive of the Fabian Society. The Vedrenne-Barker management closed at the Court Theatre in May, re-opening at the Savoy Theatre in autumn. *Waste*, scheduled for November, was banned by the Lord Chamberlain.

1908   Visited USA on invitation of would-be sponsors of an American national theatre, but the scheme fell through for lack of a suitable building. On tour in Dublin, Barker almost died of typhoid fever.

1909   Visited theatres in Germany. Returned to direct Galsworthy's *Strife* to be followed by *Justice*. Albert Barker, his father, died of tuberculosis in France.

1910   Principal director of plays for Charles Frohman's Repertory Theatre at the Duke of York's. *The Madras House* produced, alongside Shaw's *Misalliance*. Season closed prematurely at the death of King Edward VII. Visited Royalty Theatre, Glasgow, as actor and director, lecturing on 'A Citizens' Theatre'.

1911   Translated Schnitzler's *Anatol* dialogues, performing them at the Little Theatre, with Nigel Playfair and Lillah McCarthy. *Rococo* presented there in October.

1912   Revolutionary productions of Shakespeare's *A Winter's Tale* and *Twelfth Night* at the Savoy Theatre.

1913   In management at the St James's Theatre, until money ran out, directing Molière, Ibsen, Shaw, Maeterlinck, *etc.*, including *The Harlequinade* by D C Calthrop and Granville Barker. Took a long lease of the Kingsway Theatre, with Lillah, and produced Arnold Bennett's *The Great Adventure*, which ran there for twenty months.

1914   Visited Russia to observe Stanislavsky's Moscow Art Theatre at work. Celebrated production of *A Midsummer Night's Dream* at the Savoy Theatre. In November, presented Masefield's *Philip the King*, at Covent Garden, and Hardy's *The Dynasts* at the Kingsway. Wrote *Vote by Ballot*, probably early in the year.

1915   American tour, most remarkable for outdoor, arena performances of Greek tragedies.

1916   Wrote *Farewell to the Theatre*. Enlisted in the Army, later transferred to Intelligence. Wrote *The Red Cross in France*, based on a visit to the Front.

1917   Grace Barker, his sister, died of tuberculosis, in France.

1918   Translated Sacha Guitry's *Deburau*, first produced in America. Divorce from Lillah McCarthy and marriage to wealthy American authoress, Helen Huntington.

1919   Became first Chairman of the British Drama League.

1920   Directed G M Sierra's *The Romantic Young Lady* (first of the translations of Spanish plays made collaboratively with Helen) at the Royalty Theatre. Began to hyphenate his name.

1921   Directed Maeterlinck's *The Betrothal* at the Gaiety Theatre. The Granville-Barkers acquired a country house in Devon.

1922   Published *The Exemplary Theatre*.

1923   Published *The Secret Life*, 'The Heritage of the Actor', in the *Quarterly Review*, and long Prefaces

to the first three volumes of *The Players'
Shakespeare*; also, with Helen, *Collected Plays* of
Sierra in English.

1925   Revised and directed *The Madras House* at the
Ambassadors' Theatre. Gave British Academy
lecture, 'From *Henry V* to *Hamlet*'. Break with
Shaw. Published English version of Jules
Romains's *Doctor Knock*. His mother died at her
home in Monte Carlo.

1926   Re-wrote *Waste* for a production which did not
materialise.

1927   Publication of first collected volume of revised
Prefaces to Shakespeare, English version of *Six
Gentlemen in a Row* by Jules Romains and
English versions of *Four Plays* by Serafín and
Joaquín Álvarez Quintero, with Helen.

1928   *His Majesty* published.

1929   Elected President of the Royal Society of
Literature.

1930   Published *A National Theatre* and second series
of *Prefaces to Shakespeare*. Gave Clark Lectures
at Cambridge, published as *On Dramatic Method*.

1932   Publication of *Four Comedies* by S and J Á
Quintero, in English versions by Helen and
Harley Granville-Barker.

1934   Co-directed *The Voysey Inheritance* with Harcourt
Williams at the Old Vic. Co-edited *A Companion
to Shakespeare Studies* with G B Harrison.

1936   Co-directed the first public production of *Waste*
with Michael MacOwan at the Westminster
Theatre.

1937   Became Director of the British Institute in Paris.
Gave Romanes Lecture at Oxford (*On Poetry in
Drama*).

1940   Directed *King Lear* at the Old Vic in association
            with Lewis Casson (John Gielgud as Lear,
            Jessica Tandy as Cordelia). He and Helen
            escaped from France and made their way to New
            York.

1941–2   Worked for British Information Services in New
            York.

1942–44   Gave lectures at Toronto, Harvard and
            Princeton, which formed the basis of further
            Prefaces to Shakespeare.

1945   Published 'A Theatre that Might Be' in *Theatre
            Arts Monthly*, July. Returned to England and
            thence to Paris.

1946   Died of arterio-sclerosis on 31 August.

1947   Fifth series of *Prefaces to Shakespeare* published
            posthumously.

                                    compiled by Margery Morgan

Introduction

Granville Barker was thrust into the theatre with as little option as an organ grinder's monkey. No one in his generation did more to change it. On the basis of outstanding, persistently acquired theatrical expertise, he wrote a handful of original plays. Like Bernard Shaw's, which Barker introduced to the theatre-going public, these are not just period pieces but present issues thought through from first principles which concern us today as much as ever they did; and they bring to bear the viewpoint of an unusual mind and personality.

His mother was the dominant figure in Granville Barker's upbringing. Twenty-nine when she married her twenty-one-year-old husband, she was an early example of those children of the clergy who were attracted into the theatre in the second half of Queen Victoria's reign. (Violet and Irene Vanbrugh and Sybil Thorndike were later instances of the trend.) One of a large family, whose father had become encumbered with debts on the building of a church in a poor part of London, Mary Elizabeth Bozzi-Granville turned to a peculiarly Victorian form of entertainment as a reciter of poetry on public platforms, or engaged to entertain guests in private drawing-rooms. As Mrs Albert Barker, she was well-known and admired by fellow professionals, and many remembered her bringing on her small son, dressed in a sailor suit, to recite 'The boy stood on the burning deck . . .' Ellen Terry's son, Gordon Craig, made his first stage appearance, with Henry Irving's company, at about the same age, but fitted in an education at Bradfield College and Heidelberg before taking up acting regularly at seventeen. Granville Barker seems to have had no such opportunities. We get a glimpse of him at thirteen, in Harrogate, playing Dr Grimstone in Anstey's *Vice Versa*, a fantasy of schoolboys changing places with their masters, which may have been more fun.

By the standards of his own family, he was under-educated. Both his grandfathers were university men who had written and published books. His paternal grandfather's bent was scientific; his mother's father had published a three-volume 'political and social' novel anonymously, under the title of *The Dawn of the Twentieth Century*, when Granville Barker was nearly five. The great man of the family, the Italian *émigré*, Augustus Bozzi (1783–1870), who took the name of Granville along with British nationality, had been of another order of distinction: a Fellow of the Royal Society, widely travelled friend of great men, a physician to British and Russian royalty, founder of clinics for the poor of London, and a voluminous author. The child on the stage had models to kindle his ambitions.

Mrs Barker drew on her theatrical contacts and knowledge to launch her son carefully. She took him for some months before his fourteenth birthday to Sarah Thorne, lessee of the Theatre Royal, Margate, a respected professional who ran a school to train aspirants for the stage. Here he met Berte Thomas, nine years older, but also a novice, who wrote a play which Sarah Thorne put on at the theatre. Barker took note and later approached Thomas with the suggestion that they should try writing plays together. Manuscripts of three survive from about 1895 to 1898 and make it clear that the younger man was always the dominant partner in this enterprise. Thomas admitted to becoming little more than a sounding-board and an amanuensis. One play, *The Weather-Hen*, was produced in London in 1899, over both their names, and was praised for its freshness and individuality.

Meanwhile, Barker had served a further apprenticeship under Ben Greet, an ex-schoolmaster whose touring companies had, since 1886, offered young players the best opportunity there was at that time for gaining wide experience in Shakespeare and the classics of English drama. Small parts in several West End productions gave him a taste of the conditions prevailing in the London theatre and led him, with a group of like-minded friends, to join the Stage Society, founded in 1899 to give club performances of Ibsen's *Ghosts* and other distinguished modern plays which had no chance of production in the English public theatre of that period. In the context of the Stage Society he got to know Bernard Shaw, who had written a number of unperformed plays – some said unactable – and William Archer, theatre critic and proselytiser for Ibsen, and he renewed acquaintance with the Greek scholar, Gilbert Murray.

Out of this conjunction came a revolution in the theatre. The term, 'National Theatre', is now identified with a 'brutalist' building on London's South Bank, though it is occasionally remarked that the Royal Shakespeare Company is a national theatre company too. The building has provided an image of 'Establishment' power, more than paternalism, open to attack apart from any record of work. Ironically, the subsequent prefixing of 'National' with 'Royal' has further blurred the meaning the original term had for the National Theatre Committee, on which the young Barker sat alongside his more distinguished seniors at the beginning of this century. They were in fierce and total agreement that what they wanted was a living theatre, not a monument (for which there was a rival committee). They wanted to break the stranglehold of purely commercial managements on imagination, innovation and artistic quality, which actively discouraged authors of talent from writing plays. They were also keenly aware of the limitations upon actor-managers ever fearful of bankruptcy, which drove them, also, to cut rehearsal time to a minimum and to rely on long-running productions in order to maximise profits. Another enemy was the 'star' system, responsible – even in Irving's theatre – for neglect of the standard of acting among 'supporting' players. Audiences, too, were at fault: ignorant of the general excellence which could be achieved under other conditions, they allowed 'what the public wants' to become an excuse for poverty of material and slovenliness of execution.

The existence of the Comédie Française in Paris certainly cast its shadow on the Committee's discussions and on the decision that Archer and Granville Barker should prepare a 'blue book' (like the report and recommendations of a parliamentary commission) dealing with the unit of a single theatre, for distribution to politicians open to persuasion, leaders of the theatrical profession and other persons of influence who were seriously interested in the arts. A note in the text of *A National Theatre, Scheme and Estimates*, on sale to the public in 1907, pointed out that the model offered could be used for any number of other theatres, in the provinces or in other parts of the Empire. By that time, Granville Barker had given a practical demonstration, at the Court Theatre from 1904 to 1907, of what their alternative theatre would be like. It put him at the head of the theatrical *avant-garde* and identified him with a cause he was to pursue in various ways throughout the rest of his life, even in his final years as the 'king over the water'. This dedication may well have limited the number of plays he wrote; certainly it helped determine some of their characteristics. These plays are sometimes criticised for the size of cast they require and the 'uneconomical' introduction of characters who appear in one scene only – as if this were an artistic failing, rather than a financial consideration. (The same criticism is not levelled at Chekhov or Brecht.) The dirtiest words the young Granville Barker knew were 'commercial' and 'market'. He wanted a large, permanent company, giving employment and training to many actors – training through such a rich variety of experience that any of them could take on the demanding roles of *Waste*, for instance, which even today are thought to require expensive talent. Yet it is significant that the Court Theatre enterprise went by the title of 'the Vedrenne-Barker Seasons', J E Vedrenne being the business manager.

The idea of opposing the long-run system with a repertory of plays alternating in the programmes – a pattern now familiar from the practice of the main subsidised theatres – proved possible only in modified form. But room was made for new work to be seen which showed promise rather than achievement, and actors were given a variety of parts in different types of play, which saved them from the staleness of repetition. Although there was a regular core of actors, paid equally, it was not possible to cast all the plays from a permanent company; guest actors' sympathy with the experiment was tested by their willingness to take a much lower fee than they could expect elsewhere. Granville Barker himself had to play a number of leading roles for economic reasons, when no one else suitable was available. So he appeared, for instance, as Tanner in *Man and Superman*, Professor Cusins in *Major Barbara* (the character based on Gilbert Murray) and Dubedat in *The Doctor's Dilemma* and became closely identified in the public mind with Bernard Shaw, the writer he had proved to be a brilliant, actable dramatist, and who had indeed become a close associate and friend.

Much of Barker's time at the Court was taken up in seeking out new plays, persuading established authors who had made their reputations as novelists to come up with pieces for the theatre, or working with novices to get their efforts into stageworthy shape and, as a dramatist himself, supplying original plays to go into the repertory: first, completing *The Voysey Inheritance*, then going on to write *Waste*, only to have performance banned by the Lord Chamberlain at the last moment. (In essentials, this history was to be repeated by George Devine's English Stage Company at the same theatre in the 1950s and 1960s.) He would have preferred not to act, but to be a full-time director in the modern sense, bringing unity of conception and style to serve the play, and helping the actors to realise it as fully as possible. He was the first of a new breed in the English public theatre. Gordon Craig had pointed the way with a number of semi-private performances, from 1900 to 1902. Deciding that this country did not want the kind of work he wished to do, Craig took himself abroad for the rest of his life and, in fact, achieved few more theatrical productions. Primarily a designer-director, Craig made it clear in an essay *On the Art of the Theatre*, first published in 1905, that he had little time for actors, whose oversize egos were likely to destroy the harmony of effect he wanted in the theatre. During the past decade there has been a strong reaction from players against 'director's theatre', a modern variant on the protests which greeted Craig's contemptuous dismissal of the flesh-and-blood medium of drama. The testimony of many actors who worked with Barker at different periods confirms the evidence from critics who urged the public to visit the Court Theatre if they wished to see much the finest acting in London, consistently and even in the smallest roles; he was certainly not open to the same charge as Craig. His attitude is most fully stated in the essay, 'The Heritage of the Actor' (1923), which he originally intended as a Shavian-length preface to *The Secret Life*. One passage may be quoted here:

> If this is the dramatist's day, he will be wise to consider the actor, not as a mere appendage to his work, but as its very life-giver. Let him realise that the more he can learn to ask of the actor the more will he gain for his play. But asking is giving. He must give opportunity.

Craig's ideas on the new art of the theatre, though doubtless affected by the aesthetic aspect of Irving's theatre, were closely related to the theories of contemporary symbolist poets and painters: by bringing all the arts into unity, the artist hoped to address the soul, beyond the senses and the intellect. The essays of Wagner, the 'father' of the symbolist movement, published in English in 1892, seem to have been Craig's direct source in their presentation of the music-drama, in which all the arts combine, as re-creating the genius and power of ancient Greek theatre in the modern world. The soul Wagner was concerned to address and nourish was that of nascent German unity, after the failure of the 1848 revolution. This concept of a national theatre inspired Yeats, particularly, in the foundation of the Abbey Theatre, Dublin. Though the English National Theatre Committee, in the early years of this century, might have claimed to be Wagnerites all, they took the ancient theatre of Athens as a model in a considerably less mystical and less nationalistic spirit. Under the guidance of Gilbert Murray (Professor of Greek at Glasgow, then at Oxford), they regarded the theatre of the city state as offering opportunity for airing and debating public issues, educating and enlivening the citizens of a democracy, civilising them through excellence in the arts. Granville Barker and his friends were always aware that they were concerned with the general nature and structure of British society and its economy, in their attempt to change the theatre. Fabian socialist ideas combined with

the influence of Gilbert Murray in the aspiration voiced by
Philip Madras in the new Barker play, *The Madras House*,
which was to be presented at the Duke of York's Theatre in
1910:

> I want an art and a culture that . . . must spring in good
> time from the happiness of a whole people.

In 1907, celebrating the end of their tenancy of the Court
Theatre, and again when the Vedrenne-Barker management's funds ran out after the continuation of its work at the
Savoy Theatre, the theatrical reformers looked hopefully
towards the Government, which in turn did nothing to
encourage notions that the people might finance their own
theatres through the tax system. Only after two world wars
did that come about.

   Barker considered leaving the country, as Craig had done.
He seized such chances as came up: notably at the Duke of
York's, when a commercial impresario, Charles Frohman,
briefly intoxicated by optimism after observing Vedrenne
and Barker's success with the public, mounted and then
abruptly curtailed a season of new plays in repertory,
engaging Barker to direct some of them. A wealthy aristocrat
sponsored three Shakespeare productions, directed by
Barker, at the Savoy Theatre in 1912 and 1914. Fast-moving
and rapidly spoken on an open stage in decorative or abstract
settings and imaginatively costumed, these caused an immediate sensation and revolutionised the staging and speaking of Shakespeare for the future. There had been little
money to spend on designers at the Court, though Charles
Ricketts had been brought in for *Don Juan in Hell*. In 1910,
Granville Barker started to build up his own team of artist-
designers to work closely with him: Ricketts again, William
and Albert Rothenstein, Norman Wilkinson of Four Oaks
(who went on, later, to Nigel Playfair's Lyric Theatre at
Hammersmith and then to Stratford) and, as an apprentice,
young Paul Nash. Then, during an American tour in 1915,
Barker gave a start to the theatrical career of Robert Edmond
Jones, who was to become the most famous of these

designers. No playwright has worked with fuller awareness of all the aspects of a play in performance.

He got together enough money for an uncompromising thirteen weeks at the St James's Theatre, in 1913; and for a while he and his actress wife, Lillah McCarthy, in joint management, had plays running concurrently in three London theatres. They were emboldened to take the Kingsway Theatre on a twenty-five year lease, in 1914, and presented Hardy's epic drama, *The Dynasts*, and Arnold Bennett's *The Great Adventure* there, before war swept everything away. For the rest of Granville Barker's life he was to be seen in London only as an occasional visiting director. He would not try to repeat what he had already done, but left his followers to continue as he had shown them – in Manchester, Liverpool, Birmingham, Glasgow, at Stratford, in London at the Lyric, Hammersmith, in the Phoenix Society and, later, the Arts Theatre Club, or in Australia. He was less in the public eye, but continued resolutely to plan, campaign, advise and write. His authority grew among decision makers; the Universities of Oxford, Edinburgh and Reading gave him honorary doctorates; with his second wife, he lived in Paris as Director of the British Institute, while the British public forgot that he had ever been an actor and in theatrical management. His contribution to productions of Shakespeare has been enormous over at least two generations, as actors and directors turned first to his *Prefaces to Shakespeare*. He did not foresee the extent to which power in society would pass from theatre to television, or else did not acknowledge what he saw. Though the focus of the old debate has shifted, the arguments and demonstrations retain some relevance.

According to one widespread view, Granville Barker's life was split across in 1916, when his marriage to Lillah McCarthy broke up. Their careers had been closely intertwined since 1904. Under his direction, she had been a superb and versatile actress in very many leading roles, ranging from the naturalism of Galsworthy to Masefield's grim psychological tragedy, from Shaw to Ibsen to

Shakespeare and, perhaps best of all, to Euripides. When they were divorced her own career in the theatre withered away. (Her social status, as Lady Keeble, was undiminished but not what she most wanted.) At the end of the war, Barker married the wealthy and cultured American, Helen Huntington. This, it has been asserted, marked the end of his creativity: he repudiated his past activities and took on a new 'establishment' identity, soon confirmed by the introduction of a hyphen into his name.

The selection of plays in this volume invites measurement of the distance and the continuity between Barker and Granville-Barker, between *The Voysey Inheritance* and *The Secret Life* (published in 1923, re-issued in 1928). The text of *Waste* included here looks both ways. It is the revised version, used for the very first production of the play in a public theatre, as late as 1936. It was made for an earlier project which did not materialise and has qualities of 1920's drama; it can be thought of as contemporary with Noël Coward's *The Vortex*. In the note to H M Harwood (reprinted before the play in the present edition) Granville Barker writes of it as almost a distinct play from the virtually untried original, which has long been the more accessible in print: 'I doubt if one scrap of the old dialogue survives; the story and the characters are here, that is all.' This ignores the themes, though Barker's next sentence may encompass them: 'it is a thing I had – dramatically – to say twenty years ago, said as I'd say it now.' Then he adds, 'But now I'd have something different to say.' Given its similarities to *Waste*, we may wonder if he had not, already in 1926, made that different statement – dramatically – in *The Secret Life*.

Barker's rejection of formulaic construction in his plays appears, in *The Voysey Inheritance*, in the checking of plot developments, or clearing of them offstage, to give character more room: not least, the communal character of the household. He does away with authorial omniscience: Mr Voysey's motives, and even his actions, remain uncertain, matters for speculation, even as the cause of the break with his eldest son remains unknown, though we may guess at it; and the actors' guesses will inform their performances. Such means increase realism. The structure of this play depends on the contrast of personalities at the centre of the social ensemble: the expansive character of the father, a man of creative imagination and energy, a spirit liberated to the point of irresponsibility, and his son Edward, a naive idealist, rudely awakened to the world he lives in. While Barker did not go as far as portraiture, there are traces here of the contrast between Bernard Shaw's personality and his own, wryly observed. While Barker was finishing *The Voysey Inheritance*, Shaw was at work on *Major Barbara*, employing the genially diabolic character of Undershaft to test youthful idealism. In Shaw's earlier play, *Mrs Warren's Profession*, Vivie – apparently stronger and clearer-sighted than Edward Voysey – reacts to enlightenment, which is also disillusionment, with emotional revulsion from life and barricades herself in the work of her City office, whereas Edward, whose fate looks quite similar, in fact continues in a struggle for integrity in order to change society. Granville Barker had acted in the Stage Society production of *Mrs Warren's Profession*: as Frank Gardner, the young man who resembles Mr Voysey in having no reverence for money as property, but a great liking for playing with it. No simple judgment on any of these characters is in order. Indeed *The Voysey Inheritance* is so written that judgment becomes less a matter of decision between right and wrong than a task of holding disparate and contradictory elements in suspense within the mind, recognising complexities.

The Voysey Inheritance has been established in the theatrical repertoire from the time of its first production and has never failed, though major professional revivals were well spaced from the beginning of the Second World War until quite recently, and the theatres which staged them had policies that the dramatist would have approved: the Arts Theatre Club put on *The Voysey Inheritance* in 1952, under the direction of John Fernald, when Tony Britton played Edward, Alec Macowen was Hugh and Rachel Kempson (Lady Redgrave) played Alice Maitland; the English Stage Company presented it at the Royal Court Theatre in 1960, with John Castle as Edward, Sebastian Shaw as Mr Voysey and Avril Elgar as Alice, Jane Howell directing. The last three years have seen three major productions: two in 1989, both staged in-the-round and rather similarly conceived, the first opened on 11 May at the Royal Exchange Theatre, Manchester, directed by Gregory Hersov, with James Maxwell as Mr Voysey, a production which managed to be both sharp and relaxed, and the second at the Cottesloe Theatre in June (Royal National Theatre Company, directed by Richard Eyre), memorable for its integrity and for Michael Bryant's portrait of Peacey, the solicitor's clerk, who outdid his employer in dignity (a minor role played as imaginatively and lovingly as Barker the director could have wished). Stuart Burge's production for the 1992 Edinburgh International Festival subsequently toured England. Jeremy Irons was Edward on TV in 1979.

The Voysey Inheritance offers a study of the late Victorian or Edwardian upper-middle-class family to be set beside Galsworthy's *Man of Property* and subsequent tales of the Forsytes. *Waste* presents the mainly aristocratic governing class of the period, beginning to be infiltrated by commercial magnates, occasionally bringing in middle-class talent, but unready to widen its power-base. The picture was sufficiently convincing to contemporaries for the rumour to spread that Barker's behind-the-scenes view of government was the unadmitted reason, beyond the distasteful subject of abortion, for the official banning of public performances of *Waste*: the danger sensed was as much political as moral. A private performance was given by the Stage Society in November 1907: then, to secure theatrical copyright, a reading of the butchered text 'licensed by the Lord Chamberlain' was given at the Savoy Theatre, on 28 January 1908, the cast including:

Mrs O'Connell	Miss Charlotte Payne-Townshend (Mrs G B Shaw)
Blackborough	John Galsworthy
Trebell	Laurence Housman (co-author of *Prunella* with Granville Barker)
Wedgecroft	H G Wells

*Cantelupe	Professor Gilbert Murray
Horsham	Bernard Shaw
O'Connell	William Archer

Barker proceeded to publish the text, together with *The Marrying of Ann Leete* and *The Voysey Inheritance*. Censorship, as usual, was good publicity, and *Waste* soon acquired the reputation of being the finest English tragedy since *Hamlet*. In one respect, at least, the comparison was apt. Both plays present a strongly subjective view of the hero, locating the drama to a great extent within his personality and consciousness, and compelling empathy; critical judgment has a hard struggle to hold the balance. Barker's hero, Henry Trebell, is a cross-bench politician of independent mind, who cares more for policy than party. The Tories, while out of office, persuade him to join them, temporarily perhaps, for a specific purpose: to take responsibility for a Bill to disestablish the Church of England. With this in their manifesto, they hope to outflank the Liberals and so win the next election. Trebell's price is the chance to put through a positive measure dear to his heart, using the Church's surplus revenues for an ambitious educational programme.

The play was originally set in a period before the rise of the Labour Party, and audiences in 1907 would have been aware that Church disestablishment had been on the Liberal agenda since the mid-nineteenth century, though the leadership had jibbed at the challenge. (The issue had been raised in an acute form by events in Barker's grandfather's old parish of Hatcham, in the late 1870s, when his successor, the Rev. Arthur Tooth, was imprisoned by the State for persisting in Anglo-Catholic liturgical practices and so causing street riots and general public disorder.) The notion of severing the historic bonds of Church to State was currently on the public mind, as the movement to release the Anglican Church from its position of privilege in largely nonconformist Wales was gaining urgency. During the 1992 debate on the ordination of women as priests in the Church of England, voices were occasionally heard among clerics and

* Cantelupe changed to Cantilupe in 1926 revision.

politicians (including Tony Benn) lamenting the constitutional position which still involves the State in Church business. But the future towards which Trebell's post-Christian attitude points, within the play, is now with us, and only in relation to other faiths, or in other countries, are such matters likely to be of general concern.

Waste also contains a tragic victim, Amy O'Connell, who dies as a result of an illegal abortion and so gives those Tories who dislike, or are nervous about, the Church Bill a chance to use the possibility of a scandal involving Trebell to destroy both the man and his measure. Abortion remains a campaigning issue today. One result of this is that Amy becomes an even stronger focus of interest than Barker may have intended, drawing the centre of the play a little away from the hero. He is a hero in the sense that all the play's concerns are most fully summed up in him. Abortion and disestablishment are the key concepts on which *Waste* is structured and as, through his experience, they acquire deeper meaning for Trebell, so they generate metaphoric values for the audience to ponder.

It was 1936 before the theatre-going public had its first chance to see the play, directed by the author jointly with Michael MacOwan, at the Westminster Theatre, with Nicholas Hannen in the main role and Harcourt Williams as Wedgecroft. The production was based on the revised text (given in the present edition), as representing Barker's more considered thoughts, clarifying motives and strengthening the general structure where this was weak in the original version. Inevitably, choice involves the sacrifice of much that is fine and distinctive in the rejected version. This led John Barton to devise a hybrid script, combining passages from both versions, with considerable re-arrangement, for his 1985 production in The Pit at the Barbican, when Daniel Massey as Trebell and Judi Dench, rather unsuitably cast as Amy, led the RSC company. Critics who had seen both found it less impressive than the fine BBC television broadcast of *Waste* in 1977 (produced by David Jones, directed by Don Taylor, with Paul Daneman as Trebell and Hannah Gordon as Amy O'Connell, individual members of a very strong cast), for which Barker's revised text was deliberately selected. The Barton hybrid version was blamed by some for yielding less than had been expected; but also this play was less well adapted to performance in the round than *The Voysey Inheritance* proved to be.

It may well have been Granville Barker's publication of the revised *Waste* in 1927 that led to Shaw's inclusion of a scene at 10 Downing Street, in his 1933 play, *On the Rocks*, in which Cabinet ministers with different vested interests are first persuaded and then combine to defeat their Prime Minister and his unexpectedly socialist programme. This was clearly influenced by the parallel scene in *Waste*, but also shows the enormous difference between Shaw's art and Barker's.

Topicality is, as yet, hardly a problem with these plays. If the scandal threatening Trebell originally carried reminders of Parnell, or Charles Dilke, as statesmen brought down by sexual involvements, the names of Ashdown and Mellor, or Clinton, come immediately to mind in 1992. Despite vast cultural changes, questions of public and private morality have not ceased to be used to manipulate public opinion and undermine policies, or particular measures, by destruction of individuals entrusted with the task of carrying them through; such methods were then, and are now, unofficial but not uncommon in the operation of modern 'democracy'. Similarly, fraudulent trustees and City scandals seem always with us, but no 1905 scandal was as startlingly reflected in *The Voysey Inheritance* as was the Robert Maxwell affair in recent times. *The Secret Life* was written before the splitting of the atom, but its hero, Evan Strowde anticipates that and the world it will usher in, even as he goes back to Machiavelli's *The Prince* for the 'creed' of politicians in power that he proposes in Act II, scene v.

The political society of *The Secret Life*, with its academic and transatlantic affiliations, seems as authentic as that of *Waste*. William Archer mischievously wondered if Lloyd George would be tempted to sue, but keeping Bellingham out of sight was a happy act of discretion. Barker was also as well acquainted with Winston Churchill as with Balfour and Asquith and expressed strong views on him in his private

correspondence. Oliver Gauntlett, in *The Secret Life*, bears a
marked resemblance to the brilliant yet aberrant young
'Tom' Mosley (Sir Oswald, when he succeeded to the
baronetcy), then an anxiety to the aristocratic statesmen in
his family on account of his involvement with radical left-
wing groups. The war left him maimed in the leg; Oliver in
the play, has lost an arm. Like Granville Barker, young
Mosley was a keen supporter of Gilbert Murray's League of
Nations Union in its early days. He was already recognised as
a future political leader, though not of a fascist party. The
parallel gives a potentially more sinister ring to Oliver's wish
for 'One crack battalion . . . temptation proof' to 'make an
end of the muddle . . .'

All the plays Barker had written before *The Voysey
Inheritance* have a woman as central character, who grows
towards an understanding of herself and the world, and an
acceptance of responsibility. With *The Voysey Inheritance*
came a shift of focus to an immature, rather priggish young
man, who has to pass through the double process of
disillusionment and enlightenment and learn to deal with
society as it is without abandoning his sense of justice. The
play certainly derives a piquancy from the emancipated
consciousness given to two of the women characters, Beatrice
and Alice. New women, career women, are important figures
in the later plays, but Amy O'Connell in *Waste* is not one of
them. Yet this has a fair claim to be the finest part Barker ever
wrote for a woman, certainly the most disturbing: a thorough
Edwardian, a woman of the world, witty and sophisticated,
yet also a feral creature, isolated and terrified, caught in the
trap of a society that despises women. The end of the play is a
record of the dramatist's own struggle to transcend the limits
of his vision and to reach a clearer understanding of how the
life and activity of even the most able man is wrenched apart
and invalidated by the fate, by the divided nature, of the
woman, as he has come to see it.

The distance between actual woman and symbol is much
greater in *The Secret Life*. Joan Westbury bears little
superficial resemblance to her romantic prototype, Isolde,
invoked by the Wagnerian music which starts the play. Yet

she sees the moon as mirror to herself: 'Burnt out inside' –
not the expected, conventional reading. In the iterative
imagery, of which the dialogue is so largely composed, the
motif of death-in-life figures prominently in many variant
forms, interlinked particularly with the language of commerce (buying and selling, valuation and the market) and
with images of the cosmic span of time through which the
armies of mankind have marched – generations in chains.
The first scene is as resonant with echoes of the Roman
triumvirate drinking aboard Pompey's galley, in *Antony and
Cleopatra*, as with the Wagnerian *Liebestod*.

The spirit of strain and search after understanding per-
meates *The Secret Life* and is one of the austere attractions of
Granville Barker's plays. When we find them difficult, it is
usually because they are moving beyond the commonplaces
of living and conventional patterns of thought more familiar
in the theatre. It can be glibly said that Strowde is a
disillusioned idealist who has to find a way of holding to his
vision, loving the dream, while knowing it is unattainable;
and only so is it possible that he can bring something of value
into the troubled world of his time. But the play calls to its
actors for aid in involving the audience in the confusions,
horror and despair from which Strowde has to escape.
Disillusionment in *The Secret Life* has a much deeper
emotional charge than in *The Voysey Inheritance*. There are
parallels in other literature of the time, registering the effect
of the First World War on minds away from the battlefields:
in D H Lawrence's equally apocalyptic *Women in Love*,
which makes similar use of Wagnerian imagery and textural
patterning to aid expression, and in W B Yeats's 'Nineteen
Hundred and Nineteen':

> We pieced our thoughts into philosophy,
> And planned to bring the world under a rule,
> Who are but weasels fighting in a hole.

The recurrent theme of idealism and the image of the moon
lady are links between Barker's plays and the late, symbolist
plays of Ibsen, particularly *Rosmersholm* (the last Act) and
When We Dead Awaken. In his deployment of large casts and

skilful orchestration of ensembles, together with the reduction of conventional plot-development and obvious forms of dramatic action, they invite comparison with Chekhovian drama. What Barker requires of actors is close to the aim of Stanislavsky's mature work on Chekhov's plays. His dialogue anticipates Samuel Beckett's or Harold Pinter's in the frequent use of pauses – though it is not always an actual pause that Barker's punctuation signals: rather, these are reminders to the actors that there is a continuous undercurrent of inner life to be projected, thoughts and feelings crowding up behind the words. In a rehearsed reading of *The Secret Life* given by members of the RSC at the 1992 Edinburgh Festival, Alan Howard demonstrated how lines which may seem merely sententious on the page can in the utterance carry the full weight of the experience from which they were formulated, if the challenge of the script is answered.

Only one brave professional production, by Sam Walters in the cramped conditions of the old Orange Tree pub theatre (with Geoffrey Beevers as Strowde and Vivien Heilbron as Joan), has yet explored *The Secret Life* beyond a rehearsed reading. It was broadcast on the old BBC Third Programme in 1948. While radio might give the greater flexibility Granville Barker required in the staging of this play of eleven scenes (compared with the solid act-structure of *The Voysey Inheritance*) the over-arching dramatic rhythm, encompassing the whole play, can hardly be realised until the pattern of visual movement in defined stage areas is combined with the major and minor rhythms of dialogue. For the plays Barker wrote in his mature years are not only long, they are ever more carefully composed as symphonies in dramatic form.

The lengthy stage directions, or descriptions, attached to these plays were written by Granville Barker on the advice of Bernard Shaw, who had been forced to publish his plays in the early years before he could get them produced. They were originally intended simply to make reading easier for those unaccustomed to playscripts, and character descriptions give hints to actors. The scene descriptions in Barker's plays reflect a director's consciousness of how performance is controlled and meanings may be developed through the shape of an acting area, the structure of a set, a piece of furniture, like the dining-table in *The Voysey Inheritance*. Act Two of *The Secret Life* demonstrates something of the variety of visual and vocal effects these elements can generate. The descriptions need not be taken as prescriptive in all circumstances, but we neglect them to our loss.

Finally, a word about the two short plays included here. They owe their existence to the kind of theatrical enterprise Barker was engaged in, when a play of unconventional length, not long enough to provide a full evening's entertainment, required a curtain-raiser; or a one-act play by a prentice playwright might need companion pieces to make up a programme. There was a will, in the management, to include good popular drama in the repertoire (and Granville Barker, Lillah McCarthy and Nigel Playfair did make one venture into a music hall bill at the Palace Theatre with a little comedy by Schnitzler); hence the farcical *Rococo*, which has its own truth regarding aspects of English family life. Both this and *Vote by Ballot* are carefully crafted. The latter is an example of what Barker called his 'miniaturising' technique, deliberately creating a slight, light piece in the setting of local politics and on the themes of waste and a secret life.

Margery Morgan, 1992

Note

This edition follows the printing convention of the original Granville Barker texts in reserving the use of italics for stage directions and employing letter spacing as an unobstrusive indication of particular emphasis within passages of dialogue.

The Voysey Inheritance

(Revised 1934)

1903–5
revised 1913
and again in
1934

The Voysey Inheritance was first played at the Court Theatre, Sloane Square on the afternoon of 7 November, 1905.

The play was revived at the Shaftesbury Theatre, London in a revised version of the text (that of the present edition) on 25 May 1934, with the following cast:

Mr Voysey	Felix Aylmer
Mrs Voysey	May Whitty
Trenchard Voysey, KC	Harcourt Williams
Honor Voysey	Antonia Brough
Major Booth Voysey	Archibald Batty
Mrs Booth Voysey (Emily)	Joan Harben
Christopher	Horace McBane
Edward Voysey	Maurice Evans
Hugh Voysey	Marius Goring
Mrs Hugh Voysey (Beatrice)	Joyce Bland
Ethel Voysey	Hermione Hannen
Denis Tregoning	Ernest Hare
Alice Maitland	Beatrix Thomson
Mr George Booth	O B Clarence
Rev. Evan Colpus	George Devine
Peacey	Frank Napier
Phoebe	Joan Leister
Mary	Freda Silcock

Directed by the author and Harcourt Williams

The First Act

The office of Voysey and Son is in the best part of Lincoln's Inn. Its panelled rooms give out a sense of grandmotherly comfort and security, very grateful at first to the hesitating investor, the dubious litigant. **Mr Voysey**'s *own room, into which he walks about twenty past ten of a morning, radiates enterprise besides. There is polish on everything; on the windows, on the mahogany of the tidily packed writing-table that stands between them, on the brasswork of the fireplace in the other wall, on the glass of the firescreen which preserves only the pleasantness of a sparkling fire, even on* **Mr Voysey**'s *hat as he takes it off to place it on the little red-curtained shelf behind the door.* **Mr Voysey** *is sixty or more and masterful; would obviously be master anywhere from his own home outwards, or wreck the situation in his attempt. Indeed there is sometimes a buccaneering air in the twist of his glance, not altogether suitable to a family solicitor. On this bright October morning,* **Peacey**, *the head clerk, follows just too late to help him off with his coat, but in time to take it and hang it up with a quite unnecessary subservience. Relieved of his coat,* **Mr Voysey** *carries to his table the bunch of beautiful roses he is accustomed to bring to the office three times a week and places them for a moment only near the bowl of water there ready to receive them while he takes up his letters. These lie ready too, opened mostly, one or two private ones left closed and discreetly separate. By this time the usual salutations have passed,* **Peacey**'s *'Good morning, sir';* **Mr Voysey**'s *'Morning, Peacey.' Then as he gets to his letters* **Mr Voysey** *starts his day's work.*

Mr Voysey Any news for me?

Peacey I hear bad accounts of Alguazils Preferred, sir.

Mr Voysey Oh . . . who from?

Peacey Merrit and James's head clerk in the train this morning.

Mr Voysey They looked all right on . . . Give me the *Times*. (**Peacey** *goes to the fireplace for the* Times; *it is warming there.* **Mr Voysey** *waves a letter, then places it on the table.*) Here, that's for you . . . Gerrard's Cross business. Anything else?

Peacey (*as he turns the* Times *to its Finance page*) I've made the usual notes.

Mr Voysey Thank'ee.

Peacey Young Benham isn't back yet.

Mr Voysey Mr Edward must do as he thinks fit about that. Alguazils, Alg – oh, yes.

He is running his eye down the columns. **Peacey** *leans over the letters.*

Peacey This is from Mr Leader about the codicil . . . You'll answer that?

Mr Voysey Mr Leader. Yes. Alguazils. Mr Edward's here, I suppose.

Peacey No, sir.

Mr Voysey (*his eye twisting with some sharpness*) What!

Peacey (*almost alarmed*) I beg pardon, sir.

Mr Voysey Mr Edward.

Peacey Oh, yes, sir, been in his room some time. I thought you said Headley; he's not due back till Thursday.

Mr Voysey *discards the* Times *and sits to his desk and his letters.*

Mr Voysey Tell Mr Edward I've come.

Peacey Yes, sir. Anything else?

Mr Voysey Not for the moment. Cold morning, isn't it?

Peacey Quite surprising, sir.

Mr Voysey We had a touch of frost down at Chislehurst.

Peacey So early!

Mr Voysey I want it for the celery. All right, I'll call through about the rest of the letters.

Peacey *goes, having secured a letter or two, and* **Mr Voysey** *having sorted the rest (a proportion into the wastepaper basket) takes up the forgotten roses and starts setting them into a bowl with an artistic hand. Then his son* **Edward** *comes in.* **Mr Voysey** *gives him one glance and goes on arranging the roses, but says cheerily . . .*

Mr Voysey Good morning, my dear boy.

Edward *has little of his father in him and that little is undermost. It is a refined face, but self-consciousness takes the place in it of imagination, and in suppressing traits of brutality in his character it looks as if the young man had suppressed his sense of humour too. But whether or no, that would not be much in evidence now, for* **Edward** *is obviously going through some experience which is scaring him (there is no better word). He looks not to have slept for a night or two, and his standing there, clutching and unclutching the bundle of papers he carries, his eyes on his father, half-appealingly but half-accusingly too, his whole being altogether so unstrung and desperate, makes* **Mr Voysey's** *uninterrupted arranging of the flowers seem very calculated indeed. At last the little tension of silence is broken.*

Edward Father . . .

Mr Voysey Well?

Edward I'm glad to see you.

This is a statement of fact. He doesn't know that the commonplace phrase sounds ridiculous at such a moment.

Mr Voysey I see you've the papers there.

Edward Yes.

Mr Voysey You've been through them?

Edward As you wished me . . .

Mr Voysey Well? (**Edward** *doesn't answer. Reference to the papers seems to overwhelm him with shame.* **Mr Voysey** *goes on with cheerful impatience.*) Now, now, my dear boy, don't take it like this. You're puzzled and worried, of course. But why didn't you come down to me on Saturday night? I expected you . . . I told you to come. Your mother was wondering why you weren't with us for dinner yesterday.

Edward I went through everything twice. I wanted to make quite sure.

Mr Voysey I told you to come to me.

Edward (*he is very near crying*) Oh, Father!

Mr Voysey Now look here, Edward, I'm going to ring and dispose of these letters. Please pull yourself together. (*He pushes the little button on his table.*)

Edward I didn't leave my rooms all day yesterday.

Mr Voysey A pleasant Sunday! You must learn, whatever the business may be, to leave it behind you at the office. Life's not worth living else.

Peacey *comes in to find* **Mr Voysey** *before the fire ostentatiously warming and rubbing his hands.*

Oh, there isn't much else, Peacey. Tell Simmons that if he satisfies you about the details of this lease it'll be all right. Make a note for me of Mr Granger's address at Mentone.

Peacey Mr Burnett . . . Burnett and Marks . . . has just come in, Mr Edward.

Edward (*without turning*) It's only fresh instructions. Will you take them?

Peacey All right.

Peacey *goes, lifting his eyebrows at the queerness of* **Edward's**

manner. This **Mr Voysey** *sees, returning to his table with a little scowl.*

Mr Voysey Now sit down. I've given you a bad forty-eight hours, have I? Well, I've been anxious about you. Never mind, we'll thresh the thing out now. Go through the two accounts. Mrs Murberry's first . . . how do you find it stands?

Edward (*his feelings choking him*) I hoped you were playing some joke on me.

Mr Voysey Come now.

Edward *separates the papers precisely and starts to detail them; his voice quite toneless. Now and then his father's sharp comments ring out in contrast.*

Edward We've got the lease of her present house, several agreements . . . and here's her will. Here's an expired power of attorney . . . over her securities and her property generally . . . it was made out for six months.

Mr Voysey She was in South Africa.

Edward Here's the Sheffield mortgage and the Henry Smith mortgage with banker's receipts . . . her banker's to us for the interest up to date . . . four and a half and five per cent. Then . . . Fretworthy Bonds. There's a note scribbled in your writing that they are at the bank; but you don't say what bank.

Mr Voysey My own.

Edward (*just dwelling on the words*) Your own. I queried that. There's eight thousand five hundred in three and a half India stock. And there are her banker's receipts for cheques on account of those dividends. I presume for those dividends.

Mr Voysey Why not?

Edward (*gravely*) Because then, Father, there are her banker's half-yearly receipts for other sums amounting to an average of four hundred and twenty pounds a year. But I find no record of any capital to produce this.

Mr Voysey Go on. What do you find?

Edward Till about three years back there seems to have been eleven thousand in Queenslands which would produce . . . d i d produce exactly the same sum. But after January of that year I find no record of them.

Mr Voysey In fact the Queenslands are missing, vanished?

Edward (*hardly uttering the word*) Yes.

Mr Voysey From which you conclude?

Edward I supposed at first that you had not handed me all the papers. . . .

Mr Voysey Since Mrs Murberry evidently still gets that four-twenty a year, somehow; lucky woman.

Edward (*in agony*) Oh!

Mr Voysey Well, we'll return to the good lady later. Now let's take the other.

Edward The Hatherley Trust.

Mr Voysey Quite so.

Edward (*with one accusing glance*) Trust.

Mr Voysey Go on.

Edward Father . . .

His grief comes uppermost again and **Mr Voysey** *meets it kindly*.

Mr Voysey I know, my dear boy. I shall have lots to say to you. But let's get quietly through with these details first.

Edward (*bitterly now*) Oh, this is simple enough. We're young Hatherley's trustees till he comes of age. The property was thirty-eight thousand invested in Consols. Certain sums were to be allowed for his education; we seem to be paying them.

Mr Voysey Regularly?

Edward Quite. But where's the capital?

Mr Voysey No record?

Edward Yes . . . a note by you on a half-sheet: Refer Bletchley Land Scheme.

Mr Voysey Oh . . . we've been out of that six years or more! He's credited with the interest on his capital?

Edward With the Consol interest.

Mr Voysey Quite so.

Edward The Bletchley scheme paid seven and a half.

Mr Voysey At one time. Have you taken the trouble to calculate what will be due from us to the lad?

Edward Yes . . . capital and interest . . . about forty-six thousand pounds.

Mr Voysey A respectable sum. In five years' time?

Edward When he comes of age.

Mr Voysey That gives us, say, four years and six months in which to think about it.

Edward *waits, hopelessly, for his father to speak again; then says . . .*

Edward Thank you for showing me these, sir. Shall I put them back in your safe now?

Mr Voysey Yes, you'd better. There's the key. (**Edward** *reaches for the bunch, his face hidden.*) Put them down. Your hand shakes . . . why, you might have been drinking. I'll put them away later. It's no use having hysterics, Edward. Look your trouble in the face.

Edward's *only answer is to go to the fire, as far from his father as the room allows. And there he leans on the mantelpiece, his shoulders heaving.*

Mr Voysey I'm sorry, my dear boy. I wouldn't tell you if I could help it.

Edward I can't believe it. And that you should be telling me . . . such a thing.

Mr Voysey Let yourself go . . . have your cry out, as the women say. It isn't pleasant, I know. It isn't pleasant to inflict it on you.

Edward (*able to turn to his father again; won round by the kind voice*) How long has it been going on? Why didn't you tell me before? Oh, I know you thought you'd pull through. But I'm your partner . . . I'm responsible too. Oh, I don't want to shirk that . . . don't think I mean to shirk that, Father. Perhaps I ought to have discovered . . . but those affairs were always in your hands. I trusted . . . I beg your pardon. Oh, it's us . . . not you. Everyone has trusted us.

Mr Voysey (*calmly and kindly still*) You don't seem to notice that I'm not breaking my heart like this.

Edward What's the extent of . . . ? Are there other accounts . . . ? When did it begin? Father, what made you begin it?

Mr Voysey I didn't begin it.

Edward You didn't? Who then?

Mr Voysey My father before me. (**Edward** *stares.*) That calms you a little.

Edward But how terrible! Oh, my dear Father . . . I'm glad. But . . .

Mr Voysey (*shaking his head*) My inheritance, Edward.

Edward My dear Father!

Mr Voysey I had hoped it wasn't to be yours.

Edward But you mean to tell me that this sort of thing has been going on here for years? For more than thirty years!

Mr Voysey Yes.

Edward That's a little hard to understand . . . just at first, sir.

Mr Voysey (*sententiously*) We do what we must in this world, Edward. I have done what I had to do.

Edward (*his emotion well cooled by now*) Perhaps I'd better just listen while you explain.

Mr Voysey (*concentrating*) You know that I'm heavily into Northern Electrics.

Edward Yes.

Mr Voysey But you don't know how heavily. When I got the tip the Municipalities were organising the purchase, I saw of course the stock must be up to a hundred and forty-five – a hundred and fifty in no time. Now Leeds has quarrelled with the rural group . . . there'll be no general settlement for ten years. I bought at ninety-five. What are they today?

Edward Seventy-two.

Mr Voysey Seventy-one and a half. And in ten years I may be . . . ! I'm not a young man, Edward. That's mainly why you've had to be told.

Edward With whose money are you so heavily into Northern Electrics?

Mr Voysey The firm's money.

Edward Clients' money?

Mr Voysey Yes.

Edward (*coldly*) Well . . . I'm waiting for your explanation, sir.

Mr Voysey (*with a shrug*) Children always think the worst of their parents, I suppose. I did of mine. It's a pity.

Edward Go on, sir, go on. Let me know the worst.

Mr Voysey There's no immediate danger. I should think anyone could see that from the figures there. There's no real risk at all.

Edward Is that the worst?

Mr Voysey (*his anger rising*) Have you studied these two accounts or have you not?

Edward Yes, sir.

Mr Voysey Well, where's the deficiency in Mrs Murberry's income . . . has she ever gone without a shilling? What has young Hatherley lost?

Edward He stands to lose. . . .

Mr Voysey He stands to lose nothing if I'm spared for a little, and you will only bring a little common sense to bear and try to understand the difficulties of my position.

Edward Father, I'm not thinking ill of you . . . that is, I'm trying not to. But won't you explain how you're justified . . . ?

Mr Voysey In putting our affairs in order?

Edward Are you doing that?

Mr Voysey What else?

Edward (*starting patiently to examine the matter*) How bad were things when you came into control?

Mr Voysey Oh, I forget.

Edward You can't forget.

Mr Voysey Well . . . pretty bad.

Edward How was it my grandfather . . . ?

Mr Voysey Muddlement . . . timidity! Had a perfect mania for petty speculation. He'd no capital . . . no real credit . . . and he went in terror of his life. My dear Edward, if I hadn't found out in time, he'd have confessed to the first man who came and asked for a balance sheet.

Edward How much was he to the bad then?

Mr Voysey Oh . . . a tidy sum.

Edward But it can't have taken all these years to pay off. . . .

Mr Voysey Oh, hasn't it!

Edward (*making his point*) Then how does it happen, sir, that such a recent trust as young Hatherley's has been broken into?

Mr Voysey Well, what could be safer? There is no one to interfere, and we haven't to settle up for five years.

Edward (*utterly beaten*) Father, are you mad?

Mr Voysey Mad? I wish everybody were as sane. As a trustee the law permits me to earn for a fund three and a half per cent. . . . and that I do . . . punctually and safely. Now as to Mrs Murberry . . . those Fretworthy Bonds at my bank . . . I've borrowed five thousand on them. But I can release them tomorrow if need be.

Edward Where's the five thousand?

Mr Voysey I needed it . . . temporarily . . . to complete a purchase . . . there was that and four thousand more out of the Skipworth fund.

Edward But, my dear Father –

Mr Voysey Well?

Edward (*summing it all up very simply*) It's not right.

Mr Voysey *considers his son for a moment with a pitying shake of the head.*

Mr Voysey That is a word, Edward, which one should learn to use very carefully. You mean that from time to time I have had to go beyond the letter of the law. But consider the position I found myself in. Was I to see my father ruined and disgraced without lifting a finger to help him? I paid back to the man who was most involved in my

father's mistakes every penny of his capital . . . and he
never even knew the danger he'd been in . . . never had
one uneasy moment. It was I that lay awake. I have now
somewhere a letter from that man written as he lay dying
. . . I'll tell you who it was, old Thomson the physiologist
. . . saying that only his perfect confidence in our conduct
of his affairs had enabled him to do his life's work in
peace. Well, Edward, I went beyond the letter of the law
to do that service . . . to my father . . . to old Thomson
. . . to Science . . . to Humanity. Was I right or wrong?

Edward In the result, sir, right.

Mr Voysey Judge me by the result. I took the risk of
failure . . . I should have suffered. I could have kept clear
of the danger if I'd liked.

Edward But that's all past. The thing that concerns me is
what you are doing now.

Mr Voysey (*gently reproachful*) My boy, can't you trust me
a little? It's all very well for you to come in at the end of
the day and criticise. But I who have done the day's work
know how that work had to be done. And here's our firm,
prosperous, respected and without a stain on its honour.
That's the main point, isn't it?

Edward (*quite unresponsive to this pathetic appeal*) Very well,
sir. Let's dismiss from our minds any prejudice about
behaving as honest firms of solicitors do behave. . . .

Mr Voysey We need do nothing of the sort. If a man gives
me definite instructions about his property I follow them.
And more often than not he suffers.

Edward But if Mrs Murberry knew . . .

Mr Voysey Well, if you can make her understand her
affairs . . . financial or other . . . it's more than I ever
could. Go and knock it into her head, then, if you can,
that four hundred and twenty pounds of her income
hasn't, for the last eight years, come from the place she
thinks it's come from, and see how happy you'll make her.

Edward But is that four hundred and twenty a year as safe as it was before you . . . ?

Mr Voysey Why not?

Edward What's the security?

Mr Voysey (*putting his coping stone on the argument*) My financial ability.

Edward (*really not knowing whether to laugh or cry*) Why, one'd think you were satisfied with this state of things.

Mr Voysey Edward, you really are most unsympathetic and unreasonable. I give all I have to the firm's work . . . my brain . . . my energies . . . my whole life. I can't, so to speak, cash in my abilities at par . . . I wish I could. If I could establish every one of these people with a separate and consistent bank balance tomorrow . . . naturally I should do it.

Edward (*thankfully able to meet anger with anger*) Do you mean to tell me that you couldn't somehow have put things straight before now?

Mr Voysey So easy to talk, isn't it?

Edward If thirty years of this sort of thing hasn't brought you hopelessly to grief . . . why, there must have been opportunities . . .

Mr Voysey Must there! Well, I hope that when I'm under the ground, you may find them.

Edward I?

Mr Voysey And put everything right with a stroke of your pen, if it's so easy!

Edward I!

Mr Voysey You're my partner and my son. You inherit the problem.

Edward (*realising at last that he has been led to the edge of this abyss*) Oh no, Father.

Mr Voysey Why else have I had to tell you all this?

Edward (*very simply*) Father, I can't. I can't possibly. I don't think you've any right to ask me.

Mr Voysey Why not, pray?

Edward It's perpetuating the dishonesty.

Mr Voysey *hardens at the unpleasant word.*

Mr Voysey You don't believe that I've told you the truth.

Edward I want to believe it.

Mr Voysey It's no proof . . . my earning these twenty or thirty people their incomes for the last . . . how many years?

Edward Whether what you've done has been wrong or right . . . I can't meddle in it.

For the moment **Mr Voysey** *looks a little dangerous.*

Mr Voysey Very well. Forget all I've said. Go back to your room. Get back to your drudgery. A life's work – my life's work – ruined! What does that matter?

Edward Whatever did you expect of me?

Mr Voysey (*making a feint at his papers*) Oh, nothing. (*Then he slams them down with great effect.*) Here's a great edifice built up by years of labour and devotion and self-sacrifice . . . a great arch you may call it . . . a bridge to carry our firm to safety with honour. My work! And it still lacks the key-stone. Just that! And it may be I am to die with my work incomplete. Then is there nothing that a son might do? Do you think I shouldn't be proud of you, Edward . . . that I shouldn't bless you from . . . wherever I may be, when you had completed my life's work . . . with perhaps just one kindly thought of your father?

In spite of this oratory, the situation is gradually impressing **Edward.**

Edward What will happen if I leave the firm now?

Mr Voysey I shall see that you are not held responsible.

Edward I wasn't thinking of myself, sir.

Mr Voysey Well, I shan't mind the exposure. It won't make me blush in my coffin. And you're not so quixotic, I hope, as to be thinking of the feelings of your brothers and sisters. Considering how simple it would have been for me to go to my grave and let you discover the whole thing afterwards, the fact that I didn't, that I take thought for the future of you all . . . well, I did hope it might convince you that I . . . ! But there . . . consult your own safety.

Edward *has begun to pace the room; indecision growing upon him.*

Edward It's a queer dilemma to be facing.

Mr Voysey My dear boy . . . don't think I can't appreciate the shock it has been to you. After all, I had to go through it, you know. And worse!

Edward Why worse?

Mr Voysey Well . . . I was a bit younger. And my poor dear Dad was on the edge of the precipice . . . all but over it. I'm not landing you in any such mess, Edward. On the contrary! On the contrary!

Edward Yes, I came this morning thinking that next week would see us in the dock together.

Mr Voysey And I suppose if I'd broken down and begged your pardon for my folly, you'd have done anything for me, gone to prison smiling, eh?

Edward I suppose so.

Mr Voysey Oh, it's easy enough to forgive. I'm sorry I can't assume sack-cloth and ashes to oblige you. (*Now he begins to rally his son; easy in his strength.*) My dear Edward, you've lived a quiet, humdrum life up to now, with your poetry and your sociology and your agnosticism and your ethics of this and your ethics of that! . . . and you've never before been brought face to face with any really vital question. Now don't make a fool of yourself just through inexperience. I'm not angry at what you've said to me. I'm willing to forget it. And it's for your own sake and not for mine, Edward, that I do beg you to . . . to . . . be a man and take a man's view of the position you find yourself in. It's not a pleasant position, I know . . . but we must take this world as we find it, my dear boy.

Edward You should have told me before you took me into partnership.

Oddly enough it is this last flicker of rebellion which breaks down **Mr Voysey**'s *caution. Now he lets fly with a vengeance.*

Mr Voysey Should I be telling you at all if I could help it? Don't I know you're about as fit for the job as a babe unborn? I've been hoping and praying for these three years past that you'd show signs of shaping into something. But I'm in a corner . . . and am I to see things come to smash simply because of your scruples? If you're a son of mine you'll do as I tell you. Hadn't I the same choice to make? D'you suppose I didn't have scruples? If you run away from this, Edward, you're a coward. My father was a coward and he suffered for it to the end of his days. I was more of a sick-nurse to him here than a partner. Good Lord! . . . of course it's pleasant and comfortable to keep within the law . . . then the law will look after you. Otherwise you have to look pretty sharp after yourself. You have to cultivate your own sense of right and wrong . . . deal your own justice. But that makes a bigger man of you, let me tell you. How easily . . . how easily could I have walked out of my father's office and left him to his fate! But I didn't. I thought it my better duty to stay and . . . yes, I say it with all reverence . . . to take up my cross. Well, I've carried that cross pretty successfully. And what's more, it's made a happy . . . a self-respecting man of me. I don't want what I've been saying to influence you, Edward. You are a free agent. You must consult your conscience and decide upon your own course of action.

Now don't let's discuss the matter any more for the moment.

Edward *looks at his father with clear eyes.*

Edward Don't forget to put these papers away.

Mr Voysey Are you coming down to Chislehurst soon? We've got Hugh and his wife, and Booth and Emily, and Christopher for two or three days, till he goes back to school.

Edward How is Chris?

Mr Voysey All right again now . . . grows more like his father. Booth's very proud of him. So am I.

Edward I think I can't face them all just at present.

Mr Voysey Nonsense.

Edward (*a little wave of emotion going through him*) I feel as if this thing were written on my face. How I shall get through business I don't know!

Mr Voysey You're weaker than I thought, Edward.

Edward (*a little ironically*) I've always wondered why I was such a disappointment to you, Father. Though you've been very kind about it.

Mr Voysey No, no. I say things I don't mean sometimes.

Edward You should have brought one of the others into the firm . . . Trenchard or Booth.

Mr Voysey (*hardening*) Trenchard! (*He dismisses that.*) Heavens, you're a better man than Booth. Edward, you mustn't imagine that the whole world is standing on its head merely because you've had an unpleasant piece of news. Come down to Chislehurst tonight . . . well, say tomorrow night. It'll be good for you . . . stop your brooding. That's your worst vice, Edward. You'll find the household as if nothing had happened. Then you'll remember that nothing really has happened. And presently you'll see that nothing need happen, if you keep your head. I remember times . . . when things have seemed at their worst . . . what a relief it's been to me . . . my romp with you all in the nursery just before your bed-time. And, my dear boy, if I knew that you were going to inform the next client you met of what I've just told you . . .

Edward (*with a shudder*) Father!

Mr Voysey . . . and that I should find myself in prison tomorrow, I wouldn't wish a single thing I've ever done undone. I have never wilfully harmed man or woman. My life's been a happy one. Your dear mother has been spared to me. You're most of you good children and a credit to what I've done for you.

Edward (*the deadly humour of this too much for him*) Father!

Mr Voysey Run along now, run along. I must finish my letters and get into the City.

He might be scolding a schoolboy for some trifling fault.
Edward *turns to have a look at the keen, unembarrassed face.*
Mr Voysey *smiles at him and proceeds to select from the bowl a rose for his buttonhole.*

Edward I'll think it over, sir.

Mr Voysey That's right! And don't brood.

So **Edward** *leaves him; and having fixed the rose in his buttonhole to his satisfaction he rings his table telephone and calls through to the listening clerk.*

Mr Voysey Send Atkinson to me, please.

Then he gets up, keys in hand, to lock away Mrs Murberry's and the Hatherley Trust papers.

The Second Act

*The Voysey dining-room at Chislehurst, when children and
grandchildren are visiting, is dining-table and very little else.
And at the moment in the evening when five or six men are
sprawling back in their chairs, and the air is clouded with
smoke, it is a very typical specimen of the middle-class English
domestic temple. It has the usual red-papered walls, the usual
varnished woodwork which is known as grained oak; there is
the usual hot, mahogany furniture; and, commanding point of
the whole room, there is the usual black-marble sarcophagus of
a fireplace. Above this hangs one of the two or three oil-
paintings, which are all that break the red pattern of the walls,
the portrait, painted in 1880, of an undistinguished-looking
gentleman aged sixty; he is shown sitting in a more graceful
attitude than it could ever have been comfortable for him to
assume.* **Mr Voysey**'s *father it is, and the brass plate at the
bottom of the frame tells us that the portrait was a presentation
one. On the mantelpiece stands, of course, a clock; at either
end a china vase filled with paper spills. And in front of the
fire – since that is the post of vantage – stands at this moment*
Major Booth Voysey. *He is the second son, of the age that it
is necessary for a Major to be, and of the appearance of many
ordinary Majors in ordinary regiments. He went into the Army
because he thought it would come up to a schoolboy's idea of it;
and, being there, he does his little all to keep it to this. He
stands astride, hands in pockets, coat-tails through his arms,
half-smoked cigar in mouth, moustache bristling. On either side
of him sits at the table an old gentleman; the one is* **Mr Evan
Colpus**, *the vicar of their parish, the other* **Mr George
Booth**, *a friend of long standing and the Major's godfather.*
Mr Colpus *is a harmless enough anachronism, except for the
comparative waste of £400 a year in which his stipend involves
the community. Leaving most of his parochial work to an*

energetic curate, he devotes his serious attention to the composition of two sermons a week. **Mr George Booth**, *on the contrary, is as gay an old gentleman as can be found in Chislehurst. An only son, his father left him at the age of twenty-five a fortune of a hundred thousand pounds. At the same time he had the good sense to dispose of his father's business, into which he had been most unwillingly introduced five years earlier, for a like sum before he was able to depreciate its value. It was* **Mr Voysey**'s *invaluable assistance in this transaction which first bound the two together in great friendship. Since that time* **Mr Booth** *has been bent on nothing but enjoying himself. He has even remained a bachelor with that object. Money has given him all he wants, therefore he loves and reverences money; while his imagination may be estimated by the fact that he has now reached the age of sixty-five, still possessing more of it than he knows what to do with. At the head of the table, meditatively cracking walnuts, sits* **Mr Voysey**. *He has his back to the conservatory door. On* **Mr Voysey**'s *left is* **Denis Tregoning**, *a nice enough young man. And at the other end of the table sits* **Edward**, *not smoking, not talking, hardly listening, very depressed. Behind him is the ordinary door of the room, which leads out into the dismal, draughty hall. The* **Major**'s *voice is like the sound of a cannon through the tobacco smoke.*

Major Booth Voysey Certainly . . . I am hot and strong for conscription . . . and the question will be to the fore again very shortly.

Mr George Booth My dear boy . . . the country won't hear of it . . .

Major Booth Voysey I differ from you. If we . . . the Army . . . if the men who have studied the subject . . . the brains of the Army . . . say as one man to the country: Conscription is once more necessary for your safety . . . what answer has the country? What? There you are! None.

Tregoning You try . . . and you'll see.

Major Booth Voysey If the international situation grows more threatening I shall seriously consider going on half-

pay for a bit and entering the House. And . . . I'm not a
conceited man . . . but I believe that if I speak out upon a
subject I understand, and only upon that subject, the
House . . . and the country . . . will listen.

Mr George Booth The gentlemen of England have always
risen to an emergency. Why . . . old as I am . . . I would
shoulder a musket myself if need be. But . . .

Major Booth Voysey Just one moment. Our national
safety is not the only question. There's the stamina of the
race . . . deplorably deteriorated! You should just see the
fellars that try to enlist nowadays. Horrid little runts . . .
with their stinkin' little fags . . . hangin' out of the corners
of their slobberin' little mouths. What England wants is
chest. Chest and discipline. And conscription . . .

Mr Voysey (*with the crack of a nut*) Your godson talks a
deal, don't he? You know, when our Major gets into a
club, he gets on the committee . . . gets on any committee
to enquire into anything . . . and then goes on at 'em just
like this. Don't you, Booth?

Booth *knuckles under easily enough to his father's sarcasm.*

Major Booth Voysey Well, sir, people tell me I'm a useful
man on committees.

Mr Voysey I don't doubt it . . . your voice must drown all
discussion.

Major Booth Voysey You can't say I don't listen to you,
sir.

Mr Voysey I don't . . . and I'm not blaming you. But I
must say I often think what a devil of a time the family will
have with you when I'm gone. Fortunately for your poor
mother, she's deaf.

Major Booth Voysey Well, sir . . . it might be my duty
. . . as eldest son . . . Trenchard not counting . . .

Mr Voysey (*with the crack of another nut*) Trenchard not
counting. Oh, certainly . . . bully them. Never mind

whether you're right or wrong . . . bully them. I don't
manage things that way myself, but I think it's your best
chance.

Major Booth Voysey (*with some discomfort*) Ha! If I were a
conceited man, sir, I could trust you to take it out of me.

Mr Voysey (*as he taps* **Mr Booth** *with the nut-crackers*)
Help yourself, George, and drink to your godson's health.
Long may he keep his chest notes! Never heard him on
parade, have you?

Tregoning There's one thing you learn in the Army . . .
and that's how to display yourself. Booth makes a perfect
firescreen. But I believe after mess that position is
positively rushed.

Major Booth Voysey (*cheered to find an opponent he can
tackle*) If you want a bit of fire, say so, you sucking Lord
Chancellor. Because I mean to allow you to be my
brother-in-law, you think you can be impertinent.

So **Tregoning** *moves to the fire and that changes the
conversation.*

Mr Voysey Vicar, the port's with you. Help yourself and
send it on.

Mr Colpus Thank you . . . I have had my quantum.

Mr Voysey Nonsense!

Mr Colpus Well . . . a teeny weeny drain!

Mr Voysey By the way . . . did you see Lady Mary
yesterday? Is she going to help us clear off the debt on the
chapel?

Mr Colpus Well, no . . . I'm afraid she isn't.

Mr Voysey Why not?

Mr Colpus Well . . . the fact is she's quite angry.

Mr Voysey What about?

Mr Colpus I regret to tell you . . . it's about Hugh's fresco.

Major Booth Voysey Ah . . . I knew there'd be trouble!

Mr Colpus Someone has let it out to her that the Apostles are all portraits of people . . . and she strongly disapproves.

Major Booth Voysey So do I.

Mr Colpus Indeed, I fear she's writing to you to say that as Hugh is your son she thinks you should have kept him under better control. I said I'd done all I could. And I did argue with him. First of all, you know, he wanted to make them local people . . . the butcher and the plumber and old Sandford. He said the fifteenth-century Florentines always did it. I said: My dear Hugh, we are not fifteenth-century Florentines . . .

Major Booth Voysey Hugh's no good at a likeness. I don't believe anyone would have known.

Mr Colpus But all he said was: Ha! Ha! Then I didn't see the thing for a week, and . . . oh, far worse! . . . he'd made them all quite well-known public characters! And as it was in tempera, he couldn't alter it without taking the wall down.

Mr Voysey What's the debt now?

Mr Colpus Three hundred pounds nearly.

Mr Voysey I shall have to stump up, I suppose.

Major Booth Voysey Anonymously. What?

Mr Voysey George Booth . . . will you go halves?

Mr George Booth Certainly not. I can't see what we wanted the chapel at all for. Eight hundred pounds and more . . . !

Mr Colpus People do drop in and pray. Oh . . . I've seen them.

Mr George Booth Well, Vicar . . . it's your business, of
course . . . but I call it a mistake to encourage all this extra
religion. Work on week-days . . . church on Sundays.
That was the rule when I was young.

Mr Voysey You can't stop people praying.

Mr George Booth But why make a show of it? What's the
result? Hugh's a case in point. When he was a boy . . .
mad about religion! Used to fast on Fridays! I remember
your punishing him for it. Now look at him. What his
beliefs are now . . . well, I'd rather not know. And with
Edward here . . .

Edward With me?

Mr George Booth Up at Cambridge . . . wanted to turn
Papist, didn't you? And now . . . I suppose you call
yourself a free-thinker.

Edward I don't call myself anything.

Mr George Booth Keep to the middle of the road . . .
that's what I'd tell any young man.

Tregoning Safety first.

Mr George Booth Certainly. For what should be a man's
aim in life? I have always known mine, and . . . though far
be it from me to boast . . . I look back to nothing I need
regret . . . nothing the whole world might not know. I
don't speak of quite personal affairs. Like most other men,
I have been young. But all that sort of thing is nobody's
business but one's own. I inherited a modest fortune. I
have not needed to take the bread out of other men's
mouths by working. My money has been wisely
administered . . . well, ask your father about that . . . and
has . . . not diminished. I have paid my taxes without
grumbling. I have never wronged any man. I have never
lied about anything that mattered. I have left theories to
take care of themselves and tried to live the life of an
English gentleman. And I consider there is no higher . . .
at any rate no more practical ideal.

Major Booth Voysey (*not to be outdone by this display of virtue*) Well, I'm not a conceited man, but –

Tregoning I hope you're sure of that, Booth.

Major Booth Voysey Shut up. I was going to say when my young cub of a brother-in-law-to-be interrupted me, that training, for which we all have to be thankful to you, sir, has much to do with it. (*Suddenly he pulls his trousers against his legs.*) I say, I'm scorching. Try one of those new cigars, Denis?

Tregoning. No, thank you.

Major Booth Voysey I will.

He glances round; **Tregoning** *sees a box on the table and reaches it. The Vicar gets up.*

Mr Colpus Must be taking my departure.

Mr Voysey Already!

Major Booth Voysey (*frowning upon the cigar-box*) No, not those. The Ramon Allones. Why on earth doesn't Honor see they're here?

Mr Voysey Spare time for a chat with my wife before you go. She has ideas about a children's tea-fight.

Mr Colpus Certainly I will.

Major Booth Voysey (*scowling helplessly around*) My goodness! . . . one can never find anything in this house.

Mr Voysey My regards to Mrs Colpus. Hope her lumbago will be better.

Mr Colpus These trials are sent us.

He is sliding through the half-opened door when **Ethel** *meets him, flinging it wide. She is the younger daughter, the baby of the family, but twenty-three now.*

Mr Voysey I say! It's cold again tonight! An ass of an architect who built this place . . . such a draught between these two doors.

He gets up to draw the curtain. When he turns **Mr Colpus** *has disappeared, while* **Ethel** *has been followed into the room by* **Alice Maitland**, *who shuts the door after her.* **Miss Alice Maitland** *is a young lady of any age to thirty. Nor need her appearance alter for the next fifteen years; since her nature is healthy and well-balanced. It mayn't be a pretty face, but it has alertness and humour; and the resolute eyes and eyebrows are a more innocent edition of* **Mr Voysey**'s, *who is her uncle.* **Ethel** *goes straight to her father (though her glance is on* **Denis** *and his on her) and chirps, birdlike, in her spoiled-child way.*

Ethel We think you've stayed in here quite long enough.

Mr Voysey That's to say, Ethel thinks Denis has been kept out of her pocket much too long.

Ethel Ethel wants billiards. . . . Father . . . what a dessert you've eaten. Greedy pig!

Alice *is standing behind* **Edward**, *considering his hair-parting apparently.*

Alice Crack me a filbert, please, Edward . . . I had none.

Edward (*jumping up, rather formally well-mannered*) I beg your pardon, Alice. Won't you sit down?

Alice No.

Mr Voysey (*taking* **Ethel** *on his knee*) Come here, puss. Have you made up your mind yet what you want for a wedding present?

Ethel (*rectifying a stray hair on his forehead*) After mature consideration, I decide on a cheque.

Mr Voysey Do you!

Ethel Yes. I think that a cheque will give most scope to your generosity. If you desire to add any trimmings in the shape of a piano or a Persian carpet you may . . . and Denis and I will be grateful. But I think I'd let yourself go over a cheque.

Mr Voysey You're a minx.

Major Booth Voysey (*giving up the cigar search*) Here, who's going to play?

Mr George Booth (*pathetically, as he gets up*) Well, if my wrist will hold out . . .

Major Booth Voysey (*to* **Tregoning**) No, don't you bother to look for them. (*He strides from the room, his voice echoing through the hall.*) Honor, where are those Ramon Allones?

Alice (*calling after*) She's in the drawing-room with Auntie and Mr Colpus.

Mr Voysey Now I suggest that you and Denis go and take off the billiard-table cover. You'll find folding it up a very excellent amusement.

He illustrates his meaning with his table napkin and by putting together the tips of his forefingers, roguishly.

Mr George Booth Ah ha! I remember that being done in some play . . .

Ethel Dear Father . . . you must try not to be roguish. You won't get a blush or a giggle out of either of us. Denis . . . come here and kiss me . . . before everybody.

Tregoning I shall do nothing of the sort.

Ethel If you don't I swear I won't marry you. Come along. I detest self-conscious people. Come on. (**Denis** *gives her a shamefaced peck on one cheek.*) That's a nice sort of kiss, too! If it wasn't for having to send back the presents I wouldn't marry you.

She goes off.

Tregoning Women have no shame.

The **Major** *comes stalking back, followed in a fearful flurry by his elder sister,* **Honor**. **Denis** *follows* **Ethel**. *Poor* **Honor** (*her female friends are apt to refer to her as Poor* **Honor**) *is a phenomenon common to most large families. From her earliest years she has been bottle-washer to her brothers. They were expensively educated, but she was grudged* *schooling. Her fate is a curious survival of the intolerance of parents towards daughters until the vanity of their hunger for sons has been gratified. In a less humane society she would have been exposed at birth. Yet* **Honor** *is not unhappy in her survival, even if at this moment her life is a burden.*

Major Booth Voysey Honor, they are not in the dining-room.

Honor But they m u s t be! – where else c a n they be?

She has a habit of accentuating one word in each sentence and often the wrong one.

Major Booth Voysey That's what you ought to know.

Mr Voysey (*as he moves towards the door*) Well . . . will you have a game?

Mr George Booth I'll play you fifty up, not more. I'm getting old.

Mr Voysey (*stopping at a dessert dish*) Yes, these are good apples of Bearman's. Six of my trees spoilt this year.

Honor Here you are, Booth.

She triumphantly discovers the discarded box, at which the **Major** *becomes pathetic with indignation.*

Major Booth Voysey Oh, Honor, don't be such a fool. I want the Ramon Allones.

Honor I don't know the difference.

Major Booth Voysey No, you don't, but you might learn.

Mr Voysey (*in a voice like the crack of a very fine whip*) Booth!

Major Booth Voysey (*subduedly*) What is it, sir?

Mr Voysey Look for your cigars yourself. Honor, go back to your reading or your sewing or whatever you were fiddling at, and fiddle in peace.

Mr Voysey *departs, leaving the room rather hushed.*

Mr Booth *has not waited for this parental display. Then* **Alice** *insinuates a remark very softly.*

Alice Have you looked in the library?

Major Booth Voysey (*relapsing to an injured mutter*) Where's Emily?

Honor Upstairs with little Henry, he woke up and cried.

Major Booth Voysey Letting her wear herself to rags over the child . . .

Honor Well, she won't let m e go.

Major Booth Voysey Why don't you stop looking for those cigars?

Honor If you don't mind I want a lace doily now I am here.

Major Booth Voysey I daresay they're in the library. What a house!

He departs.

Honor Booth is so trying.

Alice Honor, why do you put up with it?

Honor Someone has to.

Alice (*discreetly nibbling a nut, which* **Edward** *has cracked for her*) I'm afraid I think Master Major Booth ought to have been taken in hand early . . . with a cane.

Honor (*as she vaguely burrows into corners*) Papa did. But it's never prevented him booming at us . . . oh, ever since he was a baby. Now he's flustered me so I simply can't remember which set of them it was.

Alice The Pettifers wished to be remembered to you, Edward.

Honor I'd better take one of each. (*But she goes on looking.*) I sometimes think, Alice, that we're a very difficult family . . . except perhaps Edward.

Edward Why except me?

Honor And you were always difficult . . . to yourself. (*Then she starts to go, threading her way through the disarranged chairs.*) Mr Colpus will shout so at Mother, and she doesn't like people to think she's so very deaf. . . . I thought Mary Pettifer looking old . . .

She talks herself out of the room.

Alice (*after her*) She's getting old. I was glad not to spend August abroad for once. We drove into Cheltenham to a dance. I golfed a lot.

Edward How long were you with them?

Alice A fortnight. It doesn't seem three months since I was here.

Edward I'm down so seldom.

Alice I might be one of the family . . . almost.

Edward You know they're always pleased.

Alice Well, being a homeless person! But what a cartload to descend . . . yesterday and today. The Major and Emily. . . . Emily's not at all well. Hugh and Mrs Hugh. And me. Are you staying?

Edward No. I must get a word with my father.

Alice Edward . . . you look more like half-baked pie-crust than usual. I wish you didn't sit over your desk quite so much.

Edward (*a little enviously*) You're very well.

Alice I'm always well and nearly always happy.

Major Booth *returns. He has the right sort of cigar in his mouth and is considerably mollified.*

Alice You found them?

Major Booth Voysey Of course they were there. Thank you very much, Alice. Now I want a knife.

Alice I must give you a cigar-cutter for Christmas, Booth.

Major Booth Voysey Beastly things, I hate 'em. (*He eyes the dessert disparagingly.*) Nothing but silver ones. (**Edward** *hands him a carefully opened pocket-knife.*) Thank you, Edward. And I must take one of the candles. Something's gone wrong with the library ventilator and you never can see a thing in that room.

Alice Is Mrs Hugh there?

Major Booth Voysey Writing letters. Things are neglected here, Edward, unless one is constantly on the look-out. The Pater only cares for his garden. I must speak seriously to Honor.

He has returned the knife, still open, and having now lit his cigar at the candle he carries this off.

Edward (*giving her a nut, about the fifteenth*) Here. 'Scuse fingers.

Alice Thank you. (*Looking at him, with her head on one side and her face more humorous than ever.*) Edward, why have you given up proposing to me?

He starts, flushes; then won't be outdone in humour.

Edward One can't go on proposing for ever.

Alice Have you seen anyone you like better?

Edward No.

Alice Well . . . I miss it.

Edward What satisfaction did you find in refusing me?

Alice (*as she weighs the matter*) I find satisfaction in feeling that I'm wanted.

Edward Without any intention of giving . . . of throwing yourself away.

Alice (*teasing his sudden earnestness*) Ah, now we come from mere vanity to serious questions.

Edward Mine was a very serious question.

Alice But, Edward, all questions are serious to you. You're a perfect little pocket-guide to life . . . every question answered; what to eat, drink and avoid, what to believe and what to say. Some things are worth bothering over . . . and some aren't.

Edward One lays down principles.

Alice I prefer my plan. I always do what I know I want to do. Crack me another nut.

Edward Haven't you had enough?

Alice I know I want one more.

He cracks another with a sigh which sounds ridiculous in that connection.

I know it just as I knew I didn't want to marry you . . . each time. I didn't say no on principle . . . or because I thought it wouldn't be wise. That's why I want you to keep on asking me. Because at any moment I might say yes. And then I suppose I should find that it was simply a habit you'd got into . . . and that you didn't want me after all. Still, take another chance. Take it now!

Edward No . . . I think not . . . now.

Alice Edward! There's nothing wrong, is there?

Edward Nothing at all.

They are interrupted by the sudden appearance of **Mrs Hugh Voysey**, *a brisk, bright little woman, in an evening gown which she has bullied a cheap dressmaker into making look exceedingly smart.* **Beatrice** *is hard and clever. But if she keeps her feelings buried pretty deep it is because they are precious to her; and if she is impatient with fools it is because her own brains have had to win her everything in the world, so perhaps she does overvalue them a little. She speaks always with great decision and little effort.*

Beatrice I believe I could write business letters upon an

island in the middle of Fleet Street. But while Booth is
poking at a ventilator with a billiard cue . . . no, I can't.
The Vicar's in the drawing-room . . . and my bedroom's
like an ice-house.

She goes to the fireplace, waving her half-finished letter. **Booth**
appears at the door, billiard cue in hand, and says
solemnly . . .

Major Booth Voysey Edward, I wish you'd come and
have a look at this ventilator, like a good fellow.

Then he turns and goes again, obviously with the weight of an
important matter on his shoulders. With the ghost of a smile
Edward *gets up and follows him.*

Alice No one has a right to be as good and kind as Edward
is. It encourages the rotters.

With which comment she joins **Beatrice** *at the fireplace.*

Beatrice A satisfactory day's shopping?

Alice 'M. The baby bride and I bought clothes all the
morning. Then we had lunch with Denis and bought
furniture.

Beatrice Nice furniture?

Alice Very good and very new. They neither of them know
what they want. (*Then suddenly throwing up her chin and*
exclaiming.) Beatrice . . . why d o women get married?
Oh, of course . . . if you're caught young! With Ethel and
Denis now . . . they're two little birds building their nest
and it's all ideal. They'll soon forget they've ever been
apart.

Now **Honor** *flutters into the room, patient but wild-eyed.*

Honor Mother wants last week's Notes and Queries. Have
you seen it?

Beatrice (*exasperated at the interruption*) No.

Honor It ought not to be here. (*So she proceeds to look for*
it.) Hugh had it.

Beatrice Lit his pipe with it.

Honor Oh, d'you t h i n k so?

So she gives up the search and flutters out again.

Alice This is a most unrestful house.

Beatrice I once thought of putting the Voyseys into a book of mine. Then I concluded they'd be as dull there as they are anywhere else.

Alice They're not duller than most of the rest of us.

Beatrice But how very dull that is!

Alice They're a little noisier and perhaps not quite so well-mannered. But I love them . . . in a sort of way.

Beatrice I don't. I should have thought love was just what they couldn't inspire.

Alice Hugh's not like the others.

Beatrice He has most of their bad points. But I don't love Hugh.

Alice (*her eyebrows up, though she smiles*) Beatrice, you shouldn't say so.

Beatrice Sounds affected, doesn't it?

Alice (*her face growing a little thoughtful*) Beatrice . . . were you in love with Hugh when you married him? Don't answer if you don't want to.

Beatrice I married him for his money.

Alice He hadn't much.

Beatrice I had none . . . and I wanted to chuck journalism and write books. Yes, I loved him enough to marry him. But with some of us . . . that's not much.

Alice But you thought you'd be happy?

Beatrice (*considering carefully*) No, I didn't. I hoped he'd

be happy. Dear Alice, how ever should you understand
these things? You've eight hundred a year.

Alice What has that to do with it?

Beatrice (*putting her case very precisely*) Fine feelings, my
dear, are as much a luxury as clean gloves. From seventeen
to twenty-eight I had to earn my own living . . . and I'm
no genius. So there wasn't a single thing I ever did quite
genuinely for its own sake. No . . . always with an eye to
bread-and-butter . . . pandering to the people who were to
give me that. I warned Hugh . . . he took the risk.

Alice What risk?

Beatrice That one day I'd find I could get on better
without him.

Alice And if he can't without you?

Beatrice One should never let one's happiness depend on
other people. It's degrading . . .

The conservatory door opens and through it come **Mr Voysey**
and **Mr Booth** *in the midst of a discussion.*

Mr Voysey My dear man, stick to the shares and risk it.

Mr George Booth No, of course if you seriously advise
me. . . .

Mr Voysey I never advise greedy children; I let 'em
overeat 'emselves and take the consequences.

Alice (*shaking a finger*) Uncle Trench, you've been in the
garden without a hat after playing billiards in that hot
room.

Mr George Booth We had to give up . . . my wrist was
bad. They've started pool.

Beatrice Is Booth going to play?

Mr Voysey We left him instructing Ethel how to hold a
cue.

Beatrice I can finish my letter.

Off she goes. **Alice** *is idly following with a little paper her hand has fallen on behind the clock.*

Mr Voysey Don't run away, my dear.

Alice I'm taking this to Auntie. . . . Notes and Queries . . . she wants it.

Mr Voysey This room's cold. Why don't they keep the fire up? (*He proceeds to put coals on it.*)

Mr George Booth It was too hot in the billiard-room. You know, Voysey . . . about those Alguazils?

Mr Voysey (*through the rattling of the coals*) What?

Mr George Booth (*trying to pierce the din*) Those Alguazils.

Mr Voysey *with surprising inconsequence points a finger at the silk handkerchief across* **Mr Booth**'s *shirt front.*

Mr Voysey What have you got your handkerchief there for?

Mr George Booth Measure of precau – (*At that moment he sneezes.*) Damn it . . . if you've given me a chill dragging me through your infernal garden . . .

Mr Voysey (*slapping him on the back*) You're an old crock.

Mr George Booth Well, I'll be glad of a winter in Egypt. (*He returns to his subject.*) And if you think seriously that I ought to sell out of the Alguazils before I go . . . ? Well . . . you'll have them. You can sell out if things look bad.

At this moment **Phoebe,** *the middle-aged parlourmaid, comes in, tray in hand. Like an expert fisherman* **Mr Voysey** *lets loose the thread of the conversation.*

Mr Voysey D'you want to clear?

Phoebe It doesn't matter, sir.

Mr Voysey No, go on . . . go on.

So **Mary,** *the young housemaid, comes in as well, and the two start to clear the table. All of which fidgets poor* **Mr Booth** *considerably. He sits shrivelled up in the armchair by the fire; and now* **Mr Voysey** *attends to him.*

Mr Voysey George . . . I've told you again and again that you ought not to run after high interest as you do.

Mr George Booth Yes . . . but one ought to see that one's money's put to good use.

Mr Voysey You're an old gambler.

Mr George Booth (*propitiatingly*) Ah, but then I've you to advise me. I do what you tell me in the end . . . you can't deny that.

Mr Voysey The man who don't know must trust in the man who do.

Mr George Booth (*modestly insisting*) There's ten thousand in Alguazils. What else could we put it into?

Mr Voysey I can get you something at four and a half.

Mr George Booth Oh, Lord!

Mr Voysey (*with a sudden serious friendliness*) I sometimes wish, George, that you'd look after your own affairs a little more than you do. You leave far too much in my hands. If I were a crook I could play Old Harry with them . . . and I doubt if you'd ever find out.

Mr George Booth But, of course, I shouldn't trust anybody. It's a question of knowing one's man . . . as I know you. Ah, my friend, what'll happen to your firm when you depart this life! . . . not before my time, I hope.

Mr Voysey (*with a little frown*) What d'ye mean?

Mr George Booth Edward's no use.

Mr Voysey I beg your pardon . . . very sound in business.

Mr George Booth May be . . . but I tell you he's no use. No personality.

Mr Voysey I fear you don't much like Edward.

Mr George Booth (*with pleasant frankness*) No, I don't.

Mr Voysey That's a pity. That's a great pity.

Mr George Booth (*with a flattering smile*) He's not his father and never will be. What's the time?

Mr Voysey Twenty past ten.

Mr George Booth I must be trotting.

As he goes to the door he meets **Edward**, *who comes in apparently looking for his father; at any rate he catches his eye immediately, while* **Mr Booth** *obliviously continues.*

Mr George Booth I'll look into the drawing-room for a second. Stroll home with me?

Mr Voysey I can't.

Mr George Booth (*mildly surprised at the short reply*) Well, good-night. Good-night, Edward.

He trots away.

Mr Voysey Leave the table, Phoebe.

Phoebe Yes, sir.

Mr Voysey You can come back in ten minutes.

Phoebe *and* **Mary** *depart and the door is closed. Alone with his son* **Mr Voysey** *does not move. His face grows a little keener, that's all.*

Mr Voysey Well, Edward?

Edward *starts to move restlessly about, like a cowed animal in a cage; silently for a moment or two. Then when he speaks his voice is toneless, and he does not look at his father.*

Edward Would you mind, sir, dropping with me for the future all these protestations about putting the firm's affairs straight . . . about all your anxieties and sacrifices. I see now, of course . . . a cleverer man than I could have seen it yesterday . . . that for some time, ever since, I suppose, you recovered from the first shock and got used to the double dealing, this hasn't been your object at all. You've used your clients' capital to produce your own income . . . to bring us up and endow us with. That ten thousand pounds to Booth for his boys; what you're giving Ethel on her marriage . . . ! It's odd it never struck me yesterday that my own pocket-money as a boy must have been drawn from some client's account. I suppose about half the sum you've spent on us first and last would have put things right?

Mr Voysey No, it would not.

Edward (*appealing for the truth*) Come now . . . at some time or other!

Mr Voysey Well, if there have been good times there have been bad. At present the three hundred a year I'm to allow your sister is going to be rather a pull.

Edward Three hundred a year . . . with things as they are! Since it isn't lunacy, sir, I can only conclude that you're enjoying yourself.

Mr Voysey Three trusts . . . two of them big ones . . . have been wound up within this last four years and the accounts have been above suspicion. What's the object of this rodomontade, Edward?

Edward If I'm to remain in the firm it had better be with a very clear understanding of things as they are.

Mr Voysey (*firmly, not too anxiously*) Then you do remain?

Edward (*in a very low voice*) I must remain.

Mr Voysey (*quite gravely*) That's wise of you. . . . I'm very glad.

Edward But I make one condition. And I want some information.

Mr Voysey Well?

Edward Of course no one has ever discovered . . . and no one suspects this state of things?

Mr Voysey Peacey knows.

Edward Peacey!

Mr Voysey His father found out.

Edward Oh. Does he draw hush-money?

Mr Voysey (*curling a little at the word*) I have made him a little present from time to time. But I might well have done that in any case. (*He becomes benevolent.*) Peacey's a devoted fellow. I couldn't do without him.

Edward (*with entire comprehension*) No . . . it would hardly be wise to try. Well . . . the condition I make is a very simple one. It is that we should really try . . . as unobtrusively as you like . . . to put things straight.

Mr Voysey (*with a little polite shrug*) I've no doubt you'll prove an abler man of business than I have been.

Edward To begin with we can halve what I draw from the firm.

Mr Voysey As you please.

Edward And it seems to me that you can't give Ethel this thousand pounds dowry.

Mr Voysey (*shortly, with one of the quick twists of his eye*) I have given my word to Denis . . .

Edward Since the money isn't yours to give.

Mr Voysey (*in an indignant crescendo*) I should not dream of depriving Ethel of what, as my daughter, she has every right to expect. I am surprised at your suggesting such a thing.

Edward (*pale and firm*) I am set on this, Father.

Mr Voysey Don't be such a fool, Edward. What would it look like . . . suddenly refusing without rhyme or reason? What would old Tregoning think?

Edward Oh, can't you see it's my duty to prevent this?

Mr Voysey Well . . . you can prevent it . . . by telling the nearest policeman. It is my duty to pay no more attention to such folly than a nurse pays to her child's tantrums. Understand, Edward, I don't want to force you to go on. Come with me gladly, or don't come at all.

Edward (*dully*) It is my duty to be of what use I can to you, sir. Father, I want to save you if I can.

He flashes into this exclamation of almost broken-hearted affection. **Mr Voysey** *looks at his son for a moment and his lip quivers. Then he steels himself.*

Mr Voysey Thank you! I have been saving myself quite satisfactorily for the last thirty years, and you must please believe that by this time I know my own business best.

Edward (*hopelessly*) Can't we find the money some other way? How do you manage for your own income?

Mr Voysey I have a bank balance and a cheque book, haven't I? I spend what I think well to spend. What's the use of earmarking this or that as my own? You say none of it is my own. I might say it's all my own. I think I've earned it.

Edward (*anger coming on him*) That's what I can't forgive. If you'd lived poor . . . if you'd really done all you could for your clients and not thought of your own pocket . . . then, even though things were no better than they are now . . . why, in a queer sort of way, I could have been proud of you. But, Father, do own the truth . . . I've a right to that from you at least. Didn't you simply seize this chance as a means of money-making?

Mr Voysey (*with a sledge-hammer irony*) Certainly. I sat that morning in my father's office, studying the helmet of the policeman in the street below, and thinking what a glorious path I had happened on to wealth and honour and renown. (*Then he begins to bully* **Edward** *in the kindliest way.*) My dear boy, you don't grasp the A.B.C. of my position. What has carried me to victory? The confidence of my clients. What has earned me that confidence? A decent life, my integrity, my brains? No, my reputation for wealth . . . that, and nothing else. Business now-a-days is run on the lines of the confidence trick. What makes old George Booth so glad to trust me with every penny he possesses? Not affection . . . he's never cared for anything in his life but his collection of French prints.

Edward (*stupefied, helpless*) Is he involved?

Mr Voysey Of course he's involved, and he's always after high interest, too . . . it's little one makes out of him. But there's a further question here, Edward. Should I have had confidence in myself, if I'd remained a poor man? No, I should not. In this world you must either be the master of money or its servant. And if one is not opulent in one's daily life one loses that wonderful . . . financier's touch. One must be confident oneself . . . and I saw from the first that I must at any cost inspire confidence. My whole public and private life has tended to that. All my surroundings . . . you and your brothers and sisters that I have brought into, and up, and put out in the world so worthily . . . you in your turn inspire confidence.

Edward I sat down yesterday to try and make a list of the people who are good enough to trust their money to us. From George Booth with his money piling up while he sleeps . . . so he fancies . . . to Nursie with her savings, which she brought you so proudly to invest. But you've let those be, at least.

Mr Voysey Five hundred pounds. I don't know what I did with it.

Edward But that's damnable.

Mr Voysey Indeed? I give her seventy-five pounds a year for it. Would you like to take charge of that account, Edward? I'll give you five hundred to invest tomorrow.

Edward, *hopelessly beaten, falls into an almost comic state of despair.*

Edward My dear Father, putting every moral question aside . . . it's all very well your playing Robin Hood in this magnificent manner; but have you given a moment's thought to the sort of inheritance you'll be leaving me?

Mr Voysey (*pleased for the first time*) Ah! that's a question you have every right to ask.

Edward If you died tomorrow could we pay eight shillings in the pound . . . or seventeen . . . or five? Do you k n o w?

Mr Voysey And the answer is, that by your help I have every intention, when I die, of leaving a personal estate that will run into six figures. D'you think I've given my life and my talents for a less result than that? I'm fond of you all . . . and I want you to be proud of me . . . and I mean that the name of Voysey shall be carried high in the world by my children and grandchildren. Don't you be afraid, Edward. Ah, you lack experience, my boy . . . you're not full-grown yet . . . your impulses are a bit chaotic. You emotionalise over your work, and you reason about your emotions. You must sort yourself. You must realise that money-making is one thing, and religion another, and family life a third . . . and that if we apply our energies whole-heartedly to each of these in turn, and realise that different laws govern each, that there is a different end to be served, a different ideal to be striven for in each . . .

His coherence is saved by the sudden appearance of his wife, who comes round the door smiling benignly. Not in the least put out, in fact a little relieved, he greets her with an affectionate shout, for she is very deaf.

Mr Voysey Hullo, Mother!

Mrs Voysey Oh, there you are, Trench. I've been deserted.

Mr Voysey George Booth gone?

Mrs Voysey Are you talking business? Perhaps you don't want me.

Mr Voysey No, no . . . no business.

Mrs Voysey (*who has not looked for his answer*) I suppose the others are in the billiard-room.

Mr Voysey (*vociferously*) We're not talking business, old lady.

Edward I'll be off, sir.

Mr Voysey (*genial as usual*) Why don't you stay? I'll come up with you in the morning.

Edward No, thank you, sir.

Mr Voysey Then I'll be up about noon.

Edward Good-night, Mother.

Mrs Voysey *places a plump, kindly hand on his arm and looks up affectionately.*

Mrs Voysey You look tired.

Edward No, I'm not.

Mrs Voysey What did you say?

Edward (*too weary to repeat himself*) Nothing, Mother dear.

He kisses her cheek, while she kisses the air.

Mr Voysey Good-night, my boy.

Then he goes. **Mrs Voysey** *is carrying her Notes and Queries. This is a dear old lady, looking older too than probably she is. Placid describes her. She has had a life of little joys and cares, has never measured herself against the world, never even questioned the shape and size of the little corner of it in which she lives. She has loved an indulgent husband and borne eight children, six of them surviving, healthy. That is her history.*

Mrs Voysey George Booth went some time ago. He said he thought you'd taken a chill walking round the garden.

Mr Voysey I'm all right.

Mrs Voysey D'you think you have?

Mr Voysey (*in her ear*) No.

Mrs Voysey You should be careful, Trench. What did you put on?

Mr Voysey Nothing.

Mrs Voysey How very foolish! Let me feel your hand. You are quite feverish.

Mr Voysey (*affectionately*) You're a fuss-box, old lady.

Mrs Voysey (*coquetting with him*) Don't be rude, Trench.

Honor *descends upon them. She is well into that nightly turmoil of putting everything and everybody to rights which always precedes her bed-time. She carries a shawl which she clasps round her mother's shoulders, her mind and gaze already on the next thing to be done.*

Honor Mother, you left your shawl in the drawing-room. Oh . . . can't they finish clearing?

Mr Voysey (*arranging the folds of the shawl with real tenderness*) Now who's careless!

Phoebe *comes into the room.*

Honor Phoebe, finish here and then you must bring in the tray for Mr Hugh.

Mrs Voysey (*having looked at the shawl and* **Honor**, *and connected the matter in her mind*) Thank you, Honor. You'd better look after your father; he's been walking round the garden without his cape.

Honor Papa!

Mr Voysey Phoebe, you get that little kettle and boil it, and brew me some whiskey and water. I shall be all right.

Honor (*fluttering more than ever*) I'll get it. Where's the whiskey? And Hugh coming back at ten o'clock with no dinner. No wonder his work goes wrong. Here it is! Papa, you do d e s e r v e to be ill.

Clasping the whiskey decanter she is off again. **Mrs Voysey** *sits at the dinner-table and adjusts her spectacles. She returns to Notes and Queries, one elbow firmly planted and her plump hand against her plump cheek. This is her favourite attitude; and she is apt, when reading, to soliloquise in her deaf woman's voice. At least, whether she considers it soliloquy or conversation is not easy to discover.* **Mr Voysey** *stands with his back to the fire, grumbling and pulling faces.*

Mrs Voysey This is a very perplexing correspondence about the Cromwell family. One can't deny the man had good blood in him . . . his grandfather Sir Henry, his uncle Sir Oliver . . .

Mr Voysey There's a pain in my back.

Mrs Voysey . . . and it's difficult to discover where the taint crept in.

Mr Voysey I believe I strained myself putting in those strawberry plants.

Mary, *the house-parlourmaid, carries in a tray of warmed-up dinner for* **Hugh** *and plants it on the table.*

Mrs Voysey Yes, but then how was it he came to disgrace himself so? I believe the family disappeared. Regicide is a root and branch curse. You must read the letter signed CWA . . . it's quite interesting. There's a misprint in mine about the first umbrella-maker . . . now where was it . . . (*And so the dear lady will ramble on indefinitely.*)

The Third Act

The dining-room looks very different in the white light of a July noon. Moreover, on this particular day, it isn't even its normal self. There is a peculiar luncheon spread on the table and on it are decanters of port and sherry; sandwiches, biscuits and an uncut cake; two little piles of plates and one little pile of napkins. There are no table decorations, and indeed the whole room has been made as bare and as tidy as possible. Such preparations denote one of the recognised English festivities, and the appearance of **Phoebe,** *the maid, who has just completed them, the set solemnity of her face and the added touches of black to her dress and cap, suggest that this is probably a funeral. When* **Mary** *comes in, the fact that she has evidently been crying and that she decorously does not raise her voice above an unpleasant whisper makes it quite certain.*

Mary Phoebe, they're coming back . . . and I forgot one of the blinds in the drawing-room.

Phoebe Well, pull it up quick and make yourself scarce. I'll open the door.

Mary *got rid of,* **Phoebe** *composes her face still more rigorously into the aspect of formal grief and with a touch to her apron as well goes to admit the funeral party. The first to enter are* **Mrs Voysey** *and* **Mr Booth,** *she on his arm; and the fact that she is in widow's weeds makes the occasion clear. The little old man leads his old friend very tenderly.*

Mr George Booth Will you come in here?

Mrs Voysey Thank you.

With great solicitude he puts her in a chair; then takes her hand.

Mr George Booth Now I'll intrude no longer.

Mrs Voysey You'll take some lunch?

Mr George Booth No.

Mrs Voysey Not a glass of wine?

Mr George Booth If there's anything I can do just send round.

Mrs Voysey Thank you.

He reaches the door only be be met by the **Major** *and his wife. He shakes hands with them both.*

Mr George Booth My dear Emily! My dear Booth!

Emily *is a homely, patient, pale little woman of about thirty-five. She looks smaller than usual in her heavy black dress and is meeker than usual on an occasion of this kind. The* **Major**, *on the other hand, though his grief is most sincere, has an irresistible air of being responsible for, and indeed rather proud of, the whole affair.*

Major Booth Voysey I think it all went off as he would have wished.

Mr George Booth (*feeling that he is called on for praise*) Great credit . . . great credit.

He makes another attempt to escape and is stopped this time by **Trenchard Voysey**, *to whom he is extending a hand and beginning his formula. But* **Trenchard** *speaks first.*

Trenchard Have you the right time?

Mr George Booth (*taken aback and fumbling for his watch*) I think so . . . I make it fourteen minutes to one. (*He seizes the occasion.*) Trenchard, as a very old and dear friend of your father's, you won't mind me saying how glad I was that you were present today. Death closes all. Indeed . . . it must be a great regret to you that you did not see him before . . . before . . .

Trenchard (*his cold eye freezing this little gush*) I don't think he asked for me.

Mr George Booth (*stoppered*) No? No! Well . . . well . . .

At this third attempt to depart he actually collides with someone in the doorway. It is **Hugh Voysey.**

Mr George Booth My dear Hugh . . . I won't intrude.

Determined to escape, he grasps his hand, gasps out his formula and is off. **Trenchard** *and* **Hugh,** *eldest and youngest son, are as unlike each other as it is possible for Voyseys to be, but that isn't very unlike.* **Trenchard** *has the cocksure manner of the successful barrister;* **Hugh** *the sweetly querulous air of diffidence and scepticism belonging to the unsuccessful man of letters or artist. The self-respect of* **Trenchard**'*s appearance is immense, and he cultivates that air of concentration upon any trivial matter, or even upon nothing at all, which will some day make him an impressive figure upon the Bench.* **Hugh** *is always vague, searching Heaven or the corners of the room for inspiration; and even on this occasion his tie is abominably crooked. The inspissated gloom of this assembly, to which each member of the family as he arrives adds his share, is unbelievable.* **Hugh** *is depressed partly at the inadequacy of his grief:* **Trenchard** *conscientiously preserves an air of the indifference which he feels;* **Booth** *stands statuesque at the mantelpiece; while* **Emily** *is by* **Mrs Voysey,** *whose face in its quiet grief is nevertheless a mirror of many happy memories of her husband.*

Major Booth Voysey I wouldn't hang over her, Emily.

Emily No, of course not.

Apologetically she sits by the table.

Trenchard I hope your wife is well, Hugh?

Hugh Thank you, Trench: I think so. Beatrice is in America . . . giving some lectures there.

Trenchard Really!

*Then comes in a small, well-groomed, bullet-headed schoolboy.
This is the* **Major's** *eldest son. Looking scared and solemn, he
goes straight to his mother.*

Emily Now be very quiet, Christopher.

Then **Denis Tregoning** *appears.*

Trenchard Oh, Tregoning, did you bring Honor back?

Tregoning Yes.

Major Booth Voysey (*at the table*) A glass of wine,
Mother?

Mrs Voysey What?

Booth *hardly knows how to turn his whisper decorously into
enough of a shout for his mother to hear. But he manages it.*

Major Booth Voysey Have a glass of wine?

Mrs Voysey Sherry, please.

*While he pours it out with an air of its being medicine on this
occasion and not wine at all,* **Edward** *comes quickly into the
room, his face very set, his mind obviously on other matters
than the funeral. No one speaks to him for the moment and he
has time to observe them all.* **Trenchard** *is continuing his talk
to* **Denis.**

Trenchard Give my love to Ethel. Is she ill that . . .

Tregoning Not exactly, but she couldn't very well be with
us. I thought perhaps you might have heard. We're
expecting . . .

He hesitates with the bashfulness of a young husband.

Trenchard Indeed. I congratulate you. I hope all will be
well. Please give my best love to Ethel.

Major Booth Voysey (*in an awful voice*) Lunch, Emily?

Emily (*scared*) I suppose so, Booth, thank you.

Major Booth Voysey I think the boy had better run away

and play . . . (*He checks himself on the word.*) Well, take a book and keep quiet; d'ye hear me, Christopher?

Christopher, *who looks incapable of a sound, gazes at his father with round eyes.* **Emily** *whispers 'Library' to him and adds a kiss in acknowledgement of his good behaviour. After a moment he slips out, thankfully.*

Edward How's Ethel, Denis?

Tregoning A little smashed, of course, but no harm done . . . I hope. The doctor's a bit worried about her, though.

Alice Maitland *comes in, brisk and businesslike; a little impatient of this universal cloud of mourning.*

Alice Edward, Honor has gone to her room; I must take her some food and make her eat it. She's very upset.

Edward Make her drink a glass of wine, and say it is necessary she should come down here. And d'you mind not coming back yourself, Alice?

Alice (*her eyebrows up*) Certainly, if you wish.

Major Booth Voysey (*overhearing*) What's this? What's this?

Alice *gets her glass of wine and goes. The* **Major** *is suddenly full of importance.*

Major Booth Voysey What is this, Edward?

Edward I have something to say to you all.

Major Booth Voysey What?

Edward Well, Booth, you'll hear when I say it.

Major Booth Voysey Is it business? . . . because I think this is scarcely the time for business.

Edward Why?

Major Booth Voysey Do you find it easy to descend from your natural grief to the consideration of money? . . . I do not. (*He finds* **Trenchard** *at his elbow.*) I hope you are getting some lunch, Trenchard.

Edward This is business and rather more than business, Booth. I choose now, because it is something I wish to say to the family, not write to each individually . . . and it will be difficult to get us all together again.

Major Booth Voysey (*determined at any rate to give his sanction*) Well, Trenchard, as Edward is in the position of trustee . . . executor . . . I don't know your terms . . . I suppose . . .

Trenchard I don't see what your objection is.

Major Booth Voysey (*with some superiority*) Don't you? I should not call myself a sentimental man, but . . .

Edward You had better stay, Denis; you represent Ethel.

Tregoning (*who has not heard the beginning of this*) Why?

Honor *has obediently come down from her room. She is pale and thin, shaken with grief and worn out besides; for needless to say the brunt of her father's illness, the brunt of everything, has been on her. Six weeks' nursing, part of it hopeless, will exhaust anyone. Her handkerchief is to her eyes, and every minute or two they flood over with tears.* **Edward** *goes and affectionately puts his arm round her.*

Edward My dear Honor, I am sorry to be so . . . so merciless. There! . . . there! (*He hands her into the room; then turns and once more surveys the family, who this time mostly return the compliment. Then he says shortly.*) I think you might all sit down. (*And then, since* **Booth** *happens to be conveniently near . . .*) Shut the door, Booth.

Major Booth Voysey Shut the door!

But he does so, with as much dignity as possible. **Edward** *goes close to his mother and speaks very distinctly, very kindly.*

Edward Mother, we're all going to have a little necessary talk over matters . . . now, because it's most convenient. I hope it won't . . . I hope you won't mind. Will you come to the table?

Mrs Voysey *looks up as if understanding more than he says.*

Mrs Voysey Edward . . .

Edward Yes, Mother dear?

Major Booth Voysey (*commandingly*) You'll sit here, Mother, of course.

He places her in her accustomed chair at the foot of the table. One by one the others sit down, **Edward** *apparently last. But then he discovers that* **Hugh** *has lost himself in a corner of the room and is gazing into vacancy.*

Edward (*with a touch of kindly exasperation*) Hugh, would you mind attending?

Hugh What is it?

Edward There's a chair.

Hugh *takes it. Then for a moment – while* **Edward** *is trying to frame in coherent sentences what he must say to them – for a minute there is silence, broken only by* **Honor**'s *sniffs, which culminate at last in a noisy little cascade of tears.*

Major Booth Voysey Honor, control yourself.

And to emphasise his own perfect control he helps himself majestically to a glass of sherry. Then says . . .

Major Booth Voysey Well, Edward?

Edward I'll come straight to the point which concerns you. Our father's will gives certain sums to you all . . . the gross amount would be something over a hundred thousand pounds. There will be no money.

He can get no further than the bare statement, which is received only with varying looks of bewilderment; until **Mrs Voysey**, *discovering nothing from their faces, breaks this second silence.*

Mrs Voysey I didn't hear.

Hugh (*in his mother's ear*) Edward says there's no money.

Trenchard (*precisely*) I think you said . . . 'will be.'

Major Booth Voysey (*in a tone of mitigated thunder*) Why will there be no money?

Edward (*letting himself go*) Because every penny by right belongs to the clients Father spent his life in defrauding. I mean that in its worst sense . . . swindling . . . thieving. And now I must collect every penny, any money that you can give me; put the firm into bankruptcy; pay back all we can. I'll stand my trial . . . it'll come to that with me . . . and the sooner the better. (*He pauses, partly for breath, and glares at them all.*) Are none of you going to speak? Quite right, what is there to be said? (*Then with a gentle afterthought.*) I'm sorry to hurt you, Mother.

The **Voysey** *family seems buried deep beneath this avalanche of horror. All but* **Mrs Voysey**, *who has been watching* **Edward** *closely, and now says very calmly* . . .

Mrs Voysey I can't hear quite all you say, but I guess what it is. You don't hurt me, Edward . . . I have known of this for a long time.

Edward (*with a muted cry*) Oh Mother, did he know you knew?

Mrs Voysey What do you say?

Trenchard (*collected and dry*) I may as well tell you, Edward; I suspected everything wasn't right about the time of my last quarrel with my father. As there was nothing I could do I did not pursue my suspicions. Was Father aware that you knew, Mother?

Mrs Voysey We never discussed it. There was once a great danger, I believe . . . when you were all younger . . . of his being found out. But we never discussed it.

Edward (*swallowing a fresh bitterness*) I'm glad it isn't such a shock to all of you.

Hugh (*alive to the dramatic aspect of the matter*) My God
. . . before the earth has settled on his grave!

Edward I thought it wrong to put off telling you.

Honor, *the word swindling having spelt itself out in her mind,
at last gives way to a burst of piteous grief.*

Honor Oh, poor Papa! . . . poor Papa!

Edward (*comforting her kindly*) Honor, we shall want your
help and advice.

The **Major** *has recovered from the shock, to swell with
importance. It being necessary to make an impression, he
instinctively turns first to his wife.*

Major Booth Voysey I think, Emily, there was no need
for you to be present at this exposure, and that now you
had better retire.

Emily Very well, Booth.

*She gets up to go, conscious of her misdemeanour. But as she
reaches the door, an awful thought strikes the* **Major**.

Major Booth Voysey Good Heavens . . . I hope the
servants haven't been listening! See where they are, Emily
. . . and keep them away . . . distract them. Open the
door suddenly. (*She does so, more or less, and there is no one
behind it.*) That's all right.

*Having watched his wife's departure, he turns with gravity to
his brother.*

Major Booth Voysey I have said nothing as yet, Edward. I
am thinking.

Trenchard (*a little impatient at this exhibition*) That's the
worst of these family practices . . . a lot of money
knocking around and no audit ever required. The wonder
to me is to find an honest solicitor of that sort anywhere.

Major Booth Voysey Really, Trenchard!

Trenchard Well, think of the temptation.

Edward And most people are such innocents . . .

Trenchard Of course the whole world is getting more and more into the hands of its experts . . .

Edward Here were these funds . . . a kind of lucky bag into which he dipped.

Trenchard But he must have kept accounts of some sort.

Edward Scraps of paper. The separate funds . . . most of them I can't even trace. The capital doesn't exist.

Major Booth Voysey Where's it gone?

Edward (*very directly*) You've been living on it.

Major Booth Voysey Good God!

Trenchard What can you pay in the pound?

Edward As we stand? . . . six or seven shillings, I daresay. But we must do better than that.

To which there is no response.

Major Booth Voysey All this is very dreadful. Does it mean beggary for the whole family?

Edward Yes, it should.

Trenchard (*sharply*) Nonsense.

Edward (*joining issue at once*) What right have we to a thing we possess?

Trenchard He didn't make you an allowance, Booth? Your capital's your own, isn't it?

Major Booth Voysey (*awkwardly placed between the two of them*) Really . . . I . . . I suppose so.

Trenchard How long have you had it?

Major Booth Voysey Oh . . . when I married . . .

Trenchard Then that's all right.

Edward (*vehemently*) It was stolen money . . . it must have been.

Trenchard Possibly . . . but possibly not. And Booth took it in good faith.

Major Booth Voysey I should hope so!

Edward (*dwelling on the words*) It's stolen money.

Major Booth Voysey (*bubbling with distress*) I say, what ought I to do?

Trenchard Do . . . my dear Booth? Nothing.

Edward (*with great indignation*) Trenchard, we owe reparation.

Trenchard No doubt. But to whom? From which client's account was Booth's money taken? You say yourself you don't know.

Edward (*grieved*) Trenchard!

Trenchard My dear Edward . . . the law will take anything it has a right to and all it can get; you needn't be afraid. But what about y o u r position . . . can we get you clear?

Edward Oh . . . I'll face the music.

Booth's *head has been turning incessantly from one to the other and by this he is just a bristle of alarm.*

Major Booth Voysey But I say, you know, this is awful! Will the thing have to be made public?

Trenchard No help for it.

The **Major**'s *jaw drops; he is speechless.* **Mrs Voysey**'s *dead voice steals in.*

Mrs Voysey What is all this?

Trenchard I am explaining, Mother, that the family is not called upon to beggar itself in order to pay back to every client to whom Father owed a pound perhaps eight shillings instead of seven.

Mrs Voysey He will find that my estate has been kept separate.

Trenchard I'm very glad to hear it, Mother.

Edward *hides his face in his hands.*

Mrs Voysey When Mr Barnes died, your father agreed to appointing another trustee.

Tregoning (*diffidently*) I suppose, Edward, I'm involved?

Edward (*lifting his head quickly*) Denis, I hope not. I didn't know that anything of yours. . . .

Tregoning Yes . . . all I got under my aunt's will.

Edward See how things are . . . I've not found a trace of that yet. We'll hope for the best.

Tregoning (*setting his teeth*) It can't be helped.

Major Booth Voysey *leans over the table and speaks in the loudest of whispers.*

Major Booth Voysey Let me advise you to say nothing of this to Ethel at such a critical time.

Tregoning Thank you, Booth . . . naturally I shan't.

Hugh, *by a series of contortions, has lately been giving evidence of a desire or intention to say something.*

Edward Well, what is it, Hugh?

Hugh I have been wondering . . . if he can hear this conversation.

Up to now it has all been meaningless to **Honor**, *in her nervous dilapidation; but this remark brings a fresh burst of tears.*

Honor Oh, poor Papa . . . poor Papa!

Mrs Voysey I think I'll go to my room. I can't hear what any of you are saying. Edward can tell me afterwards.

Edward Would you like to go too, Honor?

Honor (*through her sobs*) Yes, please, I would.

Tregoning I'll get out, Edward. Whatever you think fit to do . . . ! I'm on one side of the fence and Ethel's on the other, so to speak. I wish I'd more work on hand . . . for her sake . . . and the child's. That's all.

By this time **Mrs Voysey** *and* **Honor** *have been got out of the room.* **Tregoning** *follows them, and the four brothers are left together.* **Hugh** *is vacant,* **Edward** *does not speak,* **Booth** *looks at* **Trenchard,** *who settles himself to acquire information.*

Trenchard How long have things been wrong?

Edward He told me the trouble began in his father's time and that he'd been battling with it ever since.

Trenchard (*smiling*) Oh, come now . . . that's hardly possible.

Edward I believed him. Of course I've barely begun on the papers yet. But I doubt if I'll be able to trace anything more than twenty years back . . . unless it's to do with old George Booth's business.

Major Booth Voysey But the Pater never touched his money . . . why, he was a personal friend.

Trenchard How long now since he told you?

Edward Last autumn.

Trenchard What has been happening since?

Edward He got ill in November . . . which didn't make him any easier to deal with. I began by trying to make him put some of the smaller people right. He said that was penny wise and pound foolish. So I've been doing what I could myself this last month or so. Oh . . . nothing to count.

Trenchard He didn't think you'd actually take a hand?

Edward First it was that he was in a corner and I was to help him out. Then we were to clean up the whole mess and have a quarter of a million to the good. That was in February . . . when the new Kaffir boom was on.

Trenchard He was in that, was he?

Edward Up to the neck. And I believe he'd have made a pile if he hadn't been ill. As it was, he got out fifteen thousand to the good.

Major Booth Voysey Really!

Edward I'm not sure he didn't only tell me because he wanted someone to boast to about his financial exploits.

Trenchard Got more reckless as he got older, I suppose.

Edward Oh . . . mere facts meant nothing to him. He drew up this will in May. He knew then he'd nothing to leave . . . on the balance. But there it all is . . . legacies to servants . . . and charities. And I'm the sole executor . . . with an extra thousand for my trouble!

Trenchard Childish! Was I down for anything?

Edward No.

Trenchard (*without resentment*) How he did hate me!

Edward You're spared the results of his affection anyway.

Trenchard What on earth made you stay with him once you knew?

Edward *does not answer for a moment.*

Edward I thought I might prevent things getting worse.

Trenchard I'm afraid your position . . . at the best . . . is not a pleasant one.

Edward (*bowing his head*) I know.

Trenchard, *the only of the three who comprehends, looks at his brother for a moment with something that might almost be admiration. Then he stirs himself.*

Trenchard I must be off. Work waiting . . . end of term.

Major Booth Voysey Shall I walk to the station with you?

Trenchard I'll spend a few minutes with Mother. (*He says,*

at the door, very respectfully.) You'll count on me for any
professional help I can give, please, Edward.

Edward (*simply*) Thank you, Trenchard.

So **Trenchard** *goes. And the* **Major,** *who has been
endeavouring to fathom his final attitude, then comments –*

Major Booth Voysey No heart, y'know! Great brain! If it
hadn't been for that distressing quarrel, he might have
saved our poor father. Don't you think so, Edward?

Edward Perhaps.

Hugh (*giving vent to his thoughts at last with something of a
relish*) The more I think this out, the more devilishly
humorous it gets. Old Booth breaking down by the grave
. . . Colpus reading the service. . . .

Edward Yes, the Vicar's badly hit.

Hugh Oh, the Pater had managed his business for years.

Major Booth Voysey Good God . . . how shall we ever
look old Booth in the face again?

Edward I don't worry about him; he can die quite
comfortably enough on our six shillings in the pound. It's
one or two of the smaller fry who will suffer.

Major Booth Voysey Now, just explain to me . . . I didn't
interrupt while Trenchard was speaking . . . of what
exactly did this defrauding consist?

Edward Speculating with a client's capital. You pocket the
gains . . . and you keep paying the client his ordinary
income.

Major Booth Voysey So that he doesn't find out?

Edward Quite so.

Major Booth Voysey In point of fact, he doesn't suffer?

Edward He doesn't suffer till he finds it out.

Major Booth Voysey And all that's wrong now is that
some of their capital is missing.

Edward (*half-amused, half-amazed at this process of reasoning*) Yes, that's all that's wrong.

Major Booth Voysey What is the – ah – deficit? (*The word rolls from his tongue*).

Edward Anything between two and three hundred thousand pounds.

Major Booth Voysey (*impressed, and not unfavourably*) Dear me . . . this is a big affair!

Hugh (*following his own line of thought*) Quite apart from the rights and wrongs of this, only a very able man could have kept a straight face to the world all these years, as the Pater did.

Major Booth Voysey But he often made money by these speculations?

Edward Very often. His own expenditure was heavy . . . as y o u know.

Major Booth Voysey (*with gratitude for favours received*) He was a very generous man.

Hugh Did nobody ever suspect?

Edward You see, Hugh, when there was any pressing danger . . . if a trust had to be wound up . . . he'd make a great effort and put the accounts straight.

Major Booth Voysey Then he did put some accounts straight?

Edward Yes, when he couldn't help himself.

Booth *looks very enquiring, and then squares himself up to the subject.*

Major Booth Voysey Now look here, Edward. You told us that he told you that it was the object of his life to put these accounts straight. Then you laughed at that. Now you tell me that he did put some accounts straight.

Edward (*wearily*) My dear Booth, you don't understand.

Major Booth Voysey Well, let me understand . . . I am anxious to understand.

Edward We can't pay ten shillings in the pound.

Major Booth Voysey That's very dreadful. But do you know that there wasn't a time when we couldn't have paid five?

Edward (*acquiescent*) Perhaps.

Major Booth Voysey Very well, then! If it was true about his father and all that . . . and why shouldn't we believe him if we can? . . . and he did effect an improvement, that's to his credit, isn't it? Let us at least be just, Edward.

Edward (*patiently polite*) I am sorry if I seem unjust. But he has left me in a rather unfortunate position.

Major Booth Voysey Yes, his death was a tragedy. It seems to me that if he had been spared he might have succeeded at length in this tremendous task and restored to us our family honour.

Edward Yes, Booth, he sometimes spoke very feelingly of that.

Major Booth Voysey (*irony lost upon him*) I can well believe it. And I can tell you that now . . . I may be right or I may be wrong . . . I am feeling far less concerned about the clients' money than I am at the terrible blow to the family which this exposure will strike. Money, after all, can to a certain extent be done without . . . but honour. . . .

This is too much for **Edward**.

Edward Our honour! Does any one of you mean to give me a single penny towards undoing all the wrong that has been done?

Major Booth Voysey I take Trenchard's word for it that that . . . is quite unnecessary.

Edward Then don't talk to me about honour.

Major Booth Voysey (*somewhat nettled at this outburst*) I am thinking of the public exposure. Edward, can't that be prevented?

Edward (*with quick suspicion*) How?

Major Booth Voysey Well, how was it being prevented before he died . . . before we knew anything about it?

Edward (*appealing to the spirits that watch over him*) Oh, listen to this! First Trenchard . . . and now you! You've the poison in your blood, every one of you. Who am I to talk! I daresay so have I.

Major Booth Voysey (*reprovingly*) I am beginning to think that you have worked yourself into rather an hysterical state over this unhappy business.

Edward (*rating him*) Perhaps you'd have been glad . . . glad if I'd gone on lying and cheating . . . and married and begotten a son to go on lying and cheating after me . . . and to pay you your interest in the lie and the cheat.

Major Booth Voysey (*with statesmanlike calm*) Look here, Edward, this rhetoric is exceedingly out of place. The simple question before us is . . . what is the best course to pursue?

Edward There is no question before us. There's only one course to pursue.

Major Booth Voysey (*crushingly*) You will let me speak, please. In so far as our poor father was dishonest to his clients, I pray that he may be forgiven. In so far as he spent his life honestly endeavouring to right a wrong which he had found already committed . . . I forgive him . . . I admire him, Edward . . . and I feel it my duty to – er – reprobate most strongly the – er – gusto with which you have been holding him up in memory to us . . . ten minutes after we'd been standing round his grave . . . as a monster of wickedness. I think I knew him as well as you . . . better. And . . . thank God! . . . there was not between him and me this . . . this unhappy business to

warp my judgment of him. (*He warms to his subject.*) Did
you ever know a more charitable man . . . a larger-
hearted? He was a faithful husband . . . and what a father
to all of us! . . . putting us out into the world and fully
intending to leave us comfortably settled there. Further
. . . as I see this matter, Edward . . . when as a young man
he was told this terrible secret and entrusted with such a
frightful task . . . did he turn his back on it like a coward?
No. He went through it heroically to the end of his life.
And, as he died, I imagine there was no more torturing
thought than that he had left his work unfinished. (*He is
pleased with this peroration.*) And now . . . if all these
clients can be kept receiving their natural incomes . . . and
if Father's plan could be carried out, of gradually replacing
the capital. . . .

Edward *at this raises his head and stares with horror.*

Edward You're asking me to carry on this. . . ? Oh, you
don't know what you're talking about.

The **Major,** *having talked himself back to a proper eminence,
remains good-tempered.*

Major Booth Voysey Well, I'm not a conceited man . . .
but I do think that I can understand a simple financial
problem when it has been explained to me.

Edward You don't know the nerve . . . the unscrupulous
daring it requires to. . . .

Major Booth Voysey Of course, if you're going to argue
round your own incompetence. . . .

Edward (*very straight*) D'you want your legacy?

Major Booth Voysey (*with dignity*) In one moment I shall
get very angry. Here am I doing my best to help you and
your clients . . . and there you sit imputing to me the most
sordid motives. Do you suppose I should touch, or allow
to be touched, the money which Father has left us till
every client's claim was satisfied?

Edward My dear Booth, I know you mean well . . .

Major Booth Voysey I'll come down to your office and work with you.

*At this cheerful prospect even poor **Edward** can't help smiling.*

Edward I'm sure you would.

Major Booth Voysey (*feeling that it is a chance lost*) If the Pater had ever consulted me. . . .

*At this point **Trenchard** looks round the door to say . . .*

Trenchard Are you coming, Booth?

Major Booth Voysey Yes, certainly. I'll talk this over with Trenchard. (*As he gets up and automatically stiffens, he is reminded of the occasion and his voice drops.*) I say . . . we've been speaking very loud. You must do nothing rash. I've no doubt he and I can devise something which will obviate . . . and then I'm sure I shall convince you. . . . (*Glancing into the hall he apparently catches his eldest brother's impatient eye, for he departs abruptly, saying. . . .*) All right, Trenchard, you've eight minutes.

Booth's *departure leaves **Hugh**, at any rate, really at his ease.*

Hugh This is an experience for you, Edward!

Edward (*bitterly*) And I feared what the shock might be to you all! Booth has made a good recovery.

Hugh You wouldn't have him miss such a chance of booming at us.

Edward It's strange that people will believe you can do right by means which they know to be wrong.

Hugh (*taking great interest in this*) Come, what do we know about right and wrong? Let's say legal and illegal. You're so down on the governor because he has trespassed against the etiquette of your own profession. But now he's dead . . . and if there weren't any scandal to think of . . . it's no use the rest of us pretending to feel him a criminal. Because we don't. Which just shows that money . . . and property . . .

At this point he becomes conscious that **Alice Maitland** *is standing behind him, her eyes fixed on his brother. So he interrupts himself to ask . . .*

Hugh D'you want to speak to Edward?

Alice Please, Hugh.

Hugh I'll go.

He goes; a little martyr-like, to conclude the evolution of his theory in soliloquy. His usual fate. **Alice** *still looks at* **Edward**, *and he at her rather appealingly.*

Alice Auntie has told me.

Edward He was fond of you. Don't think worse of him than you can help.

Alice I'm thinking of you.

Edward I may just escape.

Alice So Trenchard says.

Edward My hands are clean, Alice.

Alice I know that.

Edward Mother's not very upset.

Alice She'd expected a smash in his lifetime.

Edward I'm glad that didn't happen.

Alice Yes. I've put Honor to bed. It was a mercy to tell her just at this moment. She can grieve for his death and his disgrace at the same time . . . and the one grief will soften the other perhaps.

Edward Oh, they're all shocked enough at the disgrace . . . but will they open their purses to lessen the disgrace?

Alice Will it seem less disgraceful to have stolen ten thousand pounds than twenty?

Edward I should think so.

Alice I should think so; but I wonder if that's the Law. If

it isn't, Trenchard wouldn't consider the point. I'm sure
Public Opinion doesn't say so . . . and that's what Booth is
considering.

Edward (*with contempt*) Yes.

Alice (*ever so gently ironical*) Well, he's in the Army . . .
he's almost in Society . . . and he has got to get on in both;
one mustn't blame him.

Edward (*very serious*) But when one thinks how the money
was obtained!

Alice When one thinks how most money is obtained!

Edward They've not e a r n e d it.

Alice (*her eyes humorous*) If they had they might have given
it you and earned more. Did I ever tell you what my
guardian said to me when I came of age?

Edward I'm thankful you're out of the mess.

Alice I shouldn't have been, but I was made to look after
my affairs myself . . . much against my will. My guardian
was a person of great character and no principles, the best
and most lovable man I've ever met . . . I'm sorry you
never knew him, Edward . . . and he said once to me:
You've no moral right to your money . . . you've not
earned it or deserved it in any way. So don't be either
surprised or annoyed when any enterprising person tries to
get it from you. He has at least as much moral right to it as
you . . . if he can use it better perhaps he has more.
Shocking sentiments, aren't they? But perhaps that's why
I've less pity for some of these clients than you have,
Edward.

Edward *shakes his head, treating these paradoxes as they
deserve.*

Edward Alice . . . one or two of them will be beggared.

Alice (*sincerely*) Yes, that is bad. What's to be done?

Edward There's old nurse . . . with her poor little savings
gone!

Alice Something can be done for her . . . surely.

Edward The Law's no respecter of persons . . . that's its boast. Old Booth with more than he wants will keep enough and to spare. My old nurse, with just enough, may starve. But it'll be a relief to clear out this nest of lies, even though one suffers one's self. I've been ashamed to walk into that office. I'll hold my head high in prison though.

He shakes himself stiffly erect, his chin high. **Alice** *quizzes him.*

Alice Edward, I'm afraid you're feeling heroic.

Edward I!

Alice You looked quite like Booth for the moment. (*This effectually removes the starch.*) Please don't glory in your martyrdom. It will be very stupid to send you to prison, and you must do your very best to keep out. (*Her tone is most practical.*) We were talking about these people who'll be beggared.

Edward (*simply*) I didn't mean to be heroic.

Alice I know. But there's the danger in acting on principle . . . one begins to think more of one's attitude than of the use of what one is doing.

Edward But I've no choice in the matter. There's only the one thing I can do.

Alice Run the ship ashore? Well . . . if you say so!

Edward Unless you expect me to t a k e Booth's advice . . . turn honest cheat . . . jiggle and speculate in the hope that . . . ! Oh, my dear Alice . . . no! If it were only a question of a few thousands . . . ! But I'm no good at that sort of thing anyway. It'd simply make matters worse. I've been sitting down . . . self-pityingly . . . under the shame of it all these months. I did . . . take a hand . . . and stop one affair going from bad to worse. I'd no right to. Sheer favouritism! I shall suffer for it now.

Alice That's nobody's business but your own.

Edward I could go on doing that . . . putting the worst
cases straight . . . say for a year . . . or till I'm found out
. . . as I almost certainly should be. For don't think I'd be
any good at the game, Alice. (*Then his tone changes; he is
glancing inward.*) But you know . . . there's something in
me that'd rather like to try. (*He looks her full in the face.*)
What do you say?

Alice (*catching her breath*) Dear Edward . . . I can't advise.

Edward (*with grimly whimsical humour*) You've undermined
my principles. I must have some help in exchange.

Alice I'm lawless at heart, I fear. Most women are. What
would happen at the end of the year?

Edward Then I should have to do what I ought to do now
. . . send round a polite letter: Dear Sir or Madam . . . I
am a thief . . . please call the police. For I can't succeed.
Understand that. I can't make up a quarter of a million by
careful management.

Alice Will it be much worse for you . . . if at last they do
call the police?

Edward That . . . as you said . . . would be nobody's
business but my own.

Alice I'd do anything to help you . . . anything. That
sounds like dear Booth . . . and it's just as silly.

Edward Suppose I tackle the job?

Alice Not because I want you to?

Edward Do you? No . . . you shan't have to think that.

Alice But my dear . . . I shall be so proud of you.

Edward When I've failed?

Alice I shan't think it failure.

Edward Booth and Hugh and the rest must hold their
tongues. I needn't have told them.

Alice They'll do that much for you.

Edward But I rather liked telling them too.

She is looking at him with suddenly shining eyes.

Alice Edward . . . I'm so happy. Suddenly . . . you're a different man.

Edward Am I?

Alice You've begun to be. It was in you to be . . . and I knew it.

His face darkens.

Edward I wonder . . . I wonder if I'm not . . . already!

Alice Why . . . ?

Edward And if my father didn't begin . . . just like this? He told me he did. Doing the right thing in the wrong way . . . then doing the wrong thing . . . and coming to be what he was . . . and bringing me to this. Alice, suppose it's not failure I'm risking . . . but success. Yes, you're right . . . I feel a different man.

She brings him help.

Alice I'll take that risk, my dear. I'll risk your turning crook. And it's a pretty big risk now for me.

He accepts it.

Edward Then there's no more to be said, is there?

Alice Not for the moment. (*He does not ask what she means by this.*) I must go back to Honor. Horrid . . . if one knew it . . . to look comic when one is suffering. (*As she opens the door.*) And here's Booth back again.

Edward Shall I tell him he has convinced me?

Alice (*mischievously*) It would delight him. But I shouldn't.

The Fourth Act

Mr Voysey's *room at the office is* **Edward**'s *room now. It has somehow lost that brilliancy which the old man's occupation seemed to give it. Perhaps it is only because this December morning is dull and depressing; but the fire isn't bright and the panels and windows don't shine as they did. There are no roses on the table either.* **Edward**, *walking in as his father did, hanging his hat and coat where his father's used to hang, is certainly the palest shadow of that other masterful presence. A depressed, drooping shadow, too. This may be what* **Peacey** *feels; for he looks very surly as he obeys the old routine of following his chief to this room on his arrival. Nor has* **Edward** *so much as a glance for his confidential clerk. They exchange the most formal of greetings.* **Edward** *sits at his desk, on which lies the morning's pile of letters, unopened now.*

Peacey Good morning, sir.

Edward Good morning, Peacey. Any notes for me?

Peacey Well, I've hardly been through the letters yet sir.

Edward (*his eyebrows meeting*) Oh . . . and I'm late myself.

Peacey I'm very sorry, sir.

Edward If Mr Bullen calls, you had better show him those papers. Write to Metcalfe; say I've seen Mr Vickery this morning and that we hope for a decision from Mr Booth within a day or so. Better show me the letter.

Peacey Very good, sir.

Edward That's all, thank you.

Peacey *gets to the door, where he stops, looking not only surly but nervous now.*

Peacey May I speak to you a moment, sir?

Edward Certainly.

Peacey, after a moment, makes an effort, purses his mouth and begins.

Peacey Bills are beginning to come in upon me as is usual at this season, sir. My son's allowance at Cambridge is now rather a heavy item of my expenditure. I hope that the custom of the firm isn't to be neglected now that you are the head of it, Mr Edward. Two hundred your father always made it at Christmas . . . in notes if you please.

Towards the end of this **Edward** *begins to pay attention. When he answers his voice is harsh.*

Edward Oh to be sure . . . your hush-money.

Peacey (*bridling*) That's not a very pleasant word.

Edward This is an unpleasant subject.

Peacey Well, it's not one I wish to discuss. Mr Voysey would always give me the notes in an envelope when he shook hands with me at Christmas.

Edward Notes I understand. But why not a rise in salary?

Peacey Mr Voysey's custom, sir, from before my time. My father . . .

Edward Yes. It's an hereditary pull you have over the firm, isn't it?

Peacey When my father retired . . . he's been dead twenty-six years, Mr Edward . . . he simply said: I have told the governor you know what I know. And Mr Voysey said . . . I treat you as I did your father, Peacey. Never another word with him on the subject.

Edward A very decent arrangement . . . and the thriftiest no doubt. Of the raising of salaries there might have been no end.

Peacey Mr Edward, that's uncalled for. We have served

you and yours most faithfully. I know my father would
sooner have cut off his hand than do anything to embarrass
the firm.

Edward But business is business, Peacey. Surely he could
have had a partnership for the asking.

Peacey That's another matter, sir.

Edward Why?

Peacey A matter of principle, if you'll excuse me. I must
not be taken to approve of the firm's conduct. Nor did my
dear father approve. And at anything like a partnership he
would certainly have drawn the line.

Edward My apologies.

Peacey That's all right, sir. Always a bit of friction in
coming to an understanding about anything, isn't there,
sir?

He is going when **Edward**'s *question stops him.*

Edward Why didn't you speak about this last Christmas?

Peacey You were so upset about your father's death.

Edward My father died the summer before that.

Peacey Well . . . truthfully, Mr Edward?

Edward As truthfully as you think suitable.

The irony of this is wasted on **Peacey**, *who becomes pleasantly
candid.*

Peacey Well, I'd always thought there must be a smash
when your father died . . . but it didn't come. I couldn't
make you out. So I thought I'd better keep quiet for a bit
and say nothing.

Edward I see. Your son's at Cambridge?

Peacey Yes.

Edward I wonder you didn't bring him into the firm.

Peacey (*taking this very kind*) Thank you. But James will go to the bar. He'll have to wait his chance, of course. But he's a clever lad. And it's a good use for one's savings.

Edward I feel sure he'll do well. I'm glad to have had this little talk with you, Peacey. I'm sorry you can't have the money.

He returns to his letters, a little steely-eyed. **Peacey**, *quite at his ease, makes for the door yet again, saying . . .*

Peacey Oh, any time will do, sir.

Edward You can't have it at all.

Peacey (*brought up short*) Can't I?

Edward No. This was one of the first things I made up my mind about. The firm's business is not carried on quite as it used to be. You may have noticed that you don't get the same little matters passing through your hands. In fact, we no longer make illicit profits out of our clients. So there are none for you to share.

Peacey *bridles*

Peacey Mr Edward . . . I'm sorry we began this discussion. You'll give me my two hundred, please . . . and we'll drop the subject.

Edward Yes . . . I've no more to say.

Peacey I want the money. And it's hardly gentlemanly in you, Mr Edward, to try and get out of giving it me. Your father'd never have made such an excuse.

Edward D'you think I'm lying to you?

Peacey That is no business of mine, sir.

Edward As long as the dividend is punctually paid.

Peacey And there's no need to be sarcastic.

Edward Would you rather I told you plainly what I think of you?

Peacey That I'm a thief because I've taken money from a thief?

Edward Worse! You're content to have others steal for you.

Peacey And who isn't?

Edward *is really pleased with the retort. He relaxes and changes his tone, which had indeed become a little bullying.*

Edward Ah, my dear Peacey . . . I fear we mustn't begin to talk economics. The present point is that I myself no longer receive these particular stolen goods. Therefore I can throw a stone at you. I have thrown it.

Peacey, *who would far sooner be bullied than talked to like this, turns very sulky indeed.*

Peacey Then I resign my position here.

Edward Very well.

Peacey And I happen to think the secret's worth its price.

Edward Perhaps someone will pay it you.

Peacey (*feebly threatening*) Don't presume upon it's not being worth my while to make use of what I know.

Edward (*not unkindly*) But, my good fellow, it happens to be the truth I'm telling you. I am doing a thankless . . . and an unpleasant . . . and a quite unprofitable job here. How can you hope to blackmail a man who has everything to gain by exposure and nothing to lose?

Peacey (*peeving*) I don't want to ruin you, sir, and I have a great regard for the firm. But you must see that I can't have my income reduced in this way without a struggle.

Edward (*with great cheerfulness*) Very well . . . struggle away.

Peacey (*his voice rising high and thin*) But is it fair dealing on your part to dock the money suddenly like this? I have been counting on it most of the year, and I have been led into heavy expenses. Why couldn't you have warned me?

Edward Yes, that's true, Peacey . . . it was stupid of me. I'm sorry.

Peacey *is a little comforted by this quite candid acknowledgment.*

Peacey Things may get easier for you by and by.

Edward Possibly.

Peacey Will you reconsider the matter then?

At this insinuation **Edward** *looks up, more than a little exasperated.*

Edward Then you don't believe what I tell you?

Peacey Yes, I do.

Edward But you think that the fascination of swindling one's clients will finally prove irresistible?

Peacey That's what your father found, I suppose you know.

This gives **Edward** *such pause that he drops his masterful tone.*

Edward I didn't.

Peacey He got things as right as rain once.

Edward Did he?

Peacey So my father told me. But he started again.

Edward Are you sure of this?

Peacey (*expanding pleasantly*) Well, sir, I knew your father pretty well. And when I first came into the firm I simply hated him. He was that sour . . . so snappy with everyone . . . as if he had a grievance against the whole world.

Edward (*pensively*) He had then . . . in those days!

Peacey His dealings with his clients were no business of

mine. I speak as I find. He came to be very kind to me . . .
thoughtful and considerate. He was pleasant and generous
to everyone . . .

Edward So you have hopes of me yet?

Peacey (*who has a simple mind*) No, Mr Edward, no.
You're different from your father . . . one must make up
one's mind to that. And you may believe me or not, but I
should be very glad to know that the firm was going
straight again. I'm getting on in years myself, now. I'm not
much longer for the business, and there've been times
when I have sincerely regretted my connection with it. If
you'll let me say so, I think it's very noble of you to have
undertaken the work you have. (*Then, as everything seems
smooth again.*) And if you'll give me enough to cover this
year's extra expense, I think I may promise you that I
shan't expect money again.

Edward (*good-tempered, as he would speak to an importunate
child*) No, Peacey, no.

Peacey (*fretful again*) Well, sir, you make things very
difficult for me.

Edward Here is a letter from Mr Cartwright which you
might attend to. If he wants an appointment with me,
don't make one till the New Year. His case can't come on
before February.

Peacey (*taking the letter*) I show myself anxious to meet you
in every way. . . . (*He is handed another.*).

Edward 'Perceval Building Estate' . . . that's yours too.

Peacey (*putting them both down, resolutely*) But I refuse to
be ignored. I must consider my whole position. I hope I
may not be tempted to make use of the power I possess.
But if I am driven to proceed to extremities . . .

Edward (*breaking in upon this bunch of tags*) My dear
Peacey, don't talk nonsense . . . you couldn't proceed to
an extremity to save your life. You've comfortably taken
this money all these years. You'll find you're no longer

capable of doing even such a slightly uncomfortable thing
as tripping up your neighbour.

*This does completely upset the gentle blackmailer. He loses one
grievance in another.*

Peacey Really, Mr Edward, I am a considerably older man
than you. These personalities . . . !

Edward I'm sorry. Don't forget the letters.

Peacey I will not, sir.

He takes them with great dignity and is leaving the room.

Peacey There's Mr Hugh waiting.

Edward To see me? Ask him in.

Peacey Come in, Mr Hugh, please.

Hugh *comes in,* **Peacey** *holding the door for him with a frigid
politeness of which he is quite oblivious. At this final slight*
Peacey *goes out in dudgeon.*

Edward How are you?

Hugh I don't know.

And he throws himself into the chair by the fire. **Edward,** *quite
used to this sort of thing, goes quietly on with his work, adding
encouragingly after a moment . . .*

Edward How's Beatrice?

Hugh Ink to the elbows. She's half-way through her new
book.

*He studies his boots with the gloomiest expression. And indeed,
they are very dirty and his turned-up trousers are muddy at the
edge. As he is quite capable of sitting silently by the fire for a
whole morning* **Edward** *asks him at last . . .*

Edward Do you want anything?

Hugh Yes . . . I want five bob. I left home without a
penny. I've walked.

Edward From Highgate?

Hugh Yes . . . by Hornsey and Highbury and Hackney and Hoxton. And I must have some lunch.

Edward I can manage five bob . . .

He puts them on his table.

Hugh And Upper Holloway and Lower Holloway . . . and Pentonville . . . and Clerkenwell . . .

Edward I don't know any of them.

Hugh Nobody does . . . except the million people who live there. But that's London. And I also, my dear Edward, want it destroyed.

Edward We are warned that . . . under certain circumstances . . . it may be.

Hugh But why wait for mere foreigners to do the job? Why not tackle it ourselves . . . and, in the inspiring words of Mr Rockefeller, d o i t n o w?

Edward And what about the people who live there?

Hugh Why should they live there . . . or anywhere? Why should they live at all?

Edward Well, they've their work to do . . . most of them. Incidentally . . . much as I love your society . . . so have I mine. And this morning I'm rather busy.

Hugh Aha! There's the fatal word. We don't work, Edward, not one in a thousand of us. Work is creation. Is that what an outworn civilisation requires of us? Obviously not. It asks us to keep busy . . . and forget that to all these means there is no creative end at all. We've to keep our accounts straight . . . as you have to now . . . to keep the streets clean . . . and ourselves clean . . .

Edward That at least may be called an end in itself.

Hugh I'm not so sure. If it's merely a habit . . . all habits are bad habits. Why wash?

Edward I seem to remember that, as a small boy, washing was not your strong point.

Hugh I'm glad I had that much moral courage. On principle a man should not wash unless he feels an inward urge to wash. Did Michelangelo wash? Seldom!

Edward Better his work than his company, then.

Hugh I'm sick of this endless sham. But one can put some sort of an end to it . . . if not to all of it . . . to one's own small share in it. And I mean to. So that's that.

Edward Suicide?

Hugh Oh dear me no! Life's great fun if you could only live it. I mean to live it. Thanks for the five bob. (*He pockets it.*) And my first step is to hand you back for your wretched clients the money that the Pater settled on me . . . what there is left of it. And don't let me forget that I owe you this too.

Edward But my dear Hugh, you can't afford . . .

Hugh Aha! Another fatal word. Afford! Give a man an income . . . big or small . . . and he passes half his time thinking what he can or can't afford. The money has been a curse to me. It has never belonged to me . . .

Edward No.

Hugh Oh, never mind the legal . . . I mean in the r e a l sense. How could it belong to me? I didn't create it . . . or even earn it. I've belonged to it. So there's the first step to being free. My spiritual history is a very interesting one, Edward. If it weren't for Beatrice I'd make a book of it.

Edward Would it show her up badly?

Hugh No . . . but writing's h e r job. One mustn't poach.

Edward She might make a book of it.

Hugh Oh, it doesn't interest h e r. D'you remember the row there was at home when I said I meant to paint?

Edward Very well.

Hugh However . . . the Pater came down at last with two hundred a year. Studio rent, velvet coat, mutton chop cooked on the gas stove, and sardines for supper . . . that's what the art of painting meant to him. Then I got married to Beatrice . . . which was so unexpectedly moral of me that he sprang another two hundred. Well . . . I've kept busy. And I've learnt how to paint. And I do paint . . . other men's pictures.

Edward Forgery?

Hugh Yes . . . it is.

Edward Are you joking?

Hugh Not at all. Forty-nine out of fifty of us . . . if you put us to paint that table and chair . . . to begin with we don't s e e that table and chair! What we see is what we remember of some painting by Matisse or Picasso of some other table and chair. This world, my dear Edward, is growing fuller and fuller of paintings of paintings . . . and of paintings of paintings of paintings. And a couple of hundred of them must be mine. If I could afford it . . . aha, afford! . . . I'd buy them back and burn them. But the critics, dear Edward, much prefer paintings of paintings to paintings . . . for they know what to say about them. They rejoice when they see that bastard great-grandchild of Picasso's . . .

Edward's *table telephone rings.*

Edward Yes? Yes . . . in two minutes. I must turn you out, Hugh. What does Beatrice say, by the bye?

Hugh About the money? Yes, there's that. I can't quite leave her with nothing.

Edward Are you leaving her?

Hugh We got married with the idea that we'd separate some time. And I can't be free unless I do.

Edward I thought you were so fond of each other.

Hugh I suppose in a sort of way we still are. We've always disagreed about everything. That used to be stimulating. But now when we argue we quarrel. And that's tiring.

Edward Do they know at home that you're not getting on?

Hugh Emily may.

Edward For Heaven's sake keep a good face on things for Christmas.

Hugh I don't believe I'll go down for Christmas.

Edward Nonsense! You can't hurt Mother's feelings by . . .

Hugh Do not expect me to pay homage to the Voysey family feelings. If we must have a hollow fraud to kow-tow before, there are many less brassy ones. Good Lord . . . you're not still taken in by them, surely . . . after the way we've all treated you? Even I've shirked asking you how you've been getting on here . . . for fear you'd start telling me. How are things, though?

Edward I've not done so badly. Better than I thought I should, really! I've righted what I thought the four most scandalous cases . . . somewhat to the prejudice of the rest.

Hugh Then can't you cut free?

Edward And go to gaol?

Hugh (*really startled by this*) But they won't . . .

Edward But they will.

Hugh And at any moment . . . ?

Edward Yes. I live on the brink. For the first month or so I thought every knock at the door meant a push over it. But nothing happens. There are days . . . you wouldn't believe it . . . when I quite forget that I'm a criminal. And . . . it's possible . . . nothing may happen. And . . . at this moment . . . I really don't know whether I want it to or not.

Hugh I should take the plunge.

Edward Why?

Hugh The longer you wait the worse it'll be for you, won't it?

Edward Yes.

Hugh The thing's telling on you too.

Edward I know. My barber tries to sell me hair restorer.

Hugh On your faculties. The damn thing is swallowing you up. Don't let it. You've no right to let your life be brought to nothing.

Edward Does my life matter?

Hugh But of course.

Edward (*the iron in his soul*) That's where we differ. Still, now I've scavenged up the worst of the mess . . . and can only sit here drudging . . . improving things by thirty shillings here . . . and by seven pounds two and sixpence there . . . I do begin to understand Father a little better.

Hugh (*cheerfully*) Oh . . . I'm all for the Pater. He played a great game. And what this civilisation needs . . . if we can't smash it up altogether . . . is a lot more men like him. . . .

The door is opened and **Mr George Booth** *comes in. He looks older than he did and besides is evidently not in a happy frame of mind.*

Mr George Booth Hullo, Hugh. How are you, Edward?

Hugh But what I'm going to do is to step out of my front door with five bob in my pocket. And I'll tramp . . . and I'll paint for my bread . . . the farmer . . . the farmer's wife . . . or his dog or his cow . . . an honest bit of work done with despatch for just what he thinks it's worth to him. And if I can earn my bread I'll know I'm some good . . . and if I can't I'll drown myself.

Edward I should wait till the summer comes.

Hugh I'll begin with your office boy. For two shillings I will do him a sketch of his spotty little countenance. Edward, may I propose it to him?

Edward You may not. To begin with he can't afford two shillings . . .

Hugh Aha! Afford! And of course he's very busy too?

Edward If he isn't, I'll sack him.

Hugh Good God . . . what a world! Good-bye.

Hugh *departs, not, we may be sure, to tramp the roads; but he has thoroughly enjoyed hearing himself talk.*

Edward Will you come here . . . or will you sit by the fire?

Mr George Booth This'll do. I shan't keep you long.

Edward Well . . . here's the Vickery correspondence. He will pay the extra rent, but . . .

Mr George Booth (*nervously*) Yes . . . it isn't really that I've come about.

Edward No?

Mr George Booth Something less pleasant, I'm afraid.

Edward Litigation? I trust not.

Mr George Booth No. . . . I'm getting too old to quarrel. No! I've made up my mind to withdraw my securities from the custody of your firm. I don't know what notice is usual.

He has got it out and feels better. **Edward** *has awaited such a shock for so long that now it has come he finds he feels nothing.*

Edward To a good solicitor . . . five minutes. Ten for a poor one. Have you any particular reason for doing this, Mr Booth?

Mr George Booth (*thankful to be able to talk and, so he thinks, stave off reproaches*) Oh . . . naturally . . . naturally!

You can't but know, Edward, that I have never been able
to feel that implicit confidence in you . . . in your abilities,
your personality, that's to say . . . which I reposed in your
father. Well . . . hardly to be expected, was it?

Edward (*grimly acquiescent*) Hardly.

Mr George Booth It's nothing against you. Men like your
father are few and far between. I don't doubt that things
go on here as they have always done. But since he died . . .
I have not been happy about my affairs. It is a new
experience for me . . . to feel worried . . . especially about
money. The possession of money has always been
something of a pleasure to me. And my doctor . . . I saw
him again yesterday . . . he keeps me on a diet now . . .
quite unnecessary . . . but he said that above all things I
was not to worry. And, as I made up my mind upon the
matter some time ago . . . in point of fact more than a year
before your father died it was clear to me that I could not
leave my interests in your hands as I had in his. . . .

Edward (*but this strikes* **Edward** *with the shock of a bullet*)
Did he know that?

Mr George Booth He must have guessed. I practically
told him so. And I hoped he'd tell you . . . and so spare
me the unpleasant necessity of hurting your feelings . . . as
I fear I must be doing now.

Edward Not at all. But we'll take it, if you please, that he
never guessed. (*For with that thought of his father he really
could not live.*) I can't induce you to change your mind?

Mr George Booth No. And I'd sooner you wouldn't try. I
shall make a point of telling the family that you are in no
way to blame. My idea is for the future to let my bank . . .

Edward For it's my duty to if I can. . . .

Mr George Booth Heavens above us, my dear Edward
. . . the loss of one client . . . however important . . . !

Edward I know. Well . . . here's the way out. And it isn't
my fault.

Mr George Booth Forgive me for saying that your conduct seems to me a little lacking in dignity.

Edward (*patient; ironic*) I'm sure it must. Will you walk off with your papers now? They'll make rather a cart-load.

Mr George Booth You'll have to explain matters a bit.

Edward (*grimly*) Yes. I'd better. How much . . . Mr Booth . . . do you think you're worth?

Mr George Booth God bless me . . . I k n o w what I'm worth. I'm not a baby . . . or a woman. I have it all written down . . . more or less . . . in a little book.

Edward I should like to see that little book. You'll get not quite half of that out of us.

Mr George Booth Don't be perverse, Edward. I said I had made up my mind to withdraw the whole. . . .

Edward You should have made it up sooner.

Mr George Booth What's this all about?

Edward The greater part of what is so neatly written down in that little book doesn't exist.

Mr George Booth Nonsense. It must exist. I don't want to realise. You hand me over the securities. I don't need to reinvest simply because . . .

Edward (*dealing his blow not unkindly, but squarely*) I can't hand you over what I haven't got.

The old man hears the words. But their meaning . . . ?

Mr George Booth Is anything . . . wrong?

Edward How many more times am I to tell you that we have robbed you of half your property?

Mr George Booth (*his senses almost failing him*) Say that again.

Edward It's quite true.

Mr George Booth My money . . . gone?

Edward Yes.

Mr George Booth (*clutching at a straw of anger*) You've been the thief . . . you . . . you . . . ?

Edward I wouldn't tell you so if I could help it . . . my father.

This actually calls **Mr Booth** *back to something like dignity and self-possession. He thumps* **Edward***'s table furiously.*

Mr George Booth I'll make you prove that.

Edward Oh, you've fired a mine.

Mr George Booth (*scolding him well*) Slandering your dead father, and lying to me . . . revenging yourself by frightening me . . . because I detest you!

Edward Why . . . haven't I thanked you for pushing me over the edge? I do . . . I promise you I do.

Mr George Booth (*shouting; and his courage fails him as he shouts*) Prove it . . . prove it to me. You don't frighten me so easily. One can't lose half of all one has and then be told of it in two minutes . . . sitting at a table. (*His voice tails off to a piteous whimper.*)

Edward (*quietly now and kindly*) If my father had told you this in plain words, you'd have believed him.

Mr George Booth (*bowing his head*) Yes.

Edward *looks at the poor old thing with great pity.*

Edward What on earth did you want to do this for? You need never have known . . . you could have died happy. Settling with all those charities in your will would have smashed us up. But proving your will is many years off yet, we'll hope.

Mr George Booth (*pathetic and bewildered*) I don't understand. No, I don't understand . . . because your father . . . ! But I m u s t understand, Edward.

Edward I shouldn't try to, if I were you. Pull yourself

together, Mr Booth. After all, this isn't a vital matter to you. It's not even as if you had a family to consider . . . like some of the others.

Mr George Booth (*vaguely*) What others?

Edward Don't imagine your money has been specially selected for pilfering.

Mr George Booth (*with solemn incredulity*) One has read of this sort of thing. But I thought people always got found out.

Edward (*brutally humorous*) Well . . . you've found us out.

Mr George Booth (*rising to the full appreciation of his wrongs*) Oh . . . I've been foully cheated!

Edward (*patiently*) Yes . . . I've told you so.

Mr George Booth (*his voice breaks, he appeals pitifully*) But by you, Edward . . . say it's by you.

Edward (*unable to resist his quiet revenge*) I've not the ability or the personality for such work, Mr Booth . . . nothing but the remains of a few principles, which forbid me even to lie to you.

The old gentleman draws a long breath and then speaks with great awe, blending into grief.

Mr George Booth I think your father is in Hell. I loved him, Edward . . . I loved him. How he could have had the heart! We were friends for fifty years. And all he cared for was to cheat me.

Edward (*venturing the comfort of an explanation*) No . . . he didn't value money quite as you do.

Mr George Booth (*with sudden shrill logic*) But he took it. What d'you mean by that?

Edward *leans back in his chair and changes the tenor of their talk.*

Edward Well, you are master of the situation now. What are you going to do?

Mr George Booth To get the money back?

Edward No, that's gone.

Mr George Booth Then give me what's left and –

Edward Are you going to prosecute?

Mr George Booth (*shifting uneasily in his chair*) Oh, dear . . . is that necessary? Can't somebody else do that? I thought the law . . . ! What'll happen if I don't?

Edward What do you suppose I'm doing here now?

Mr George Booth (*as if he were being asked a riddle*) I don't know.

Edward (*earnestly*) When my father died, I began to try and put things straight. Then I made up my accounts . . . they can see who has lost and who hasn't and do as they please about it. And now I've set myself to a duller sort of work. I throw penny after penny hardly earned into the half-filled pit of our deficit. I've been doing that . . . for what it's worth . . . till this should happen. If you choose to let things alone . . . and hold your tongue . . . I can go on with the job till the next threat comes . . . and I'll beg that off too if I can. I've thought this my duty . . . and it's my duty to ask you to let me go on. (*He searches* **Mr Booth**'*s face and finds there only disbelief and fear. He bursts out.*) Oh, you might at least believe me. It can't hurt you to believe me.

Mr George Booth You must admit, Edward, it isn't easy to believe anything in this office . . . just for the moment.

Edward (*bowing to the extreme reasonableness of this*) I suppose not. I can prove it to you. I'll take you through the books . . . you won't understand them . . . but I could prove it.

Mr George Booth I think I'd rather not. Ought I to hold any further friendly communication with you now at all?

And at this he takes his hat.

Edward (*with a little explosion of contemptuous anger*) Certainly not. Prosecute . . . prosecute!

Mr George Booth (*with dignity*) Don't lose your temper. It's my place to be angry with you.

Edward I shall be grateful if you'll prosecute.

Mr George Booth It's all very puzzling. I suppose I must prosecute. I believe you're just trying to practise on my goodness of heart. Certainly I ought to prosecute. Oughtn't I? I suppose I must consult another solicitor.

Edward (*his chin in the air*) Why not write to *The Times* about it?

Mr George Booth (*shocked and grieved at his attitude*) Edward, how can you be so cool and heartless?

Edward (*changing his tone*) D'you think I shan't be glad to sleep at night?

Mr George Booth You may be put in prison.

Edward I am in prison . . . a less pleasant one than Wormwood Scrubs. But we're all prisoners, Mr Booth.

Mr George Booth (*wagging his head*) Yes. This is what comes of your free-thinking and philosophy. Why aren't you on your knees?

Edward To you?

This was not what **Mr Booth** *meant, but he assumes a vicarious dignity of that sort.*

Mr George Booth And why should you expect me to shrink from vindicating the law?

Edward (*shortly*) I don't. I've explained you'll be doing me a kindness. When I'm wanted you'll find me here at my desk. (*Then as an afterthought.*) If you take long to decide . . . don't alter your behaviour to my family in the meantime. They know the main points of the business, and. . . .

Mr George Booth (*knocked right off his balance*) Do they? Good God! And I'm going there to dinner the day after tomorrow. It's Christmas Eve. The hypocrites!

Edward (*unmoved*) I shall be there . . . that will have given you two days. Will you tell me then?

Mr George Booth (*protesting violently*) But I can't go . . . I can't have dinner with them. I must be ill.

Edward (*with a half-smile*) I remember I went to dine at Chislehurst to tell my father of my decision.

Mr George Booth (*testily*) What decision?

Edward To remain in the firm when I first learned what was happening.

Mr George Booth (*interested*) Was I there?

Edward I daresay.

Mr Booth *stands, hat, stick, gloves in hand, shaken by this experience, helpless, at his wits' end. He falls into a sort of fretful reverie, speaking half to himself, but yet as if he hoped that* **Edward**, *who is rapt in his own thoughts, would have the decency to answer, or at least listen to what he is saying.*

Mr George Booth Yes, how often I dined with him! Oh, it was monstrous! (*His eyes fall on the clock.*) It's nearly lunchtime now. D'you know I can still hardly believe it all. I wish I hadn't found it out. If he hadn't died, I should never have found it out. I hate to have to be vindictive . . . it's not my nature. I'm sure I'm more grieved than angry. But it isn't as if it were a small sum. And I don't see that one is called upon to forgive crimes . . . or why does the law exist? This will go near to killing me. I'm too old to have such troubles. It isn't right. And if I have to prosecute. . . .

Edward (*at last throwing in a word*) Well . . . you need not.

Mr George Booth (*thankful for the provocation*) Don't you attempt to influence me, sir. (*He turns to go.*)

Edward And what's more . . . with the money you have left . . .

Edward *follows him politely.* **Mr Booth** *flings the door open.*

Mr George Booth You'll make out a cheque for that at once, sir, and send it me.

Edward You might . . .

Mr George Booth (*clapping his hat on, stamping his stick*) I shall do the right thing, sir . . . never fear.

So he marches off in fine style, he thinks, having had the last word and all. But **Edward**, *closing the door after him, mutters . . .*

Edward Save your soul . . . I'm afraid I was going to say.

The Fifth Act

Naturally it is the dining-room which bears the brunt of what an English household knows as Christmas decorations. They consist chiefly of the branches of holly, stuck cock-eyed behind the top edges of the pictures. The one picture conspicuously not decorated is that which hangs over the fireplace, a portrait of **Mr Voysey**, *with its new gilt frame and its brass plate marking it also as a presentation. Otherwise the only difference between the dining-room's appearance at half-past nine on Christmas Eve and on any other evening in the year is that little piles of queer-shaped envelopes seem to be lying about, and quite a lot of tissue paper and string is to be seen peeping from odd corners. The electric light has been reduced to one bulb, but when the maid opens the door showing in* **Mr George Booth** *she switches on the rest.*

Mr George Booth No, no . . . in here will do. Just tell Mr Edward.

Phoebe Very well, sir.

She leaves him to fidget towards the fireplace and back, not removing his comforter or his coat, scarcely turning down the collar, screwing his cap in his hands. In a very short time **Edward** *comes in, shutting the door and taking stock of the visitor before he speaks.*

Edward Well?

Mr George Booth (*feebly*) I hope my excuse for not coming to dinner was acceptable. I did have . . . I have a very bad headache.

Edward I daresay they believed it.

Mr George Booth I have come at once to tell you my decision.

Edward What is it?

Mr George Booth I couldn't think the matter out alone. I went this afternoon to talk it over with the Vicar. After your father, he's my oldest friend now. (*At this* **Edward**'s *eyebrows contract and then rise.*) What a terrible shock to him!

Edward Oh, three of his four thousand pounds are quite safe.

Mr George Booth That you and your father . . . you, whom he baptised . . . should have robbed him! I never saw a man so utterly prostrate with grief. That it should have been your father! And his poor wife . . . though she never got on with your father.

Edward (*with cheerful irony*) Oh, Mrs Colpus knows too, does she?

Mr George Booth Of course he told Mrs Colpus. This is an unfortunate time for the storm to break on him. What with Christmas Day and Sunday following so close they're as busy as can be. He has resolved that during this season of peace and good-will he must put the matter from him if he can. But once Christmas is over. . . ! (*He envisages the old* **Vicar** *giving* **Edward** *a hell of a time then.*)

Edward (*coolly*) So you mean to prosecute. If you don't, you've inflicted on the Colpuses a lot of unnecessary pain and a certain amount of loss by telling them.

Mr George Booth (*naïvely*) I never thought of that. No, Edward, I have decided not to prosecute.

Edward *hides his face for a moment.*

Edward And I've been hoping to escape! Well, it can't be helped. (*And he sets his teeth.*)

Mr George Booth (*with touching solemnity*) I think I could not bear to see the family I have loved brought to such disgrace. And I want to ask your pardon, Edward, for some of the hard thoughts I have had of you. I consider this effort of yours a very striking one. You devote all the firm's earnings, I gather, to restoring the misappropriated capital. Very proper.

Edward Mr Booth . . . as I told you, you could help me . . . if you would. Your affairs, you see, are about the heaviest burden I carry.

Mr George Booth Why is that?

Edward My father naturally made freest with the funds of the people who trusted him most.

Mr George Booth Naturally . . . you call it. Most unnatural, I think.

Edward (*finely*) That also is true. And if you really want to help me, you could cut your losses . . . take interest only on the investments which do still exist. . . .

Mr George Booth No . . . forgive me . . . I have my own plan.

Edward By prosecuting you'd be no better off . . .

Mr George Booth Quite so. The very first thing the Vicar said. He has an excellent head for business. Of course his interests are small beside mine. But we stand together . . .

Edward *scents mischief and he looks straight at* **Mr Booth** . . . *very straight indeed*.

Edward What is your plan?

Mr George Booth Its moral basis . . . I quote the Vicar . . . is this. You admit, I take it, that there were degrees of moral turpitude in your father's conduct . . . that his treachery was blacker by far in some cases than in others.

Edward I think I won't make that admission for the moment.

Mr Booth What . . . to cheat and betray a life-long friend . . . and . . . and a man of God like the Vicar . . . is that no worse than a little ordinary trickiness? Now where are

my notes? Our conditions are . . . one: we refrain from
definitely undertaking not to prosecute . . . two: such
securities as you have intact are to be returned to us at
once . . .

Edward Oh, certainly.

Mr George Booth Three: the interest upon those others
that have been made away with is to be paid.

Edward As it has been so far.

Mr George Booth We admit that. Four: the repayment of
our lost capital is to be a first charge upon the . . . surplus
earnings of the firm. There you are. And the Vicar and I
both consider it very fair dealing.

Edward D o you!

He goes off into peals of laughter.

Mr George Booth Edward . . . don't laugh!

Edward But it's very, very funny!

Mr George Booth Stop laughing, Edward.

Edward You refrain from undertaking n o t to prosecute
. . . that's the neatest touch. That would keep me under
your thumb, wouldn't it? (*Then with a sudden, savage
snarl.*) Oh, you Christian gentlemen!

Mr George Booth Don't be abusive, sir.

Edward I'm giving my soul and body to restoring you and
the rest of you to your precious money-bags. And you'll
wring me dry . . . won't you? Won't you?

Mr George Booth Don't be rhetorical. The money was
ours . . . we want it back. That's reasonable.

Edward (*at the height of irony*) Oh . . . most!

Mr George Booth Any slight amendments to the plan . . .
I'm willing to discuss them.

Edward (*as to a dog*) Go to the devil.

Mr George Booth And don't be rude.

Edward I'm sorry.

There is a knock at the door.

Edward Come in.

Honor *intrudes an apologetic head.*

Honor Am I interrupting business?

Edward (*mirthlessly joking*) No. Business is over . . . quite over. Come in, Honor.

Honor *puts on the table a market basket bulging with little paper parcels, and, oblivious of* **Mr Booth**'s *distracted face, tries to fix his attention.*

Honor I thought, dear Mr Booth, perhaps you wouldn't mind carrying round this basket of things yourself. It's so very damp underfoot that I don't want to send one of the maids out tonight if I can possibly avoid it . . . and if one doesn't get Christmas presents the very first thing on Christmas morning quite half the pleasure in them is lost, don't you think?

Mr George Booth Yes . . . yes.

Honor (*fishing out the parcels one by one*) This is a bell for Mrs Williams . . . something she said she wanted so that you can ring for her, which saves the maids; cap and apron for Mary; cap and apron for Ellen; shawl for Davis when she goes out to the larder . . . all useful presents. And that's something for you . . . but you're not to look at it till the morning.

Having shaken each of them at the old gentleman, she proceeds to re-pack them. He is now trembling with anxiety to escape before any more of the family find him there.

Mr George Booth Thank you . . . thank you. I hope my lot has arrived. I left instructions . . .

Honor Quite safely . . . and I have hidden them. Presents are put on the breakfast-table tomorrow.

Edward (*with an inconsequence that still further alarms* **Mr Booth**) When we were children our Christmas breakfast was mostly made off chocolates.

Before the basket is packed, **Mrs Voysey** *sails slowly into the room, as smiling and as deaf as ever.* **Mr Booth** *does his best not to scowl at her.*

Mrs Voysey Are you feeling better, George Booth?

Mr George Booth No. (*Then he elevates his voice with a show of politeness.*) No, thank you; . . . I can't say I am.

Mrs Voysey You don't look better.

Mr George Booth I still have my headache. (*With a distracted shout.*) Headache!

Mrs Voysey Bilious, perhaps. I quite understand you didn't care to dine. But why not have taken your coat off? How foolish in this warm room!

Mr George Booth Thank you. I'm . . . just going.

He seizes the market basket. At that moment **Mrs Hugh** *appears.*

Beatrice Your shawl, Mother. (*And she clasps it round* **Mrs Voysey's** *shoulders.*)

Mrs Voysey Thank you, Beatrice. I thought I had it on. (*Then to* **Mr Booth**, *who is now entangled in his comforter.*) A merry Christmas to you.

Beatrice Good evening, Mr Booth.

Mr George Booth I beg your pardon. Good evening, Mrs Hugh.

Honor (*with sudden inspiration, to the company in general*) Why shouldn't I write in here . . . now the table's cleared?

Mr George Booth (*sternly, now he is safe by the door*) Will you see me out, Edward?

Edward Yes.

He follows the old man and his basket, leaving the others to distribute themselves about the room. It is a custom of the female members of the **Voysey** *family, about Christmas time, to return to the dining-room, when the table has been cleared, and occupy themselves in various ways which involve space and untidiness.* **Beatrice** *has a little work-basket containing a buttonless glove and such things, which she is rectifying.* **Honor**'s *writing is done with the aid of an enormous blotting book, which bulges with apparently a year's correspondence. She sheds its contents upon the end of the dining-table and spreads them abroad.* **Mrs Voysey** *settles to the table near to the fire, opens the Nineteenth Century and is instantly absorbed in it.*

Beatrice If there's anywhere else left in this house where one can write or sew or sit, I'd be glad to know of it. Christmas tree in the back drawing-room and all the furniture in the front! Presents piled up under dusters in the library! My heap is very soft and bulgy. Honor . . . if you've given me an eiderdown quilt I'll never forgive you.

Honor Oh, I haven't . . . I shouldn't t h i n k of it.

Beatrice And tomorrow this room will look like a six P.M. bargain counter.

Honor But . . . Beatrice . . . it's Christmas.

Beatrice Noël . . . Noël! Where's Emily?

Honor Well . . . I'm afraid she's talking to Booth.

Beatrice If you mean that Booth is listening to her, I don't believe it. She has taken my fine scissors.

Honor And I think she's telling him about you.

Beatrice What . . . in particular . . . about me?

Honor About you and Hugh.

Beatrice Now whose fault is this? We agreed that nothing more was to be said till after Christmas.

Honor But Edward knows . . . and Mother knows . . .

Beatrice I warned Mother a year ago.

Honor And Emily told me. And everyone seems to know except Booth. And it would be fearful if he found out. So I said: Tell him one night when he's in bed and very tired. But Emily didn't seem to think that would . . .

At this moment **Emily** *comes in, looking rather trodden upon.* **Honor** *concludes in the most audible of whispers . . .*

Honor Don't say anything . . . it's my fault.

Beatrice (*fixing her with a severe forefinger*) Emily . . . have you taken my fine scissors?

Emily (*timidly*) No, Beatrice.

Honor (*who is diving into the recesses of the blotting book*) Oh, here they are! I must have taken them. I do apologise!

Emily (*more timidly still*) I'm afraid Booth's rather cross. He's gone to look for Hugh.

Beatrice (*with a shake of her head*) Honor . . . I've a good mind to make you do this sewing for me.

In comes the **Major**, *strepitant. He takes, so to speak, just enough time to train himself on* **Beatrice** *and then fires.*

Major Booth Voysey Beatrice, what on earth is this Emily has been telling me?

Beatrice (*with elaborate calm*) Emily, what have you been telling Booth?

Major Booth Voysey Please . . . please do not prevaricate. Where is Hugh?

Mrs Voysey (*looking over her spectacles*) What did you say, Booth?

Major Booth Voysey I want Hugh, Mother.

Mrs Voysey I thought you were playing billiards together.

Edward *strolls back from despatching* **Mr Booth**, *his face thoughtful.*

Major Booth Voysey (*insistently*) Edward, where is Hugh?

Edward (*with complete indifference*) I don't know.

Major Booth Voysey (*in trumpet tones*) Honor, will you oblige me by finding Hugh and saying I wish to speak to him here immediately.

Honor, *who has leapt at the sound of her name, flies from the room without a word.*

Beatrice I know quite well what you want to talk about, Booth. Discuss the matter by all means if it amuses you . . . but don't shout.

Major Booth Voysey I use the voice Nature has gifted me with, Beatrice.

Beatrice (*as she searches for a glove button*) Nature did let herself go over your lungs.

Major Booth Voysey (*glaring round with indignation*) This is a family matter . . . otherwise I should not feel it my duty to interfere . . . as I do. Any member of the family has a right to express an opinion. I want Mother's. Mother, what do you think?

Mrs Voysey (*amicably*) What about?

Major Booth Voysey Hugh and Beatrice separating.

Mrs Voysey They haven't separated.

Major Booth Voysey But they mean to.

Mrs Voysey Fiddle-de-dee!

Major Booth Voysey I quite agree with you.

Beatrice (*with a charming smile*) Such reasoning would convert a stone.

Major Booth Voysey Why have I not been told?

Beatrice You have just been told.

Major Booth Voysey (*thunderously*) Before.

Beatrice The truth is, dear Booth, we're all so afraid of you.

Major Booth Voysey (*a little mollified*) Ha . . . I should be glad to think that.

Beatrice (*sweetly*) Don't you?

Major Booth Voysey (*intensely serious*) Beatrice, your callousness shocks me. That you can dream of deserting Hugh . . . a man who, of all others, requires constant care and attention.

Beatrice May I remark that the separation is as much Hugh's wish as mine?

Major Booth Voysey I don't believe that.

Beatrice (*her eyebrows up*) Really!

Major Booth Voysey I don't imply that you're lying. But you must know that it's Hugh's nature to wish to do anything that he thinks anybody wishes him to do. All my life I've had to stand up for him . . . and, by Jove, I'll continue to do so.

Edward (*from the depths of his arm-chair*) Booth . . . if you could manage to let this alone . . .

The door is flung almost off its hinges by **Hugh**, *who then stands stamping and pale green with rage.*

Hugh Look here, Booth . . . I will not have you interfering with my private affairs. Is one never to be free from your bullying?

Major Booth Voysey You ought to be grateful.

Hugh Well, I'm not.

Major Booth Voysey This is a family affair.

Hugh It is not!

Major Booth Voysey (*at the top of his voice*) If all you can do is to contradict me . . . you'd better listen to what I've got to say . . . q u i e t l y.

Hugh, *quite shouted down, flings himself petulantly into a chair. A hushed pause.*

Emily (*in a still small voice*) Would you like me to go, Booth?

Major Booth Voysey (*severely*) No, Emily. Unless anything has been going on which cannot be discussed before you. (*More severely still.*) And I trust that is not so.

Beatrice Nothing at all appropriate to that tone of voice has been . . . going on. We swear it.

Major Booth Voysey Why do you wish to separate?

Hugh What's the use of telling you? You won't understand.

Beatrice (*who sews on undisturbed*) We don't get on well together.

Major Booth Voysey (*amazedly*) Is that all?

Hugh (*snapping at him*) Yes, that's all. Can you find a better reason?

Major Booth Voysey (*with brotherly contempt*) I've given up expecting common sense from you. But Beatrice. . . ! (*His tone implores her to be reasonable.*)

Beatrice Common sense is dry diet for the soul, you know.

Major Booth Voysey (*protesting*) My dear girl . . . that sounds like a quotation from your latest book.

Beatrice It isn't. I do think you might read that book . . . for the honour of the family.

Major Booth Voysey (*successfully side-tracked*) I bought it at once, Beatrice, and . . .

Beatrice That's the principal thing, of course.

Major Booth Voysey (. . . *and discovering it*) But do let us keep to the subject.

Beatrice (*with flattering sincerity*) Certainly, Booth. And there is hardly any subject that I wouldn't ask your advice about. But upon this . . . please let me know better. Hugh and I will be happier apart.

Major Booth Voysey (*obstinately*) Why?

Beatrice (*with resolute patience, having vented a little sigh*) Hugh finds that my opinions distress him. And I have at last lost patience with Hugh.

Mrs Voysey (*who has been trying to follow this through her spectacles*) What does Beatrice say?

Major Booth Voysey (*translating into a loud sing-song*) That she wishes to leave her husband because she has lost patience.

Mrs Voysey (*with considerable acrimony*) Then you must be a very ill-tempered woman. Hugh has a sweet nature.

Hugh (*shouting self-consciously*) Nonsense, Mother.

Beatrice (*shouting good-humouredly*) I quite agree with you, Mother. (*She continues to her husband in an even, just tone.*) You have a sweet nature, Hugh, and it is most difficult to get angry with you. I have been seven years working up to it. But now that I am angry I shall never get pleased again.

The **Major** *returns to his subject refreshed by a moment's repose.*

Major Booth Voysey How has he failed in his duty? Tell us. I'm not bigoted in his favour. I know your faults, Hugh. (*He wags his head at* **Hugh**, *who writhes with irritation.*)

Hugh Why can't you leave them alone . . . leave us alone?

Beatrice I'd state my case against Hugh if I thought he'd retaliate.

Hugh (*desperately rounding on his brother*) If I tell you, you won't understand. You understand nothing! Beatrice thinks I ought to prostitute my art to make money.

Major Booth Voysey (*glancing at his wife*) Please don't use metaphors of that sort.

Beatrice (*reasonably*) Yes, I think Hugh ought to earn more money.

Major Booth Voysey (*quite pleased to be getting along at last*) Well, why doesn't he?

Hugh I don't want money.

Major Booth Voysey How can you not want money? As well say you don't want bread.

Beatrice (*as she breaks off her cotton*) It's when one has known what it is to be a little short of both . . .

Now the **Major** *spreads himself and begins to be very wise; while* **Hugh,** *to whom this is more intolerable than all, can only clutch his hair.*

Major Booth Voysey You know I never considered art a very good profession for you, Hugh. And you won't even stick to one department of it. It's a profession that gets people into very bad habits, I consider. Couldn't you take up something else? You could still do those wood-cuts in your spare time to amuse yourself.

Hugh (*commenting on this with two deliberate shouts of simulated mirth*) Ha! Ha!

Major Booth Voysey Well, it wouldn't much matter if you didn't do them at all.

Hugh True!

Mrs Voysey *leaves her arm-chair for her favourite station at the dining-table.*

Mrs Voysey Booth is the only one of you that I can hear at all distinctly. But if you two foolish young people think you want to separate . . . try it. You'll soon come back to each other and be glad to. People can't fight against nature for long. And marriage is a natural state . . . once you're married.

Major Booth Voysey (*with intense approval*) Quite right, Mother.

Mrs Voysey I know.

She resumes the Nineteenth Century. And the **Major,** *to the despair of everybody, makes yet another start; trying oratory this time.*

Major Booth Voysey My own opinion is, Beatrice and Hugh, that you don't realise the meaning of the word marriage. I don't call myself a religious man . . . but, dash it all, you were married in church. And you then entered upon an awful compact. . . ! Surely, as a woman, Beatrice, the religious point of it ought to appeal to you. Good Lord . . . suppose everybody were to carry on like this! And have you considered that . . . whether you are right, or whether you are wrong . . . if you desert Hugh you cut yourself off from the family.

Beatrice (*with the sweetest of smiles*) That will distress me terribly.

Major Booth Voysey (*not doubting her for a moment*) Of course.

Hugh *flings up his head, and finds relief at last in many words.*

Hugh I wish to God I'd ever been able to cut myself off from the family! Look at Trenchard!

Major Booth Voysey (*gobbling a little at this unexpected attack*) I do not forgive Trenchard for his quarrel with the Pater.

Hugh He quarrelled because that was his best way of escape.

Major Booth Voysey Escape from what?

Hugh From tyranny . . . from hypocrisy . . . from boredom! . . . from his Happy English Home.

Beatrice (*kindly*) Now, my dear . . . it's no use . . .

Major Booth Voysey (*attempting sarcasm*) Speak so that Mother can hear you!

But **Hugh** *isn't to be stopped now.*

Hugh Why are we all dull, cubbish, uneducated . . . hopelessly middle-class!

Major Booth Voysey (*taking this as very personal*) Cubbish!

Beatrice Middle-class! Hugh . . . do think what you're saying.

Hugh U p p e r middle-class, then. Yes . . . and snobbish too! What happens to you when you're born into that estate? What happened to us, anyhow? We were fed . . . we were clothed . . . we were taught and trained . . . and we were made comfortable. And that was the watchword given us: Comfort! You must work for a comfortable livelihood. You must practise a comfortable morality . . . and go to your parson for spiritual comfort . . . and he'll promise you everlasting comfort in Heaven. Far better be born in a slum . . . with a drunkard for a father and a drab for a mother . . .

Major Booth Voysey I never heard such lunacy.

Hugh If you're nothing and nobody, you may find it in you to become something and somebody . . . and at least you learn what the world wants of you and what it doesn't. But do you think the world today couldn't do without u s? Strip yourself of your comfortable income . . . as Edward here told you to . . . and step out into the street and see.

Major Booth Voysey (*ponderously*) I venture to think . . .

Hugh Oh no, you don't. You don't do either . . . and you'd better not try . . . for a little thinking might tell you that we and our like have ceased to exist at all. Yes, I mean it. Trenchard escaped in time. You went into the Army . . . so how could you discover what a back number you are? But I found out soon enough . . . when I tried to express myself in art . . . that there was nothing to express

. . . except a few habits, and tags of other people's thoughts and feelings. There is no Me . . . that's what's the matter. I'm an illusion. Not that it does matter to anyone but me. And look at Honor . . .

Major Booth Voysey Honor leads a useful life . . . and a happy one. We all love her.

Hugh Yes . . . and what have we always called her? Mother's right hand! I wonder they bothered to give her a name. By the time little Ethel came they were tired of training children. She was alive . . . in a silly, innocent sort of way. And then . . .

Beatrice Poor little Ethel!

Major Booth Voysey Poor Ethel!

They speak as one speaks of the dead.

Hugh And though your luck has been pretty poor, Edward, you've come up against realities at least . . . against something that could make a man of you. (*Then back to his humorous savagery.*) But if Booth thinks this world will stand still because he and his like want to be comfortable . . . that's where he's wrong.

Major Booth Voysey (*dignified and judicious*) We will return, if you please, to the original subject of discussion. This question of a separation . . .

Hugh *jumps up, past all patience.*

Hugh Beatrice and I mean to separate. And nothing you may say will prevent it. The only trouble is money. She says we must have enough to live apart comfortably.

Beatrice (*in kindly irony*) Yes . . . comfortably!

Hugh And I daresay she's right . . . she generally is. So the question is: Can we raise it?

Major Booth Voysey Well?

Hugh Well . . . for the moment we can't.

Major Booth Voysey Well then?

Hugh So we can't separate.

Major Booth Voysey Then what in Heaven's name have we been discussing it for?

Hugh I haven't discussed it. I don't want to discuss it. Why can't you mind your own business? Now I'll go back to the billiard-room and my book.

He is gone before the **Major** *can recover his breath.*

Major Booth Voysey I am not an impatient man . . . but really. . . !

Beatrice Hugh's tragedy is that he is just clever enough to have found himself out . . . and no cleverer.

Major Booth Voysey (*magnanimous but stern*) I will be frank. You have never made the best of Hugh.

Beatrice No . . . at the worst it never came to that.

Major Booth Voysey I am glad . . . for both your sakes . . . that you can't separate.

Beatrice As soon as I am earning enough I shall walk off from him.

The **Major's** *manly spirit stirs.*

Major Booth Voysey You will do nothing of the sort, Beatrice.

Beatrice (*unruffled*) How will you stop me, Booth?

Major Booth Voysey I shall tell Hugh he must command you to stay.

Beatrice (*with a little smile*) I wonder would that make the difference. It was one of the illusions of my girlhood that I'd love a man who would master me.

Major Booth Voysey Hugh must assert himself.

He begins to walk about, giving some indication of how it should be done. **Beatrice's** *smile has vanished.*

Beatrice Don't think I've enjoyed wearing the breeches
. . . to use that horrid phrase . . . all through my married
life. But someone had to plan and make decisions and do
accounts. We weren't sparrows or lilies of the field. . . .
(*She becomes conscious of his strutting and smiles rather
mischievously.*) Ah . . . if I'd married you, Booth!

Booth's *face grows beatific.*

Major Booth Voysey Well, I own to thinking that I am a
masterful man . . . that it's the duty of every man to be so.
(*He adds forgivingly.*) Poor old Hugh!

Beatrice (*unable to resist temptation*) If I'd tried to leave
you, Booth, you'd have whipped me . . . wouldn't you?

Major Booth Voysey (*ecstatically complacent*) Ha . . .
well. . . !

Beatrice Do say yes. Think how it will frighten Emily.

The **Major** *strokes his moustache and is most friendly.*

Major Booth Voysey Hugh's been a worry to me all my
life. And now . . . as head of the family . . . well, I
suppose I'd better go and give the dear chap a quiet talking
to. I see your point of view, Beatrice.

Beatrice Why disturb him at his book?

Major Booth *leaves them, squaring his shoulders as becomes a
lord of creation. The two sisters-in-law go on with their work
silently for a moment; then* **Beatrice** *adds . . .*

Beatrice Do you find Booth difficult to manage, Emily?

Emily (*putting down her knitting to consider the matter*) No.
It's best to let him talk himself out. When he has done that
he'll often come to me for advice. But I like him to get his
own way as much as possible . . . or think he's getting it.
Otherwise he becomes so depressed.

Beatrice (*quietly amused*) Edward shouldn't be listening to
this. (*Then to him.*) Your presence profanes these
Mysteries.

Edward I won't tell . . . and I'm a bachelor.

Emily (*solemnly, as she takes up her knitting again*) Do you really mean to leave Hugh?

Beatrice (*slightly impatient*) Emily, I've said so.

They are joined by **Alice Maitland**, *who comes in gaily.*

Alice What's Booth shouting about in the billiard-room?

Emily (*pained*) Oh . . . on Christmas Eve, too!

Beatrice Don't y o u take any interest in my matrimonial affairs?

Mrs Voysey *shuts up the Nineteenth Century and removes her spectacles.*

Mrs Voysey That's a very interesting article. The Chinese Empire must be in a shocking state. Is it ten o'clock yet?

Edward Past.

Mrs Voysey (*as* **Edward** *is behind her*) Can anyone see the clock?

Alice It's past ten, Auntie.

Mrs Voysey Then I think I'll go to my room.

Emily Shall I come and look after you, Mother?

Mrs Voysey If you'd find Honor for me, Emily.

Emily *goes in search of the harmless, necessary* **Honor**, *and* **Mrs Voysey** *begins her nightly chant of departure.*

Mrs Voysey Good-night, Alice. Good-night, Edward.

Edward Good-night, Mother.

Mrs Voysey (*with sudden severity*) I'm not pleased with you, Beatrice.

Beatrice I'm sorry, Mother.

But without waiting to be answered the old lady has sailed out of the room. **Beatrice**, **Edward** *and* **Alice**, *now left together, are attuned to each other enough to be able to talk with ease.*

Beatrice But there's something in what Hugh says about this family. Had your great-grandfather a comfortable income, Edward?

Edward I think so. It was his father made the money . . . in trade.

Beatrice Which has been filtering away ever since. But fairly profitably, surely . . . to the rest of the world. You'd a great-aunt who was quite a botanist and an uncle who edited Catullus, hadn't you?

Edward Yes.

She is beginning to work out his theme.

Beatrice Well, that didn't pay them. Then there was the uncle killed in the Sudan. A captain's pension and no more wouldn't have been much for a widow and four children. . . .

Alice Five.

Beatrice Was it? Dear me . . . how prolific we were! And though I chaff Booth . . . I've seen him with his regiment giving weedy young slackers chest and biceps and making them 'decent chaps'. It takes a few generations, you know, to breed men who'll feel that it pays to do that for its own sake . . . and who'll be proud to do it. Oh, I can find a lot to say for the Upper Middle Class.

Edward The family's petering out as its income does. D'you notice that? Six of us. But there are only Booth's two children.

Beatrice It's more than the shrinking income that's doing it . . . more even than Hugh's 'worship of comfort'. Some fresh impulse to assert itself . . . I expect that is what a class needs to keep it socially alive. Well . . . your father developed one.

Edward Not a very happy one!

Beatrice It might have been . . . if he'd had the good sense to borrow the money for his financial operations just a little less casually.

Edward D'you know what I think I've found out about him now?

Beatrice Something interesting, I'm sure.

Edward He did save my grandfather and the firm from a smash. That was true. A pretty capable piece of heroism! Then . . . six years after . . . he started on his own account . . . cheating again. I suppose he found himself in a corner. . . .

Beatrice (*psychologically fascinated*) Not a bit of it! He did it deliberately. One day when he was feeling extra fit he must have said to himself: Why not? . . . well, here goes! You never understood your father. I do . . . it's my business to.

Edward He was an old scoundrel, Beatrice, and it's sophistry to pretend otherwise.

Beatrice But he was a bit of a genius too. You can't be expected to appreciate that. It's tiresome work, I know . . . tidying up after these little Napoleons. He really did make money, didn't he, besides stealing it?

Edward Lord, yes! And I daresay more than he stole. An honest two thousand a year from the firm. He had another thousand . . . and he spent about ten. He must have found the difference somewhere.

Beatrice There you are, then. And we all loved him. You did, too, Alice.

Alice I adored him.

Edward He was a scoundrel and a thief.

Alice I always knew he was a scoundrel of some sort. I thought he probably had another family somewhere.

Beatrice Oh . . . what fun! Had he, Edward?

Edward I fancy not.

Beatrice No, he wasn't that sort . . . and it spoils the picture to overcrowd it.

Edward Pleasant to be able to sit back and survey the business so coolly.

Beatrice Somebody has to . . . some time or other . . . try to find a meaning in this and everything that happens . . . or we should run mad under what seems the wicked folly of it all. But it's only the flippant and callous little bit of me which writes my flippant and callous little books that sits back so coolly, Edward. And even that bit . . . when you're not looking . . . stands up to make you a pretty low bow. Aren't matters any better . . . aren't you nearly through?

Edward Yes, they are better.

Beatrice I'm glad. Have you ever been sorry that you didn't do the obviously wise thing . . . uncover the crime and let the law take its course?

Edward Often.

Beatrice Why did you take up the challenge single-handed . . . lawlessly . . . now that perhaps you can look back and tell?

Edward *rather unwillingly, rather shyly, confesses . . .*

Edward I think that I wanted . . . quite selfishly . . . a little vaingloriously, I daresay . . . to prove what my honesty was worth . . . what I was worth. And I was up against it. (*After which comes, perhaps, a more inward truth.*) And then, you know, I loved the Pater.

Beatrice (*touched*) In spite of all?

Edward Oh, yes. And I felt that if the worst of what he'd recklessly done was put right . . . it might be the better for him somehow.

Beatrice, *who has no such superstitious beliefs, lets this sink in on her nevertheless.*

Beatrice Silence in the court.

Another moment, and she collects her sewing, gets up and goes.
Alice *has had all the while a keen eye on* **Edward**.

Alice But something has happened since dinner.

Edward Could you see that?

Alice Tell me.

Edward (*as one throwing off a burden*) The smash has come
. . . and it's not my fault. Old George Booth . . .

Alice I knew he'd been here.

Edward He found out . . . I had to tell him. You can
imagine him. I told him to take what was left of his money
and prosecute. Well . . . he'll take what he can get and he
won't prosecute. For he wants to bleed me, sovereign by
sovereign as I earn sovereign by sovereign, till he has got
the rest. And he has told the Vicar . . . who has told his
wife . . . who has told the choirboys by this time I
daresay. So it's a smash. And I thank God for it.

Alice (*quiet but intent*) And what'll happen now?

Edward One can't be sure. Gaol, possibly. I'll be struck
off the Rolls anyhow. No more Lincoln's Inn for me.

Alice And what then?

Edward I don't know . . . and I don't care.

Alice (*still quieter*) But I do.

Edward Oh, I shan't shoot myself. I've never cared
enough about my life to take the trouble to end it. But I'm
damned tired, Alice. I think I could sleep for a week. I
hope they won't undo what I've done, though. They won't
find it very easy to . . . that's one thing. And I shan't help
them. Well, there it is. Nobody else knows yet. I like you
to be the first to know. That's all. A Merry Christmas.
Good-night.

As he takes no more notice of her, **Alice** *gets up and goes to the* *door. There she pauses, and turns; and then she comes back to him.*

Alice I'm supposed to be off to Egypt on the twenty-eighth for three months. No. I'm not ill. But, as I've never yet had anything to do except look after myself, the doctor thinks Egypt might be . . . most beneficial.

Edward Well, you may find me still at large when you come back.

Alice Oh, I'm not going . . . now.

Edward (*sharply*) Why not? Good God . . . don't make it worse for me. To have you about while I'm being put through this . . . have you reading the reports the next morning . . . coming into court perhaps to look pityingly at me! Go away . . . and stay away. That's all I ask.

Alice (*unperturbed*) At the best, I suppose, you'll be left pretty hard up for the time being.

Edward If His Majesty doesn't find me a new suit, they'll leave me the clothes on my back.

Alice What a good thing I've my eight hundred a year!

Edward (*with a gasp and a swallow*) And what exactly do you mean by that?

Alice Could they take my money as well . . . if we were married already? I've never been clear about married women's property. But you know. It's your business to. Could they?

Edward (*choking now*) Are you . . . are you. . . ?

Alice Because if they could it would be only sensible to wait a little. But if not . . .

Edward *hardens himself.*

Edward Look here, now. Through these two damnable years there's only one thing I've been thanking God for . . . that you never did say yes to me.

Alice (*chaffing him tenderly*) Four times and a half you proposed. The first time on a walk we took down in Devon . . . when you cut a stick of willow and showed me how to make a whistle from it. I have that still . . . and there are four and a half notches in it. The half was only a hint you dropped. But I could have caught you on it if I'd wanted to.

Edward Well . . . you didn't.

Alice No. But I kept the stick.

Edward If you didn't care enough for me to marry me then . . .

Alice Well . . . I didn't.

Edward You don't suppose that now your eight hundred a year . . .

Alice Are you still in love with me, Edward?

Edward *sets his teeth against temptation.*

Edward The answer must be no.

She smiles.

Alice You're lying.

Edward Can't we stop this? I've had about as much as I can stand.

Alice Don't be so difficult. If I ask you to marry me, you'll refuse. And then what can I do? I can't coquette and be alluring. I don't know how.

Edward (*trying to joke his way out*) Something to be thankful for!

Alice But, my dear . . . I love you. I didn't before. I thought you were only a well-principled prig. I was wrong. You're a man . . . and I love you with all my heart and soul. Oh . . . please . . . please ask me to be your wife.

Edward (*for he resists happiness no more*) If I've luck . . . if they let me go free . . .

Alice No . . . now . . . now . . . while you're in trouble. I won't take you later . . . when the worst is over. I'm dashed if I do. I'll marry you tomorrow.

Edward (*objecting but helplessly*) That's Christmas Day.

Alice And Boxing Day's next. Well, the old wretch of a Vicar can marry us on Saturday.

Edward (*giving his conscience one more hysterical chance*) I haven't asked you yet.

Alice I don't believe, you know, that they will put you in prison. It would be so extraordinarily senseless.

Edward But now the scandal's out, we must go smash in any case.

Alice You couldn't call them all together . . . get them round a table and explain? They won't all be like Mr Booth and the Vicar. Couldn't we bargain with them to let us go on?

The 'we' and the 'us' come naturally.

Edward But . . . heavens above . . . I don't want to go on. You don't know what the life has been.

Alice Yes, I do. I see when I look at you. But it was partly the fear, wasn't it . . . or the hope . . . that this would happen. Once it's all open and above-board. . . ! Besides . . . you've had no other life. Now there's to be ours. That'll make a difference.

Edward (*considering the matter*) They just might agree . . . to syndicate themselves . . . and to keep me slaving at it.

Alice You could make them.

Edward I! I believe my father could have . . . if that way out had taken his fancy.

Alice (*her pride in him surging up*) My dear . . . don't you know yourself yet . . . as I now know you, thank God? You're ten times the man he ever was. What was he after all but a fraud?

Edward (*soberly*) Well . . . I'll try.

Alice (*gentle and grave*) I'm sure you should. (*For a moment they sit quietly there, thinking of the future, uncertain of everything but one thing.*) The others must have gone up to bed. This is no way for an Upper Middle-Class Lady to behave . . . sitting up hob-nobbing with you. Good-night.

Edward Good-night. God bless you.

She is going again, but again she stops, and says half-humorously.

Alice But even now you haven't asked me.

Edward (*simply*) Will you marry me?

Alice (*as simply in return*) Yes. Yes, please. (*Then, moving nearer to him.*) Kiss me.

Edward (*half-humorously too*) I was going to.

And he does, with a passion that has reverence in it too.

Alice Oh, my dear. My very dear. Till tomorrow then.

Edward Till tomorrow.

She leaves him sitting there; a man conscious of new strength.

Waste

(Revised 1926)

Written 1906
Revised 1926

My dear H M Harwood

You are responsible, though unwittingly, for this revision of *Waste*. When we agreed you should revive it, I never thought of reading it through. Did you? I said lightly that one or two alterations might be needed. Then, later, I turned to the job – and this is the result. I doubt if one scrap of the old dialogue survives; the story and the characters are here, that is all. So it is a thing I had – dramatically – to say twenty years ago, said as I'd say it now. But now I'd have something different to say.

Yours very gratefully (if I ought to be!)

Harley Granville-Barker

Waste was first presented by the Stage Society at the Imperial Theatre, Westminster, on 24 November 1907, under the direction of the author.

The play was first given a full public production (in the revised text of the present edition) at the Westminster Theatre, 1 December 1936, with the following cast:

Walter Kent	Stephen Murray
Countess Mortimer	Nina Boucicault
Lady Julia Farrant	Mary Hinton
Frances Trebell	Gillian Scaife
Lucy Davenport	Mary MacOwen
Amy O'Connell	Catherine Lacey
George Farrant	A. Scott Gatty
Russell Blackborough	Cecil Trouncer
Butler	Robert Dalzell
Henry Trebell	Nicholas Hannen
Betha	Bridget Phelps
Sir Gilbert Wedgecroft	Harcourt Williams
Lord Charles Cantilupe	Gibb McLaughlin
Cyril Horsham	Felix Aylmer
Vivian Saumarez	Alfred Gray
Justin O'Connell	Mark Dignam

Produced by Harley Granville-Barker and Michael MacOwan

Act One

Shapters, which is thirty miles or so from London, is a typically English home. Its kitchens are Tudor; it faces the world looking seventeenth century; from the garden you would call it Queen Anne. But the sanctity of age is upon even this last and not least ruthless of its patchings and scrappings, and the effect of the whole is beautiful.

It is a Sunday evening in summer, and in one of the smaller sitting-rooms **Lady Julia Farrant** *has been playing to some of her weekend guests. She is a woman of fifty; she plays very well for an amateur, she has just launched into Chopin's shortest prelude (Op. 28, No. 20). Her listeners are her mother,* **Lady Mortimer**, *a genuinely old lady and dowered with all the beauty of age;* **Frances Trebell**, *a woman in the fifties who has nothing smart about her, her face showing more thought than feeling;* **Mrs O'Connell**, *a charming woman, who takes care she does charm;* **Lucy Davenport**, *a girl in her twenties, more grave than gay; and* **Walter Kent**, *just such a young man as the average English father would wish his son to be. They are all attentive. The room is not so brightly lit but that one can see in the moonlight – for the curtains are drawn back and the long windows are open – a paved garden set in a courtyard of some sort, and lights in the rooms beyond. The room is evidently a woman's room, and its owner's taste, one would guess, was formed in the school of Burne-Jones. Having finished the prelude,* **Lady Julia** *shuts the piano and, after a moment, leaves it.*

Walter Kent Oh . . . was that 'God save the King'? I'd have stood up.

Lady Mortimer Thank you, my dear Julia.

Lady Julia Thank you for listening, Mamma. That's the polite reply, isn't it?

Frances Trebell Chopin for a finish, Julia . . . after John Sebastian!

Lady Julia Allow us that much emotional indulgence.

Walter Kent Romantic moonrise into a starlit sky.

Lucy Davenport Five marks to you for an epigram, Walter.

Walter Kent Don't be so frightfully surprised when I say something clever.

Frances Trebell I prefer the stars.

Amy O'Connell And I'd been wondering what was missing.

Lady Julia *finds herself a chair; it happens not to be very near* **Mrs O'Connell**.

Lady Julia Don't you like Bach? Why didn't you say so?

Amy O'Connell I respect the old gentleman . . . but he makes me feel a demi-semi-quaver of a creature.

Lady Julia *catches sight of a book – a quite severe-looking book – upon* **Lucy Davenport**'s *lap*.

Lady Julia Lucy . . . were you reading while I played?

Lucy Davenport No, indeed, Cousin Julia. But I keep hold of it . . . it soaks in up the arm.

Amy O'Connell I spent half a fugue trying to make out the title.

The book is handed to her; **Lucy**'s *arm at full stretch will just do it.*

Amy O'Connell Walter Bagehot . . . the English Constitution. Bagehot and Bach! What company I'm in! Dear Lucy, are you doing it for a bet?

Lucy Davenport No; it's good stuff.

Amy O'Connell So all the authorities declare. Yes . . . and one ought to be able to say: I've read Bagehot. You can say that, Julia, can't you?

Lady Julia I can . . . even truthfully. But I don't.

Amy O'Connell And Frances has lectured on Bagehot.

Frances Trebell No. Mathematics were my bread and butter.

Amy O'Connell And Lady Mortimer will tell us that she once saw Bagehot plain. And I'm sure he was plain.

Lady Mortimer Yes . . . he used to come to my father's house . . . with Mr Richard Hutton . . . when I was small. They had long beards . . . which frightened me.

Amy O'Connell That's better. Now, Mr Kent . . . what's your contribution?

Walter Kent I have been lectured on Bagehot . . . and examined on Bagehot. And it never, please Heaven, can happen again.

Lucy Davenport Shame!

Amy O'Connell Well . . . if I'd only thought of it I might have put all you clever, well-brought-up people in the shade by protesting loudly at dinner to the distinguished statesmen each side of me that I'd never even heard of Bagehot! Though I have . . . oh yes, in my hot youth, I have!

Lady Julia Who did bring you up, Amy?

Her tone is ever so slightly tart, as **Mrs O'Connell** *is quick to hear – and she counters.*

Amy O'Connell Dear Julia . . . there's no scandal about it! I was orphaned at two and bequeathed to a great-uncle, who was a parson and an atheist and too clever for his job and too conceited to ask for a better one. And he thought the whole duty of woman was to be pretty . . .

Lady Mortimer You gave him no trouble there, my dear.

Amy O'Connell Kind Lady Mortimer! Pretty and agreeable and helpless. He drank casks of Madeira . . . and that was old-fashioned, too . . . and had a dreadful temper.

Frances Trebell Cause and effect, possibly.

Amy O'Connell I think suppressed atheism was worse for it. So I married at seventeen and turned Catholic and went to Ireland with Justin. Then Justin turned Sinn Fein and I came back . . . and everyone was so kind. And that's enough about me. But if I'd only been sent to Cambridge instead . . . and been lectured at by Frances, perhaps, on mathematics and morals . . . what a very different woman I should be! More like Lucy . . . though never so nice. Or I might have gone in for politics and been a power in the land.

Frances Trebell I don't see you tramping the Lobbies in those pretty shoes.

Amy O'Connell No, no . . . a power behind the throne . . . like Julia. But, of course, never so powerful.

Lady Julia (*a shade wryly; only a shade*) I'm not so powerful, I fear.

Amy O'Connell (*who can be very innocent at times*) Aren't you? Don't you make history? I thought all the diaries that can't possibly be published for heaven knows how long must be full of you. I thought we were all here this weekend helping you make history. The election coming . . . this horrid, hypocritical Lib-Labour government to be beautifully beaten . . . dear Mr Horsham to be sent for again to save the country . . . with Mr Blackborough to find the money and Mr Trebell to find the brains. And that you were arranging it all, Julia.

Lady Julia I wish the country's salvation were so simple a matter.

This may sound a little smug; but **Lady Julia** *does not like you to chaff her unless she likes you very much.* **George Farrant**'s *arrival breaks the conversation. He is about his wife's age; a pleasant, very honest fellow, bred to big affairs, but with no other particular qualification for them. Yet this, allied to his honesty and good nature, has let him hold his place among them respectably enough.*

Farrant Blackborough's going, Julia.

Lady Julia I thought he must have gone. What time is it?

Farrant Ten past eleven.

Lady Julia Well . . . you've had something of a talk, you four.

Amy O'Connell What about . . . or can't we be told?

Farrant About the Goths in Italy and the Normans in Sicily . . . Maltese fever . . . Marriage in Morocco . . . Witchcraft . . . Oliver Cromwell and the Jews . . . William III's love affairs and Bergson's philosophy. I forget what else.

Russell Blackborough *follows his host into the room. One might more suitably say that he arrives. For to arrive is his vocation, and he by no means agrees with the proverb-maker that to travel is better. He is an able man; he has all the virtues that make for success, and, if sensitiveness is not among them, yet he is not an unkindly man. His voice, perhaps, is louder than it need be; and even when he is silent you always know he is there.*

Blackborough Good-bye, Lady Julia. A delightful weekend.

Lady Julia Whatever hour will you be home?

Blackborough Not before the moon's down. But I'm due in Birmingham bright and early tomorrow. Good-bye, Lady Mortimer.

He is rounding the room with his good-byes.

Lady Mortimer You're a marvel, Mr Blackborough. And never a holiday, you were telling me.

Blackborough I hate holidays. Want to know my secret?

Amy O'Connell Oh . . . please!

Blackborough Learn to sleep at odd moments.

Amy O'Connell In public?

Blackborough Yes.

Amy O'Connell That's no advice to give a woman.

Blackborough Why not?

Amy O'Connell I saw you asleep after tea. Good-bye.

The pin-point does not prick him. Thick-skinned he may be, but, to do him justice, he has no unmanly vanities.

Blackborough Besides . . . we poor politicians must work double shifts for our bread and butter while we're in opposition. It's hardly safe when you're in office to hold on to a share . . . much less a directorship. How's the wretched capitalist to live? We can't all have copper magnates for great-grandfathers like you, Farrant . . . or be company lawyers like your brother . . . and they'd not have him in public life in America, Miss Trebell. Sorry I missed the music.

He really is. He likes music and the vigour of it. He sang in the Leeds choir in his young days.

Lady Julia I left you alone. I thought you'd be talking shop.

Blackborough No, no, no . . . we'd no shop to talk. And when will Horsham talk shop if he can help it? Idealist philosophy we finished with. That counts me out . . . I don't know the jargon. But I strongly suspect there's not too much sense in anything that can't be discussed in language the ordinary educated man can understand.

The **Butler** *has entered.*

Butler Mr Blackborough's car, my lady.

Blackborough *has finished his round, but for* **Walter Kent**. *Standing by him, he addresses* **Lady Julia**.

Blackborough Do you go campaigning? No . . . Farrant's seat is safe. Come and speak for me.

Lady Julia (*as who should say, with all courtesy: The impudence!*) I have never spoken in public in my life . . . and I never shall.

Blackborough (*almost welcoming the snub;* **Lady Julia** *can impress him, though it would not become him to own it*) Ah . . . that's the true Tory tradition. We've to leave it to you ladies, though, to keep it up nowadays.

Farrant A September dissolution, too! Labour w o u l d let us in for that.

Lady Mortimer Is it to please the partridges? But they have no votes yet, have they?

Amy O'Connell Poor partridges . . . with nobody but nobodies left to shoot at them!

Farrant I mean to get a fortnight, though . . . whatever happens.

Blackborough We shall come back this time, I don't doubt. (*Then with masterful suddenness to* **Walter**.) Are we to find you a seat, young man?

Walter Kent Not yet, thank you. I've my trade to learn.

Blackborough Trebell's taking you on.

Walter Kent Yes.

Blackborough (*though somehow he doesn't seem to mean quite – quite – what he says*) Lucky fellow! You'll learn a lot.

Farrant Classical tripos at Cambridge. Now he has to go to Pitman's for shorthand and type-writing.

Blackborough A year at the Central Office would have done you some good. I could have got you in there. Our

young men in the House don't start by learning . . . as
they ought . . . how a party is run and how votes are got.

Walter Kent (*very simply: one likes him for it*) I think I'm
more interested in ideas.

Blackborough Then why go in for politics?

Lady Julia Really, Mr Blackborough!

Blackborough (*genially*) I know, I know . . . that raises a
laugh from the intellectual snobs. Ideas have their place,
undoubtedly. We need them to draw upon. But the
statesman's task is the accommodation of stubborn fact to
shifting circumstance . . . and in effect to the practical
capacities of the average stupid man. Democracy involves
the admission of that.

Lady Julia (*whose patience is being tried*) I am at least not a
democrat, Mr Blackborough.

Blackborough Nor I . . . more of a democrat than I need
to be. We've all to bow down a bit nowadays in the House
of Rimmon. But, stampede a people with ideas. . . ! Why
. . . look at the Russian Revolution . . . look at the
Chinese Revolution . . . look at India . . . look at Poplar.
We live in dangerous times.

Lady Mortimer So my dear grandfather used to say.

Blackborough And no doubt he was right. The salvation
of this country so far has been its imperviousness to
abstract ideas. The difficulty of doing anything definite by
party politics . . . strange as this sounds . . . is what keeps
us sane and lets us get on with our business. I am a good
enough democrat to wish to save democracy from itself
. . . and from the ideologue and the doctrinaire. And I
wish very much that this present government weren't
leaving us such a crop of problems to deal with. The
Dominion Treaties . . . the Emigration muddle . . .
Disestablishment! They've shown great political wisdom in
leaving us to tackle them. Well . . . we must just keep our

heads and go slow . . . go slow. Good-night . . . good-night.

These last farewells have the savour of businesslike blessings. He departs, and **Farrant** *hardly allows himself a smile as he follows him to see him off. But the rest of the company is visibly relieved.*

Lady Mortimer Most impressive.

Amy O'Connell Shouldn't we have cheered, or said 'Order' or 'Divide' or something?

Frances Trebell Alas . . . one must never suppose a man a fool because he t a l k s nonsense.

Lady Julia And I begged George to see he had his say after dinner. He'd been saving that up for t h e m . . . and he empties it over u s. I will not be called an intellectual snob by Mr Blackborough. Is he out of my house yet?

Walter Kent I expect so.

Lady Julia Then I consider him a hog of a man.

Having said so, she forgives **Mr Blackborough**.

Lady Mortimer But why have you let the Blackboroughs of this world become a power in your party, Julia?

Lady Julia They think they are.

Lady Mortimer I should give this one a peerage without more delay.

Lady Julia Heavens . . . he wouldn't take it. I know . . . we used to quiet them that way. He wants the Treasury . . . and he'll get it some day, I suppose. He's useful . . . he knows where the votes come from . . . and he does raise funds from people that one really couldn't truckle to oneself. And if it pleases him to imagine that he 'bosses' us . . .

Lady Mortimer Julia, don't be complacent. The man rattles you in his pocket with the rest of his loose change.

Lady Julia Well, Mamma . . . if you'll tell me how to prevent undesirable people joining a party . . . we'll all be very much obliged to you.

Farrant *has returned, and finds himself opposite* **Mrs O'Connell**.

Farrant How's the headache?

Amy O'Connell Oh, had I a headache? So I had. No one pitied me. That must have cured it.

Farrant Come and play one game of pool. Good exercise. Come along, you two.

This last is to **Lucy** *and* **Walter**. **Lady Julia**'s *eyebrows go up*.

Lady Julia Dear George . . . at this hour!

Lucy Davenport I'll play.

Lady Julia Send Mr Trebell in to us. He won't, I'm sure.

Farrant He said he'd a brief to look through. Shocking Sabbath-breaking!

Amy O'Connell What a wonderful moon!

The suggestion of pool has shifted **Amy O'Connell** *Come and play one game of pool. Good exercise. Come along, you two.*

This last is to **Lucy** *and* **Walter**. **Lady Julia**'s *eyebrows go up*.

Lady Julia Dear George . . . at this heparted. . . ?

Farrant Who's that? Oh, Blackborough.

Lady Julia Did they get on any sort of terms, d'you think?

Farrant I daresay. There's often more gained by not talking about a thing than just by talking.

Lady Julia We really ought to have got one step further.

Farrant Don't scold me . . . I did my devil-most. Why didn't you ask His Eminence Charles Cantilupe down? Then we'd have had Disestablishment hot for breakfast

and cold for lunch . . . and Disestablishment nicely
warmed up again for dinner.

Lady Julia Yes . . . just what we didn't want at this
juncture.

Farrant Oh! Sorry I'm not subtle. (*Grumbling contentedly.*)
I'm sick of politics. Nothing but a safe seat and devotion to
my country . . .

Lucy Davenport Why don't you take a peerage, Cousin
George?

Farrant I'd love it. Julia won't let me.

Frances Trebell Oh . . . why not?

Farrant Julia, the daughter of a hundred earls . . . Julia,
the wife of a pinchbeck modern peer! No, no! She married
me for my money . . . and I must keep in my place.

Lady Julia George . . . your humour is old-fashioned. Run
away.

*The two of them must be very happy together if he can joke
with the truth like that. He turns towards the window.* **Mrs
O'Connell** *is standing right out in the moonlight now, but
when he speaks to her she frames herself in the window again
to answer him.*

Farrant Come and take a cue, dear lady.

Amy O'Connell Kind gentleman . . . did you never
remark that I have a pointed elbow?

Farrant (*who is perhaps not quite so simple as he seems*) No
. . . have you?

Amy O'Connell If I took a cue, you would. My headache's
back . . . and the moon's very good for it. I shall stroll
once round the fountain. And so to bed, Julia?

Lady Julia Yes . . . biscuits are by the billiard-room. We'll
pick you up there.

Amy O'Connell I may be rude and not wait for you.

She vanishes into the moonlight and the garden. **Farrant** *departs.* **Lucy** *and* **Walter** *are about to follow him.*

Lady Julia Oh dear, oh dear! I'm growing old . . . I'm growing clumsy. Here's the weekend over . . . and nothing has happened. And I thought I'd made up the mixture so nicely too. Lucy! Take Amy O'Connell her lace . . . or she'll catch a cold next.

Lucy *returns and picks up the lace scarf as if, it would seem, she had a certain contempt for it.*

Lucy Davenport Colds are unbecoming.

Lady Julia Lucy!

Lucy Davenport Sorry! My claws need cutting. Here, Walter . . . you take it. Be gallant. You're forgetting how . . . hob-nobbing with me.

Walter Kent That's your fault.

There is a happy, triumphant confidence in his voice which can have nothing to do, surely, with what he says. He goes after **Mrs O'Connell** *and* **Lucy** *after her Cousin* **George**. *The three women left together settle at once into cosier friendliness.*

Lady Mortimer Are those two young people engaged or are they not, Julia?

Lady Julia No . . . but they settled when they were children that neither of them would ever marry anybody else. They haven't twopence. He thinks he ought to go into the City for a few years. She won't have that . . . he's to start for a career straight away. She's to have babies . . . two boys and a girl, she tells me.

Lady Mortimer Science is so accommodating nowadays.

Lady Julia She has the brains really . . . but he wants to please her. He'll be somebody before she has done.

Lady Mortimer It was good of your Henry to give him such a chance.

Frances Trebell My Henry wanted to please. And likes Walter. He doesn't like many people.

Lady Julia Your Henry has been very naughty this weekend.

Frances Trebell Julia, I did warn you . . . you may be wasting your time.

Lady Mortimer Julia . . . if a brutal question is permissible: What are you up to?

Lady Julia I hoped it was obvious. The successful intriguer, Mamma, does nothing underhand. If Cyril Horsham forms a cabinet, Mr Trebell must be in it.

Lady Mortimer But he doesn't belong to your party.

Lady Julia He doesn't belong to any other. He sits as an Independent . . . Ellesmere's his pocket-borough. He always has got in as an Independent, hasn't he, Frances?

Frances Trebell During the war . . .

Lady Julia Oh, that doesn't count. And I want him to have charge of the Disestablishment Bill.

Lady Mortimer That'll be a bold stroke.

Lady Julia It's high time we made one . . . if we're not to be Blackboroughed to death.

Lady Mortimer But won't it be Cyril's own affair?

Lady Julia He can't . . . he must take the Foreign Office. Do you mean to tell me, Frances, that if Henry's made the offer point-blank, he'll say no?

Frances Trebell I think it quite likely.

Lady Julia But what is he in public life for at all, then? He can't stay in the House and make speeches that count . . . count for votes! . . . and always refuse office. It's not right. He needn't join the party even. Disestablishment is an exceptional thing . . . there'll be a lot of cross voting.

Lady Mortimer But sanctified by office, he might stay in it, you think?

Lady Julia (*countering her mother with perfect frankness*) Yes . . . I hope. Practical politics are party politics. And we'd be the better off for him. Can't you use your influence, Frances?

Frances Trebell Julia . . . though such a thing must seem to you against nature . . . I have no influence with Henry . . . and never have had, from the days when we played in our suburban nursery together.

Lady Julia But what does he want of life? He doesn't like society . . .

Frances Trebell No.

Lady Julia He dislikes women, apparently.

Frances Trebell He's pretty indifferent to them.

Lady Julia He can't suspect m e of wanting to flirt with him, I hope. But whenever I try to talk to him the temperature drops.

Lady Mortimer He flattered an old lady at tea-time yesterday with some very pleasant attentions.

Lady Julia He considers you safe, Mamma.

Lady Mortimer Then he has no right to. Mine is the perfect age for a love affair.

Lady Julia How old is he, Frances?

Frances Trebell Fifty-one.

Lady Julia Well . . . he has made himself a unique position. If it's going to be a barren one . . . what a pity! And here's a chance of the premiership for him . . . nothing less in the end. Isn't that good enough? If you can't do better with him, Frances . . . marry him off to some vulgar ambitious woman who will.

Frances Trebell I think I have never really known what

Henry believed in. We all disbelieve in so much . . . and believe in so little nowadays.

The **Butler** *comes in.*

Butler Dr Wedgecroft has telephoned, my lady. His thanks . . . they stopped the express for him and he reached town in good time.

Lady Julia Thank you.

The **Butler** *goes.*

Lady Mortimer Was he sent for?

Lady Julia No . . . it's his point of honour not to sleep out of town during what he calls his duty months.

Frances Trebell Gilbert can do as much with Henry as any one.

Lady Julia I know. That's why I fetched him down today. They had a talk before dinner. Bed, Mamma?

Lady Mortimer I think so.

Lady Julia I must go by the billiard-room. Is our lovely Amy still star-gazing? Mr Blackborough didn't seem to be so very 'took' with her.

Lady Mortimer He eyed her as if he thought she'd try to borrow money from him.

Frances Trebell I don't see her.

The suggestion of bed has brought them to their feet; **Lady Mortimer** *is collecting her spectacles and such-like;* **Frances** *has moved out into the courtyard, she now comes back.*

Lady Julia I only asked her in the hope that she'd amuse him.

Frances Trebell Julia . . . how brutal!

Lady Julia People must expect to be made use of. She sets out to be amusing . . . to men. A house-party needs just a dash of . . . her sort of thing.

Lady Mortimer Your cunning is too consistent, Julia. You really should do something single-minded occasionally. Why, by the way, did you ask m e?

Lady Julia I love you, Mamma.

Lady Mortimer That may be your salvation yet.

Lady Julia But the lovely Amy bores me. I wonder you like her so, Frances.

Frances Trebell I like all sorts of people.

Lady Julia Why doesn't she go back to her Justin?

Frances Trebell He's impossible.

Lady Julia I doubt it.

Frances Trebell My dear . . . with a housemaid for his mistress . . . even an Irish housemaid!

Lady Julia She could give her a month's notice.

Lady Mortimer And this is the result of bringing up my daughter upon the novels of Miss Charlotte M Yonge!

Frances Trebell But for all Amy's airs and graces one feels sorry for her at times. There's something of the waif about her.

Lady Mortimer Good-night, dear Miss Trebell.

Frances Trebell Good-night.

Lady Julia I'll come in and kiss you, Mamma. And I will not sit up watching Lucy play pool . . .

And so they talk themselves out of the room.

It must be an hour later, or nearly, for the moon has sunk behind the little wooded hills which bound the gardens. The room is empty. Some thrifty hand has turned out a light or two. In the courtyard there appear **Amy O'Connell** *and* **Henry Trebell**. *The lace scarf that* **Walter** *took her is wrapped round her head and shoulders: she looks nun-like. They pause outside the window.*

Amy There goes the moon . . . so there goes romance! I'm cold. Doesn't moonshine warm the night just a little?

Trebell No.

Amy Sure?

Trebell Quite.

Amy I like to think it does.

She comes into the room; he follows her. We are all built up on contradictions; hence our equilibrium. But with most of us the opposing qualities are fused in compromise. What one remarks in **Trebell** *is that with him this is not so. The idealist and the cynic, the sensualist and the ascetic, gentleness and cruelty, could any one of them have undisputed sway if he'd let them. But not the least remarkable thing about him is the rigid control which some inner man seems to exercise over this outer man, yet with indifference, almost with disdain. At this moment, however, he is flirting with a pretty woman. He flirts a little grimly. There is something, one would say, cat-like about* **Mrs O'Connell**, *and one might compare her flirting – the metaphor is none the worse for being old – to the cat playing with its mouse. But a tiger is playing with her.*

Amy Everyone in bed?

Trebell The billiard-room lights are out.

Amy How rude of Julia! What's the time?

Trebell Twenty past twelve.

Amy (*happily horror-struck*) Never! Then how dare you keep me gallivanting in the garden all this while? No one told you I was down there?

Trebell No.

Amy That's as well.

Trebell They thought you'd carried your headache to bed. . . .

Amy I hope.

Trebell I went off to finish some work. I slipped out for a breath of air . . . and took a bee-line to you.

Amy In the dark!

Trebell By instinct.

Amy Well, good-night.

Trebell Goodnight.

She gives him her hand, which he holds a moment longer than he need.

Amy But you've been dodging me this whole weekend . . . publicly.

Trebell I have been dodging you . . . privately . . . for these last six months.

Amy Then . . . let me tell you . . . you began to dodge long before there was any need.

Trebell I felt the need.

Amy Thank you. I'm such a siren, am I . . . malgré moi? I'll see there's no more need. How long since we first met?

Trebell I fear I forget.

Amy It's a year or more. I disliked you then exceedingly.

Trebell I make no complaint of that.

Amy Last January I began to like you a little . . . and for one whole evening I thought you liked me. After that I disliked you till about April . . . then for a week or two I liked you a lot. But I think I'd better finish by disliking you.

Trebell Perhaps you had.

Amy Have you any friends?

Trebell Only old friends.

Amy You'll chaff and flatter and gibe at me for an hour. But you don't like me . . . so why not say so? Good-night.

She is close to him. Without preliminaries, he seizes her and

*kisses her, full on the lips. Having done so he releases her as
suddenly. She stands there, a challenger, whose challenge has
been accepted. But there is to be manoeuvring yet.*

Amy And you'll do that! I might have known.

Trebell Didn't you?

Amy One has to risk it.

Trebell I've not kissed a woman for ten years . . . just
about.

Amy (*pursing her numbed lips prettily*) So I should suppose!

Trebell I apologise. No, I don't. You knew that I'd kiss
you.

Amy Really! Which is the worst? The kiss . . . or the
apology . . . or that? I wonder if I could be as brutal as
you, Henry. Shall I try?

Trebell Do try.

Amy If you meant to . . . why didn't you . . . before? It
was wonderful there by the fountain. I'll confess, when we
turned down by the yew trees . . . I did think you would.

Trebell No! I've no use for romance in the moonlight. Nor
any time . . . nor taste for semi-intellectual flirtations.
You're quite right . . . you'd better keep away from me.

Amy What has made you so afraid of women? Did some
selfish creature try to marry you? I wonder any man gets
married. Why should he? But I rather wonder you weren't
married young . . . and married wrong. Almost any
woman could have married you . . . if she'd put her mind
to it.

Trebell I was engaged for a year or more when I was
twenty-two. For I was a nice young man. . . .

Amy Never!

Trebell By bringing up . . . by habit . . . heading for
domesticity. Yes . . . and it was by moonlight in a garden
I proposed.

Amy Such an indelicate word, I always think! Did she jilt you, the silly? Did you suffer?

Trebell No . . . I broke it off . . . I had the pluck to.

Amy Why?

Trebell I never can want to see things but just starkly as they are. She was a nice young woman through and through . . . and full of sentiments that she thought were feelings and of shop-soiled ideas. Incurably suburban and incurably unreal. And she wasn't for babies and housekeeping. We were to be life-long companions in culture. I should have broken her heart. She never married. Frances keeps in touch with her. She settled in Surrey . . . has a garden . . . and belongs to the Labour Party. Later . . . if this interests you . . .

Amy But of course it interests me.

Trebell It ought not to . . . at the moment.

Amy Why not?

Trebell The past has no place in love-making . . . nor the future.

Amy Oh . . . are we love-making?

Trebell I'm waiting to begin again.

Amy Then I'd better hear about your past . . . while there's still time.

Trebell It's not interesting. I had an affair . . . as they're called . . . with a woman, which worked out like the plot of a cheap novel. Really we might have been reading it up as we went . . . she and her husband and I. It must have been about their sixth volume. He'd been the first one's hero. Then he had to encourage successors . . . or the useless, unhappy creature would have taken to drink or religion or something. I escaped. Good honest harlotry is more tolerable than that. No . . . thank you very much . . . no more hectic half-hours or moonlit moments for me.

Amy But has no woman ever made you suffer? Not that you'd tell me!

Trebell I daresay I shouldn't.

Amy Never a heartache?

Trebell When you talk of stomach-ache I know what you mean. When you talk of heartache . . . I'm not so sure y o u do!

Amy I do not talk of stomach-aches . . . and I never have one.

Trebell Lucky woman!

Amy There's no luck in it . . . I'm particular about my food. But I wonder if I couldn't make you suffer . . . just a little.

Trebell I doubt it.

Amy You'd come to thank me. All that is best in my character I owe to unhappiness.

Trebell This is where I kiss you again.

Amy Thank you for the warning. It's where you don't.

Trebell Silly talk of some sort seems a necessary prelude . . . though I never could make out why. I've obliged with my share . . . I hoped we were through with it. But do let us avoid cant!

Amy Henry . . . you're right . . . I'd better have done with you. You're a cold-blooded brute. . . .

Trebell Far from it.

Amy Well . . . you've given what you'd call your heart, then, to politics and the law. I daresay you're quite sentimental about tariffs and the gold standard. But wherever should I come in? Join the Tories and let Julia patronise you. You'll find that frightfully thrilling. I wish I'd never begun to like you. Heavens . . . you must be horrid to live with! Poor Frances!

Trebell She has not been complaining, I hope.

Amy Not she! I love Frances.

Trebell I constantly hear you say so.

Amy And she adores you.

Trebell With the subtlety of vanity I divined what you and she had in common.

Amy I wish I thought you were vain. There'd be that much humanity about you.

Trebell The very first time I saw you . . . you were sitting on the sofa by the fireplace in Berkeley Street . . . Frances was giving you tea . . . there were three or four other women there. You wore a pink dress with frills to it . . .

Amy Lilac!! Heavens . . . I never wore pink in my life!

Trebell It was pink to me! And when you arched your instep . . . it's a trick you have . . . I could hear the stocking rustle.

Amy I'd forgotten you were there. I'm so glad I'd forgotten.

Trebell If I'd followed my instinct then I should have sat down and made love to you before them all . . . which wouldn't quite have done.

Amy And since then you've had so much else to do!

Trebell My day's work's pretty dull. I've grown so used to doing it.

Amy Such brilliant speeches to make!

Trebell I've grown so used to making 'em. No . . . I rather regretted then that the temptation of you wasn't overwhelming. But we have our wintry seasons . . . long ones, often!

Amy I don't want to tempt you. Yes, I do. But you don't look one bit . . . even now . . . as if you were in love with me. Yes, you do . . . yes, you do. But you've not said you love me. Why don't you say so?

Trebell I'll say whatever's necessary.

Amy Don't gibe! I hate you when you gibe. Not even asked me if I love you!

Trebell Don't you? Do you? Don't you?

Amy We don't mean the same thing by it, I'm afraid.

Trebell It comes to the same thing.

Amy Henry . . . you have a coarse mind! No . . . I'll have nothing to do with you.

Trebell Very well.

Amy I won't be played with. Oh . . . it has always been the same. I was petted and bullied as a child . . . one or the other or both at a time. Justin petted and spoiled and bullied me till he got sick of it . . . and I got sick of it and left him. I was very unhappy with Justin. Well . . . I made him unhappy, I suppose.

Trebell Still, he was able in the intervals to write two books that count on Plantagenet Charters.

Amy Do they? I'm sure I'm very glad. I suppose it would be kinder now to divorce him. But I can't make up my mind to . . . for we're Catholics . . . and I haven't any money of my own. And whatever I did he'd never divorce me.

Trebell Well . . . that gives you scope.

Amy Oh no, no . . . you don't take me seriously! I'm good for something more than to be treated like this. And I will be!

They have been sitting together on the sofa, close together. But all this time he has not even touched her hand. Now, though, he takes her in his arms and begins to kiss her, not once but again and again, not hastily either.

Trebell This is how I take you . . . seriously . . . very seriously. Isn't this serious enough?

She gasps, half-ecstatic, or a little frightened.

Amy Let me get my breath.

Trebell No, I won't.

He holds her still, and still kisses her.

Isn't this good enough . . . almost?

He half-releases her at last. If he quite let her go she would fall.

Say something.

Amy (*softly*) I've nothing to say.

Trebell Kiss me.

She is lifting her lips obediently when she hears footsteps.

Amy Good Heavens . . . somebody's coming.

Trebell One of the servants. Sit still.

Amy No, no . . . he'll notice . . . ! Oh, what a fool . . . to be caught . . . !

She has vanished through the window. **Trebell** *is sitting at his ease as the* **Butler** *comes in, evidently to close the room. This promises a dilemma. As* **Trebell** *does not move, after a moment the* **Butler** *asks discreetly . . .*

Butler You're sitting up, sir?

Trebell No . . . I've just been for a walk . . . round the ponds . . . I didn't know it was so late. The house looks its best by moonlight.

Butler Yes, sir . . . the Inigo Jones wing especially . . . so it's considered.

Trebell It is Inigo Jones?

Butler Most houses that can like to call themselves

that . . . but there's his accounts for the work in the library. I have the drawing-rooms to see closed yet, sir.

He is on his way out by the other door.

Trebell Oh . . . what about trains in the morning?

Butler There's the 8.45 . . . the 9.30's a slow . . . and a 10.14.

Trebell What time in town?

Butler Ten past eleven.

Trebell I must take the early one. I don't want breakfast. A cup of coffee.

Butler Very good, sir.

The **Butler** *departs.* **Trebell,** *after two seconds' assurance that he has departed, goes up to the window.*

Trebell All clear!

Amy *slips back through the window, and is making a bee-line for the door when he catches her hand. She is tremulous, but too stirred to be frightened. She tugs, though.*

Amy Good-night . . . good-night!

Trebell No.

Amy My darling . . . good-night.

Trebell Not at all.

Amy Henry . . . let me go.

Trebell Your room's the last on the left?

She gasps.

Amy Oh no! No . . it isn't.

Trebell Never mind . . . there are cards on the doors . . . most sensible custom!

Amy No, no . . . oh, for heaven's sake, no! Not here!

Trebell Why ever not!

Amy Not tonight, though . . . Henry . . . please!

Trebell We may both be dead by tomorrow. I'll wait half an hour.

Amy Don't make me ashamed. Let's be patient a little. That'll make it more beautiful. I promise . . . I promise you . . . very soon.

Trebell I can't stop you turning your key.

Amy Then you'll say I'm heartless. Is he coming back?

Trebell Yes.

The advent of the **Butler** *whips her share of the dispute to a small frenzy. He holds her still, but if she struggled a little harder, surely she could break away. It is not his hand's grip that holds her, distracted, possessed, pathetic.*

Amy . . . and I'm not. No, nor patient . . . in my heart. I love you . . . it hurts me to love you so. Yours . . . all of me . . . whenever . . . whenever . . . ! Oh, I can't stop here arguing!

With which sudden break into the commonplace and almost with a stamp of the foot she breaks free and vanishes. He is finding a book to take up to bed with him when the **Butler** *returns one moment later.*

Trebell Good-night.

Butler Good-night, sir.

Trebell *goes off with his book. The* **Butler** *starts to close the room.*

Act Two

Trebell *has just moved into a fresh working room in his house in Berkeley Street, though* **Frances**, *to be sure, did the moving. The room shows new, but not aggressively. It shows also in its white paint, its plain beige walls, its barely-curtained windows, its spareness of ornament, his taste (and hers) for simplicity in such matters, above all, for plentiful light by which to work. You can read a book in any corner of it.*

The two long windows on your left throw their light well across the room. Facing you is a double door; when this is opened another door is seen across the landing (we are on the first floor); and when this is opened you can see a writing-table with its furnishings. And the walls of this smaller room, which is, so to speak, an under-study, are lined with bookcases filled with law reports and such-like. Between the two rooms a window throws light on the landing and up and down the staircase. In **Trebell**'s *room the bookcases are low, they run all around it, and the books are of every sort and kind. On one side of the bright fire, which is on your right, there is an arm-chair. On the other a chaise-longue sticks out, and by each are tables piled with books. There is yet another table with newspapers ranged on it in order. And, standing out in the room is a very large writing-table, covered – besides its proper belongings, its big ink-stand, its telephone – with books, blue-books, pamphlets and a hundred letters or so, opened and unopened, neatly placed in packets, elastic-banded. And at the table sits* **Trebell** *himself, surveying the work he has evidently just come back to, and beginning to nibble at it.* **Frances** *looks in on him. She is dressed to go out; by the look of her dress it is a fine autumn morning.*

Frances Henry . . . I'm off now. I've ordered lunch for you. There's enough for two if you want to feed Walter.

Trebell I've given him this morning to spend with his beloved. But I do wish that nice young man hadn't settled to marry just as this job was starting. And he didn't tell me till the ship was half-way to Naples . . . or I'd never have taken him the jaunt.

Frances Lucy made him go.

Trebell I wish they were married, then, and had got their romancing over.

Frances You're their romance.

Trebell Heaven help me!

Frances And your job. It's a big job.

Trebell It has the makings of a job in it.

Frances Is this room all right? The paint still smells a bit. I had to put Hansard and the big dictionaries and most of the books from the Temple in there.

Trebell I admire my wastepaper basket (*which is, indeed, magnificently capacious*).

Frances The statesman's companion. Everything has been answered that could be. There are the press-cuttings. You do look the sounder for six weeks Italy.

Trebell That stretch east of Rome that nobody ever sees is worth seeing. I escaped the election babel anyhow. Thank Heaven I didn't have to fight.

Frances It was a near thing, though, they didn't run that Labour man against you.

Trebell But when the car broke something . . . which it did most days . . . Kent and I would climb up out of the dust and sit making up fifteenth-century campaigning speeches to the citizens of Cassino or Lanciano or Bovino or wherever it was we ought to have been getting to while Giacomo Giuseppe Giusti tied it up again with bits of string.

Frances It rained hard here all September. This month has been beautiful so far.

Trebell How long did you stay at Winfield?

Frances Till Mary was up again.

Trebell A boy or a girl? You did tell me.

Frances Another girl.

Trebell A dull holiday for you.

Frances No . . . I'm not sure I wasn't meant to live in a Dorset rectory.

Trebell Sorry I took the wrong turning. The thing to remember about the Renaissance Italian is that he was a realist . . . a financier . . . a passionate politician . . . who took beauty and art and literature and the rest in his stride. An immoral fellow . . . Hullo!

This last is to **Walter Kent**, *who has just bounded up the stairs, glanced into the little room, which is his own, and now turns into this. He is in fine trim, and happy beyond words: not so much at being on the threshold of his own career as in his share of his hero's.*

Walter Kent I got Lord Charles on the telephone. He'd rather come and see you. He said eleven-thirty.

Trebell That'll do.

Walter Kent I'd better begin on these.

He takes a packet or so of the already opened letters from the table.

Trebell What about Wedgecroft?

Walter Kent He's here.

Trebell I gave you the morning off, you know.

Walter Kent I know.

Walter carries his letters into his room. **Frances** *stands watching him, affectionately amused; time was when she*

*dashed at work like that. He does not deliberately ignore her,
of course; they have evidently met before this morning. A maid
now announces* '**Dr Wedgecroft**', *whom* **Frances** *turns to
greet.* **Wedgecroft** *is a man of* **Trebell**'s *age, if to outward
appearance rather older, but alert in body and mind; a born
healer, his bedside manner real and not assumed; one discerns
an intellectual ruthlessness in him too.*

Wedgecroft How are you?

Frances You need never ask.

Wedgecroft You wait! Once I start physicking you. . . !
Have y o u come back ill?

He has passed on to **Trebell**. *Not having met for months, they
are yet too close friends for any hand-shaking.*

Trebell No.

Wedgecroft Then how dare you drag me from Wimpole
Street?

Trebell I've a better use for you. Give me five minutes.

Frances *is departing.* **Walter** *comes to the door of his room.*
Wedgecroft *goes up for a word with him.* **Trebell** *has not
moved from his table.*

Frances In to dinner, Henry?

Trebell Yes . . . no . . . I don't know.

Frances I'll ask Julia . . . if she's doing nothing . . . and
your young lady (*this to* **Walter**). You'll be here . . . let me
tell you . . . till midnight.

Wedgecroft How long have I to decide between a set of
fish-knives and a sugar-sifter?

Walter Kent I should start to think about it.

Frances Oh . . . and, Walter, if Amy O'Connell rings up
. . . No . . . never mind. I'll leave a message downstairs.
She asked us to Charles Street . . . vaguely. Whatever time
she wakes in the morning. . . !

Frances *is already half-way downstairs.* **Walter** *goes back into his room.* **Wedgecroft** *returns to* **Trebell**, *and the two are at ease for their talk.* **Trebell** *looks at the other a little quizzically as if he expected* **Wedgecroft** *to have something to say to him – and he has.*

Trebell Well?

Wedgecroft Henry . . . I consider you owe me an apology.

Trebell Do you?

Wedgecroft When did you settle this?

Trebell With Horsham . . . definitely? . . . though, of course, it can't be definite till he is sent for. Ten days before I left.

Wedgecroft And just about three weeks before that I was walking you round the garden at Shapters . . . persuading you . . .

Trebell The good Lady Julia having set you on.

Wedgecroft And you quite persuaded me that you'd be wrong to.

Trebell Did I? What excellent arguments did I use?

Wedgecroft You said you were no Tory. . . .

Trebell Notoriously no Tory!

Wedgecroft Psychologists declare the punning habit to be a sign of failing intellect.

Trebell They're wrong. The passionate pun is a feature of great literature. But I'm not a Liberal, am I?

Wedgecroft I have never accused you of altruism.

Trebell I might join the Liberals . . . if I were twenty.

Wedgecroft You said you'd made Labour loathe you by ten years' damning of the Trades Unions. . . .

Trebell And I've been right! Look at their candidates this last election. Good God . . . a feudal system working from the bottom up! Who wants that?

Wedgecroft So you could be no help to Horsham there.

Trebell Oh . . . the Labour front bench loves to hear me damning the Unions. They look down their noses like pleased pussy-cats. They daren't do it themselves.

Wedgecroft What made you change your mind?

Trebell That's my secret. Have you been seeing Horsham?

Wedgecroft Once or twice. He's been at Lympne . . . pretty tired out.

Trebell These present fellows mean to meet Parliament . . .

Wedgecroft Apparently.

Trebell He'll have to beat 'em on the Address.

Wedgecroft You won't be in office till mid-November.

Trebell I'm not in all that hurry. It's a simple secret, Gilbert. I found I'd fallen in love. No . . . not with a woman, you old sentimentalist! With this job. I am in love with a Bill for the Disestablishment of the Church of England . . . and for doing sundry other more interesting things. And I mean to make an honest Act of Parliament of the little darling. I'm as joyful . . . as that lad is in there at his prospect of answering my letters for a year or two. But I don't show it.

Wedgecroft Don't you . . . my innocent!

Trebell Do I? Well, I don't care if I do.

Wedgecroft I'm glad . . . I'm damned glad. I'd begun to wonder about you. I seem to have watched so many rivers run into the sand.

Trebell Men get what they want in this world mostly. The hard thing is to want it . . . and to keep on wanting it . . . and to want nothing else. I thought the law altogether lovely once . . . till I learned to make twelve thousand a year out of it. I went into the House quite hopefully. But

my only choice there came to be between gibing at the
fools and becoming one of them.

Wedgecroft Now, now . . . are they all fools?

Trebell There are the worse than fools . . . that see the
facts and shirk them. Do our bodies ever come to
disbelieve in life?

Wedgecroft Sometimes.

Trebell Then you've soon done with them?

Wedgecroft Not always.

Trebell Better to be. From barrenness of mind and
emptiness of will, at any rate, I'd pray . . . if I knew how
to pray . . . for death to deliver me. But we cling on . . .
and sometimes life delivers us. Most men's temptation, I
suppose, is to make for success . . . to learn the official
creed of what we do n o t believe . . . to attune themselves
to the mob mind . . . till they have earned their place
among the parasites upon power that call themselves
governments today. It's not so hard a path . . . to the
dead end of success. But I wasn't tempted. I'm not built
that way.

Wedgecroft And what's to be the difference now?

Trebell You'll see. I hope you'll see.

Wedgecroft Horsham's doing a plucky thing, Henry.
What will the real old Tories make of you?

Trebell Oh, they'd kick . . . if they'd the spirit of their
own sheep.

Wedgecroft And the rest of the crew? Blackborough?

Trebell I'm not afraid of him.

Wedgecroft He'll be at the Treasury?

Trebell I hope not. He and his ca' canny business kind
. . . they've no right in a government at all . . . they're as

bad as the Trades Unions every bit. Blackborough's a
getter . . . not a giver.

Wedgecroft Cut out for the Treasury, then . . . he may
think. He doesn't love you.

Trebell I daresay not.

Wedgecroft There's a Cabinet sweepstake at the Club. I
drew Farrant.

Trebell Oh . . . he'll be in. Nice fellow. No good, of
course. Agriculture, probably.

Wedgecroft I sold him for a fiver.

Trebell There'll have to be a fair lot of fresh men. Walter
and I sat in the Galleria at Milan last Thursday drinking
chocolate and trying to make a list. Yes . . . I can pull this
Bill through the House . . . I can face the public . . . I can
stand up to the press! But the thought of one's colleagues
keeps one awake at nights. I want Cantilupe in.

Wedgecroft Good heavens . . . no!

Trebell Why not?

Wedgecroft My dear Henry! His Eminence . . . with
every incense-swinger in England at his back . . . in a
Cabinet . . . that's to disestablish the Church!

Trebell He has come round to it.

Wedgecroft Even so . . . will Broad Church and Low
Church and pretty-nearly-no-Church stomach his official
finger in the pie?

Trebell They're to be bought. Endow their good works
department. The mammon of righteousness!

Wedgecroft And the bishops?

Trebell I can deal with the bishops. A bishop's a man of
business. He has to be . . . and it's all he has much chance
to be. But there's life in Cantilupe and his lot. They
believe in something bigger than the multiplication table.

So do I . . . though they don't give me credit for it. I can get something out of t h e m.

Wedgecroft But, Henry . . . from your own standpoint . . . when you've done this job . . . and it's going to be the devil of a job . . . what's to happen then?

Trebell What do you see happening then?

Wedgecroft Why is it offered you?

Trebell *up to now has been shrewd, amused, reflective. This rouses in him a certain dialectical pugnacity.*

Trebell Because they've not a man among them that doesn't funk it. Why must democracy grow us these crops of political cowards? Two governments have shirked the thing . . . Horsham would shirk it now if he could . . . though it has been plain these ten years that something drastic must be done . . . ever since the Jackson case . . . ever since the Anglo-Catholics began to keep out non-communicants. And what has been done? The Liberals meet at Manchester and cry: Down with Dogma . . . Free Trade in Religion for ever . . . Take the endowments to pay off the War Debt. . . !

Wedgecroft Now, now . . . be fair.

Trebell Never be fair to your opponents . . . it wastes time. All Labour can think of is: Pity the poor pew-opener . . . double her old-age pension. I talk some sense on the subject. So Horsham turns to me . . . and I may take any sort of a settlement that will save him thinking of the thing again. And then Blackborough and his back-scratching friends will pick a quarrel with me . . . and out I may go into the wilderness with whatever odium's in the Act when it's working on my back.

Wedgecroft Well . . . as long as you foresee that part of the programme too!

Trebell That part mayn't come off, though.

Wedgecroft Oh, they'll be glad enough to turn you Tory.

Dear Lady Julia will take you gently in hand . . . to add you to the list of reformers she has reformed.

Trebell I know! Damn all these women. Though she has brains . . . of the ornamental sort. I don't think, though, she has been good for Horsham. These spiritual adulteries debilitate the mind. She'd better have been his mistress for a year or two and have done with it.

Wedgecroft But I do not see you leavening the Tory lump.

Trebell Gilbert . . . when you fall in love don't look too far ahead. Let your faith have its will of you. Here's a problem in high politics . . . the first for how long that has not been mere bread-and-butter business . . . set me to solve. I'm in love with solving it. And my creed is belief in the thing done . . . well and truly done as a means to the next. Not in the thing shirked . . . in this fashionable fog of good-will . . . this power, not ourselves, that makes for statesmanship. I believe if I dare do this job ruthlessly . . . for its own sake . . . I can make the thing done a living thing . . . a hopeful thing. And with a few more such for a sign this dazed generation might pluck up and face the future again. And I'll face a soft old age. But look here . . . this is what I want you for. How about Brampton?

Wedgecroft I'm on my way round there.

Trebell I thought you might be. How ill is he?

Wedgecroft He's seventy-four.

Trebell What's that nowadays? Is he really ill . . . is he going to die?

Wedgecroft Sir . . . I am attending him.

Trebell And why the devil do you let him get ill just now? Is he too ill to look through my figures? Horsham says he has had them three weeks.

At this moment the table telephone rings. **Trebell** *mechanically puts the receiver to his ear, and holds it there while the talk goes on. But he receives nothing apparently.*

Wedgecroft He has been ill enough to do nothing he didn't want to do.

Trebell (*to the telephone*) Hullo? Yes? Hullo? Won't he stomach me as a colleague? Is that what's the matter with him?

Wedgecroft Professional etiquette forbids me to disclose what a patient may confess in the sweat of his agony. But you may take it his stomach is sound.

Walter Kent *comes in and, seeing his chief clinging to the receiver, says, cheerfully . . .*

Walter Kent Sorry . . . I wasn't sure if it worked.

Trebell You and your new toy! Cantilupe?

Walter Kent No. This from Mr Horsham. And Mrs O'Connell's downstairs. Miss Trebell's out. Are you both dining with her in Charles Street or not?

Trebell *opens the large envelope and goes through its contents as he talks.*

Trebell I haven't the remotest idea. I shall work here till eight. Then I shall go where I'm taken . . . till ten.

Walter Kent I could telephone to Lady Julia's . . . Miss Trebell may be there.

He goes back to his room to do so.

Wedgecroft Does Horsham expect to bring the old man in?

Trebell I want him at the Treasury.

Wedgecroft In Blackborough's place?

Trebell It isn't Blackborough's place.

Wedgecroft You want all the troublesome fellows.

Trebell I want all the first-rate fellows. These are my figures . . . sent back through Horsham. He has not made a note on them. What the devil's he up to?

Wedgecroft I can tell you a bit of his mind. He knew I
should see you . . . I fancy he meant me to. He detests this
political generation. He thinks you're mad . . . but he
rather admires you. He'll come back, he says, if he comes
back at all, to knock your finance into shape and some of
the nonsense out of you. But for you, he thinks,
Horsham's not got a man who won't muddle the job
anyhow. So why the blankety blank blank . . . but for you
. . . shouldn't he make ready to meet his God in peace?

Trebell Good. . . !

During this **Mrs O'Connell** *has come quietly up the stairs to
stand, smiling and composed, on the landing. At this point they
turn to see her.*

Amy Oh . . . this is y o u r room now? And I'm
interrupting . . . I'm so sorry. Where's the drawing-room,
then? And how are you? Had a good holiday? Not being
physicked? How are y o u, dear Dr Wedgecroft? Do you
and Frances dine with me? Nothing's ordered now . . . so
you can't. Why doesn't she answer my messages?

*Still smiling, still composed – is she a little too composed? – she
has come into the room for these greetings and questions.*
Trebell *is familiarly polite.*

Trebell Kent is telephoning to Frances. I'm very well,
thank you. The new drawing-room is downstairs. I've had
an excellent holiday. I think nothing of Gilbert as a doctor;
but his political intelligence . . . in both senses . . . I
prize.

*She is surveying the big writing-table now with mock-childish
admiration.*

Amy What a tableful! If I sit here, shall I know what it
feels like to be a great man?

Wedgecroft How is Ireland?

Amy Beautiful always, isn't it? But sad!

Wedgecroft I used to feel sad there. But that was my bad British conscience. I'm off, Henry.

Trebell *joins him at the door, and* **Mrs O'Connell** *is left sitting at the table. She takes up a pencil and a bit of paper and begins to scribble idly.*

Trebell The old man's my man . . . I don't mind what he thinks of me. He has forgotten more than I've ever learnt. He's got courage . . . he's got character. I'd sooner have him to fight than these political tradesmen to chaffer with. Get him out of bed . . . or give me half an hour with him and I'll get him out for you.

Walter Kent *has emerged from his room.*

Walter Kent I'm sorry . . . Miss Trebell's not there.

Amy Thank you ever so much . . . it doesn't matter in the least.

Walter *goes back again.*

Wedgecroft Well . . . when the thermometer's in his mouth I'll say a word.

Trebell Thank you for coming . . . and always thank you.

Now, as upon impulse, the two do shake hands; and then **Wedgecroft**, *half in fun, slips professional fingers to his friend's wrist.*

Wedgecroft I have backed you from the start. No, not for a place . . . you could have had that any time, I knew . . . but to win. Pulse . . . seventy. I'd prefer it a thought quicker.

Trebell Why?

Wedgecroft Good balance is good . . . but the power of recovery is better . . . and Nature likes us to have a little practice in it now and then. I've never yet seen you thrilled or rattled.

Mrs O'Connell, *her scribbling over, has picked up from the* *table between finger and thumb what looks like a large flint stone, used as a paper weight evidently.*

Amy Whatever is this, Henry?

Trebell I don't get rattled. I will at the next chance to please you. That? . . . won me my first seat . . . flung at me out of the first crowd I spoke to.

Amy Did your head make this chip in it?

Trebell The fellow was a good shot. I wore a bandage for a month. I owed him five hundred votes by polling day. But he never let me thank him.

Wedgecroft *has gone. Beckoned by her voice* **Trebell** *moves towards her, and a tapping finger tells him to read over her shoulder what she has scribbled on the scrap of paper. When he has read it he looks up to find* **Walter Kent** *standing in the doorway as if waiting instructions.*

Walter Kent No answer to Mr Horsham?

Trebell No.

The word has perhaps an odd ring in it; but **Walter** *does not notice and goes downstairs to dismiss* **Mr Horsham**'s *messenger.* **Trebell** *goes, not too quickly, to the door to shut it after him, while* **Amy O'Connell** *tears the scrap of paper into small bits, and throws them – a first sacrifice – into the so capacious wastepaper basket.*

Amy Don't shut the door. Yes . . . you'd better.

He does; then faces her. Her mask drops off.

Trebell What's wrong?

Amy Why have you been away . . . these ages? I couldn't write. Come nearer to me. You'll hate me, Henry.

Trebell Trouble with your husband?

Amy Not yet. No . . . I've not been near him. But you'd stopped loving me before you went away . . . after that one week. I knew. And you'll hate me now.

Her voice, too flat, too sharp, is hardly under her control. She is near the edge, indeed, of a nervous collapse.

Trebell My dear girl . . . if you've anything to tell me that won't wait, tell it quickly. We shall be interrupted . . . at any moment.

She tells him . . .

Amy There's a danger of my having a child . . . your child . . . sometime in April. That's all.

Trebell In April?

Amy The first week in April.

Trebell You're sure?

Amy My God . . . d'you think I want it to be true? Say something.

He does not recognise, nor she, this echo of his own demand at a certain auspicious moment. But if he is silent, it is that his thoughts are racing.

Trebell When did you last . . . see your husband?

Amy A year ago . . . and more.

Trebell Yes. We must consider.

His tones are dry. Her voice is dead.

Amy I knew you'd hate me.

He is kindlier, but his mind is set neither to kindness nor unkindness.

Trebell Nonsense, my dear! You've had a hard month or so . . . with no one to talk to. I'm sorry.

Amy I kept telling myself: It's not possible. Then . . . last Thursday week . . . I went to a doctor . . . down at Southampton . . . picked him out of the telephone book . . . gave him another name . . . told him I was off abroad. A kind old thing . . . said it was all quite satisfactory. But I've to keep telling myself it's true . . . or I shouldn't

believe it. Though when I wake at night . . . each time I
wake, I'm saying: Yes, of course it's true . . . you've
known it all along. How can things happen so . . . in spite
of one?

Trebell Yes . . . you've not been sleeping . . . I can see.

Amy Kind of you to tell me . . . most consoling! No, I've
not been. I've taken stuff . . . all I dare . . . all I could get.
You can't get much.

Trebell That won't do. You must be looked after.

Amy Who's one to trust? I nearly bolted when I saw
Gilbert Wedgecroft. He stood there mum as a maggot.
Heaven knows what these doctors can't tell just by
glancing at you. Why did he ask me about Ireland?
Doesn't he know I never go back?

Trebell Probably not. We could trust Gilbert.

Amy I don't like him.

Trebell Why?

Amy Because he doesn't like me, I suppose. He's your
friend . . . he'd think of what suited you. I won't have him
told. Give me your word, please, you won't even hint
things to him.

Trebell Very well.

*They are at odds, hopelessly apart; she querulous and
distraught, he considerate, but incapable of soft phrase. Now,
though, her voice rises in the wail of a lost child.*

Amy But what am I to do . . . what am I to do?

Trebell There are half a hundred sensible things we can do
. . . when you've steadied your nerves.

Amy If only you still loved me a little it would help! You
think I've had lovers . . . besides you. It's not true . . .
whoever has told it you. I've been near enough to the edge
of it. I don't really like men . . . that's the silly thing. But

you've to fool them . . . or they'll fool you. I did do one thing that wasn't quite right before I was married . . . though nothing happened. Then Justin wasn't fair to me. He thinks a woman should sit at home and sew baby-clothes when she's not in church praying God to send her a use for them. Still . . . being a Catholic and confessing now and then does help keep you straight. Though you can't confess everything. And what do priests know about marriage anyway? They oughtn't to! And I'd been getting to be no end of a sceptic and thinking there might be something in Science and Spiritualism and the rest. Well . . . I'm punished for that. God lets you be for a bit . . . and then does something that m a k e s you believe in him. I nearly went back to Justin to tell him all about it . . . for the sake of telling someone. But he's queer. He might have killed me . . . not that I'd mind much. Or he might kill you.

Trebell He'd likelier be off to his lawyer and start a divorce . . . and remember to be queer and Catholic again when he'd got it.

Amy And that'd smash you.

Trebell At the moment . . . yes.

Amy I'd be so sorry. Still . . . you'd marry me.

Trebell That is the usual thing.

Amy Then you'd hate me the more, I suppose, for being the smashing of you. But we could get along. People do. I'm good company . . . and I'm still pretty. I can't see why you don't love me . . . just a little.

Trebell I can say that I love you. It's easily said.

Amy You never once said it . . . you'd no need. That's pretty shameful. Did you think I wouldn't notice?

Trebell It's a sort of lying I dislike . . . using words that have no meaning to me.

Amy Oh, don't talk cleverly now, Henry . . . please! Let's be practical. Tell me what to do.

To these pitiful, ridiculous, revelations what could he find to say! But his own dry – and really rather priggish – piece of pedantry having roused her to a very wholesome impatience, he comes, readily enough, to the bearings of common sense, and, to that extent, of kindness.

Trebell Well . . . you may count on me for as much of my duty to the child . . . and to you, while the trouble lasts . . . as you'll let me do. My rights are forfeit. That's as it should be . . . the law shows some sense. You can't forfeit yours. A bad time . . . for a few months yet . . . you're bound to have. One or two people must know. If you choose to tell your husband now or later and risk the scandal . . . the rights and the wrongs of that we'd better talk out when you're calmer. But it's your duty, remember . . . whatever else happens . . . to keep yourself fit. And . . . oh, my dear girl! . . . if kindness will do it, I'll be as kind as I know how to be. Well, now . . . you're not tied down . . . you can get off abroad . . . we'll cover your tracks. . . .

Intent on her human needs he has himself become human; something more than mere kindness and common sense might be rising in him. But she has only listened with a growing horror, her eyes round and staring, her face set; till at last she breaks out, dreadfully . . .

Amy Are you expecting me to go through with this?

Trebell (*echoing*) . . . through with it?

Amy I'd sooner kill myself.

He looks at her gravely and speaks gravely.

Trebell You've no choice by now, I should suppose, but to go through with it . . . no reasonable choice.

Amy I won't.

Trebell Put mischievous notions out of your head once and for all.

Amy I'll kill myself sooner.

He is stern, and no kindliness can hide it. She seems to mean precisely what she says.

Trebell Steady . . . steady! This is the trouble, then . . . just this?

You'd not call it a laugh that escapes her.

Amy Yes . . . thank you! . . . just this.

She is suffering; he can still be kind.

Trebell Try and talk frankly to me. You're not simply afraid?

Amy Why not? I'm ill as it is.

Trebell Because Nature . . . if you'll let her . . . provides against that, you know. And there's other provision in these days. What's at the back of the fear?

To her poor, twisted mind this is mere torture, and she cries out under it.

Amy Oh . . . don't question me . . . and steady me . . . as if I were a beast being broken in! But that's what I am now . . . no better!

Trebell Come . . . come!

He puts a restraining hand on her. She breaks free and turns on him; desperate, weakly violent.

Amy When I was a girl . . . and no more than a girl . . . I said to myself . . . and I didn't need to say it . . . that never, never, would I have a child.

Trebell Weren't you foolish, then, to marry?

Amy One has to marry. I was a fool to marry Justin. He found out . . . after a bit. He thinks it a sin. I said I'd a

right to choose. What do women's rights come to if that's
not their right? So I left him.

Trebell But I don't understand your dread.

Amy How should you? Love's beautiful . . . this is
beastly. Oh dear, oh dear . . . when I've always been so
clever about things that didn't matter much . . . to run up
against two such impossible men! No civilised woman
wants children growing up round her to remind her she's
growing old. If she's trapped into it she makes the best of
it . . . or pretends to. Well . . . I won't pretend to. Do you
mean to tell me I've no right to choose?

*She is growing a little shrill, shedding the daintiness that avails
her nothing. Is there something common at the core of her? He
grows graver yet.*

Trebell Here's something I've learnt to believe. We choose
and think we've chosen wisely . . . then by some grace we
blunder on a better thing. Then comes the test. Have we a
sense of it . . . and the faith to go on into the unknown?

Amy A sense of what? Faith! Faith in what?

Trebell My dear, my dear . . . beauty or brains, what are
they worth . . . if we've not enough life in us to pay Life
on demand?

Amy I'm in trouble . . . I'm in danger . . . and you talk
platitudes to me! Are you going to help me out of this hell
or are you not?

Trebell Through it.

Amy No . . . no . . . no!

Trebell You'll play no tricks. Mark that now.

Amy Who's to stop me?

Trebell You'll think of your child.

Amy There's no child . . . and there's not to be . . . if I
say so. And it's my right . . . no one else's to say so.

What answer can he make? Their anger checked by silence, she relapses into pitifulness again.

Amy And you've not even said you're sorry . . . you've not even kissed me. If you loved me just a little I mightn't feel so lost. But you don't . . . and you never did . . . I knew it all the time. So I shouldn't believe you now if you said you did. Well . . . I don't want to lie to you either. What's the use? I daresay I didn't love you very much . . . once it was over . . . and you'd gone away.

These seem to be the depths. But out of them his incorrigible intellect plucks a forlorn hope.

Trebell If that's the truth . . . let's start from that. . . .

Amy I don't see what use the truth is. I wish I were dead.

At this moment the table telephone rings.

Trebell This'll be Cantilupe.

He goes to answer. She rises wearily, and with something of the indifference of weariness.

Amy I've broken up your morning's work . . . I'm so sorry. The papers have been full of you . . . if I'd needed reminding of you. You're to save the country . . . or to ruin it. But somebody's always doing that.

Trebell He's coming up.

Amy Then for heaven's sake open the door.

Trebell Are you going home now . . . back to Charles Street?

Amy I hadn't thought of it.

Love her – how can he pretend he does? But he is touched; and to a sort of reverence for her, little as this is what she asks.

Trebell We'll find salvation for you.

But this is the last straw. She rounds on him savagely.

Amy Don't mock at me . . . don't cant! You've done for

me . . . isn't that enough? I was happy and free. You've brought me down and degraded me . . . and what do you care? I'm nothing to you now. I'm a sick beast . . . unclean . . . cancerous!

Trebell Hold your tongue, will you . . . before you believe what you're saying? You unhappy woman . . . if life only seems like death to you!

Amy Will you please open that door?

Trebell *opens it and goes out upon the landing. She braces herself – slips on the mask again – for an encounter with* **Lord Charles.**

Amy Tell Frances I waited in vain for her . . .

Trebell He's still at the bottom of the stairs.

She takes a last chance to say tensely. . . .

Amy Will you find me somebody to go to?

Trebell No.

Amy Very well, then . . . very well . . . !

Trebell How are you, Cantilupe?

With this warning to her, **Cantilupe** *appears.*

Cantilupe I'm a quarter of an hour late. I'm sorry.

Trebell It's no matter.

Amy I've been distracting him from statesmanship for ten minutes of it. How do you do and good-bye!

Cantilupe A most dangerous distraction.

Amy Sweet of you to say so. Well . . . I leave you to disestablish the Church. I'm sure that between you it'll be beautifully done.

Trebell Won't you wait . . . for Frances?

Amy What's the use . . . if you're sure she can't help me?

Trebell I should wait.

Walter Kent *has followed* **Cantilupe** *up the stairs.* **Amy** *strolls across to his room as if she might possibly wait there.*

Amy And is this your kennel? How precious! Dear Frances does spoil you. It's the big room made little. But you must get a pretty cover for your typewriter.

Walter Kent It's as if the big room had had a baby . . . I tell Miss Trebell.

Amy Quite! How witty of you!

Walter *having made this magnificent gaffe, turns to his chief.*

Walter Kent Wedgecroft has just sent back a message: will you see him for another moment on his way back to Wimpole Street?

Trebell Yes.

Walter Kent Right.

He goes downstairs again. **Amy O'Connell** *stands in the doorway of the little room.* **Trebell** *goes towards her and they are out of* **Cantilupe***'s sight if not of his hearing.*

Trebell Please wait for Frances.

Amy I've no faith in any of you.

Trebell But you'd better wait.

She gives him a little twisted smile, but turns and goes into the room. He closes the door on her and looks as if he'd like to lock it. Then he comes back to **Cantilupe** *and his work, shutting his own door too. One sees at once why* **Cantilupe** *is nicknamed His Eminence. In spite of his layman's dress – which has besides a dandified individuality about it, permissible, if well-contrived, in the man of fifty or over; and* **Cantilupe** *is over – he would be better suited by purple soutane and red cap, and his face would look well from one of El Greco's canvases. There is a natural, if constrained, courtesy in his speech and movements. He is almost the last man in London to pay old-fashioned compliments to women – and he refers to them as ladies. He has a charming mind and a subtle* *mind; but he is not a strong man and he knows it; his refuge is in obstinacy. He has the limpid eye of the enthusiast, but the mouth of a fanatic. And he is very wary of* **Trebell**.

Cantilupe How are you?

Trebell Very well. How are you?

Cantilupe A pleasant holiday?

Trebell Most. A pleasant election?

Cantilupe The usual thing. Not quite so degrading as usual, perhaps.

After which duellists' parade they settle to what **Cantilupe**, *at any rate, thinks to be a duel.*

Trebell Well . . . now?

Cantilupe I've brought you these memoranda back.

Trebell I hoped you'd keep them.

Cantilupe My cousin and I have certainly been discussing my possible inclusion in his new Cabinet. But after one turn of office twenty years ago I had made up my mind against another.

Trebell Why . . . if that's not too personal a question?

Cantilupe No. I find myself inevitably at war with the master-fallacy of a godless age . . . the belief that the things we do can be better . . . or other . . . than the thing we are. I distrust most modern legislation, that is to say.

Trebell (*appreciative but practical*). But you'd sooner have something to say to this Disestablishment business . . . if it's got to be.

Cantilupe Oh, I'm for it . . . reluctantly . . . Church and State Tory though I remain at least. But as the modern State scarcely reflects my heart's desire, I have come to think that the Church can best serve it . . . and best save her own soul . . . by breaking partnership.

Trebell Well . . . I hope you'll be in the Cabinet.

Cantilupe Horsham told me you hoped so. It was a surprise to me.

Trebell Till you read my memoranda.

Cantilupe I never expected a scheme of yours to seem so favourable to my point of view.

Trebell Could you do better for your section of the Church with a Bill of your own?

Cantilupe Not so well, as I'm sure you know. 'Section' I protest against. My friends and I are for the Church and the whole Church as we conceive the Church. But an appearance of sectionalism has been thrust on us . . . and whatever we might propose would excite prejudice. I doubt my use in a Cabinet anyway . . . I detest intrigue. I might do more for my own people . . . and for you even . . . by supporting your Bill from the back benches. Frankly, Mr Trebell . . . I want to know why you want me on the front one.

Trebell You want to know that I'm not drafting a Bill to bring you into the Cabinet . . . so that once you're in I may back down upon every item of it while I keep you in . . . till I've so bedevilled your influence that it won't much matter whether you're out or in. For you're a danger on the back benches . . . even as I was. No . . . those are the policies by which we perish. But you see me at best, I suppose, as a sceptic lawyer, content if he can fence you all with your controversies into some form of words and not caring if you starve there. No. Again, no. You're wrong, believe me . . . though it's a safe start to think the worst of any man. I want you with me because you believe in your Church. And though I've to disestablish I'm not out to destroy. I hate all destruction.

Cantilupe I do believe you . . . and I beg your pardon.

Trebell *has won the first bout, evidently.*

Trebell Thank you. Well . . . what will you examine me on? Appropriation . . . Buildings. . . ?

Cantilupe There'll be a lot of silly sentiment to combat over Buildings.

Trebell Yes. These idolaters of Art!

Cantilupe Will you show me one of them that cares a rap what goes on inside the church after he has preserved it?

Trebell No . . . they'll be a nuisance. Representation . . . pre-Restoration endowments?

Cantilupe *is fingering through the memoranda,* **Trebell** *has the whole thing in his head.*

Cantilupe The figures there are troublesome.

Trebell Very rough figures so far.

Cantilupe Your solution of the country parish problem would make a good election cry. Ten square miles and a thousand a year for a curate and a car!

Trebell It's mainly a question of locomotion. I don't much like the Rural District options, though.

Cantilupe And your disputed surplus to go to Education?

Trebell Yes.

Cantilupe That's the heart of the plan.

Trebell The very heart of it.

Cantilupe It sounds well. And the more we quarrel over the loaves and fishes the more Education may get?

Trebell Do you object?

Cantilupe It asks a little courage to object. But every big Bill in my time has had its one provision which the press would unite to praise and all parties promise to support . . . in principle . . . upon a first reading. Yet it seldom survived Committee. I have wondered if it ever was meant to. Not quite perversely, I have sometimes opposed it from the start.

Trebell I shall stand by the education proposals.

Cantilupe Or fall?

Trebell I don't think I shall fall by them.

Cantilupe Well . . . nor do I! So I've been prying into them pretty sharply.

Trebell I supposed you would.

It is genial cut and thrust – though 'genial', perhaps, is hardly the word for either of them. But they are getting on splendidly.

Cantilupe It comes to this. You think the old quarrel over the children is too dead to blaze up again over the teachers?

Trebell Things have changed. Things do change. We've learnt a little. We do learn by being brayed in the mortar of experience. I'd have been on your side in the old quarrel. Atmosphere in a school or college . . . why, it's what most matters. The first thing a child must learn is that he lives by faith. One and one makes two, don't they, by God's grace . . . I'm told there's no other proof. If we could have done with text-book teachers. . . ! But there are never enough good men to go round . . . that's the perennial trouble in this over-engined civilisation. We've to put our money into finding and training them, though.

Cantilupe How many of these colleges do you think your surplus will run to?

Trebell Fifty, I hope . . . more or less. I don't want 'em too big. And I mean to house them when I can . . . though we needn't give this away yet . . . in the country seat that the country gentleman can't sit in any longer. You're not enough of a Tory for me, Cantilupe. You were mourning last Budget over the sad fate of the big country houses. Won't it comfort you to see an abbey or two turned back after four centuries' usurpation to something of the use it was meant for?

This is fascinating, no doubt; but **Cantilupe** *follows his trail.*

Cantilupe And the Church colleges will be under Church control?

Trebell Yes . . . I'll find the money elsewhere for the secular . . . and some of the undenominational . . . balance. There's a good lump being released . . . and a lot of slack to take up. -

Cantilupe *here puts down the memoranda.*

Cantilupe Would you let me ask you, Mr Trebell . . . though I'm aware that in these days the question's thought almost an indecent one . . . what is your own attitude towards my Church?

Trebell I'd like you to know. I grew up in the late nineteenth-century, neo-Polytechnic belief that you couldn't take God seriously and be an FRS. And when I'd done wanting to be an Admiral of the Fleet and the engine-driver of the Scotch Express I wanted to be an FRS. For there were my father's books on the top shelves. He'd sold his ambitions for domesticity and a dispensary practice in West Croydon. But he died of it . . . and I foreswore poverty. Later . . . in a certain loneliness of heart . . . I began to go to church again. I didn't want to be preached at. But I did want to feel myself . . . amid week-day battlings for success . . . one of the congregation of faithful men. I'd read to the end of my prayer-book, you perceive. And after all it was m y Church as by law established. But that didn't last.

Cantilupe What lost you to us?

Trebell Intellectual conscience. I can't take your sacraments. I can't say your creeds. I've tried . . . I don't believe them. You do?

Cantilupe Certainly I do.

Trebell Damned odd you should! Without reserve?

Cantilupe With no reserve.

Trebell I can respect that. Save me from Mr Facing-both-ways. The present may be his . . . but never the future.

Cantilupe You are to set my Church free to save herself from him.

Trebell Quite so. But when that's done . . . what will you do for me and for men of my kind in return? Churchmen at heart . . . members one of another in science or statecraft . . . with no use at all for conventicles and their self-righteousness. Nor even for the promise of salvation hereafter . . . for we die pretty tired, most of us. But with much need to sanctify here on earth the world of power that our secular minds have made.

Cantilupe I have found it, I fear, to be a world of intellectual pride . . . with many simpler lessons still to learn.

Of a sudden he is on his defence, acrid and aloof. **Trebell** *breaks out in good-tempered exasperation . . .*

Trebell Heavens above! Even now you don't repent?

Cantilupe Of what?

Trebell Of these . . . how many? . . . generations of the loss of us . . . of the men who've made the world as it is.

Cantilupe As it is! As it is!!

Trebell The while your Church has been a squabbling ground for third-rate minds . . . most of them; come now! . . . fighting unreal issues into such confusion that at last all parties only want to be quit of you!

Cantilupe You are hardly refuting my accusation of arrogance.

Trebell Our issue's joined, then. Well . . . do you run away?

They are on good terms again. **Cantilupe** *takes up the memoranda to emphasise his disclaimer.*

Cantilupe No.

Trebell Good. Then let's get the issue clear. The Establishment has been your fortress . . . but it has been your prison too.

Cantilupe I admit it. Well . . . a living faith need not fear freedom.

Trebell Nor learning for its own sake?

Cantilupe Nor learning, certainly!

Trebell Very well. The statutes for your colleges are going to be the test of that. And I'll not be afraid of your faith and its dogmas either. Admit with me that hunger for knowledge is a spiritual hunger and its balking or its warping a sin against the light . . . and I ask no more of you.

> 'On a huge hill
> Cragged and steep Truth stands, and he that will
> Reach her, about it and about must go.'

Cantilupe *is really delighted.*

Cantilupe Donne!

Trebell The poet, wasn't he, of your Church's last great dilemma? I believe in your Church too, you see . . . all apart from what your Church may believe in . . . and in more Churches than one. For I believe in vocation . . . in the calling of voices from that hill, however confusedly. I dislike trade . . . the shrewd mind . . . the measuring of profit . . . and property in toil. The world's great ages have had strength to spare and to waste. And even the waste . . . imaginings, art, adventures . . . was fruitful. The fruit of it is ours today. You promise men in their poverty a future life. Why not make them the gift of it now? That's no paradox. Once we're through with youth's appetites and illusions, what does our carnal life hold for us? The past becomes a picture-book. The moment as it passes can't be very interesting . . . saving your presence

. . . for we live it ignobly chained. But the future! That we create . . . selflessly . . . out of ourselves. We can be honourably happy there. And what wise creator will want to know too much about his creation? I have strange visions of your churches, Cantilupe . . . and of week-day praises to God. Of cathedral cloisters busy with dispute. And of every parson in the country turned scholar and schoolmaster . . . with his soul really set upon eternal things. What a chance for you now . . . what a chance! And it may be a last chance . . . so I'm out to make you take it. You shall give us in your freedom what you denied us in your fetters. You shan't leave any longer the world's powers and the men that wield them to the anarchy of unbelief. It may be our civilisation's last chance too. You Churchmen shall write us a creed for our children to believe. You shall sanctify their new world for them or perish.

Though he is still speaking to **Cantilupe** *he has, in a sense, ceased to speak to him. There is silence for a moment.*

Cantilupe If my invitation stands and I join the Cabinet, it will be for the pleasure of hearing you propound this Bill to them.

There is ever such a slight touch of irony in the compliment. **Trebell** *responds to it.*

Trebell Not in these terms!

Cantilupe No . . . perhaps not. And you'll have some not too nice bargains to drive, I fear, in and out of Cabinet.

Trebell That's all in the day's work. But I needed another sort of understanding with you. Ah . . . you wanted my coat, did you, Cantilupe? You shall have my cloak also. You'd have me go with you a mile? By Jove, you shall go with me twain!

Their conference is breaking up. **Cantilupe** *has risen. He is, one remarks, taking the memoranda away with him again.*

Cantilupe We'll go very willingly, I assure you, as far as

we find we can go. Your heresy, Mr Trebell, has its
fascinations . . . as other such heresies have had. We can't
burn you, nowadays . . . we must try to profit by you.

Trebell Yes. The blood of the martyrs you've made . . .
that also has been the seed of the Church.

Trebell *has given of his best – for he felt the need – to win*
Cantilupe. *But it is hard to say how far he has succeeded.*

Cantilupe The Church's wisdom has been to know how
much, on the whole, may be expected of men. And the
hells of this world are paved, don't you think, less with
good intentions than with high ideals.

Trebell *laughs: it is a shrewd hit for a finish. He takes from*
his table the papers that **Horsham** *returned him.*

Trebell Here are more Appropriation figures . . . no, I'd
like to put these tidy. I can show you a draft of the Fabrics
scheme in a few days.

Cantilupe (*his eye twinkling coldly*) And of those statutes?

Trebell I'd like another talk first.

Cantilupe Could you lunch with me . . . on Thursday?

Trebell Yes. We must find out our differences. Hullo!

They have moved to the door, and **Trebell** *has opened it.*
There stands **Wedgecroft**, *watch in hand. And one sees that*
the door of the little room is open.

Wedgecroft I was giving you two minutes more. (*To*
Cantilupe.) How are you?

Cantilupe Is Brampton better?

Wedgecroft Much. I've just been in to see him.

Cantilupe Good-bye.

Abruptly, as his habit is, he departs. **Wedgecroft** *strolls*
towards the fire. **Trebell**, *seeing* **Cantilupe** *down the stairs, is*
alive to the little room's open door. He goes in quickly to make

sure the room is empty; then, but not quite as quickly, he comes out again.

Trebell Been here long? I'm sorry.

Wedgecroft No. No . . . not long. Converted His Eminence, have you?

Trebell I shall yet.

Wedgecroft The sight of him might explain why the early Christians took a fish for their symbol.

Trebell Did you see Mrs O'Connell?

Wedgecroft On her way out.

Trebell She was waiting for Frances. Is she coming back?

Wedgecroft She didn't say. By the way . . . is she a Catholic?

Trebell He is.

Wedgecroft Ever met him?

Trebell No.

Wedgecroft I knew him at Balliol. When he came into Irish money and land he thought it his duty to go back and live there. Then he went Republican. Does she see much of him?

Trebell Not more than she can help, I think.

Neither **Trebell** *nor, be it noted,* **Wedgecroft** *have seemed quite ingenuous in this little talk.*

Trebell Well . . . what about Brampton?

Wedgecroft Will you go and see him?

Trebell When?

Wedgecroft Now.

Trebell (*his look is dark, his thoughts are away*) No, I can't. Yes . . . I could.

Wedgecroft Then you'd better. He wants me to order him to Scotland tomorrow. He wanted me to order him pork pie and old Marsala for lunch. For God's sake give him something . . . a little more digestible . . . to occupy his m i n d. You've messed up my whole morning, Henry. Curse you . . . and farewell.

Trebell Sorry!

Wedgecroft You're not. My patients may die in dozens . . . what would you care? Hullo, young woman!

This last is evidently to someone unseen by us, whom he meets on the stairs. He is gone. **Trebell,** *left alone for a moment, his face still dark and thoughtful, fingers the telephone, then discards it as useless and sits down to write a note.* **Lucy Davenport** *appears on the landing and stands looking from one room to the other.* **Trebell,** *conscious of interruption, glances up.*

Lucy No . . . please!

Trebell D'you want your young man . . . my young man . . . our young man? He's on an errand.

Lucy He's back . . . paying his cab.

Trebell Taking him out to lunch?

Lucy May I?

Trebell Do.

He has gone back to the writing of his note. **Walter Kent** *comes upstairs and turns into his own room, saying . . .*

Walter Kent You've no right up here. Go and hide. You'll get me the sack.

Trebell Walter!

Walter Kent Sir?

Trebell Ring for a messenger boy.

Walter Kent Right!

Trebell *finishes his note and has only the envelope to address.*

Trebell But I wish you'd get married, you two . . . and have done with it.

Lucy I have named the day. We're to be the first pair tied up by your Disestablished Church. Or shall I put it off? I've come to tell you I will. For two years. And I'll go to India and come back by Japan . . . the Tyrrells have asked me to. I sent him on his holiday with you . . . that was a pledge of good faith. But if you're still so sure I'm a nuisance I'll get right out of the way.

Trebell *looks up, a little touched.* **Walter** *has come out of his room and the two stand together in the doorway, a very wholesomely happy pair.*

Trebell He'd only fret for you. D'you hear this?

Walter Kent I'm not sure I want to marry her anyhow. She takes me too seriously. I shall never go the pace. But she'd make you a perfect secretary.

Lucy I tried for that once . . . through Miss Trebell . . . when I thought you no longer loved me. He wouldn't look at me. But I'll make y o u a perfect secretary.

Walter Kent Well. . . !

Trebell Run along! The Saumarez appointment's at two?

Walter Kent Quarter past. I'll be back.

They go happily downstairs together. **Trebell** *seals his envelope, his face still very dark.*

Act Three

Mr Horsham's *drawing-room in Queen Anne's Gate, with its soft grey walls, its mellow old French carpet and furniture, its spare and formal decoration, is a fit setting for the man himself, mellow of mind, classic in his tastes, his emotions faded, of a temper sceptical and fastidious. He is standing at this moment before a noiseless fire (he dislikes noise, and the very fires in his house, even as the servants that lay and light them, seem to have learnt to conform), his head bent, his benign brow wrinkled in perplexity. If he glances up he sees on the sofa in front of him* **Wedgecroft**, *who, though it is late, is still wearing the regulation kit of his busy doctor's day, and is sitting there, nervously irritable – as he seldom is – and depressed. With his back to them both, on a sofa with its back to them, is* **George Farrant**, *knees apart, hands clasped, head bent, very glum.* **Horsham** *glances beyond him to the big double doors of the library and to the door on the left of them that leads to the passage, as if either of them might open to admit an expected visitor. And, if his gaze travels back along the room, it passes over the long black piano ranged against the wall to where, poised on the music bench, as if it were a stool of repentance, is* **Lord Charles Cantilupe**. *His face is grave and set, but calm. The general air of the conclave, however, suggests a problem discussed and discussed and yet unsolved. It is, in fact, a charged silence that* **Farrant** *breaks by asking irritably . . .*

Farrant But what time did you a s k him to come, Horsham?

Mr Horsham O'Connell?

Farrant Yes . . . we're talking of O'Connell, aren't we?

Mr Horsham (*pacifically*) Did you give him a definite time, Wedgecroft?

Wedgecroft Not before half-past ten, I told him.

Farrant (*eyeing his watch*) Twenty to eleven . . . just.

Wedgecroft He'll come.

Farrant Blackborough's not turning up, though.

Mr Horsham He was dining at Coombe . . . I sent a note after him.

Cantilupe Saumarez caught me by mere chance, Cyril . . . I was off to Tonbridge by the ten-fifteen. I happened to go home for some papers.

This little eddy of talk dies down. Then **Horsham**; *in bland recognition of the irony of life's happenings (his first apprehension of them is always of their irony, his blandness in the face of it seems never to fail him)* . . .

Mr Horsham And I interned O'Connell during the Rebellion, did I?

Wedgecroft You did.

Mr Horsham Surely . . . surely he has no grievance against me because of that!

Cantilupe But . . . Mrs O'Connell being dead . . . what is to precipitate the scandal?

Cantilupe *was a late arrival, evidently.* **Horsham** *gives him the necessary facts, cut and dry.*

Mr Horsham The inquest.

Cantilupe Which can't be avoided?

Mr Horsham It seems not.

Cantilupe Tomorrow?

Mr Horsham Tomorrow.

Wedgecroft *breaks out.*

Wedgecroft Good God! . . . I'd have risked the police-court and given the certificate if she'd died right away . . . and I thought she was gone that evening she sent for me. But O'Connell, when he came, said: Call in old Fielding Andrews. I couldn't object.

Mr Horsham How much had Sir Fielding to be told?

Wedgecroft Not about Trebell, of course.

Mr Horsham But the yet more unpleasant part of the business . . .

Wedgecroft Heavens! . . . if I'd left him to find that out he'd have suspected m e. And he'd have found out. He's half-blind and three-quarters deaf . . . but there's not much he misses. Well . . . I might have risked it . . .

Farrant Oh, my dear fellow . . . quixotic!

Wedgecroft . . . but whoever the quack was she did go to . . . the police may be on his track . . . the whole thing might have come out that way . . . and then where should I have been?

Farrant I suppose . . . even now . . . there's no getting hold of the Coroner?

Farrant, *Privy Councillor though he is, speaks for the moment as might a village schoolboy of robbing an orchard.* **Horsham** *is very definite on this point. And when he is definite upon a question – he seldom seems to be – he sings a little song . . .*

Mr Horsham No, no! No, no, no! No, no, no, no!

Farrant Brampton thought we'd better try.

This offers a pleasant opening.

Mr Horsham He would think so! I admire Brampton . . . I have even had moments of liking for Brampton . . . and I have been in four Cabinets with him. But for flippancy of mind . . . and for perversity of conduct . . . in great matters as in small . . . he is unsurpassed.

Cantilupe Was he quite too ill to come tonight?

Farrant He said Wedgecroft wouldn't hear of it.

Wedgecroft True! I didn't hear of it.

Mr Horsham Was it necessary, then, to confide in him? He's the greatest gossip in London. The one pleasure life has left him . . . apart from bullying her ladyship . . . being his scabrous little chats with the dozen or so young women whom he honours with his senile attentions!

If **Horsham** *were an old woman – and his opponents have been known to call him so – he might, one fears, be accounted a cat. But, really, this is an exceptional outburst. His temper at the moment is seriously tried. He must keep his serenity for the business in hand. A little snappishness is a safety-valve. Still, one sees well enough why his colleagues do not court the rough side of his tongue.* **Farrant**'s *own crest falls a little.*

Farrant Leave nothing undone, I thought . . .

Mr Horsham Even the unwise thing! You may be right. Sometimes one's very errors conspire to help one. Try the Coroner if you like!

Farrant No . . . I admit I don't fancy being snubbed by a Coroner.

Wedgecroft *rather roughly brings the talk back to the point.*

Wedgecroft Besides . . . this man's keen on these cases. He had one last year he kept adjourning till they did nab the culprit. And the *Mail* wrote leaders and reported him verbatim. There's a lot of birth-control propaganda in his district. That has his back up.

Cantilupe Small wonder!

There is cold passion in his voice as he says this. Two subjects so rouse him – birth-control and vivisection – and he does not argue about them.

Wedgecroft He's a Plymouth Brother.

Cantilupe (*disappointed*) Really! But that's not right either.

Mr Horsham (*his eyes upturned to the classic Adam ceiling*) Why do not the members of that distressful sect abandon a designation which does so suggest gin-drinking?

Wedgecroft (*forcibly*) You're at O'Connell's mercy . . . that's what it comes to. If he doesn't keep a guard on his tongue, there'll be an adjournment . . . and the whole story will be out. I've said all I can say to him . . . so has Farrant. If this conclave can't impress him . . . Trebell's done for.

Cantilupe Did she confess to her husband?

Wedgecroft I don't think she opened her mouth from the time he came till she died. But he found a letter Trebell wrote her . . . ten days ago . . . on her table. She'd never had it.

Mr Horsham A letter! I ask you!! Here's a lawyer and a man of the world . . . in a situation of this sort . . . writes the woman a letter!

Wedgecroft It wouldn't have meant much . . . apart from the catastrophe.

Mr Horsham (*fatherly, grandfatherly, quite patriarchal*) My dear Wedgecroft . . . when trouble begins . . . political or personal . . . write one letter only . . . the one that you know will get you safe out of it. And let that be a short one.

Wedgecroft Anyhow . . . once she was dead he told me to tell O'Connell the whole truth. And I had to . . . or he'd have gone himself to tell him. I had to stop that somehow.

Cantilupe Mrs O'Connell consulted you first of all . . . did you say?

Wedgecroft I met her at Trebell's just by chance . . . last Thursday week it was . . . the day he got back from abroad.

Cantilupe (*gravely*) I was there.

Wedgecroft Were you? So you were.

Mr Horsham You met her at Trebell's . . . at Trebell's!

Farrant She was friends with Frances.

Mr Horsham Frances?

Farrant His sister.

Wedgecroft By the way . . . Frances knows nothing yet.

Mr Horsham Ah . . . yes! An exceptional woman . . . a modestly intelligent woman!

Wedgecroft She tackled me . . . saved her face by a few lies . . . and asked me plump to help her out. I told her I couldn't . . . I knew there was no excuse. Oh . . . there are men who would have on one pretext or another.

Mr Horsham Really! Reputable men?

Wedgecroft I believe you gave one of 'em a knighthood.

He's not sorry for the chance of a dig at **Horsham. Horsham** *is horrified.*

Mr Horsham Surely not!

Wedgecroft No . . . it wasn't you.

Mr Horsham But are these practices known to their colleagues?

Wedgecroft Oh, my dear Horsham! When I retire . . . if you're in office . . . I shall write you an open letter entitled: How not to organise the Medical Profession.

Mr Horsham Please don't! What unkindness have I ever done you? Please, my dear Wedgecroft, don't!

Wedgecroft I suppose I might have sent her to one of them . . . and I wish I had now. Then if things had gone wrong she'd have died in the odour of sanctified science . . . and there'd have been an end of that.

Cantilupe Where did she go?

Wedgecroft I've no notion.

Cantilupe Who did send her?

Wedgecroft I've no idea. She bolted out of sight and knowledge for a week . . . without even a maid . . . to some dirty little country lodging. That's what put her in the cart. Then she dragged herself back with a temperature of a hundred and three . . . and sent for me. Even then she didn't tell me the full facts. So when O'Connell came I spoke to him quite openly. All he said was that it wouldn't have been his child.

Trebell *and their own troubles vanish from their minds for a moment.*

Farrant Poor devil!

Mr Horsham Poor woman!

Farrant There's one thing more you might make clear, Wedgecroft . . . that Trebell didn't even know of her going to this quack.

Wedgecroft She'd threatened to go . . . he was trying to stop her. His letter shows that. She disappeared . . . he was trying to find her . . .

Farrant Otherwise I'd not be lifting a finger to save him.

Mr Horsham How long have you known O'Connell, George?

Farrant I was with him at Harrow . . . we found together. I've hardly seen him since. And I wouldn't have spoken to him now . . . after what he did in the Rebellion . . . but for this.

Mr Horsham Oh . . . why? Still, I wish I hadn't interned him.

Cantilupe But may I ask, Cyril, why I am here?

Before **Horsham** *can answer,* **Saumarez**, *his secretary, comes* *quietly from the library.* **Saumarez** *is a man of forty. He has abandoned a normally distinguished career in the Civil Service out of devotion to* **Horsham** *and from a dislike of routine. In his spare moments – he has few – he walks disinterestedly in the more removed paths of literature.*

Saumarez Mr O'Connell's come.

Mr Horsham In there, is he?

Saumarez Will you see him alone first?

Mr Horsham I think not. And do go home now, Saumarez. You've had a long day . . . and two hours of it with your dentist!

Saumarez I'm all right, sir. Besides . . . what about Blackborough? You must be pretty tired yourself.

Saumarez *returns to the library.*

Mr Horsham I a m very tired. I left Lympne at seven this morning . . . I've been at it ever since. I read the whole Nigeria report on the way up . . . I detest reading in a car.

Cantilupe Cyril . . . what is m y position. . . ?

Mr Horsham Sh!

For the library door has opened and **Saumarez**'s *voice can be heard saying* 'Mr O'Connell, sir.' *And* **Justin O'Connell** *comes in. He is a man, as we have just heard, of Farrant's age, but he looks older; an Irish gentleman and scholar, and no foreigner could look more foreign among these Englishmen than he does. His face is lined by more than thought, by intellectual passion. A man capable of devotion and of suffering, but not, one would say, of happiness. Whatever his thoughts or feelings are now, however, they are masked in a frigid, formal politeness.* **Horsham**, *sensitive to this, subdues his welcome and his introductions to tonelessness.*

Mr Horsham How do you do? Let me see . . . do you know my cousin, Charles Cantilupe? Farrant? . . . yes. We are still expecting Russell Blackborough. Sir Henry Brampton is ill. Do sit down.

O'Connell *does so; and the rest re-settle themselves – all but* **Wedgecroft**, *who in the ensuing pause says, half-aloud, to* **Horsham** . . .

Wedgecroft I could wait a bit for Blackborough and tell him all he need know. That'll free Saumarez. Then you won't want me again.

Mr Horsham Thank you so much.

O'Connell If you're not still busy at this hour, Dr Wedgecroft, would you perhaps wait a few minutes also for me? . . . but a very few, I think, it will need to be.

Wedgecroft All right.

This little speech of **O'Connell**'s *only deepens the chill with which his very appearance affected the gathering; and* **Wedgecroft**'s *intentionally off-hand response as he passes into the library does nothing to lift it. Yet another silence follows;* **Horsham** *is still feeling his way. But* **O'Connell** *himself breaks it.*

O'Connell You sent for me, Mr Horsham.

This allows the pleasantest of responses, which comes promptly and charmingly.

Mr Horsham My message gave you, I hope, no impression of being sent for.

But charm he never so wisely, **Horsham** *will charm here in vain.*

O'Connell As an Irishman I am happily less concerned nowadays to know by what persons, in or out of office, this country is governed. Very well . . . you did not send for me. But I am here.

Mr Horsham And you know what we have to ask you.

O'Connell I think I do. Farrant and Wedgecroft at least have not spared energy in impressing upon me that if this man's adultery with my wife becomes as notorious tomorrow as its consequences for her are to be . . . public

opinion may make it hard for you to add him to your
government.

Mr Horsham Public opinion . . . so called . . . so called!
. . . would, rightly or wrongly, but quite unfailingly, oust
him from public life for some years to come at least.

O'Connell It is your business to be aware of such things.

Horsham *now faces his task.*

Mr Horsham Mr O'Connell . . . a great wrong has been
done you . . . and no one here will say a word to excuse it.
Nor have we any title to ask your forgiveness for the guilty
man. But for the reputation . . . and so for the very
existence . . . not of the man, but of the statesman, I am
prepared to plead with you . . . and I do.

But **O'Connell** *will have none of these subtleties either.*

O'Connell My wife is dead. For Mr Trebell . . . I do not
know the man . . . in the statesman I am uninterested. But
I am to cover their sin tomorrow . . . am I . . . with a lie?

This is really rather brutal, and **Farrant** *brings good British
common sense into the account.*

Farrant No . . . you won't have to lie as far as I can see.
The Coroner must keep his questions within bounds. Well
. . . you'll have to lie by implication. In a good cause! So
that won't imperil your immortal soul, I take it.

O'Connell *turns to him with grave disdain.*

O'Connell Our souls are in constant peril. That is not
troubling me.

Farrant Well, what is the worry, then? I've talked myself
to a standstill with you. So has Wedgecroft. We've not
found out.

O'Connell No? It was not the way, perhaps.

Irony is lost on **Farrant***: the more credit to his good heart.*

Farrant I haven't excused Trebell . . . I'm not defending

that sort of thing. There's the old sign still stuck up:
Trespassers will be prosecuted. Mostly they're not. If the
game amuses you . . . you run the risk. But no one expects
this sort of consequence. If you won't think of his
reputation . . . think of your wife's. Why make a perfectly
unprofitable mess of things now?

It does not occur to dear **Farrant** *that to talk himself to a
standstill yet again will be profitless; it does, however, to*
Horsham.

Mr Horsham May we hear your difficulties, please, Mr
O'Connell . . . if you think we can help you in them?

Cantilupe *breaks silence, pale-voiced.*

Cantilupe May I just say, Cyril . . . all, I think, that I
shall want to say. You are a Catholic, I believe, Mr
O'Connell . . . you are a Christian gentleman. Trebell will
have need of your forgiveness. I cannot tell you he is
asking it . . . and we are told (*a glance at* **Horsham**) we
have no right to. He may yet be thinking . . . even as we
seem to be . . . of less profitable things. But . . . after
God's forgiveness . . . he will need yours. And if you
forgive him you will know better than we whether you
should then save him from such clumsy vengeance as this
world takes.

For the first time a little life stirs in **O'Connell**'s *face.*

O'Connell You are an apt advocate, Lord Charles.

From the library comes **Mr Blackborough**, *businesslike as
usual, but too businesslike to emphasise his interruption
needlessly.*

Mr Horsham Ah! You've met Russell Blackborough?

O'Connell No.

Blackborough How d'you do?

Mr Horsham . . . who joins us, I'm sure, in this appeal to
you.

Blackborough Heartily. I've seen Wedgecroft.

When one says 'Heartily' with such convinced gravity but with so little heartiness as that, one means to imply that really the matter is too near one's heart for easy emotional expression. With **Blackborough**, *of course, this may be so. He sits, with equal conviction, in the nearest chair.* **Horsham**, *now gently dominating, proceeds . . .*

Mr Horsham And . . . to sum up . . . with forty years of public life to look back upon . . . I have seen men come and I have seen them go . . . but I do not remember a career of more potent promise than is Trebell's at this moment. A certain eccentricity of attitude may have hampered him so far. But office with its exigencies will cure that. I approached him upon this Disestablishment question last July with much misgiving, I confess. But his reduction of the problem . . . fraught, as we know, with the passions of centuries . . . to practical terms has so far been more than remarkable. Talent for politics is not uncommon. Genius is rare . . . how rare! I do not hesitate to say that I discern it in Trebell. Your country needs him, Mr O'Connell. My country, then . . . if you, unhappily, now count yourself a stranger here. What more can I say?

With another man the unfortunate anti-climax would have spoiled the whole effect. But **Horsham** *has a way of making even his blunders effective, by investing his recovery from them with an appealing, helpless charm. Yet* **O'Connell** *shows no response, and* **Farrant** *has another simple try.*

Farrant Oh . . . be a good fellow. Come!

And now they definitely wait for his reply.

O'Connell Do I seem stubborn? I'm sorry . . . it is not quite that. But I am now a stranger to your time as to your country, Mr Horsham . . . and such talk as this means nothing to me. I have chosen for my refuge a century in which men had to have the courage even of their sins . . . and my statecraft has been studied under the f i r s t Edward.

Mr Horsham (*so comprehending*) Yes . . . yes, indeed. And

only the other day, in a little address I had to make at
Gray's Inn, I referred to that remarkable chapter upon the
Confirmatio Cartarum. . . .

O'Connell, *it is to be regretted, quite ignores this compliment.*

O'Connell What, then, are your politics to me? And, if
you must rouse me from my indifference to you . . . better
think, perhaps, what you may rouse.

Farrant I know! You're a Republican . . . you hate the lot
of us . . . we're your Saxon oppressors . . .

O'Connell I am not a Republican . . . nor any other sort of
lunatic. But it was just possible, Farrant, to prefer the folly
and passion of my own people to the sloven good humour
which is the boast of yours. Yes, you can rouse me to hate
you . . . for all you do . . . and for what you are. And the
hate will come from beyond me . . . so that I will be
justified of it.

Farrant *can endure it no longer. He flings out of his chair.*

Farrant O'Connell . . . I'm sorry for your trouble. But
what you're talking about now I'm damned if I know. This
conversation had better finish without me.

Mr Horsham Patience . . . George . . . !

Farrant No, if it gratifies him to wreck Trebell's career
and put your government in Queer Street . . . let him. He
can. Good God Almighty!

*This last exclamation springs from him as he opens the library
door for escape; and it seems to have nothing to do with his
main protest – though it just might have. But he does not
escape. On the contrary he shuts the door again quickly.*

Cantilupe What's the matter?

Farrant Nothing. Go ahead. I'll hold my tongue. I'll try to.

He sits down incontinently. **Cantilupe** *had wondered for a
moment if he felt ill.* **Horsham**, *however, calmly
continues . . .*

Mr Horsham Mr O'Connell will not yield, I am sure, to any such vulgar temptation.

Cantilupe But what is it you hate in us, may I ask, Mr O'Connell?

O'Connell What . . . when even you can speak to me of forgiveness as if it were a penny in my pocket . . . and a ransom for him from the jealous and ignorant mob that you've made your masters!

As incontinently **Farrant** *gets up again and vanishes into the library.* **Horsham** *is growing a little fretful.*

Mr Horsham Whatever is the matter with George?

O'Connell This clever fellow with his clever scheme! Is the fate of the two of them worth a lie? For your time breeds such . . . and will . . . till its corruption burst. You might better thank me to rid you . . .

Once again the library door is opened, this time with a sort of violent difficulty. There might be a tussle taking place. There is; though it is an all but noiseless one. In a second the result of it is evident. **Trebell** *stands in the doorway, and* **Farrant** *behind him, rather dishevelled. The assembly is speechless; well it may be. But* **O'Connell** *and* **Trebell** *himself seem the least concerned.* **Trebell** *speaks at last and casually enough.*

Trebell Forgive me, Horsham, for thrusting myself in. Wedgecroft did his best. Sorry I've wrecked your collar.

This over his shoulder to **Farrant**, *who proceeds to adjust it. A collar escaped from its stud would discompose an archangel.* **O'Connell** *is now standing isolated facing* **Trebell**, *who faces him full.*

O'Connell You are the man?

Trebell Yes.

O'Connell Better we should meet.

Trebell Simpler. I thought so.

Farrant For God's sake, Trebell . . . come away!

Trebell What's happening?

Mr Horsham Mr O'Connell . . . how Trebell knew of your presence here I can't say. No one of us, I'm sure, is responsible for t h i s.

Trebell You're begging me off. Is that the way?

Farrant This isn't.

The two ignore the rest. They might be alone together. The Irish voice keeps its level irony.

O'Connell What then can I do for you?

Trebell What she was to you . . . you know. Tell the truth of it tomorrow. She has had to die to trap me. I'll tell the truth of that if need be.

If no one else understands, **O'Connell** *does; and he blazes into a white fire of passion.*

O'Connell Yes, indeed . . . yes, indeed . . . a worthless woman! Had she borne you your child I could better have forgiven her. She could cheat me of mine and leave me. Is the curse of barrenness to be nothing to a man? God forgive her now. What have I left to forgive? I think we are brothers in misfortune, sir. (*Then, as an afterthought, and as if grown aware of the rest.*) I shall say nothing tomorrow that will compromise Mr Trebell.

A silence; then, as no one else will, **Horsham** *has to speak.*

Mr Horsham Thank you. Each one of us thanks you, I'm sure . . . for your magnanimity.

Cantilupe Thank you.

Blackborough Most magnanimous.

Farrant Good fellow . . . I knew you would be!

Mr Horsham Thank you . . . once again, thank you.

Trebell, *be it noted, has not thanked him. Instead, and with a queer edge upon his voice, he says . . .*

Trebell So all's well! And I'm to go ahead, am I, Horsham? I'd like to know.

Farrant Why not?

Trebell It's what I came about.

Mr Horsham You feel . . . I hope . . . under every obligation to go ahead.

Trebell If you say so.

Farrant But what's the trouble?

Trebell What do you say, Blackborough?

Blackborough *sees his drift. So does* **Cantilupe**, *but he is silent. So does* **Horsham**, *but he'd ignore it.* **Farrant** *soon begins to and refuses to.* **O'Connell**, *motionless, watches him keenly.*

Blackborough I'm glad . . . heartily glad . . . that Mr O'Connell sees his way to keep silent. Frankly . . . not for your sake only. You're one of us already in a sense. Besides . . . these scandals weaken confidence in the whole governing class. . . .

Trebell You're not answering my question.

Blackborough No . . . it's for Horsham to answer . . . not for me.

Farrant What question?

Blackborough Why, my good Farrant . . . it's pretty plain, I take it, that however considerate Mr O'Connell here may be, this thing will be gossiped around . . . garbled, what's more . . . in the clubs and the Lobbies . . . among all the people that count . . . and want to count . . . and have it thought they count. No such thing as a secret nowadays! That's what's in your mind, isn't it, Trebell? Can you still carry through a Bill of this sort in an atmosphere of that sort? It's a question, no doubt.

Farrant *takes up the cudgels.*

Farrant Why need there be gossip if we keep our mouths shut?

Blackborough The tighter we shut 'em the more there'll be.

Farrant Then we must find means to stop it.

Blackborough If you make that discovery, Farrant, I'll see a statue's put up to you.

Farrant Well . . . whatever the gossip . . . if we stand solid behind Trebell we can pull him through.

Blackborough Oh . . . if we could postpone the Bill . . . !

Farrant You know that's impossible.

Blackborough Or if it were any sort of a Bill but a Church Bill . . . ! I may be wrong. I'd like to think so. I don't enjoy saying the unpleasant thing. But as well say it now as six weeks hence if it has to be said. However . . . it's for Horsham to decide . . . in the first place.

Is there a little sting in the tail of the sentence? Why should one suppose so? What he says sounds honest common sense.
Horsham *is lulling.*

Mr Horsham I think we might perhaps wisely leave both well and ill alone just for this evening. And Mr O'Connell may be feeling that we have wandered from the point that concerns him.

From the beginning the situation has been on **Cantilupe**'s *nerves, none the less because he could speak calmly. But he now speaks his mind; distaste for the whole affair, and for his part in it, sounding in every word.*

Cantilupe Cyril . . . you never should have brought me here. I hate to embarrass you further. I am thankful Mr O'Connell has decided as he has. But let it be clear, please, that I cannot now sit in a Cabinet with Mr Trebell.

No one shows surprise. **Trebell** *is, indeed, not surprised.*
O'Connell *listens and looks, as a stranger in court may look
on, tensely, at the climax of a trial. Only* **Farrant** *finds words.*

Farrant Well . . . I'm damned!

Cantilupe I'm sorry . . . and this may not seem the
moment to say it. But we've been at work upon the Bill
together . . . for three hours today we were at work upon
it . . . we were to meet again tomorrow. And I cannot . . .
I cannot!

Horsham *is bitter-sweet.*

Mr Horsham Thank you, my dear Charles . . . you do
embarrass me. The moment i s ill-chosen . . . so far I agree
with you. I note your decision.

The position now gives **Blackborough** *the best of openings.*

Blackborough But, my dear Cantilupe, why rush to these
extremes?

Cantilupe I cannot discuss the matter.

Blackborough No, no . . . let's be helpful! I don't know
much about the Bill . . . I've not been consulted. Frankly
. . . what little I do know I don't like . . . and I wish we
weren't pledged to it. But now Trebell's out of the worst of
his mess . . . let's do the best we can . . . though it mayn't
be all we'd like to do . . . for him . . . and the Bill . . . and
the party . . . and the country in general.

This all-embracing friendliness exasperates **Cantilupe** *beyond
bearing.*

Cantilupe Convictions apart . . . how . . . how! . . . can I
sit in Cabinet with a man . . . and canvass my friends for
his Bill . . . for this Bill! . . . with such a scandal for an
unspoken end and beginning of my every talk with them?
It's impossible.

It is clearly time **O'Connell** *took his leave.*

O'Connell Will Dr Wedgecroft still be waiting for me?

May I wish you good evening, gentlemen? No, sir, you were right . . . I can do nothing for you. And had revenge been what I wanted . . . could I be leaving my interests in better hands?

He says this and passes by **Trebell** *towards the library door, at which* **Horsham** *is standing.*

Mr Horsham Yes . . . he's here.

But at the door **O'Connell** *turns.*

O'Connell Why don't you, though?

Trebell Do what?

O'Connell Speak the truth . . . if it's in you to? Outface the British lion in his smugness. If he didn't eat you . . . you could put your friends here in your pocket after, I think. Thank you, Mr Horsham.

So he departs; **Horsham**, *in courtesy, following him.*

Blackborough Irish! Well . . . he would be.

Farrant He'll hold his tongue. That's the great thing! Damn it, I believe he meant to all the time.

But **Trebell** *pays no attention; he has turned to* **Cantilupe**.

Trebell Yes, Cantilupe . . . I'm an adulterer. So you'll have no more truck with me. Would our work be worthless? Is the thing in itself a deadly sin to you?

Cantilupe Living in the world I live in, I have little right, perhaps, to call that a strange question. Yes . . . it is.

Trebell And what's the atonement? Can you and your wise Church help me there?

Cantilupe I fear not . . . when you ask unrepentant.

Trebell Oh, I can repent . . . the thing done . . . and the folly of it. But the thing that I am . . . to repent that is to die.

Cantilupe God help you, Trebell . . . God help you!

This talk between the two has been strangely like a talk between friends. **Horsham** *returns – returns to his troubles; but* **O'Connell** *at least he is rid of.*

Mr Horsham He's gone . . . they've both gone. I remember now why I interned him.

It is **Trebell**'s *turn now to say his say, and he says it without wasting time.*

Trebell Horsham . . . I've not made you the usual gentlemanly offer to stand aside. This job means more to me. I wasn't sent into the world to make things easy for you. I warn you, Cantilupe . . . I can carry this Bill as it stands . . . and no one else will. You care for what's in it . . . and I care. You'll find no one else does. But if you do stick to me, Horsham . . . and Blackborough thinks this incongruous catastrophe and his kind help out of it will turn me into a biddable underling . . . he's mistaken.

Blackborough (*tartly*) That's uncalled for.

Trebell That mediæval Irishman is right. There'll be poisonous gossip. Well . . . I'll tell the truth. I'll stand up in my place in the House and say: This I've done . . . this I am . . . this and no more I repent. Will you back me after?

Farrant By God . . . I believe we might!

Trebell As a piece of policy I recommend it you. For if I win I'd carry the Bill for you without one bargain struck. If I go under . . . you'll be rid of a most uncomfortable colleague. I'll do it . . . I'm serious.

Blackborough My dear fellow!

Mr Horsham Public life is not to be lived nowadays, I fear, on such heroic heights.

Trebell Would that count for atonement, Cantilupe . . . would you stand by me then? Yes, indeed . . . we might put Worldly Wiseman and Facing-both-ways in our pockets afterwards. Well, Horsham . . . it's up to you. But make up your mind as quick as you can, please. You must, though, mustn't you? The job won't wait.

And he leaves them.

Blackborough Half off his head!

Farrant Do you wonder?

Blackborough I met him on the doorstep. I thought Wedgecroft would get him away.

Farrant He nearly throttled m e!

Horsham's *thoughts are already a little removed.*

Mr Horsham I'm afraid, you know, that I always found her a detestable little woman.

Farrant (*sturdily*) I liked her. (*then candidly*) My wife never liked her.

Mr Horsham A harlot at heart! How much better then . . . for all concerned . . . just to be a harlot.

Farrant Well, whatever she was . . . and she's dead . . . and I disagree with you . . . if he gets through tomorrow, you're not going back on him, I trust. For that'd be damnable.

He has shot an angry glance at **Blackborough**.

Blackborough I haven't suggested you should go back on him . . . farther than you need go. Find him some other job.

Farrant He won't take another job.

Blackborough Oh . . . if he's going to be pig-headed!

Cantilupe Cyril, if you think Trebell can take the Bill through . . . you can do well enough without me. And I can do as much for it from the back benches . . . and more, I daresay, for the things in it that I've at heart.

Blackborough Yes . . . I don't doubt you can.

Blackborough *lets this out with such a bang that* **Cantilupe** *turns to him, half-surprised, half-angry.*

Cantilupe What are you insinuating, may I ask?

Blackborough *now asserts himself.*

Blackborough Horsham . . . when you do form your Cabinet you'll ask whom you choose to join it. By summoning us three, though, and Brampton . . . how is Brampton, by the way?

Farrant Better.

Blackborough I'm glad . . . to this rescue party, you imply, I may take it, that you count on us?

Mr Horsham Quite.

Blackborough Very good. We're pledged to a Church Bill of some sort. I wish we weren't . . .

Cantilupe So you've told us . . . and we didn't need telling.

Horsham *grows the more pacific as* **Farrant** *grows angrier and* **Cantilupe** *snappier in his nervous distress.* **Blackborough**, *however, has no intention of losing his temper.*

Blackborough My dear fellow . . . what good can it do us? At the best it's bound to be one of those damned cross-fire measures . . . with men opposite supporting you and your own side attacking you . . . disastrous to party discipline. You and Trebell have been cooking it up together . . .

Cantilupe The Bill is his.

Blackborough Brampton besides.

Mr Horsham He has seen the figures.

Blackborough A most efficient little cabal.

Cantilupe I object to that term.

Blackborough (*with perfect good humour*) I withdraw it. And Trebell still talks of pushing the thing through the

Cabinet . . . sic volo, sic jubeo. Plump and plain, I'd better tell you there may be things in it that won't at all suit me.

Cantilupe For instance?

Blackborough Well . . . as you've not done me the honour to consult me, I can't be very precise.

Mr Horsham I didn't know you were so interested in Church questions, Blackborough.

Blackborough I'm not . . . nor in any political question till it has to be answered. But these rumours of Utopian educational schemes . . . seminaries for teachers . . . countryside universities! This isn't a time to be throwing the country's money about.

Cantilupe It is the Church's money. Do you want to relieve the rates with it?

Blackborough We might do worse mischief. Seriously, Cantilupe . . . you stand for the Church, twopence coloured. I stand for it penny plain. Mine, that's to say, is the traditional British common-sense view of religion. Well, now . . . if you're going to leave us in the lurch with this Bill on our backs . . . not to mention Trebell, if Horsham thinks he can stick to him . . . I think we ought to have a pledge from you that you and your friends won't make trouble.

Cantilupe Why should we?

Blackborough Because you'll be free from responsibility and you'll want to get all you can. And what one's friends lose one's enemies gain. That's an axiom in politics.

Cantilupe (*hotly*) I wish to get nothing for my friends that is inconsistent with justice and righteousness.

Blackborough Quite so! So we all say!

Cantilupe As long as this settlement . . . which the Bill provides for . . . as Trebell has drafted it and as Horsham

has approved it . . . as long as that stands in its integrity
. . . I shall support it.

Blackborough *casts his eyes towards the heaven which in its
inscrutable wisdom has made such men as* **Cantilupe***. But he
treats him with masterly – if slightly masterful – patience.*

Blackborough I'm sorry . . . I'm not making myself plain.
I admit no settlement. If you're keen on parts of the Bill
. . . stay in the Government and fight for them . . . and I'll
fight you fair. If Horsham does drop Trebell I suppose you
will stay. Need you insist on his being dropped altogether?
Why not wait and see if scandal does spread? We shall
soon know. Oh . . . if mine were a foxy mind . . . I'd not
be sorry, you'd think, to see a Bill I dislike made a hash of
by a man that . . . ! After all . . . from the party point of
view . . . he's an outsider. What has Brampton to say, by
the way?

Farrant About all this? Oh, it was meat and drink to him.
He kept me an hour this afternoon telling me scandals of
every Premier he'd served under. Not of you, Horsham.

Mr Horsham Whatever he may not know of me he can be
trusted to invent.

Blackborough But about the Bill . . . has Trebell been
seeing him?

Farrant Once or twice. He thinks the finance will be fun
because the Treasury will kick at it. But the fact is he's
had a grudge against Theobald Rogers there ever since his
last Budget . . . and he wants to pay him out. If Trebell
doesn't come in, Brampton won't.

Blackborough Really?

Farrant Brampton thinks a lot of him.

If **Farrant** *had not been dead tired, he'd never have done it.
As it is, he stays innocent of what he has done.* **Horsham** *sees,
but gives hardly a sign of seeing. What is the use?*
Blackborough*'s speech now is measured, his tone judicious.*

Blackborough Brampton would be a loss. His mind's not what it was . . . but he cuts a figure still. Well . . . there's nothing more to say, for the moment, is there? Good-night.

He has, indeed, no more to say.

Farrant But what is settled . . . about Trebell?

Cantilupe Cyril . . . I wish to do whatever is best. But consider my position.

Farrant And consider our position if we drop Trebell and he rounds on us. We shan't have fifty majority. And for this sort of Bill there's bound to be cross-voting.

Blackborough Then it won't be my sort of Bill. Our business is to compose our differences and bring in a Conservative Bill that a Conservative majority can vote for.

Cantilupe That will be a worthless Bill.

Farrant But we've laid down the principles of the thing and they've been approved of by the press and the public . . .

Blackborough My good Farrant . . . don't talk like a patent medicine advertisement. Praise from the press in a chorus . . . they abuse you the worse later on . . . when they want something fresh to say. The public . . . can't hold an idea in its head as long as my dogs can.

Farrant Trebell can knock now any Church Bill but his own to pieces in Committee. He could turn us out on it . . . and I shouldn't blame him.

Blackborough No . . . it's the sort of thanks one gets for saving a man from gaol . . . yes, from gaol very likely. But I don't think so. Even he'd not have the hardihood to talk Christian statesmanship with the dirt of this scandal still spattered over him. Not that we should spread it abroad, of course, unless . . . ! No . . . I should always be against such meanness. But I shouldn't . . . in that case . . . feel called upon to contradict it. Horsham . . . you've been

kindness itself to him. If you want to be kinder yet . . . in
my opinion . . . you'll drop him and let him go back to the
Bar for a bit . . . he must have been making his pile there.
Or put him on the Bench. You've a reputation as a cynic.
The Divorce Court ought to be vacant soon.
Seriously . . . ! But you don't need my advice. Still . . .
you'd rather I made my position clear.

*He has made himself, his position, and his intentions crystal
clear to* **Horsham**, *who answers very drily* . . .

Mr Horsham Much.

Blackborough Good-night.

Mr Horsham Thank you for coming.

Blackborough Can I drop you, Farrant?

Farrant No, I'll walk . . . thanks. (*The gratitude more an
effort than an afterthought.*)

Blackborough Right! Don't come down.

*He departs. He has done a good evening's work and knows it.
They detest him.*

Farrant And what sort of a very private life has he led, I
wonder.

Mr Horsham I should suppose that his relations with the
gentler sex have always been businesslike . . . most
businesslike. The social scandals of the Industrial North
do not, however, penetrate to our sophisticated world . . .
a fact, of which, we must hope, no undue advantage is
taken.

Horsham *can always salve his troubles with a little acrid
humour. Lucky man!*

Farrant Well . . . what is settled? It's very late.

Mr Horsham What's settled? . . . since you so recklessly
keep asking! Why . . . that I drop Trebell.

Farrant – *bless him!* – *is surprised.*

Farrant D'you mean it?

Mr Horsham My dear George . . . if, after listening to
Blackborough, you imagine he now means to let me form a
Cabinet with Trebell in it . . . I must admire your
innocence.

Farrant But . . . good God! . . . is one to be bullied by
Blackborough? Leave h i m out, then.

Mr Horsham I should love to . . . and his friends and
relations besides.

Farrant No . . . you can't. Get him in, then, with Trebell
. . . and assert yourself.

Mr Horsham No leader who needs to do that, George,
must ever dare to.

Farrant Oh, don't be paradoxical . . . I'm tired. I don't
see, though . . . if O'Connell stands pat . . . what more
Blackborough can do now than he always could have done.

Mr Horsham Don't you? Brampton, who despises him
. . . Charles here, with some prestige in Church matters
. . . and Trebell, till this happened . . . were a pretty
strong combination. He'd have had to knuckle under to it.
Break it up . . . and there's his chance . . . as he saw.

Cantilupe But isn't this the heart-breaking thing in
politics? Some great chance . . . if every circumstance will
conspire in its favour. One slip . . . and it's against it
they're conspiring.

Mr Horsham I am glad you appreciate that, Charles.

Horsham *has gone to a writing-table and is beginning a letter.*
Cantilupe *responds across the room rather pathetically.*

Cantilupe My saying I'd stand out made the mischief,
d'you mean?

Farrant *rounds on him quite brutally.*

Farrant Well, what else? Serve you damned well right,
Charles, if your Bill is wrecked.

Cantilupe But Blackborough saw the situation sooner than I did.

Mr Horsham Still . . . never play your opponent's game for him. Your temperament, Charles, leads you to embrace misfortunes.

Farrant *thinks a little blame may as well be put on* **Horsham**.

Farrant Why did you bring him here tonight anyhow?

Mr Horsham Oh . . . he's as touchy as a beauty losing her looks. If I'd left him out . . . ! No, no . . . no, no, no! Flattering him into playing the magnanimous . . . that was the only chance.

Cantilupe He's after the Exchequer himself, I suppose.

Mr Horsham Yes . . . and he'll get it now . . . I've no one else. When you let out we'd lose Brampton, George, he launched his ultimatum . . . did you notice? No . . . you didn't.

Farrant But . . . good God! . . . why didn't you stop me?

Poor **Farrant**; *the tables are turned on him!*

Mr Horsham I'd as soon know how I stand tonight as know it a week hence . . . and sooner. What's Trebell's number in Berkeley Street?

Farrant Forty-seven.

Then they both realise what the letter is. Veritably a funereal air falls.

Cantilupe Are you writing to tell him now?

Mr Horsham Yes.

Farrant I say! . . . can't you wait a bit? Something may happen.

Mr Horsham No.

Farrant I hate this.

They feel guilty and look it. **Horsham** *addresses his envelope.*

Cantilupe But, Cyril . . . who's to take the Bill through?

Mr Horsham I don't know yet. I can't . . . there's the
FO complication. I rather advise you to stand clear and
screw out of us any scraps of the old scheme that you'd
really set your heart on. I shall find somebody.

He says it quite cheerfully. He always has found somebody.

Farrant I don't care so much about the Bill . . . but I do
bar Trebell's being dished . . . just when we'd got him
clear from the real mess too. What fools it leaves us
looking! Surely, Horsham, with your authority . . .

Horsham *has finished his letter and addressed and closed it.*

Mr Horsham You take, I think, a romantic view of my
office, and, consequently . . . though I don't complain . . .
an unromantic one of me. What authority will make men
abler . . . or more honest . . . or less selfish than they are?
I have to match you all with . . . and against . . . each
other, so that from the heat of your differences a little
power to do something may, if possible, result. The art of
the thing lies in having such a quick sense of what won't
work that before we've all quarrelled irretrievably I have
set you to something else that will. Shall I post this . . . or
had one of you better see that he gets it tonight?

Farrant I won't face him.

Mr Horsham Dear Uncle Mark started me as his secretary
at twenty-three . . . and he taught me to nourish no
political illusions. Yet at sixty-five I am tempted to try this
rather imaginative stroke . . . and I fail. I'm not surprised.
But the calculation was such a nice one . . . such a
combining of incompatibles! What a triumph . . . and how
amusing . . . to have brought it off! Would you post this,
then, in the corner pillar-box as you pass?

*He has found a stamp in his pocket-book and has carefully
stuck it on. But these reflections are of small comfort to*
Farrant, *who is feeling savage.*

Farrant I just hope Trebell will give us hell next session . . . that's all.

Cantilupe What will happen to him, I wonder, Cyril?

Mr Horsham Hard to say. Most men's careers work to a climax . . . and if they miss their moment the best of them may sink back to nonentity. A pity in this case . . . a pity. By the bye, Charles, there was something else I wanted a word with you about. The Giorgione portrait. Your mother mustn't sell it.

They have found their way to the door. **Farrant**, *indeed, is already on his way downstairs. But the two cousins pause in the doorway.*

Cantilupe But she needs the money.

Mr Horsham But it's the copy, I do assure you. It's the original that's at Holcroft. My father told me the whole story. Fotheringham got it out of Great-aunt Jane. He was cracked about pictures after he was sixty. She'd been his mistress, undoubtedly . . . and their later relations were unspeakable. All sorts of references to them had to be cut out of Creevey and . . . what's that other book?

Cantilupe But mother must pay her income tax.

Mr Horsham Well . . . if she tries to sell that picture all these old stories will be raked up. It will be most unpleasant for her. . . .

They go out together talking.

Act Four

Trebell's *room in the evening looks as you would expect it to look, except that, this evening, the curtains of the window are drawn back and we are conscious of the strange London darkness, which is never dark, outside.* **Trebell** *and* **Wedgecroft** *come up the stairs talking.* **Wedgecroft** *carries his hat and wears his overcoat.*

Wedgecroft Yes . . . when I saw the light I whistled the tune without a thought . . . and down you came!

Trebell I was thinking . . . at the moment . . . of my old room in Gower Street. . . .

He puts a period to this preface by whistling the signal tune – all ardent Wagnerians used it in the eighteen-nineties – the Siegfried sword motif. Then **Wedgecroft** *begins . . .*

Wedgecroft Well . . . we're safe, I'm sure. O'Connell won't go back on you.

Trebell He's not committed to flat perjury, I hope. Nor you?

Wedgecroft Oh . . . I rank as an expert witness.

Trebell Has the thing hit him very hard?

Wedgecroft He's at odds with the world.

Trebell He can slip back to his thirteenth century . . . after tomorrow. Well, what more can you do for me, Gilbert? I've been a lot of trouble to you, I'm afraid.

For **Wedgecroft** *is regarding him with a quizzical and not unanxious eye, in which friendly and professional concern are mixed.* **Trebell**'s *voice has, indeed, an oddly hollow ring, and* *he walks with a curious lightness, as a man may feel himself walking in a dream.*

Wedgecroft I'd like you to get some sleep tonight. When was your last good night's sleep?

Trebell I haven't slept for a night or so.

Wedgecroft I see. You'll swallow two of these when you go to bed . . .

He has fetched a little bottle out of his pocket, taken an envelope from the writing-table and is shaking some pellets into it.

Trebell No, no. They upset my inside . . . and my dignity.

Wedgecroft . . . and two more an hour later if need be.

Trebell Why not acid drops? Just as effective! I won't go to bed . . . that's the simplest plan.

Wedgecroft Confound you! . . . I'm thinking of your job, not of you. You must keep fit for it.

Trebell I told her that.

The casual inconsequence of this is jarring. But **Wedgecroft** *holds his professional course.*

Wedgecroft It has been a bad business. But drop the curtain of one good night's sleep on it . . . and I'll soon have you back to normal. By the way . . . how much . . . now . . . is Frances to know?

Trebell How much does she know? She'd hold her tongue to me . . . and expect me to hold mine to her. But she may have to be told now. Horsham may be throwing me over after all.

This, though, does knock **Wedgecroft** *off his balance.*

Wedgecroft No!

Trebell Yes.

Wedgecroft In heaven's name . . . why?

Trebell It must be so vexing for you, Gilbert, to pull a patient through . . . and have him run over in the street a week after. And I'm told that then his executors always grumble when there's your bill to pay.

Wedgecroft Why the devil didn't I let you go to O'Connell when you wanted to? They need never have known.

Trebell True! I've been thinking of that. But they may not throw me over. I left them in conclave. So don't hint anything to Frances. She has just come in . . . I heard the car. Farrant will stroll round to tell me, I daresay. The window's for his benefit.

Wedgecroft If they throw you over now . . . the next one that calls me in . . . I'll poison him.

Trebell That's the spirit! But I rather wish I'd not given my virgin heart to a Bill of disestablishing the Church of England. Reckless of me!

Frances *comes upstairs hurriedly, a little breathless, disturbed.*

Frances Henry! Oh, Gilbert . . . I'm so glad you're here.

Trebell 'Meistersingers' over early?

Frances It's past twelve.

Trebell I said early.

Frances I'm terribly upset. I heard as I was coming out in the crowd . . . Amy O'Connell's dead.

The two men keep their composure, but the talk takes on a certain restraint.

Trebell Gilbert has been telling me.

Frances I knew she was ill. You weren't attending her?

Wedgecroft Yes.

Frances But there's to be an inquest.

Wedgecroft Tomorrow.

Frances What's been wrong? Mustn't I ask?

Trebell I'll tell you. Gilbert's tired. He has done a day's work . . . and a bit.

Wedgecroft Good-night, then. Take that stuff. I'll be round about 9.30 . . . but if I hear you snoring I'll be the better pleased.

Frances Are you ill, Henry? Hasn't he been sleeping?

Wedgecroft He's not ill. A nice little illness now and then . . . a little lowering of the physical pride . . . might be very good for him. Bless you both.

Frances Bless you, dear Gilbert.

Trebell Pull the door to, hard, would you? The lock's loose or something.

Wedgecroft *leaves them together.*

Frances What about Amy?

Trebell An unwelcome baby was on the way. She went to some quack . . . and Gilbert couldn't save her.

Frances Yes . . . that's the gossip. Terrible! Doubly terrible! The little fool! The little runaway!

One discovers in **Frances** *a taste of her brother's ruthlessness. His response is somewhat acid.*

Trebell The celibate's comment.

She has had, one must remember, half an hour in which to grieve for Amy's death; so her lively good sense is already in the ascendant.

Frances No . . . come now! One may choose one's lot in life . . . but having chosen it . . . !

Trebell True. I didn't mean to gibe.

Frances That wasn't all the trouble, though . . . surely?

Trebell I daresay not.

Frances Some affair she'd been having. . . ?

Trebell I daresay.

Frances Even so . . . couldn't she have found someone
with common sense to turn to . . . some woman? Heavens
. . . I didn't like her much . . . but I'd have done what I
could. No . . . there it was! She was pretty and popular
. . . she could make a party go . . . and men flirted with
her. But when it came to this . . . she knew none of us
liked her much. Oh . . . death leaves things so frustrate,
doesn't it? I'd meant to go round there this morning. I
think she did like m e a little. Egoist! Another debt, then,
I'll never pay.

Trebell I shouldn't worry about that. Our likes and
dislikes go the round . . . in various disguises. The sum of
the getting and giving works out pretty fairly.

This is sufficiently cryptic for **Frances** *to ask him – though
without too much intention* . . .

Frances Is this all you know?

Trebell It's all I can tell you for the moment.

*They have a habit, these two, of saying what they mean to
each other and accepting the thing said. It has been a
businesslike and not such a bad relationship.*

Frances Then I'll go to bed. Not that I'll sleep.

Trebell Try Gilbert's physic.

Frances Poor Amy! Poor little fool!

Trebell Her epitaph.

Frances Fear of life . . . the beginning of all evil.

Trebell Is it?

Frances I've come to think so.

Trebell I've wondered lately whether you did right to give
up your work to turn housekeeper for me.

Frances It's a little late to be wondering that.

Trebell You were a pretty good teacher . . . and that's moral motherhood of a sort. Your young women were fond of you. Could you go back to it?

Frances I wasn't very fond of them, I fear. Reason enough for giving up. I can spare you the self-sacrificing sister. No . . . I couldn't go back.

Trebell This need to care for people, Frankie, is the devil and all.

Frances And when did it begin to trouble y o u? And what makes you call me by my nursery name for the first time in thirty years?

Trebell I don't know. But I should have sent you packing perhaps. Why . . . we've never even had a quarrel.

To which touch of wan humour she responds.

Frances All the domestic joys missed. Never mind. You've been a credit to me. And time begins to slip by for us pretty quickly now, doesn't it? Good-night. Shall I give you these?

'These' are **Wedgecroft**'s *soporifics. But his thoughts are far from such matters.*

Trebell No . . . no, thank you.

She goes towards him, as if – though not intrusively – she would like to get a little nearer to him, in another sense, if she could.

Frances There's nothing troubling you . . . that you'd like to tell me?

Trebell No.

Nothing harsh about it; again, he just means what he says. But now, for a wonder, she does not leave it at that.

Frances Has it been my fault you've never confided in me? You hate women . . . I've heard you say . . . when you can't altogether despise them. Yet I'm not so very womanly . . . in the worst sense . . . am I? If I thought you could ever come to be unhappy . . . as other people are . . . it would make me unhappy to be such a stranger to you.

Trebell If I ever come to be . . . waste no time on me. The egoist gone soft . . . I know nothing more contemptible.

Frances No . . . you see other men so starkly as they are . . . you're not built to be disillusioned about yourself. And you've never had a failure . . . never even been crossed in love. . . .

Trebell Never come within reach of the good woman's gospel of salvation. And I think, thank you, I'll keep out of it to the end. Go to bed . . . go to bed. I've to sit up for a bit yet . . . I'm expecting a message.

Frances At this hour? And I don't even ask what about . . . though that would be human . . . even womanly! Very well. Don't work, though . . . or sit and think. You're tired. I'll choose you a book.

Trebell My mind was never clearer.

Frances The rest of you is the more tired. Mark Twain?

As she moves to the bookcase those familiar red volumes face her.

Trebell Good . . . not a woman's choice, either. 'Huck Finn', please. Mark was a sound fellow. He had comic courage. A gift. I'd choose it, I think, before any. Man's last weapon against the gods. When he's at his puniest . . . he can still laugh them into littleness . . . and come to his own standing again. Thank you. I'll give Mark his chance . . . to stop me thinking . . . if he can.

Frances But I can't help?

Trebell No.

Frances Very well.

*Still his rejection of her is not harsh, nor purposefully cold. But
the blank chill of it seems to rouse some inward anger in her
now, as if her care for him must somehow struggle for its life.
But the anger, too, stays dumb, and she turns away and leaves
him.*

*Early the next morning she finds him there. He has not moved,
to all appearances. The fire is out, the lights are out; through
the window, with its drawn-back curtains, can be seen
London's grey autumn sky.* **Frances** *has been disturbed in her
dressing and has thrown a wrap about her to come down. The
night has broken her composure, but it has set his hard.*

Frances Henry!

Trebell Yes?

Frances Bertha says you've not been to bed all night.

Trebell She's quite right. She came in to do the room. I
fear I startled her.

Frances I waited to hear you come up. I came down once
to listen. Then I fell asleep. Did you fall asleep down here?

Trebell No . . . I've not been to sleep.

Frances I must know what's wrong. What was the
message? What has happened?

Trebell The message didn't come. There might be a letter.
Are they here yet?

Frances Yes . . . I don't know . . . yours are put in
Walter's room.

Trebell I'll see.

*He goes across to the little room and returns with a pile of
twenty letters, it may be. He finds her, head bowed, face
hidden, and she does not look up. As he sees her thus, suddenly
forty years fall away: for so he has seen her time and again, in
their rather shabby nursery schoolroom, childishly grieving.
And the difference is not so great.*

Trebell My dear . . . don't cry. You've had a bad night too . . . and where was the use of that?

Frances I'm not crying. I never cry.

Trebell What then?

Frances I think I was trying to pray.

Trebell Help me to look through these. The thing may be settled . . . past praying for.

He gives her a half of the letters and they begin to open them.

Frances But I'm still angry, I'm afraid. When you said I couldn't help you . . . though God knows I knew it! . . . it made me angry to have you say it. But if I'd not been angry it would have hurt too badly. You may as well tell me the facts now about Amy O'Connell.

Mechanically, as she asks him, she is opening and glancing at the letters, putting them in an orderly pile, tearing the envelopes. He, as he answers her, is doing the same.

Trebell Yes . . . it was my child.

Frances I'm a blind fool, I suppose. I never guessed you were in love with her.

Trebell I wasn't.

Frances She with you, then.

Trebell It didn't last long. The little trull!

The thing is wrung from him. It releases her anger.

Frances Henry . . . how can you be so vile as to say that of her . . . now?

Trebell It's the truth.

Frances Whatever she was you were. And she has paid.

Trebell I've to pay. Whatever she'd done but this . . . I'd have faced it. Let's get through these letters.

Her anger is exhausted. The letter-opening has come to a standstill. Mechanically they start again.

Frances If you'd loved her . . . only a little . . . s h e might have found courage to face it.

At this he turns to her in sudden poignant uncertainty.

Trebell D'you think so?

She is honest.

Frances No. We are what we are, I suppose.

Trebell Then don't let us cant.

Frances Will you dine with the Anglican League . . . and speak?

Trebell Put it over there . . . Walter can answer it.

The letter reminds her . . .

Frances But what's to happen? Are people to know?

Trebell I've been got off that much.

Frances This is marked Private.

Trebell Begging letter probably!

Frances Oh . . . I know what she was. But you who've despised the best of us . . . and the best in us . . . you to be caught in the trap the cheapest of women can spread!

Frances *does not, perhaps, quite comprehend the masculine nature.* **Trebell** (*at this moment even*) *is a little short with her.*

Trebell The best or the worst of you, my dear . . . if you'll all but go your own way and make it a straight way . . . we know where we are with you then.

Frances This is from Mr Horsham . . . he always initials his envelopes, doesn't he?

He asks for the letter (by a gesture) precisely, and yet, it would seem, indifferently. But this is not indifference; it is something far harder to survive, detachment. **Trebell** *is now taking a cool but genuine interest – in someone else's affairs.*

Frances Don't let us be harsh with each other . . . now. That's Cousin Robert's hand.

She pushes him over another letter. He has glanced through **Horsham**'s *note, which* **Farrant** *had put in the pillar-box the night before.*

Trebell Thank you. Horsham will have no use for me in his Government.

Frances Oh! Does that follow?

Frances *is blank at the news. Having finished* **Horsham**'s *letter, he begins Cousin Robert's.*

Trebell Well . . . it has. Robert says it seems a long time since they had the pleasure of seeing me at Winfield . . . but that now I'm a greater man than ever I must of course be very busy. But he has been busy too . . . over a bazaar to raise money for his boys' club. And they've re-papered the rectory throughout . . . except the servants' rooms, which were done six years ago . . . and that has been an upset. And Mary sends you her love and hopes you've had no return of your rheumatism. And he wonders, if he could find time to run up to town, whether I wouldn't like an afternoon's talk with him upon my Disestablishment schemes. For, after all, his practical experience of the work of a country parish . . .

Slowly – for she is tired and her emotions have been stunned – the full scope of the catastrophe has opened out to **Frances**. *And his detachment from it is the more dreadful to her.*

Frances Don't, Henry . . . don't! I can't bear it.

Trebell But he's quite right. I ought to have had a talk with him. And he remains my affectionate cousin. He has the neatest little signature.

A silence.

Frances Mr Horsham's quite definite?

Trebell He is kind enough to be.

Frances Was it inevitable? Why . . . if there's to be no scandal?

Trebell A scandal half-stifled is worse than a scandal. One is at everybody's mercy. That's their excuse . . . but it isn't their reason for getting rid of me. No . . . I knew! I was trying them pretty high. Take the hard path and you can't afford to slip . . . the easier world is in a natural conspiracy against you.

Frances But Mr Horsham believed in you . . . and your plan.

Trebell Very nearly. But he'd have had a horrid time with me.

Frances It'll tumble to pieces without you.

Trebell They'll patch up something . . . they'll muddle something through.

Frances The best of it did seem too good to be true.

Trebell If I were God that's the one blasphemy I'd not forgive.

From the vengeful force of this you'd say there was hope in the man still. And – though she may not know it is this – it inspires her with a broken sort of hope.

Frances Well, my dear . . . what now? All this will lie heavy on you for a little. But I see fifty futures for you still.

Trebell *might almost be amused; it is so easy to be hopeful for others.*

Trebell Do you?

Frances You're a free lance again. You made your name fighting the lot of them.

But somehow it doesn't sound very hopeful.

Trebell We don't travel the same road twice . . . except as ghosts. Oh . . . I could still make a show of success. Have my revenge on them too! A barren business. No. I'm done. I've come to the end. Walter will finish the letters.

He says it all so simply that it might mean little – or much.

Frances To the end?

Trebell As far as I can see.

And the careless simplicity of that is suspicious.

Frances That can't mean with you . . . what one might fear it to mean. Besides . . . if it did, you wouldn't be telling me, would you? But I know the feeling. It has deadened us all at some time. It's a sign, though, that the worst's over.

He turns to her with a curious air of kindly, cold reproval.

Trebell If I'm to confide in you . . . for once! . . . better believe I mean what I say.

Frances But this one piece of work . . . had it come to mean everything to you?

Trebell More.

Frances More?

Trebell Yes. I'd never, so to speak, given myself away before. It's a dreadful joy to do that . . . to become part of a purpose bigger than your own. Another strength is added to your own . . . it's a mystery. But it follows, you see, that having lost myself in the thing . . . the loss of it leaves me a dead man.

There is the sort of logic about this that speaks of the toppling mind. She eyes him rather fearfully, but her voice is calm, is comforting.

Frances Yes . . . I understand. But these are only words.

Trebell D'you think so? Death is a fact to be faced. And what is it that dies? One may be dead for years . . . and who'll notice . . . if one keeps up appearances? It's not good manners to notice. But why cumber the ground? I once heard four doctors . . . Gilbert among them . . . disputing the moment, the exact moment, when they'd a right to say: This is death. I thought the corpse ought to know. And after some days . . . and nights . . . of consideration, I'm of the opinion that in all that matters to me I'm a dead man.

Frances You're a sick man. And suffering is so strange to you.

Trebell I'm not suffering . . . far from it. While one suffers, one lives, I suppose.

Frances Then there's a deeper hurt. Is it her death that's haunting you? But you didn't love her, you say.

He responds a little wearily: what have the dead to do with such mortal matters?

Trebell Can't you forgive me that? You'd hardly have forgiven me if I had.

Frances Oh . . . I can be callous about her . . . if it'll help. What was she but a bit of base pleasure to you? And not fit to be more! Let's forget her, then.

Trebell I keep thinking of the child.

Frances Is t h a t the trouble?

Trebell Why . . . has it no right to be?

This, oddly enough, is a new and unexpected light on the matter to **Frances**. *But, surely, there can be no incurable trouble here.*

Frances My dear . . . it was dreadful . . . the thing she did . . . dreadfully wrong. But after all . . . babies enough don't get born. We must take a practical view of it.

A ruthful little smile flickers across his face, and is gone.

Trebell Women do . . . for they have to . . . who's to
blame them? But men's travail is of the soul. And if this
new power coming to birth in me has been killed now . . .
as wantonly as she denied life to that child . . . ! I'd rather
like to think Fate could be so subtle in revenge.

Whatever answer can she make?

Frances This isn't sane! It isn't sane!

Trebell By other measure than our thrifty sanity my life
may well be of no more account than that balked scrap of
being was.

*If she can say nothing to combat these delusions – monstrous
delusions! – she must do something at least. She has hold of his
hand, she can grip his arm; and these are alive.*

Frances I shan't leave you . . . till you've promised . . . to
do nothing foolish.

This time he smiles irrefutably.

Trebell We can't sit here, you know, and hold hands for
ever. And if I meant to add that death to the other . . .
though I've not said I mean to, have I? . . . a jump from
the window and a broken neck . . . or a broken promise
. . . yes, even to you! . . . what could be simpler?

She does not loose him; she searches desperately for other help.

Frances Will you come away with me?

Trebell Where?

Frances I don't think it matters . . . as long as we cut free,
for a little, from this tangle of failure. What's to stop us
walking out of the door and away . . . this very minute?

He is provokingly patient.

Trebell Nothing.

Frances Let's break prison, my dear . . . no matter how.
D'you remember being taken from school that summer
Mother was dying . . . and sent out all day . . . and we

followed back each one of those streams in the hills there
till we found out where it rose? Well, let's go gipsying now
. . . we're not so dreadfully middle-aged. We could turn
our backs to the sea, once we'd crossed it. We could walk
up a real river now. That's the only right way to the
mountains. We'd reach them by spring-time . . . when the
passes are opening . . . and you see flowers in the snow. I
did walk down into Carinthia once . . . one Easter . . .
sleeping where I found myself when night came . . . and
the people were so simple and kind. Why stay in a prison
just because you've built it . . . when the whole world
belongs to you? We'll walk on and on . . . day after day
. . . and not talk much . . . and only be tired in body . . .
till we feel alive again . . . and in tune again . . . till the
touch of common things has healed us.

Trebell And till we finish where we started. What a pity
the world's round! The most depressing discovery ever
made. Should we write a book too? You've the romantic
touch. But a tour of the Empire's my move, surely . . . by
all the rules!

She has failed.

Frances Very well. It should be some comfort, I suppose,
to find you can still mock at me.

Trebell I'm sorry. But the fact is that, for a selfish man,
I'm not as much interested in myself as you might think.
I'm done for . . . I'm done with. I wish my job were done
. . . but, really, it would be pompous to complain. If I'd
life in me . . . nothing that has happened would matter a
straw. I've none . . . so do I matter? And I'm quite sane, I
assure you. I've not been sleeping, it's true. But I read
'Huck Finn' for an hour and had a good laugh. I was
hungry . . . and I raided the larder for some bread and
cheese. I said I'd give one more sunrise its chance. But my
light's out.

What more can she say, or do? She speaks calmly.

Frances Very well. I won't vex you any more now, as long

as I know . . . don't promise; I don't want a promise . . .
that you'll do nothing foolish . . . or irretrievable. And
we'll have another talk in a week's time, shall we? After all
. . . what's a week . . . now the worst's over? And you'll
sleep now.

Trebell I'd be glad of some sleep.

*She has freed him; and she stands by him, watchfully, would-
be trustfully.*

Frances I love you . . . you're all I've ever loved. Till you
are yourself again . . . find a little life in that.

He does not answer. There is an empty moment.

Trebell But now you must get dressed, mustn't you? And
I need a shave . . . so don't lock up my razors.

She gives a wan little laugh.

Frances I'd meant to.

Trebell What's a week . . . as you say . . . or a year . . .
or ten? Who'd bargain for life on such terms . . . even if
he could? Time's no measure, is it, of the things men have
made honourable? And whatever our failings, Frankie,
we've meant to live . . . you and I . . . in the large
freedom of the mind. So let's be true to it. My faith . . . a
man needs one when he faces the ignorance of death . . . is
that Nature is spendthrift . . . yet the God to whose
creating we travail may be infinitely economical and waste,
perhaps, less of the wealth of us when we're dead than we
waste in the faithlessness and slavery of our lives.

*That much liveliness of thought in him seems to comfort her.
And she is so ready to find comfort.*

Frances My dear! I've not been very sane myself, I think.
But all's well now . . . all's going to be.

Trebell That's a large order. Here's Bertha come to do the
room.

Bertha *had appeared, somewhat doubtfully. But hearing this* *last she takes it she is to do the room at last.* **Bertha** *has the air of a housemaid many years settled in her place, whom town life has never despoiled of her country training. The tension of their talk together thus finally broken,* **Frances** *turns to go, in ease of mind now, giving a final look at her brother and saying . . .*

Frances And we might break prison for a little . . . all the same.

When she has gone he begins to pick up the letters from the table, keeping them, as far as he can, in their tidied heaps.

Trebell Give me those, will you? Then you can dust. Did you have a good holiday?

Bertha Yes, sir . . . thank you, sir. And I hope you had the same.

To be sure; not three weeks ago he was in Italy!

Trebell Yes, thank you, Bertha . . . so I did!

He carries the letters through to leave them on **Walter Kent**'s *table, and comes out again, closing the door behind him with a certain decision. Then he goes upstairs, leaving* **Bertha** *to do the room.*

An hour or so later (the room has been done) we find **Wedgecroft** *sitting at the big table writing a letter.* **Frances**, *fully dressed now, comes upstairs and stands beside him waiting for him to finish before she speaks. But he does not keep her waiting so long. When she speaks there is death in her voice, as in her face – though not her own death.*

Wedgecroft Yes?

Frances Mr Horsham's downstairs . . . and I can't see him . . . I can't! He has come to sympathise, I suppose. What are you writing?

Wedgecroft Only a note to . . . to the police surgeon. All right . . . I'll see Horsham.

Frances I've taken the revolver out of his hand. Was that wrong . . . shouldn't I have touched it?

Wedgecroft No, of course not! You must stay out of the room. I ought to have locked the door.

Frances I'm sorry. I couldn't bear, somehow, to see the revolver in his hand. I won't go back. He's not there in the room any more, is he? But the spirit must stay by the body for a little, you'd think. And his face is so eager still.

Wedgecroft Hush . . . hush!

He puts out a soothing hand towards hers, and she pulls herself together again. **Lady Julia Farrant** *has come quietly into the room. She stands for a moment, sympathetically silent, till* **Frances,** *conscious of her, turns. Sympathy is unnerving: she droops into* **Lady Julia's** *arms.*

Frances Julia!

Lady Julia Oh . . . dear friend . . . poor friend! I brought Cyril Horsham. He felt he must come.

Wedgecroft I'll see him.

He speaks brusquely. His compassion is not at all of this kind. He has finished his letter. He gets up and goes downstairs. **Lady Julia** *makes* **Frances** *sit down and sits down by her.*

Lady Julia Don't try to talk. Walter has told me . . . just what happened.

But **Frances** *is herself again.*

Frances I don't mind talking. I was in my bedroom when I heard the shot. We'd been sitting here together not ten minutes before.

Lady Julia But why . . . oh, why? Not because he'd lost this chance of office? That wasn't like him. Oh . . . I don't want Cyril Horsham to think that! And even if the scandal had broken . . . nowadays everything's forgotten so soon. No one dreamed her death would upset him so.

Frances *turns an inquiring gaze on her friend, who now, indeed, seems more distracted – certainly more unguarded – than she.*

Frances Did you know . . . about Amy?

Lady Julia No one k n e w, of course . . . and it couldn't have lasted any time. But she always had to show off her conquests. People joked about it for a week or two.

Frances I never knew. Why didn't you tell me? I might have saved her.

Lady Julia My dear . . . how could I? Besides, you never wanted to know . . . about that sort of thing.

Frances *sits silent for a moment. Then she looks at* **Lady Julia** *again; but no longer questioningly, rather as if all questions were now answered.*

Frances We should never have had anything to do with you, Julia . . . no, not with any of you . . . he or I. We weren't your sort, I'm afraid. Will you go away now, please?

No trace of anger in her voice. But **Lady Julia** *is amazed, hurt, wounded, and bereft of words.*

Lady Julia Frances . . . dear Frances!

Frances Oh . . . I'm sure you're very fond of me. You're not heartless . . . you and the rest of you . . . nor hypocrites . . . nor even so selfish as you might be. For you've just got to be greedy, haven't you, of the things you need from the people who can help keep you where you are? And you were making good use of him. You've always been kind to me, Julia . . . and I'm fond of you, too. I never quite lost my head, did I, in your flattering world? Nor he! We both knew the worth of it, I think . . . and our worth to you. But for all that, I suppose, we weren't wise enough at heart in its ways. And now he's dead in the toils of them. Yes . . . you're sorry, I'm sure . . . and you're still kind. But he was half my life to me . . . and more. So now will you let us be strangers again for a little, please?

Lady Julia, *recovered, makes with gentleness, with dignity,* *with true kindliness and affection, what is surely the right answer.*

Lady Julia Dear Frances . . . there's nothing you mayn't say to me . . . and in anger . . . if that eases the hurt. Only don't think that things said so are true . . . for then to have said them makes the hurt worse later on.

As if the hurt mattered! As if (thinks **Frances***) anything they could feel or say or do would bring him back! But all she says is . . .*

Frances I am not angry.

Walter Kent, *head dropped, fists clenched, comes upstairs and turns into his own room.* **Wedgecroft** *follows him and comes in to fetch the letter he wrote.*

Wedgecroft Horsham is just going. He asked me to tell you he was sure he could keep the worst out of the papers. He thought you'd be staying with Frances, Lady Julia. Can he have your car?

There is something in all this, and in his tone, which does not, somehow, support **Horsham***'s reputation for sympathy – of which* **Lady Julia** *is very tender.*

Lady Julia But he's dreadfully upset, isn't he? Have you ever seen him so upset?

Wedgecroft Never.

Dear **Gilbert Wedgecroft** *is really most uncompromising. She gets up to go.*

Lady Julia Send for me soon, Frances dear. Tell Walter to. You'll have him here to help, won't you? He's heart-broken.

Frances Yes. Thank you, Julia. You're very kind.

As it happens she has said it quite mechanically; her thoughts are in that room upstairs. But poor **Lady Julia** *is flooded by self-consciousness and says in deprecating protest. . .*

Lady Julia No . . . not just kind! Do believe that . . . do try to believe that of me, Frances . . . please!

Frances Yes, yes . . . I'll believe it.

If she'll only go! She goes; a little hurt, but as sympathetic as when she came. **Wedgecroft**'s *brusqueness is a comforting change.*

Wedgecroft Don't let anyone else fuss you. I'll come back and see to things. But I have to go now . . . for an hour.

Frances To the other inquest?

Wedgecroft (*unwillingly*) Yes.

Frances Yes, of course.

Wedgecroft, *on the point of leaving, feels he must be just to* **Horsham**, *who had – though so unwittingly – angered him a little.*

Wedgecroft Horsham blamed himself bitterly . . . and he i s very, very upset. Dear Frances . . . you've pluck enough for twenty.

Frances No. I'm stunned. I shall come round . . . and it'll hurt . . . and I still want it to. Then I shall wonder why he did it. Now I know . . . glimmeringly.

Wedgecroft Do you?

Frances Why . . . when you come to think of it, Gilbert . . . life, for its own sake, is an overrated thing.

Wedgecroft, *who will not play the professional comforter, says no more but goes. As he passes* **Walter** *emerging from his room the two exchange British greetings.*

Wedgecroft Hullo.

Walter Kent Hullo.

Walter *has some papers in his hand which he is bringing, without much thinking why, to put on* **Trebell**'s *table. He is undisguisedly crying. He sees* **Frances** *sitting there, silent, still. He gulps out . . .*

Walter Kent Selfish of me to make a fool of myself before
you!

Frances No, Walter, no . . . I'll cry when I can.

Walter Kent I'm not grieving . . . I'm angry. I don't want
to whisper and hide things. I'd like to go through the
streets and shout that he's dead . . . that they've lost him
and wasted him, damn them! With his work all undone!
Who's to do it? Much they care! What did they know of
him? We knew. I cared. I was nothing to him . . . but I
cared. That's waste too. What does it matter? Oh, the
waste of him . . . oh, the waste . . . the waste!

But this is very foolish, and quite useless.

The Secret Life

1919–22

The Secret Life was first produced professionally at the
Orange Tree Theatre, Richmond, on 29 January 1988,
with the following cast:

Stephen Serocold, MP	Michael Elwyn
Sir Geoffrey Salomons	Peter Wyatt
Evan Strowde	Geoffrey Beevers
Eleanor Strowde, his sister	Auriol Smith
Joan Westbury	Vivien Heilbron
Mildred Gauntlett, Countess of Peckham	Angela Browne
Oliver Gauntlett, her son	Daniel Flynn
Dorothy Gauntlett, her daughter	Lucy Durham-Matthews
Mr Kittredge	Leon Eagles
Susan Kittredge, his granddaughter	Robin Brunskill
Sir Leslie Heriot, MP	Alan Brown
Lord Clumbermere	Barrie Cookson

Directed by Sam Walters
Designed by Anne Gruenberg

Act One

Scene One

*A house that faces the sea; the salted turf runs up to its white,
rough-cast walls. This one is cut through in the middle by steps
that lead up five feet or so to a loggia which opens on one side
to the sitting-room, on the other to the dining-room. On the
grass, at each side of the steps, a seat stands against the wall.
But as it is a warm summer night, and as the rooms are small,
the loggia, which is itself as large as a room, is being used as
one. A piano has even been run out of the window; and around
it are gathered four or five people. They cannot be seen unless
they stand up, the parapet that bounds the loggia prevents this.
But their voices can be plainly heard, and one of the party – a
man – is coming to the end of a curious, half-sung, half-spoken
performance of 'Tristan and Isolde'. He accompanies himself
on the piano. He proceeds in English when it happens to fit the
music, when it doesn't he relapses incongruously into the
German. On the white steps sits a solitary figure in white;* **Joan
Westbury**.

Stephen Serocold's voice. . . . weherndern all! And
sinking . . . be drinking . . . unbewusst . . . hochste Lust!
Uplifted, transfigured, Isolde sinks into Brangaene's arms.
Hush! Her spirit is passing. The faithful Brangaene relaxes
her hold of the lifeless body. . . .

The voice of Sir Geoffrey Salomons Always an awkward
moment!

Serocold Shut up! Awestruck in death's presence the
rough soldiers stand motionless.

Evan Strowde's voice Their hard eyes fill with tears.

Serocold (*protesting violently through the harmonies*) No!

Strowde You used to fill them with tears.

Serocold Never! King Mark, stern and noble, calm without though inwardly shaken. . . .

Strowde Wagner always must be flattering that sort of man.

Salomons Every one does.

Serocold (*drowning them with voice and piano both*) . . . raises his hand as if in benediction of the tragic lovers. The twilight deepens. The curtain falls.

He closes with some elaboration. There is, however, no applause; an ironic silence rather. After a moment, **Miss Eleanor Strowde**'s *voice is heard, saying* . . .

Eleanor Thank you.

Serocold Well . . . not so bad, considering! May I have a drink?

Eleanor They'll be in the dining-room, Evan.

Strowde *unhurriedly walks across to the dining-room and turns on the light there.*

Serocold Sir Geoffrey Salomons, KCB, your performance of King Mark . . . for all that I thumped the notes for you . . . was rotten.

Salomons Time has, I fear, added a patine to my voice.

Serocold *Patina*, sir, *et praeterea nihil*. And in future I shall address your envelopes KCB flat.

Strowde (*calling back*) What about my Kurwenal?

Serocold What, indeed!

Salomons You have been shamelessly practising, Serocold.

Serocold Certainly . . . I gave half a morning to it. Well . . . Tristan, Isolde, chorus, and orchestra . . . I ask you!

Odd . . . Eleanor's note telling me you'd be dining . . .
and that very day I'd happened on my old score.

Salomons Which I notice has my name on it.

Serocold Horrid habit it was of yours . . . writing your
name in other people's books. (*He forces a sigh, the
mocking sigh of reminiscent middle-age.*) Well, I shall never
make that noise again!

Strowde Whisky, Stephen?

Serocold Not much.

Salomons I've been trying to recall our last bout.

Serocold I came back to Balliol in the spring after Evan
got his fellowship.

Salomons I was down by then.

Serocold You were there.

Strowde Soda?

Serocold Tap.

Strowde Same for you, Geoffrey?

Salomons Soda. No whisky.

Eleanor The water looks worse than it tastes. But we have
to bring every drinkable drop from the village.

Serocold I suppose one can't sink a well so near the sea.

Salomons (*with the slightest touch of orientalism*) But it's a
charming place, Miss Strowde.

Eleanor For a summer six weeks. Evan likes the bathing.
We're getting too old for our long walks.

Salomons And with such weather.

Serocold It will start to rain next Friday . . . as I change
trains at Fayet St Gervais.

Salomons It will start to pour on Wednesday morning as I
leave Perth.

Serocold You deserve no better . . . keeping us sitting through August over your wretched Tied Industries Bill.

Salomons You should have put your trust in the Permanent Official, and passed the thing in May.

Strowde *returning with the drinks, notices the still figure on the steps. He is a man of fifty.* **Lady Westbury** *is rather younger. A woman that, in her youth, must have been very flower-like; the fragility, and a sense of fragrance about her, remains.*

Strowde Is that you, Joan?

Joan Yes.

Strowde Couldn't you endure it?

Joan I could hear perfectly. Look at the moon.

Strowde It might be a ship on fire.

Joan Burnt out.

Eleanor's voice My dear . . . I thought you'd stolen to bed. Don't sit there without something round your shoulders. You're not in Egypt now.

Joan The desert's far colder.

Eleanor I shall get you a shawl.

Joan No, Eleanor.

Eleanor And an ugly one . . . as a punishment.

Stephen Serocold *now leans over the loggia; a middle-aged man, who has kept his youth.*

Serocold I fear we made a horrid noise.

Joan I always come home hungry for music.

Salomons A horrid sight, Serocold!

Serocold What is?

Sir Geoffrey Salomons *joins him. You would know* **Sir Geoffrey** *was a Jew; but mainly because he seems a little*

*conscious of the racial difference himself. Irony is his main
conversational key.*

Salomons Romantic youth . . . dragged from its grave and
gibbeted. The three of us used to meet in my rooms at
Oxford, Lady Westbury . . . I had the piano, that's why
they put up with me . . . to find food for our
undergraduate souls. We didn't want to listen to music
. . . we wanted to make it. And Tristan was the great dish
. . . served as it has just been served to you. And I've
known us sit silent for an hour after . . . gorged with
emotion.

Strowde *having given* **Serocold** *his whisky, asks* **Joan** . . .

Strowde Whisky, lemonade, or Eleanor's butter-milk?

Joan Nothing, thank you.

Salomons Think . . . if you had but stuck to art and your
ideals, my good Serocold, you might now be worth three
pounds a week as pianist in a cinema.

Serocold And a steadier, better-paid job on the balance,
it'd be, than my present one.

Salomons You surprise me. I thought you were a venal
politician. I have always envied you.

Serocold No one will bribe me, Salomons . . . no one, at
least, has ever tried. Whether that is a compliment to my
character, or an estimate of my unimportance . . . ! No,
my beauty has faded in my country's service . . . late
hours in the House are ruinous to the complexion . . . and
I've nothing to live on but the money that ought to be
spent keeping up the family estate.

Eleanor Strowde *comes back with the shawl for* **Joan**. *She is
grey-haired; a few years older than her brother.*

Eleanor Put this on.

She wraps it round her with a certain austere tenderness.

Joan It's not ugly.

Eleanor Not on you.

Joan (*with finesse*) Thank you . . . and thank you, kind Eleanor.

Sir Geoffrey Salomons *grows playfully portentous.*

Salomons I take leave, Miss Strowde, to look upon this as a significant occasion. We sit here and celebrate with due mockery our emancipation from the toils of the wanton art that seduced our youth. Consider us. Serocold is the most popular man in London.

Serocold (*with a flourish*) Shall I deny it? No.

Salomons Why, they tell me that if you didn't light up the lobby with your smile, your poor party couldn't sometimes muster ten votes. I govern England.

Joan (*repaying him a little irony, in her turn*) All of it, Sir Geoffrey?

Salomons To be accurate, there are about a dozen such sitting in offices, signing papers. We're all the real government England has. She won't stand more. And she'd get rid of us . . . if she knew who we were.

Joan And what about you, Evan?

Strowde I have left the market-place.

Salomons Truly . . . and the dust your feet shook has been laid with our tears.

Serocold Vexing fellow. Well . . . you're fifty.

Strowde I know it. Look at the moon rising. Time on the move! Can you bear the sight of it?

Serocold Just . . . if I keep busy.

Joan And she's dead, poor thing.

Strowde A shining nonentity . . . still going on her ordered way.

Serocold The moral's as plain as the moon is, thank you.

Strowde I'm not mocking, Stephen. I envy you your restlessness. My youthful ambition was to do some one thing just as perfectly . . . before I died.

Salomons Did you assume a lunar life to do it in?

Strowde Now, it is not for one of your race, Geoffrey, to gibe at our religious fallacies.

Serocold (*with calculated despair*) Evan, that was a fatal reply. Salomons will now come the Old Testament over us. At Oxford he couldn't open his mouth without boasting he was a Jew. All the evening his ageless almond eye has been silently reminding me that beneath my clothes I am still stained with woad. Salomons, you may lend me money if you like. But if you patronise me . . . I'll have your teeth drawn . . . I will publish a pamphlet proving you to be in a world-conspiracy with Mr Judas Abramovitch of Moscow . . . I will cut your throat on the Stock Exchange.

Strowde Have you really a sense, Geoffrey, that we ultra-Europeans are so different?

Salomons Yes . . . very deep down I feel a stranger among you. But my mentality is now a little like the money you let me learn to master . . . it's a currency. By nature you're all for absolute values, for rooted virtues . . . flourish or perish! You're capable of suicide and murder . . . how seldom a Jew commits either! . . . and of all extremes. I'm for what's marketable.

Strowde And no Christian paradoxes!

Salomons But don't you want to see heroism and patriotism and altruism . . . all the kingdom of heaven that's within you . . . turned to some practical account? The marketing of ideals is the trade that matters . . . and there is a world-conspiracy of the people who know it. Join us, Miss Strowde.

Eleanor I! Why?

Salomons Then . . . for one thing . . . you wouldn't be so down as you were at dinner on poor Serocold's political morality.

Serocold My political immorality.

Salomons She will no longer . . . forgive me! . . . stand helplessly confused between the two.

Serocold Oh, Evan and Eleanor are like the man with the million pound bank note who starved.

Salomons My dear Serocold, that's not how to deal with idealists. Then they protest that they'll die with dignity. Persuade them it's we who are poor without them.

Eleanor We must all cash in our principles, must we?

Salomons Not for mere cash. Don't misunderstand me. My race and its pupils have mastered a larger technique. I'm not a money-lender nowadays . . . I'm a Civil Servant . . . a damned bureaucrat. If I weren't I'd be a philanthropist. I work with a finer currency than gold.

Strowde Stephen wants to buy me back. But I protest there's nothing left of me to sell.

Serocold Nonsense!

Strowde Not one principle.

Serocold Buy you!

Strowde You and I got into Parliament, Stephen, in nineteen-hundred and . . . peace-time. War-time got me out of it. Why?

Serocold Why indeed! I could have patched up the row with Bellingham in ten minutes if I'd been on the spot.

Strowde My beliefs proved unworkable. I have no new ones. Geoffrey thinks he knows a lot . . . that suffices him. You strike attitudes. When I hear you talk politics nowadays, Stephen, it's like hearing you sing Tristan.

Serocold As bad as that.

Strowde As incredible. Scratch off our clothes, o survivor of wrecked civilisations, and instead of the savage it's likelier you'll find nothing at all.

Salomons But, my dear good heroic fellow . . . why not be content with appearances? Why risk disillusion? Cultivate morality . . . but not religion. Elaborate your politics. And exalt good manners. The achievement in a hundred thousand years or so of the gentleman, the lady, and the leisure class with appetites turned to taste, is a most important one. Don't let democratic cant belittle that. Indulge yourselves, incidentally, in a little art . . . a few good tunes, a picture or so, a scene full of pretty girls. Provide such things . . . for now that the human brute is well-fed, his passions need distracting . . .

Strowde And a little alcohol.

Salomons Yes, if you can't be sentimental without it. But never be carried off on crusades you can't finance . . . don't overdraw on your moral credit. Don't, for one moment, let art and religion and patriotism persuade you that you mean more than you do. Stand by Jerusalem when it comes to stoning the prophets. I must be off.

Eleanor Before you're answered.

Salomons Answers are echoes.

Eleanor What does that mean?

Serocold It means that we all talk the same nonsense and all have to do the next thing there is to be done.

Salomons But thank you for a charming evening.

Eleanor Till October.

Salomons The Committee is to meet on the fifteenth. But you'll get your summons.

Eleanor My first full-fledged official committee. I feel cock-a-hoop.

A skittish phrase for **Eleanor**. **Serocold** *goes back to the*

piano to strum delicately and sing little snatches. 'Tristan',
'Isolde'.

Salomons Good-bye, Lady Westbury. Once more, my
condolences upon the catastrophe. But I must not agree
that insurance is a mockery.

Eleanor Be thankful you weren't burnt in your bed.

Joan My first fire! It's inspiriting to have to start life again
in one's dressing-gown and the gardener's boots.

Strowde Your car's round here, Geoffrey.

Salomons Good-night, Serocold.

Serocold *sings to the melody of the Liebestod . . .*

Serocold Good-night, Sir Geoffrey . . . Salomons KCB
flat . . . hidden-handed bureaucrat . . . Beast in
Revelations . . . your number will shortly be up.

Salomons Not going abroad?

Strowde I've no impulse to. Europe still reproaches one.
Perhaps . . . in the winter.

Salomons If Serocold don't recapture you.

They have gone down the steps and away round the house,
Strowde *kindling a pocket-torch. The two women lean*
together on the parapet.

Joan You've never been to Karnak, Eleanor?

Eleanor No.

Joan We break our journey at Luxor whenever there's
time. You should stand on the great gate and watch the
moon rising over the Nile . . . and then think of all the
armies that have marched . . .

Eleanor (*touching her hand*) My child, you're as cold as a
toad. Cheer up! Mark'li be home for good next year . . .
and think of the fun you'll have re-building.

Joan (*with a rather wan smile*) Energetic Eleanor! But as if he hadn't enough to worry him in Cairo at this moment.

Eleanor (*the kindly scold*) You go to bed now.

Serocold (*as he softly strums*) How many more volumes to this infernal history that Evan has found refuge in?

Eleanor One to publish . . . one to write.

Serocold How long'll that take you?

Eleanor I don't know.

Serocold Can't you finish it for him, Eleanor?

Eleanor Hardly.

Serocold (*pleasantly ironic*) Books must be written, I admit . . . but there are lots of men fit for nothing else. We philistine politicians may be a poor lot . . . but we do get things done.

Joan (*half to herself as she leans on the parapet*) I must pray now to the moon . . . as one burnt-out lady to another . . . to teach me to order my ways.

Serocold *breaks into song again; from the second act this time.*

Serocold Oh rest upon us . . . night du Liebe.

Joan Burnt out inside . . . the moon is. Gutted . . . such an ugly word!

Serocold (*singing away*) Give forgetting . . . that I live. Take me out . . . in deinen schoss . . . .

Eleanor *has gone into the sitting-room.* **Joan** *stares out to sea.*

Scene Two

It is morning, and the sun is shining. **Eleanor**, *wrapped in a fur coat, is sitting in the loggia, writing.* **Serocold**, *dressed for his journey, comes out of the house and stands by the head of the steps talking to her.*

Serocold Good morning, ma'am.

Eleanor Has the car come?

Serocold Not yet, I think.

Eleanor There's ample time. It's to pick up Joan at the Cottage Hospital.

Serocold I'm interrupting?

Eleanor No, I've just finished.

Serocold Proofs?

Eleanor Pages one to sixty . . . volume four . . . of the infernal history.

Serocold We've been in for a swim. I left Evan basking. Are you cold?

Eleanor No. I work in a fur coat all the year round. Thin blood . . . old age!

Serocold Intellectual passion, Eleanor . . . chilling but admirable. Am I to post these in London?

Eleanor I'm coming up with you . . . for the day.

Serocold My dear! Eighty miles up and eighty miles down at eighty in the shade.

Eleanor I'm going to lunch at Kate Gossett's to meet Lord Clumbermere.

Serocold (*with much meaning in the exclamation*) Oh! And what does Kate want with him?

Eleanor I want fifty thousand pounds out of him for the Institute of Social Service.

Serocold Well . . . I daresay you'll get it.

Eleanor I'm told he's a good little man.

Serocold He's good for that much.

Eleanor (*pointedly*) You should know.

Serocold (*bland*) I assure you, we got nothing for his peerage. Reward of merit! I did hope he'd be substantially grateful. But divil a threepenny bit!

Eleanor He bought his baronetcy surely.

Serocold (*bitter-sweet*) Ah . . . Egerton gave him that. (*He looks back towards the house, and lifts his voice a little.*) Good morning, fair lady!

Eleanor I hope the taxi-man didn't hurry you. How's Lester?

Joan, *to whom this has been spoken, comes from the sitting-room, and speaks first to* **Eleanor**, *then to* **Stephen Serocold**.

Joan She had a good night. My heroic maid who went back for my pearls.

Serocold Her point of honour.

Eleanor She didn't get them.

Joan I'm almost glad she didn't. Pearls at that price! (*To* **Eleanor**.) You saw her arm.

Eleanor Rather perverse of you!

Joan Is it? Yes, Lester would think so. We discuss now what we'll do with the insurance money. She's to decide!

She goes back into the house; a moment later comes out again with a parasol, goes down the steps and sits on one of the benches there silently. **Eleanor** *being now quite free of her writing-table,* **Serocold** *fixes her.*

Serocold You may take it from me, Eleanor, that the pro-Leaguers will vote against Egerton on the Japanese question . . . and he'll resign . . . and Bellingham must be sent for. He can form a government even without dissolving. And I'll lay you five to two that it all comes off before Christmas.

She lets him finish; then she shakes her head with a half-smile.

Eleanor I'm not interested, Stephen.

Serocold You definitely refuse to help shepherd Evan back to the fold.

Eleanor Yes. I'm sorry your weekend has been wasted.

Serocold I've enjoyed myself! Don't be nasty.

Eleanor If Evan chooses to go back into politics he will, whatever I say.

Serocold And of course he will . . . it's the obvious thing to do. But why drift back?

Eleanor If he ever serves under Mr Bellingham again . . . I shall be surprised.

Serocold You must serve under the man who's there! Bellingham has his failings . . . and his wife's a disaster.

Eleanor I don't call Mrs Bellingham a disaster.

Serocold She's so dull.

Eleanor (*beyond indignation even*) My objection to your respected chief is simply that he's a liar.

Serocold I shouldn't call him a liar.

Eleanor . . . that he's a trickster.

Serocold He can be tricky when he's driven to it.

Eleanor He has no principles.

Serocold (*cheerily*) I tell him that. But he says that his answer is Emerson's . . .

Eleanor It would be!

Serocold That a foolish consistency is the bugbear of little minds.

Eleanor Well . . . he is consistently disloyal to his friends.

Serocold (*with just a little heat added to the lightness*) No, Eleanor, there you're wrong. And it hurts him when they say the sort of things about him that you're saying. But how can he go on working with them afterwards?

Eleanor (*very directly*) Would you tolerate a tithe of his dishonesty in your own lawyer?

Serocold (*changing ground with the utmost grace*) Ah . . . that opens a wide question. I want an honest lawyer. I've got one, I think . . . and I do my best to deserve him. But isn't Bellingham the sort of Prime Minister that our dear public want?

Eleanor Then let the people of England cultivate political intelligence.

Serocold And what's to happen meanwhile? After all, we're responsible.

Eleanor Who are we?

Serocold The governing classes.

Eleanor Who are they?

Serocold (*with a candour that quite obliterates irony, should there by chance be any at the very bottom of his mind*) Nowadays . . . the people of good-will and energy . . . wherever they spring from . . . who'll trouble to learn the tricks of the trade. I'm a good democrat. I'll work with any one who'll work with me. And I say that the great thing is to keep things going . . . to make for righteousness somehow . . . by the line of least resistance.

Eleanor (*the moralist*) You've all deteriorated since the war.

Serocold And what sort of a morality's yours, may I ask . . . truckling to Clumbermere for money? Travelling up to London to do it, too.

Eleanor (*the realist*) I offer Lord Clumbermere social salvation . . . cheap at the price. I've nothing else to sell him. We must start. Have I got a hat on? Joan, dear, forgive my deserting you. Be nice to Evan. I'll be back to dinner . . .

Serocold With fifty thousand honest sovereigns jingling in your pocket!

Eleanor You'll find me in the car . . . in two minutes.

Eleanor *goes into the house.* **Serocold** *comes down a few steps and leans against the wall within a good range of* **Joan**.

Serocold We physicians of the body politic, you'll observe . . . of whatever school . . . are at one in our firm faith in bleeding.

Joan Who is Lord Clumbermere . . . ought I to know?

Serocold Tanner's Inks he was. God knows what else now . . . now that he himself is appropriately de-personalised into Clumbermere. An able devil.

Joan You want Evan back.

Serocold Bellingham wants to make it up with him. But he must hold out a hand.

Joan Was he trying to work with?

Serocold Infinitely.

Joan But you keep on trying!

Serocold It's my job. And the party's so loaded up nowadays with axe-grinders of all sorts . . .

Joan. D'you think Eleanor's is the right woman's way into politics?

Serocold I don't like women in public affairs, I'm afraid . . . though it's too unpopular a thing to say. They make bad worse . . . not better.

Joan Her Institute and her Guilds.

Serocold They're nice new toys.

Joan And Sir Geoffrey's Committee! She thinks you'll soon be left chattering in your clubs.

Serocold She has been devilling for Evan all her life. She's sick of it . . . that's all.

Joan You miss Mary.

Serocold Damnably.

Joan I'm so glad I was home that summer and saw her before she died.

Serocold She was very fond of you.

Joan Life's eddies are so strange. Evan and Eleanor take this cottage for August . . . I'm burnt out of house and home, and cast on their mercy.

Serocold And do you remember our first meeting?

Joan Shamelessly . . . no.

Serocold Evan and Eleanor, Mary and I, you and your husband . . . emptied together from various trains on the platform at Verona.

Joan Oh yes . . . I was on my honeymoon.

Serocold I had a vision of it this morning . . . as I floated on the sea. And of the man with the guitar who offered to pass the time for us by singing 'Rigoletto' right through for three lire. My Tristan fooleries must have reminded me. And our last meeting?

Joan Such is the blank I call my mind . . . !

Serocold Tea at the Military Tournament . . . nineteen-thirteen. Your boy was with you.

Joan Which?

Serocold The one that was killed.

Joan They were both killed.

Serocold Both!

Joan Within a month.

Serocold (*there being nothing better to say*) I forgot. I won't blunder further by saying sympathetic things. I fear I used sometimes, rather meanly, to thank God Mary had no children. Then I lost her.

Joan (*detaching her mind*) I was once taken through Vickers's to see the armour-plate making . . . and the big steam-hammer cracked a nut for my benefit. They gave me the nut, and told me just where to place it. Mighty goings on leave us, don't you think, almost too dazed to complain? Won't Eleanor be waiting for you?

Serocold Heavens . . . yes. Good-bye.

Joan Good-bye.

Serocold Come and see Braxted again some day?

Joan I'd like to.

He goes into the house and so away. **Joan** *sits looking out to sea. After a moment* **Strowde**, *in a bathing-suit covered by a voluminous dressing-gown, comes as if from the beach.* **Joan**, *motionless, is aware of him.*

Joan Good morning.

Strowde Did you sleep?

Joan Yes.

Strowde The night through?

Joan Oh no!

Strowde For how long?

Joan Three hours. Don't give me away.

Strowde I'll give you till Wednesday to get a night's rest. Then I'll tell on you.

Joan I don't want to be doctored. I'm having such a peaceful time.

Strowde Eleanor gone?

Joan With Stephen Serocold.

Strowde (*his tone changing just a little*) We've a day together.

Joan (*not indifferently*) Yes.

Strowde Our first for a while.

Joan For a long while. You're to go back into Parliament, please, Evan, and into the Cabinet . . . at once.

Strowde The voice of Stephen!

Joan Why don't you?

Strowde I must dress. Then I'll tell you.

Joan Don't you believe in yourself any longer?

Strowde Is that enough of a faith?

Joan Its revenges are simple.

Strowde I've been clearing out the wardrobe of my mind lately. I used to have quite a fashionable mind. I find worn-out stuff and stuff I've never worn. And one can't get rid of it. It mocks me from the rubbish heap.

Joan Better be burnt out.

Strowde Yes . . . you're lucky.

Joan I do feel, though, that one cannot start in collecting again. Let God's eye behold me still in my dressing-gown and the gardener's boots.

Strowde Shall we lunch out here? It won't be too hot. The parlourmaid's eye not being as God's, I will shift to a less symbolical attire. I want to talk to you, Joan.

Joan Well . . . we'll talk.

He goes in to dress. She does not move. She is, indeed, of a very still habit.

Scene Three

It is nearly midnight, and the moon is shining. **Joan**, *wrapped from the chill in a white cloak, is sitting on the steps as before.* **Strowde** *comes out of the house.*

Joan What happened? Is she very tired?

Strowde She hasn't come. He drove here to tell me.

Joan But it's the last train.

Strowde No . . . I've sent him to the Junction now. There's a nine-thirty express she might have caught.

Joan And if not?

Strowde She could motor forty miles and get here about three in the morning.

Joan Couldn't she have telegraphed?

Strowde Yes . . . up to seven.

Joan Not like Eleanor.

Strowde I'm sorry. Will you wait up?

Joan I think so . . . a little longer.

Strowde She'll come.

Joan Is she still rifling Lord What's-his-name's pockets . . . while Kate Gossett holds him down? The silly man must have been struggling.

Strowde Clumbermere's his name . . . if you ever want to thank him for our day together.

By this they have settled themselves to wait.

Joan A long day, Evan.

Strowde Has it seemed so?

Joan Eighteen years long. (*A silence; then she says, as if released from the spell of time.*) How easy to talk to you, though . . . surprisingly!

Strowde (*wholesomely matter-of-fact*) No . . . we've had something to say . . . and haven't had to repeat ourselves . . . as we'd have done talking day in and day out. . . .

Joan (*yielding again for a moment to the spell*) For eighteen years. (*Then again shaking free.*) I believe I've told you everything. You've not told me much.

Strowde Several anecdotes. Do you want more? I've a good memory. Sometimes I exercise it to see if the anecdotes strung together have any meaning.

Joan Ought I to be ashamed to have so little to tell? No spiritual adventures. Housekeeping in odd corners of the world . . . a husband and two children.

Strowde Dutiful happiness.

Joan Yes.

Strowde As we agreed then . . . all for the best.

Joan I've never doubted it.

Strowde (*his tone sharpening a little; the edge towards himself, though*) But when people say that, they're apt to mean . . . all for the second-best, aren't they?

Joan (*countering with irony*) And that's not worth clinging to . . . in these hard times?

Strowde It has also been said, Joan, that Second-Best is what the Devil relies on to keep this world his own.

There is a silence before she asks, as of things long past . . .

Joan Was it God tempted us then?

Strowde God's the great tempter. But . . . even as you now understand what you then were . . . you did love me?

Joan Yes.

Strowde And you've never doubted that either?

Joan Never.

Strowde Though the love for Mark survived. And you had your boys.

Joan (*as making final confession*) I couldn't have lived my love for you, Evan . . . it would have killed me.

Strowde Did I understand that? (*He is disposed to laugh.*) It's always hard to believe that a little human happiness will hurt one.

Joan I think some power in me would always have kept me from you . . . some innermost power.

Strowde I'd have put up a fight with it. I can be less of an altruist . . . than I was then.

Joan But what would you have brought to surrender? Nothing you loved. Nothing that loved you. (*Now she joins him in protective mockery.*) It's shocking for a woman to discover that wifehood and motherhood are really best carried through as matters of business . . . but if she loves a man she can only make him miserable.

Strowde I'd be glad enough to be made unhappy once again.

Joan (*with a touch of mischief*) Has no one managed it in these eighteen years? No, no . . . I'm not curious.

Strowde *faces her, and asks very seriously, but almost disinterestedly . . .*

Strowde Then, in the sense that you've always loved me . . . do you love me still?

Joan Yes.

Strowde Oh . . . why not!

Joan I keep it a secret from my everyday self. But . . . I love you.

Strowde Well, it's a word of all work, isn't it? . . . and we wear out its meanings one by one, as we fulfil and prove them . . . or as we fail to.

Joan Perhaps, Evan . . . for a last meaning . . . to love is to love the unattainable.

He breaks the tension.

Strowde Still, you've not much to complain of. Mark's a first-rate fellow.

Joan's *voice is never hard, nor ever dry, but sometimes it empties of all tone; as now.*

Joan My boys are gone.

Strowde Yes . . . I won't pretend to understand what that means.

Joan One's capable, you know, of uncomprehended suffering. I watched women making a sort of emotional profit out of their loss. People called me stoical . . . but it was only that I didn't understand . . . or want to. Why ask what an earthquake's for? My bitterest moment was when I came home to find their kit sent back from France. Burnt up with everything else now, I'm glad to think. The emptyings, poor dears, of their pockets . . . of a dead boy's pockets!

Strowde (*setting his teeth to this*) Death leaves us that . . . and life breeds in us fantastic hopes.

Joan The night the second news had come we lay awake holding hands . . . and Mark said suddenly: 'I'm sorry, my dear . . . I'm sorry.' And I said: 'Oh, Mark, don't apologise.' We didn't feel very sane.

Strowde (*his brows knit, but his eyes lifted a little*) Nature wastes life . . . for she can afford to. And our human nature spends loving-kindness . . . and we must afford to. You and he have each other. I'm sure he needs you.

She comes back with relief to practical things.

Joan I wish I'd not left him just now . . . but the doctor won't let me stay out the summer there. His work's a failure, he says . . . so they thought they must send him red ribbons and things. When his KCB badge came he threw it into the corner and cursed. It has been a bad three years. We used to fear that you and your party would come in to theorise us out of existence. I remember the evening

when he brought the paper to Gizeh with the news of your
by-election majority. 'Evan will take three steps into the
FO,' he said . . . 'and I shall resign.' (*A little grimly.*) It's
his friends have let him down.

Strowde Did he really picture me astraddle before the
official mantelpiece with my chest puffed out and:
Gentlemen, now I'm in power . . . ?

Joan But why aren't you, Evan?

He looks at her in silence for a moment.

Strowde If I say: Thanks to you . . . don't misunderstand.

Joan (*puzzled and ready to be hurt for his sake all the same*)
Oh, my dear!

Strowde But understand I do thank you that I am not a
popular political figure today . . . putting on all the airs of
wisdom.

Joan Was your history-writing the better choice?

Strowde Well, the Industrial History is honestly laboured
stuff. You've not read it?

Joan Horrid confession . . . no. I began to.

Strowde Shamefuller still!

Joan Three volumes.

Strowde And a fourth to come.

Joan And a fifth.

Strowde Perhaps. A job almost anyone could have done,
and nobody did. Shall I tell you why I took it on . . . even
before the other job failed me?

Joan Why?

Strowde This sounds unselfish . . . it wasn't. I really had
to find something more than housekeeping for Eleanor to
do. My marriage!

Joan It's been a happy one?

Strowde Quite.

Joan Dear Eleanor.

Strowde The best of women. And she brings some meaning to that banal praise.

Joan What's to happen when the history is finished?

Strowde (*businesslike*) Eleanor's goodness begins to be accounted wisdom of the current sort. Committees are seeking her out. Even Salomons, you see, that shrewd appraiser of what's worthwhile . . .

Joan I meant what's to happen to you?

Strowde (*with just a touch of irony, not an unkind one, though*) Eleanor, grown a power in the land and backed by much Clumbermere money, may find me employment.

Joan Nonsense. When will the last volume be done?

Strowde Ah, that's a question. (*He turns his head suddenly.*) I hear the car changing gear on Pewsey Hill.

Joan He has been very quick.

Strowde Impossibly. She'll have found a taxi at the Junction, and they've met half-way.

Joan (*her voice taking on more colour*) Evan . . . stir yourself out of this hopelessness and disbelief.

Strowde (*grimly*) When the donkey's at the end of his tether and has eaten his patch bare, he's to cut capers and kick up a dust, is he?

Joan Have you no purpose left in you?

Strowde (*grimly, indeed*) None. Have you?

Joan Second-Best has exploited me, you may say, and left me for dead. But I was firmly minded that you'd make for yourself a great career.

Strowde How shamefully romantic of you!

Joan Don't you want to be a power in the world?

Strowde Save me from the illusion of power! I once had a glimpse . . . and I thank you for it, my dear . . . of a power that is in me. But that won't answer to any call.

Joan Not to the call of a good cause?

Strowde (*as one who shakes himself free from the temptations of unreality*) Excellent causes abound. They are served . . . as they are! . . . by eminent prigs making a fine parade, by little minds watching for what's to happen next. Track such men down . . . past picture-paper privacy, and their servants' knowledge of them. Oh, never mind if they drink a little, if they're foolish over women or sordid about money . . . we won't damn them for their weaknesses. But search for their strength . . . which is not to be borrowed or bargained for . . . it must spring from the secret life . . .

Joan Yes . . . Yes, I know.

Strowde . . . and what is it, as a rule, but the old, ignorant savagery? Nothing to be ashamed of . . . but why deck it with new names? Women should know, even if we forget, what savages men still are. But you and I climbed together to a chilly height. Was it illusion . . . the truth we found there?

Joan Who am I to say . . . that never put it to the proof?

Strowde Well . . . if we loved the unattainable in each other . . . and if all we could easily have taken mattered so little besides that we let it go with hardly a murmur . . . why, I've learnt to believe, I suppose, in what's unattainable from life and nothing else can content me or stir me now.

Joan (*steadily*) It would have been better then if we never had met . . . and never loved.

Strowde No . . . that's blasphemy. At least don't join the

unbelieving mob who cry: Do something, anything, no
matter what . . . do your devil-most . . . all's well while the
wheels go round . . . while something's being done! . . .
Lord, give us increase . . . if we stop to question, barbarous
poverty will overwhelm us again. Are we so few steps
upward from the beast that gluts and starves?

Joan (*with an irony that is irony of the soul*) But seek first the
kingdom of God . . . and the desire of all things else shall
be taken from you?

Strowde (*very simply*) It has been taken from me. I don't
complain . . . and I don't make a virtue of it. I'm not the
first man who has found beliefs that he can't put in his
pocket like so much small change. But am I to deny them
for that?

Joan No . . . one can't.

Strowde (*choosing his words*) If I could be . . . call it in love
again . . . then, perhaps I'd dare stretch out my hand for
power.

Joan Don't waste time . . . next time . . . over a woman.

Strowde I promise you.

*She breaks the tension now, and lightens her distress with
something like a laugh.*

Joan I never put such fantastic value on myself. If
we'd kissed and parted . . . as we couldn't marry and
settle . . . !

Strowde (*grimly responsive to her tone*) And we never even
kissed.

*For a little now, they survey this eighteen-year span,
detachedly enough; puzzled, acquiescent, interested.*

Joan Is life meant to be so serious?

Strowde Tell me how to forget you . . . and the meaning
of you.

Joan I'm changed.

Strowde How many times have we met since that cold and desperate parting?

Joan A dozen perhaps.

Strowde (*with a lover's courtesy*) You outface the years very beautifully.

Joan Thank you . . . says my vanity.

Strowde But such things are tokens for strangers to know you by. What shines for me is the vision of the truth of you which you gave me when you said . . . weighing the words, but not sadly, I remember . . . when you said that you loved me. And that, you see, whatever it may mean, has not changed.

Joan (*firmly*) I can wish it had never come to your cutting the commonplace earth from under us, Evan, by asking the question. But that was, and it is the truth of me. I'd unsay it if I could.

Strowde Yes. We live another life from the beasts only in this tiresome belief that beyond the tokens of our living something we call truth exists. Yet there's nothing near to truth that we learn, but when we've felt the burden we'd cast it away . . . we'd unsay it if we could.

Joan (*desperately, even with some impatience showing*) But if I'm to stand to you for ever as a symbol of denial . . . of uselessness . . . of a sort of death in life! Evan, Evan . . . no recording angel will consent to write: He could not be a conquering hero all for thinking of a love affair.

Strowde It sounds absurd, doesn't it?

Her tone changes; there is pain in it now.

Joan Has it been . . . oh, but it can't have been this winter-time with you ever since? We did wisely.

Strowde We did right.

Joan (*fearlessly probing, for that may help*) No, I don't say so. I did what I felt then I could be sure of doing well.

Strowde (*putting it to the inscrutable gods*) And we must always try to do more . . . even knowing that we'll fail! A grim burden for the fledgling soul. Why not make the best of things?

Joan (*echoing*) The devil's own second-best of things. (*She turns to him again with pain in her voice and eyes.*) You've suffered.

Strowde (*shrugging*) Why . . . I've had my losses as you have. When the war came my beliefs about men and things were an enemy the more. I fought against them and beat them . . . and they're dead. And what remains? I'm rather sullen-minded.

Joan Is it right to leave present fighting to ignobler minds?

Strowde How can one go in again without purpose or conviction . . . without even ambition or vanity as an excuse . . . remount the merry-go-round?

Joan Yes . . . Mark says the most pitiful thing he meets is the well-meaning man who daren't stop. He sees him, he says, poor dear, in the mirror of a morning.

Strowde (*with a savage shake of the head*) I'd be an ill-meaning man pretty soon.

Joan Why?

Strowde Can you think of a greater driving force for evil than the man who has seen a better way and accepts the worse . . . who knows there's a wisdom that escapes him and must deny it? I'd sooner trust things to fools, if the fools would take heart, than to disillusioned men.

Joan And there's always Eleanor!

Strowde Yes, let the busy women have a try at tidying up. But, frankly, I fear they'll make a commonplace world of it.

Joan Here she is.

Strowde Weary, but cheerful.

Joan Bless her!

Strowde *goes quickly into the house. After a moment* **Eleanor** *comes out. Weary she may be, but she does not show it much. She is subduedly, and a little strangely, cheerful.*

Eleanor Dear Joan . . . forgive me.

Joan Good hunting?

Eleanor Good enough. Has Evan looked after you?

Joan Perfectly.

Strowde *returns.*

Eleanor You didn't get my message. But I missed even that train.

Joan (*merrily*) You have a callous brother. I said you might be lying cold and stiff. He said it was unlikely.

Strowde No one is ever anxious about Eleanor. There are sandwiches and barley-water for you.

Eleanor Go to bed, Joan. I didn't dream you'd sit up.

Joan Naughty of me. Good-night.

Eleanor *kisses her, more tenderly than, one would say, the occasion demanded.*

Eleanor My dear . . . !

Joan I'm sure you've most intriguing things to tell Evan about Lord Bumble-bee . . . or whatever his silly name is. Good-night, Evan.

Strowde Good-night, Joan.

She goes. There is a little pause, as if they were waiting for her to get out of earshot.

Strowde Well, what's wrong?

Eleanor Mark Westbury fell down dead in his office in Cairo this morning.

Strowde Good God!

Eleanor By pure chance I met Neville Hamerton at the corner of Whitehall, and he told me. So I went back with him to the FO to stop them sending her a telegram. That's what kept me, of course. Shall I tell her tonight or not?

Strowde Yes, I should.

Eleanor Would she take it better from you?

Strowde (*almost sharply*) Why should she?

Eleanor (*with a hint of evasion*) You knew Mark very well.

Strowde (*concluding this small excursion*) Not better than you know her.

Eleanor It'll seem like the end of the world. Both her boys . . . the house burnt down . . . and now this.

Strowde (*taking to abstractions, as his wont is*) Mark is an immeasurable loss. But all losses are . . . till one measures them by forgetting them.

Eleanor They only had each other.

Strowde The breaking of a last link brings relief with it too.

Eleanor (*her brows knitting*) Evan, don't be so callous.

Strowde (*reasonably*) I am not. It will be a great shock . . . and a great grief . . . till Nature rebels and says: Die of it, or get over it.

Eleanor Is this how I'm to talk to Joan?

Strowde Don't start talking at all. Tell her Mark's dead, kiss her, and come away the moment she loosens your hand.

Eleanor *faces her mission with misgiving, as well she may.*

Eleanor Well . . . I'll go up now. Lord Clumbermere was very sound. I think he'll give us thirty thousand.

This last inappropriate remark by no means shows an unsympathetic mind. The thought was there, and she found some support in it. **Strowde,** *though, is not unconscious of the effect of its simple utterance.*

Strowde Good. Shall I take the sandwiches to your room?

Eleanor No, thank you . . . I'm not hungry.

Eleanor *goes into the house. He now has but to put out the lights below, lock up and go to bed.*

Act Two

Scene One

Braxted Abbey, **Stephen Serocold**'s *home, is a Tudor house, built on monastic foundations. It has, on the first floor above ground, a long panelled gallery with six high embrasured windows, which overlook the broad terrace. Here is the end of the gallery, and we face the last of these windows, through which we can see the cypresses that border the terrace, and the sky. Set out from the blank wall on our left is a writing-table; sitting at it one can command the gallery's length. A small door in the panelling cuts off the corner; it opens to a small turret staircase which descends but does not ascend. The window is open, for it is a summer afternoon. On the window seat are* **Serocold** *and* **Lady Peckham**. *She is a woman over fifty, of pronounced vitality, if somewhat insensitive. By the way she is dressed she has just arrived. She is chattering.*

Lady Peckham . . . He never forgave me for ruffling his hair once at a supper party at Frankie Turnour's. I told that silly scared girl he married that she'd better learn to. But I think she prefers him pompous. He has gone very bald, though, lately.

Serocold He works hard. Bellingham gets on with him. He ballasts the Cabinet. God knows we need that.

Lady Peckham (*nodding towards the garden*) Where did Joan Westbury spring from? I've not met her for an age.

Serocold She's been about.

Lady Peckham You brought Evan and Eleanor down with you?

Serocold Yesterday.

Lady Peckham Who else is coming?

Serocold The Kittredges.

Lady Peckham I've seen them.

Serocold We only hold eight these days.

Lady Peckham Lunching tomorrow?

Serocold Bellingham.

Lady Peckham (*cocking her head*) You stick to your point, don't you?

Serocold No, never . . . but I keep on coming back to it.

Lady Peckham He hates Evan.

Serocold (*cheerfully*) Evan despises him. But I'll make it a match.

Lady Peckham (*her gaze on the garden again*) And are those two going to?

Serocold I haven't heard so. But they're walking nicely in step. It looks connubial.

Lady Peckham How long has Mark Westbury been dead?

Serocold He died in August. This is only June.

Lady Peckham They'd better hurry up. They're not getting younger. She'll want more children. And why not?

Serocold (*with mild idealism*) My dear Mildred . . . there are other objects in marrying.

Lady Peckham That's an obvious one. Why do you ask these Kittredges?

Serocold I like them . . . and it's as well to be civil to Americans.

Lady Peckham Are they rich?

Serocold I'm sure they'd hate to be thought so.

Lady Peckham That's very morbid. Who is it with Evan and Joan?

Serocold Why, Oliver!

Lady Peckham Heavens . . . I must get new spectacles. You've no right to look so young, you know, Stephen. I wasn't out of the nursery when you were born.

Serocold Mildred, I believe I may live to be a hundred. It's terrible . . .

From some way along the terrace below, **Oliver Gauntlett**'s *voice is heard calling 'Hullo, darling Mother!'* **Lady Peckham** *waves a hand to him.*

Lady Peckham Bless you, my son.

Serocold Things bore me and never tire me. I'm no real good to this government . . . but, honestly, I don't think Bellingham could get on without me. I'm happy down here. All the years Mary was ill I got into the habit of leaving myself with her on the Monday morning and she'd hand it me back well-cared for on the Friday night.

Lady Peckham Poor Stephen!

Serocold You never could stand a sick-bed, could you?

Lady Peckham Stand by one, d'you mean? Not for long.

Serocold We had more of a married life, though, than most people.

Lady Peckham You're good right through, Stephen.

Serocold I'm harmless. (*Now he broaches something which it would seem has been on his mind.*) I'm pretty vexed, Mildred, about this escapade of Oliver's.

Lady Peckham Nothing in it.

Serocold Why go to an Anarchist meeting? And if you must go, why in God's name get arrested there!

Lady Peckham They didn't charge him with anything.

Serocold Every paper had a paragraph.

Lady Peckham A fortnight ago . . . all forgotten. The tradition of the English gentleman, Stephen, is that he may go where he pleases and do what he likes.

Serocold No doubt. But England's so full of gentlemen now . . . competition has abolished these privileges. Talk to him seriously.

Lady Peckham Try it yourself.

Serocold I have.

Lady Peckham Well?

Serocold He says Anarchy interests him.

Lady Peckham Why shouldn't it?

Serocold My dear Mildred, I'm in the Cabinet, and I'm his uncle.

Lady Peckham That's not his fault.

Serocold That's what he said. I think it most courageous and forgiving of me to ask him down here.

Lady Peckham It is.

By this it is evident that **Joan**, **Strowde**, *and* **Oliver Gauntlett** *have arrived under the window; and one can talk from the gallery to the terrace with perfect ease.*

Lady Peckham How are you, Joan?

Joan's voice Do you want to know?

Lady Peckham I ask.

Joan I feel like flying.

Serocold Door's locked inside. I'll open it.

He goes down the turret stair. The exchange of compliments proceeds.

Lady Peckham Hot?

Joan No.

Lady Peckham Pretty frock.

Joan One I had dyed.

Lady Peckham You're losing a comb.

Joan Thank you. When did you get here?

Lady Peckham About six.

Joan How's London?

Lady Peckham Horrid.

Oliver Gauntlett *comes in by the turret door. He is a young man, and he has lost an arm.* **Strowde** *follows him. He carries a printed paper that has an official look about it. This he opens in a minute, and sets himself to at the writing-table.* **Oliver** *kisses his mother with real affection.*

Oliver Where's Dolly?

Lady Peckham Went down to the lake with Miss Susan Kittredge. Well, Evan?

Strowde Well, Mildred?

No greeting could be friendlier.

Oliver You look very handsome, Mother.

Lady Peckham Thank you kindly. How are you?

Oliver Kicking. Evan won't take me on.

Lady Peckham Why should he?

Serocold's voice Mildred, come and see the Alderney bull.

Lady Peckham Now?

Serocold Yes.

Lady Peckham All right.

Oliver (*hailing*) Uncle Stephen!

Serocold's voice Hullo.

Oliver I positively was not drunk.

Serocold I wish you had been.

Strowde (*looking up from his reading*) Distressing to the nice-minded historian . . . to note how aggressively moral revolutionaries become.

Oliver New Year before last at Blair I tried to get drunk and couldn't. Nor wine nor spirits has passed my lips since. I think I'll try again.

Lady Peckham Do you feel you really must?

Oliver Why did you give me such a queer head?

Lady Peckham (*as she kisses the top of it in farewell*) I sometimes wish it had been an even thicker one.

Oliver But what about my future?

Strowde Did the worthy Sir Charles Phillips positively throw you down the office steps?

Oliver He wept over me. I resigned.

Lady Peckham I shall shortly have the pleasure of telling that gentleman publicly that he's a liar.

Oliver For saying I was frolicsomely drunk! Dear Mother, he meant that kindly.

Lady Peckham Still, I shall not deny myself the pleasure.

Lady Peckham *passes down the gallery.*

Oliver Grin through a mask and explode an idea on them . . . and your Phillipses show the white scuts of their minds like rabbits.

Strowde What precise shade of red are you? Anarchy's black, by the way.

Oliver Evan, I will tell you a secret. I was down there searching for a Chinese debating society . . . and I got into the wrong meeting.

Strowde Did the Bobbies frog-march you?

Oliver Well, I'm glad they didn't give me a chance of going back on the poor scared devils. But I had to get quit of old Phillips. So I worked up Bakunin, and had a fine set-to with him.

Strowde What's wrong with the City?

Oliver What's wrong with a mine that's on a map and a cotton-field on a balance-sheet?

Strowde Not primitive enough?

Oliver Maybe. Digging potatoes might sweat all the nonsense out of me, d'you think? But I can't.

Strowde You play an amazing game of tennis, though.

Oliver I write a better hand than I did. It's harder to.

Strowde I don't see what use I can be. If politics are your game . . . won't you do better attacking the citadel of the constitution from within . . . as you happen to have the entrée?

Oliver Yes . . . the Right Honourable Brooke Bellingham's lunching tomorrow. I might wag my tail at him and be a Cabinet Minister in no time.

Strowde Why not?

Oliver There's a longer lease for the old gang in letting the youngsters in than in keeping them out, isn't there? I'm not for bombs. There's not enough difference between a dead Bellingham and a live one.

Strowde And there's something to be said, you know, for simple and vulgar ambition.

Oliver They're all twitteringly afraid of you, Evan. If your name comes up at a dinner-table, Uncle Stephen gets that genial . . . !

Strowde They flatter me.

Oliver You're going to stand again at the election?

Strowde I may.

Oliver They think you mean to give them hell.

Strowde I must manage to keep up the impression.

Oliver I want to learn what's what. I've chucked a success in the City.

Strowde You could have given them hell there. A spectacular bankruptcy. You've a name to discredit. That's real revolution.

Oliver You're spoiling for a fight, you know . . . for all you sit there writing niggling notes on that report of Eleanor's damned Committee.

Strowde I'd be setting you to type them.

Oliver I will . . . till the time comes.

Strowde And if the time never comes?

Oliver How long have you believed that?

Strowde It is my firm disbelief.

Oliver Then why don't you shoot yourself?

Strowde I must finish these notes.

Oliver I must dress.

Strowde Dinner at eight?

Oliver It takes me half an hour. But you might think me over.

Strowde Yes, I will.

Oliver Thank you.

Oliver *goes down the gallery, leaving* **Strowde** *to his note-making.*

Scene Two

Half an hour later. **Strowde** *has nearly reached the end of the report and of his notes on it.* **Lady Peckham** *comes down the gallery.*

Lady Peckham You'll be late for dinner.

Strowde No.

Lady Peckham You will. Because I want to talk to you.

And she sits on the other side of the writing-table.

Strowde What about?

Lady Peckham Oliver.

Strowde (*with more than a casual acquiescence*) Yes. What do you want me to do?

Lady Peckham Queer his turning to you . . . so instinctively.

Strowde How long since he turned fantastically minded? I've hardly seen him since he grew up.

Lady Peckham He has been very mum with me this last year or two.

Strowde Is it the strain of the war still?

Lady Peckham I don't see why it should be. He was only three months out . . . got smashed . . . came home.

Strowde He had three years among the stay-at-homes . . . growing up to it. His mind is jangled at the moment. It mayn't last.

Lady Peckham He's very unhappy. I've always wondered whether sometime he ought not to be told.

Strowde (*looking at her, so to speak, from under his brows*) D'you think that would cheer him?

Lady Peckham D'you think it's possible he knows?

Strowde Hardly possible. What gossip there was . . .

Lady Peckham How should we know what gossip there was?

Strowde Then why should very stale echoes of it drift his way? Still, it's possible.

Lady Peckham Don't think I'd mind telling him he's your son.

This plain fact – which she has purposely put so plainly – lies, one may say, for consideration on the table between them.

Strowde My dear Mildred . . . surely it would be a piece of wanton cruelty.

Lady Peckham I consider you've a right to forbid me to.

Strowde You've been seriously thinking of telling him?

Lady Peckham Yes.

Strowde Tell me why.

She turns her eyes on herself for a moment, a comparatively infrequent habit.

Lady Peckham I'm a tough old heathen . . . and I'm a sentimental fool. The two things go together, I suppose.

Strowde Often.

Lady Peckham Have you any feeling for Oliver?

Strowde Honestly?

Lady Peckham Of course.

Strowde Well . . . it's hard to define . . .

Lady Peckham Then you haven't.

Strowde I can't contradict you.

Lady Peckham Why expect it? You were pretty young. We were happy for a bit.

Strowde And you threw me over just as suddenly, Mildred.

Lady Peckham You didn't complain.

Strowde I had no right to.

Lady Peckham I took a sort of pride, Evan, in sending you off whistling. (*She relaxes to reminiscence.*) I remember my father, when I was fifteen, setting forth Great-aunt Charlotte to me . . . which had to be done as she's in the history books . . . and took some doing! He said: She was a bad lot, but a good fellow.

Strowde You have a genius, Mildred, for making things seem simple.

Lady Peckham (*summarily*) Well . . . I've more energy than brains. And I never could fuss about my immortal soul. I'm not sure that I have one. I used to think I might grow one. But if you can only get it by fussing about it . . . I don't want that sort. So when I die there'll be an end of me. I don't mind. I've done all I can for Oliver. He has lost the need for me. And the same sort of thing's to be gone through with Dolly . . . though she's no concern of yours . . . nor of anyone else's now.

Strowde (*measuring his mind in the matter*) I don't, of course, refuse responsibility, . . . if you really think I can do something for the boy that no one else can.

Lady Peckham (*grimacing, and dragging out the accusing word*) You're so dry, Evan.

Strowde (*undisturbed*) But he's twenty-six . . .

Lady Peckham Twenty-five.

Strowde And he is what he is. He's looking ahead. Why should he thank us for tying this corpse of a story round his neck?

Lady Peckham (*as businesslike as he*) He doesn't get on with the Gauntletts. And he can hardly inherit . . . what with Victor's two sons . . . and it's a third on the way, I daresay. He was dutifully fond of Peckham, and Peckham liked him . . . died when he was twelve, though . . . so that's all they knew of each other. Peckham was no fool.

Strowde (*half-humorously*) I never thought so.

Lady Peckham Except over women. But a sensible husband to me . . . and I was no end of a nuisance of a tomboy when he married me. It's my money Oliver gets. I saw to that.

Strowde But surely he'd hate me if he knew . . . whatever I might learn to feel for him.

Lady Peckham And you'd sit down under it?

Strowde What else could I do?

Lady Peckham What a question!

Strowde Give me the answer.

Lady Peckham (*with a sudden blaze of feeling*) I'm angry with you.

Strowde I retain great respect for your anger.

Lady Peckham Even in those days you always seemed to be looking for something over my shoulder.

Strowde Most ungallant of me!

Lady Peckham No . . . I hoped you'd find it.

Strowde I never did.

Lady Peckham Are you going to marry Joan Westbury?

Though this is fired at him without warning his answer is perfectly balanced.

Strowde I hope so.

Lady Peckham (*quickly*) You'd mind her knowing?

Strowde (*countering effectively*) Would you?

Lady Peckham Oliver's very fond of her.

Strowde Is he?

Lady Peckham (*her voice dropping a tone or two*) When I saw you three in the garden together just now . . .

Strowde Well?

Lady Peckham I got ready to give him up. It's far likelier, when he's told, that he'll learn to hate me.

Strowde (*a little askew*) And it's also possible, isn't it, that Joan might turn her back on the three of us.

Lady Peckham (*simply*) I hadn't thought of that.

For the first and only time he permits himself something of a score.

Strowde Hadn't you? I'm afraid I had.

Lady Peckham (*most genuinely shocked*) Good God, Evan . . . you used not to think me a cad. And you'd let her?

Strowde You credit me with the queerest powers.

Lady Peckham I've not patience with people that only seem able to live in a mix-up of the past and the future. . . .

Strowde The present!

Lady Peckham If Joan finds she's jealous of me, let her take Oliver from me . . . and from you too. I could. That ought to satisfy her.

Strowde I doubt if you understand Joan.

Lady Peckham Well enough!

Strowde . . . even though you understand me.

Lady Peckham You'd have puzzled me once if I'd let you. But we took things for granted. Well . . . you bear me no grudge, do you?

Strowde On the contrary, I apologise.

Lady Peckham (*robust, to his subtlety*) What for?

Strowde For looking over your shoulder.

Lady Peckham I can tell you this, Evan . . . whatever it was you set out to be when I sent you packing, you ought to be six times the size of it by now. I've played the fool pretty blindly, no doubt . . . but I'm wise where I need to be . . .

Strowde (*seriously*) That's a great boast.

Lady Peckham Even if I'm not very wise. And you can't put me in the wrong over my children . . . for they've had the best of me . . . and I don't have to ask questions about them . . . I k n o w.

Strowde Adopting him as my secretary or what not would prompt some people's memories . . . that was one good reason, I thought, for snubbing the boy.

Lady Peckham Thank you.

Strowde (*his eyes travelling to the gallery's end*) Here come the What's-his-names . . . American people . . . Kittredges.

Lady Peckham (*without turning*) Can they hear us?

Strowde Not yet . . . they're stopping to look at a picture.

But their talk seems at an end. **Lady Peckham** *adds a postscript.*

Lady Peckham I've wondered what the second housemaid felt like when she swore her baby on the footman.

Strowde And the footman was adjured to have the feelings of a man! I'm sorry.

Lady Peckham You'd better dress for dinner. (*Then she smiles wryly.*) I once gave you a dog. Did you get fond of it?

Strowde Very. I'm afraid you can't shame me quite so easily.

Lady Peckham Well, Oliver's going wrong . . . and it's breaking my heart.

Strowde You'd cut bits out of yourself for him.

Lady Peckham He is a bit cut out of me.

Strowde (*gravely*) We must tell him if you think it right.

Lady Peckham No. No use.

Strowde I wish that I didn't agree.

Lady Peckham (*with all her sincerity, and of this, at least, she has much*) But if you can't take what's your own when it's offered you, my friend, I don't know what else is to do you good.

Strowde (*neither lifting nor lowering his voice*) Look out!

Mr Kittredge's *voice is heard saying as he approaches, 'Is it my ignorance to suppose that a Hobbema?'*

Lady Peckham (*brightly, as she turns*) We'll hope not, Mr Kittredge, as it is earmarked for income-tax.

Mr Kittredge *and* **Susan** *appear, ready for dinner. He is an old man; of the aristocracy of New England, and of a higher aristocracy too.* **Susan** *is his granddaughter; a girl of a grave simplicity, of which she is only a little conscious and not at all ashamed.*

Mr Kittredge (*with his light touch*) Very unfair, I agree, for any mere nobody to paint such a picture.

Lady Peckham (*as one bullies one's oldest friend*) Evan, w i l l you go and get dressed?

Strowde Dear me . . . you're my hostess, aren't you?

Lady Peckham I wait dinner twenty minutes and no more. British punctuality, Miss Susan.

Strowde (*with admirable vigour*) You count a hundred and walk to the hall and pick up the others, and you'll find me waiting by the soup tureen. And I'll trust to your honour for a measured hundred, Miss Kittredge. . . .

By which time he is down the gallery and away.

Mr Kittredge (*in his musical tone*) This was your home, Lady Peckham?

Lady Peckham Mamma started married life by being restless. I got born in Venice. But I grew here.

Mr Kittredge I know better than to be enthusiastic in England . . . so I won't remind you how beautiful it is.

Lady Peckham (*with British politeness*) You needn't. I know. Though it's ramshackle, all but the kitchens. They're Norman. You must see them. A bit of a nuisance to Stephen now he can't keep it up. He could sell it to a Trade Union for a Convalescent Home. But we've a cousin who's gone into oil, and won't break the entail.

Mr Kittredge I picture a sick bricklayer meditating in the cloister upon his spiritual affinity to the men who built it . . . as a refuge from the anarchy of mind without.

Lady Peckham I can picture him asleep over the Sunday paper.

Mr Kittredge They were Hospitallers, weren't they?

Lady Peckham Order of St John . . . and I'm a something or other of that now too.

Susan *has been standing reposefully where she paused by the window. She now announces as a matter of course, though much to* **Lady Peckham**'s *astonishment* . . .

Susan One hundred.

Lady Peckham What? Oh, thank you.

Mr Kittredge I ask your approval of Susan's upbringing. She does what she is told without comment.

Lady Peckham, *once she gets what she'd call the hang of a talk, has a shrewd humour of her own.*

Lady Peckham Then she's both a very good girl and a very deceitful one.

The young woman in question now unobtrusively takes part.

Mr Kittredge She smiles. I always think that I know what she means when she smiles . . . but perhaps it's only because I'm fond of her. However, in that at least I'm not deceived.

Lady Peckham (*briskly*) Come along. (*But she has to collect the half-dozen etceteras that women, dressed for dinner, carry round in a country house.*) You're writing a book about us, aren't you, Mr Kittredge . . . somebody told me!

Mr Kittredge No, indeed . . . the warfare of my works is accomplished. They repose in the half-calf of a definitive edition upon the shelves of those gentlemanly libraries which, the advertisements inform me, cannot be considered complete without them. In my hey-day I was read, apparently, but not bought. Now I am bought but not read. Heaven forbid, though, that I should quarrel with the bread and butter I still need to consume.

Lady Peckham But you're a professor?

Mr Kittredge Emeritus.

Lady Peckham Does that mean you don't earn any money by it?

Mr Kittredge That also is implied.

Susan (*close at his side*) Your books are read, Grandfather.

Mr Kittredge (*his voice caressing her*) Family pride . . . pray pardon it, madam. (*They now make vague starts on their way to dinner.*) From sheer force of habit, though, I am collecting materials for a book I shall never write now . . . and England is rich in them at the moment.

Lady Peckham (*seeking a foothold amid the rising waters of intellect*) What's it called?

Mr Kittredge The Selection of an Aristocracy might serve for a title.

Lady Peckham What does that mean?

Mr Kittredge You must not indulge my garrulity. I believe . . . the idea is not a new one, of course . . . that a community can only be kept self-respecting and powerful by courage in the continuing selection of an aristocracy.

Lady Peckham Aren't they born?

Mr Kittredge In that case, circumstances will call for their being bred and born unconventionally at times.

Lady Peckham (*turning a sharp eye on his unconscious serenity*) Oh! Yes . . . I never thought of that.

Now they move slowly down the gallery.

Mr Kittredge In the United States, unfortunately, for the last eighty years . . . my lifetime! . . . the methods of our material advancement have been too crudely selective for anything one can call an aristocracy to adhere in the social structure. But you are somewhat luckier. Barriers break, but new classes form. The art of social sympathy flourishes just a little more easily in England. . . .

Lady Peckham (*reduced to politeness*) Ah! Yes . . . very interesting, I'm sure. . . .

By this they have disappeared.

Scene Three

It is Sunday, near lunch-time. **Eleanor** *is alone in the gallery with her letters and papers. On the terrace a very noisy game is in progress.* **Dolly Gauntlett**'s *fresh young voice is heard, crying, 'Run, Joan! No, not a straighter . . . she'll get you. Stop at Apollo. Oh, I knew she would! That's three games to them. Why didn't you stop at Apollo?' And then* **Joan**'s, *cheerful but distracted: 'But I have to do it in five, haven't I?'*

Dolly Well, you'd two to spare.

Joan No, I took three up.

Oliver's voice Yes, she did . . . one to the Faun . . . and one to Diana. . . .

Dolly Susan, you're no end of a shot. Let's play women against men . . . and Evan may run twice.

Strowde's voice Miss Dorothy Gauntlett . . . do you know my age?

Dolly Fiddle-de-dee! Look how Joan runs.

Joan Tactful child!

Eleanor *walks to the window with a letter which she waves.*

Eleanor Evan!

Strowde What's that? I'll come up.

Dolly (*raising loud protest*) No, no, no! We can't play four.

Eleanor I won't keep him long.

Dolly Why do you desecrate the Sabbath by reading reports? Come down and play Straighters.

Eleanor I believe I last played Straighters, Dolly, the year before you were born.

Dolly Mother's a dab at it still.

The game thus checked, the players seem to be resting beneath the window.

Susan Does that drawing in the library date its being invented?

Dolly It's older . . . because of the counting by chases. The tennis court was pulled down in seventeen-fifty. . . .

Strowde, *a little the worse for his bout of Straighters, comes in by the turret door, and* **Eleanor** *hands him the letter. The voices from below form a curious counterpoint to their talk.*

Oliver It's only Rounders played straight up the Terrace.

Eleanor From Sir Curtis Henry.

Strowde What's he plaguing you for?

Eleanor Duddington's been at him.

Strowde He's been at me.

Dolly The paving makes your feet so hot . . . that's the worst.

Eleanor Why Sir Curtis should suppose that I could or would persuade you to stand as the party nominee, I can't imagine.

Susan Was this how Apollo and Diana got their arms broken?

Strowde *finishes the letter and gives it back.*

Strowde Stockton-on-Crouch is growing agitated, evidently.

Dolly There used to be a rule in my young days not to touch the statues.

Eleanor But Duddington thinks you could carry it as an Independent, doesn't he?

Strowde Duddington's job as an election agent is to find the greatest common measure of agreement . . .

Dolly Oliver, fetch us a towel.

Oliver What for?

Strowde . . . and to collar votes from Anarchists, Christadelphians, Anti-vivisectionists, members of the Flat Earth Society and old Uncle Tom Cobley and all.

Dolly We three females will then go dabble our six hot feet in the fountain.

Strowde *puts his head sharply out of the window.*

Strowde Dolly, don't be a fool . . . you'll give yourselves frightful colds.

Dolly Silence, Methusaleh.

Eleanor Well, what shall I say to the valiantly tactful Sir Curtis?

Dolly Come along!

Joan No!

Dolly Joan Westbury . . . do you want me to carry you there like a sack of potatoes or a Sabine lady?

Strowde Give him a taste of your quality. You'll be a candidate yourself yet.

Joan I shall ask your mother to put you on a lowering diet, Dolly.

Strowde My part in the answer is that I'm still considering whether I'll stand at all.

Dolly I'd tuck Susan under my arm too for tuppence.

Come along. Come along!
If you stick to me you can't go wrong!

And **Dolly** *can be heard whooping triumphantly along the terrace. The other two follow her, their voices tell us.*

Susan Are you so hot?

Joan Only breathless . . . a little.

Eleanor Very well. I'll say that.

Strowde *turns to go, but turns again.*

Strowde Have you read my notes on your report?

Eleanor I was just about to. You haven't told me what you make of it as a whole.

Strowde It's dull.

Eleanor The Industrial Birth-rate is not a lively subject. Perhaps Part Two upon Wages of Young Persons will amuse you more.

Strowde When is that to be ready?

Eleanor We still have the West Riding evidence to take.

Strowde Shall I do a draft in rhyme for you?

Equal work for equal wages,
Boys and girls who read these pages!
Men and women through the ages!
Twelve disinterested sages
Have arrived by easy stages
At the . . . gages . . . cages . . .

But I fear my nonsense doesn't ring like Dolly's.

Eleanor (*who has been looking at him very steadily for the last few moments*) Evan . . . since we passed the last of those proofs in September you haven't, as far as I know, done a stroke of work. You make a mock-bow now and then to this Committee drudgery of mine . . .

Strowde It must be. But you enjoy it.

Eleanor As long as I'm busy I'm happy, I fear.

Strowde Don't be ashamed of that.

Eleanor Are we ever to begin our last volume?

Strowde Probably never. I'm sorry.

Her face does not change, magnanimity does not fail her.

Eleanor Well . . . give me good reason why, and we'll say no more about it.

His face does change. It softens; but the softening seems to age it rather. His eyes seek distances.

Strowde Do you remember the book's very first plan?

Eleanor Yes . . . if you confided it to me.

Strowde When it was to be called . . . long ago . . . The Philosophy of Machinery. A towering title!

Eleanor I was looking at your discarded chapters only the other day.

Strowde Any good?

Eleanor Very well-written.

Strowde (*with a touch of the schoolboy*) And a poser of a problem. I can quote my first sentence: How is the spirit of man to be given power over his prosperity? Most conscientiously we set to and rounded up the prosperous facts and counted the cost of them in four fat volumes. Only the problem remains.

Eleanor Quite so.

Strowde (*in a tone that might almost be thought compassionate*) You still face the future, Eleanor?

Eleanor (*with some humour*) It's coming.

Strowde (*promptly responsive*) The prospects of the break-up of the atom don't alarm you.

Eleanor If we can break it up we can teach it how to behave . . . if we choose.

Strowde I ought to respect your confident sanity. It has been as a strong wall about my more domestic self these forty years. Father bequeathed it to you.

Eleanor I think so.

Strowde I'm not a bit like him?

Eleanor Not very.

Strowde (*whimsically*) Poor Mother!

Eleanor (*gravely*) No, I believe she was a very happy woman.

Strowde (*remorseful*) My dear . . . we've been happy . . . and thank you. Forgive the gibe.

Eleanor Is there anything I could have done for you, Evan, that I have not?

Strowde (*chivalrously candid*) No indeed. You were fully yourself at sixteen. You have been unwearied in well-doing. And I'm still a naughty boy. But why is it, Eleanor, that for all your goodness and my cleverness, for all the assembled virtues of this jolly house-party, and the good-will that's going begging throughout the world . . . how is it that we shan't establish the Kingdom of Heaven on earth by Tuesday week?

Eleanor We could be content with less.

Strowde (*finely*) I used to think that was one reason we failed.

Eleanor Yes. I have some sense, even some sense of humour . . . of my own. But I am still simple enough to wonder why.

Strowde For you have never found that the whole world's turmoil is but a reflection of the anarchy in your own heart?

Eleanor No.

Strowde That's where we differ, then.

She looks rather sadly across the gulf between them.

Eleanor I fear you have always kept up appearances a little with me.

Strowde I fear you have always believed in them.

Eleanor And I'm to end by confessing I know nothing about you.

Strowde Do you want to know more than what I mean to be up to next? This time, as it happens, I can't tell you . . . for the best of reasons. Mischief, perhaps.

Eleanor Yes . . . you're a naughty boy at heart.

Strowde (*with a dash of impatience*) Where the devil else can one be anything at all? Have you never gone adventuring . . . dear, good Eleanor . . . in your secret heart?

Eleanor (*her curbed resentment just evident*) I notice you call me good in the tone you might tell your wife . . . if you had one . . . that she was pretty.

Strowde And then I escape to where there is neither prettiness nor goodness.

Eleanor I let you. Would she?

Strowde Is that why I haven't married?

Eleanor I have never enquired into your relations with women . . .

Strowde (*brotherly in the extreme*) My dear . . . don't talk like a Scottish divine addressing King Charles the Second!

Eleanor I have supposed that as a rule they weren't very civilised.

Strowde Possibly not . . . though possibly not in your sense of the word. For civilisation formulates vice as it formulates virtue, doesn't it . . . and I'm not interested in formulas.

Eleanor (*dismissing sophistry*) Our work together is to end then. Well . . . if you're going into Bellingham's government . . . if you're going to marry Joan Westbury . . .

Strowde (*not quite to be treated so, but wielding his own weapons*) And civilise the relation.

Eleanor I hadn't Joan in mind . . . and please don't pretend to think it.

Strowde But the angels in heaven, you know, are not what we should call civilised.

Eleanor When these trifles are settled, no doubt you'll tell me.

Lady Peckham, *as from church, and, as usual, in the best of spirits, comes in by the turret door. She is followed by* **Mr Kittredge.**

Lady Peckham Morning, Evan.

Strowde Been to church?

Lady Peckham Sitting among the tombs of the Serocolds. I believe I wrecked my youthful eyesight reading those epitaphs in sermon-time.

Mr Kittredge I was whisperingly commanded to translate the Latin ones.

Lady Peckham I suspect your translations, Mr Kittredge.

Mr Kittredge There are more ways than one of reading most epitaphs.

Lady Peckham I'd better write my own.

Mr Kittredge The work of a lifetime!

Strowde Stephen go with you?

Lady Peckham Haven't seen him.

Strowde In your absence the effigies are left, I fear, to set a rather chilly example.

Lady Peckham Stephen ought to go to church when he's here. It's not fair to the Rector. I like going. I much prefer saying my prayers in public . . . and it's the only place where they'll let me sing.

From the other end of the gallery comes **Dolly***'s voice, strepitant, with, 'Evan . . . stand still . . . you're the winning post . . . stick your arms out.'* **Strowde** *does as he is bid, and the rest gaze.* **Mr Kittredge** *obligingly clears a chair from the course. We hear a scurrying.* **Dolly** *and* **Joan** *are racing down the gallery neck and neck. The winning post reached,* **Joan** *flings herself in a chair, with an 'Ay de mi!'.* **Dolly** *is barefoot; a strapping young lady of twenty, abounding in healthy, thoughtless vigour.*

Dolly Did I win?

Strowde Not you!

Dolly Oh . . . I lost a pound . . . and I wanted one badly. You're nowhere!

This last is addressed to **Susan Kittredge***, who comes in conscientiously, a bad third.* **Mr Kittredge** *shakes a humorously solemn head at her.*

Mr Kittredge Susan, if you mean to invest your small capital in racing you must do better.

Dolly (*the sport*) No . . . she wasn't to pay if she lost . . . because she thinks betting's wrong.

Susan I don't. I only said I didn't bet.

Dolly What about bare feet over the gravel for a handicap anyway?

Susan I caught my dress on the big door.

Eleanor Joan . . . ought you to run like that?

Joan (*sunnily triumphant*) But I won!

Eleanor, *after this grave and spectacled remonstrance, returns to reading her report. The rest of the company settle themselves at ease,* **Dolly** *in the window seat, oblivious to chills.* **Mr Kittredge** *sets the talk to a smooth flow again.*

Mr Kittredge A granddaughter is a terrifying responsibility for an ignorant old man whose business it has been to theorise about life. But I think it a subtle form of cruelty to children to educate them in ideals that the world they will emerge into never means to abide by. So I try to fix Susan's attention upon the simple arithmetic of things. Is that wise?

Lady Peckham Mr Kittredge, you're a most accomplished flirt, and I only wish I were up to your form. Bait Eleanor for a bit . . . she's intellectual. I'll look on.

Mr Kittredge Miss Strowde is entrenched against frivolity.

Eleanor (*over the edge of the report*) No.

Mr Kittredge But it's true. As my spirit outwears its fleshly trammels I feel in it the stirrings of a quite reckless youth.

Here a towel comes flying through the window. **Dolly**, *with ready skill, catches it.*

Dolly Thank you, Oliver.

Strowde Did you feel an older man at fifty, sir?

Mr Kittredge Much.

Strowde That's cheering.

Dolly (*as a matter of general interest*) Mother . . . I've cut my great toe.

Lady Peckham Wash it with Condy.

Dolly (*and with some pride*) It's bleeding.

Lady Peckham I don't believe I've ever felt any particular age. I sleep like a log . . . I don't dream . . . and every morning at half-past seven I wake up wide and say to myself: Hullo, here I am again.

Strowde Good for you, Mildred. Be grateful.

Mr Kittredge What do you find fifty's worse symptom, Mr Strowde?

Strowde That it's easy to stop and hard to begin.

Mr Kittredge Yes . . . if one stops to think. Doing defeats itself. In disgust of mere doing men turn to destroy.

Strowde I'd enlist under Oliver for red revolution . . . but I don't think there'll be one if I enlist.

Dolly (*her head out of the window*) Do you hear that, Oliver?

Oliver's voice No.

Strowde Or I might apply for his leavings in the City. Mildred . . . do you see me as a financier-philanthropist and a secret menace to the peace of Europe?

Lady Peckham You talk worse nonsense than he does.

Mr Kittredge We're all driven to talk nonsense at times . . . when no other weapon is left us against the masters of the world . . . who have made language and logic, you see, to suit their own purposes.

Dolly Got a handkerchief, Oliver?

Oliver's voice Dash it, I fetched you a towel. Wipe your nose on the corner.

Dolly (*as one who speaks the tongue that Milton spoke*) I wish to blow my nose.

Lady Peckham Really, Dolly!

Dolly Don't you want me to be clean?

Lady Peckham Very, very clean, my darling . . . as you'll never be godly.

Dolly Thank God!

Serocold *comes down the gallery*.

Serocold Good morning, guests.

Lady Peckham Just up?

Serocold Mildred . . . I was milking a cow on behalf of your breakfast at six-thirty.

Strowde No one believes that, Stephen.

Serocold It is very nearly true.

Dolly Uncle Stephen, will you lend me a pound?

Serocold (*with ceremonially avuncular politeness*) For how long is the accommodation required?

Dolly Till I can take you on at tennis.

Serocold I do not play tennis for money.

Dolly But how mean of you when you've got some!

Serocold No Bellingham for lunch.

Lady Peckham Oh?

Dolly Well, he'd have been a bit tough . . . would Broken Bellows. That is a joke.

The joke, however, is ignored.

Serocold Telephones he has toothache. Not even neuralgia!

Lady Peckham Evan, who told him you were here?

Strowde Stephen, I trust.

Serocold He invited himself . . . he told me he wanted to meet you by accident.

Strowde You are an incorrigible intriguer.

Dolly It's Oliver! The silly old snob won't lunch with a gaol-bird. Hurrah!

Joan Perhaps he has toothache.

Serocold You've not yet met our Prime Minister, Mr Kittredge?

Mr Kittredge Not for thirty years. I shall hope for another chance.

Strowde Don't. Well . . . I'm unfair to the creature, I suppose. I retain a perverse affection for him. But the worst of democracy, don't you find, sir, is that it tends to breed these low forms of political life. You could slice bits out of Bellingham and each bit would wriggle off . . . and he'd find them all seats in Parliament and make them under-secretaries.

Dolly Vote for Brooke Bellingham . . . our only bulwark against Bolshevism.

Serocold Dolly . . . I'll send you electioneering.

Strowde Think of it. A line of alliteration between us and the abyss.

Oliver's voice A bas Belinjam! Conspuez Brooke.

Lady Peckham (*as one who is really anxious for the information*) D'you think it's coming?

Mr Kittredge Why, we are living already, you may say, under a dictation of the intellectual proletariat . . . and how few of us complain! Yes, I think we must finally be ruled by the people who provide us with what we want most in the world. Comforts, power, or wisdom. Artisan, king, or philosopher. Which will you exalt?

Strowde Not the philosopher, Mildred.

Lady Peckham Think not? Why not?

Strowde He'll always be finding fresh things for you to do without. That makes his job easy for him.

Lady Peckham (*cheerily*) I wouldn't mind a revolution . . . if Oliver and you and Stephen would run it.

Serocold I will not. I'm tired.

Lady Peckham But save us from cads.

Mr Kittredge Amen.

Strowde Yes, when we consider what the gentlemen have been capable of occasionally, God knows what the cads may do.

Eleanor (*to give – for **Mr Kittredge**'s benefit – the conversation a seemlier turn*) You're a Conservative, I fancy, Mr Kittredge . . . like most Americans I meet.

Mr Kittredge You may call me a re-actionary, Miss Strowde. Me . . . as they say in my expressive country . . . for the divine right of kings, rather than the divine rights of property.

Serocold (*the harassed farmer*) Well, anyone may have this property who likes. . . . if they'll pay me five hundred a year to manage it for them.

Lady Peckham Twenty years back, if we'd known it, was our time for a good revolution.

Dolly It's never too late to smash.

Lady Peckham I don't want any more killing.

Dolly (*radiant in the sunshine by the window*) I tell you though . . . women are going to fight in the next war. And if we hurry up I can be in the Air Force. Susan, I'll come and bomb your little head off, first thing.

Susan (*with 'New England' seriousness – as it is called elsewhere*) Please do.

From now the talk flags and loosens a little.

Serocold How long do you stay in England, Mr Kittredge?

Mr Kittredge Will you promise me a General Election by November? Susan is studying politics, and she wants to see one.

Lady Peckham (*stupent*) What on earth is she doing that for?

Serocold I can't promise.

Eleanor (*with one of her rare smiles for the girl*) I can provide you with more profitable study meanwhile.

Susan Thank you, indeed. Lady Westbury says that she'll come back to Countesbury with us, Grandfather.

Joan May I leave it at perhaps, for a little? But I've travelled Eastwards so much that it's time I went West, isn't it?

Dolly D'you mean die?

Joan I didn't.

Serocold My dear Dolly!

Dolly That's what that means.

Mr Kittredge Please do come and see us, Lady Westbury, sitting in blankets before our wigwams.

Joan What must I bring to trade with?

Mr Kittredge Your heart.

Susan Our woods are beautiful in the autumn.

Joan I thought you called it the Fall.

Mr Kittredge That sounds too sad, don't you think? But by November we're tucked up in snow very often.

Joan I may go on to Japan. Eva Currie wants me to . . . to be there by Christmas.

Lady Peckham Dolly, go and make yourself half-way decent for lunch.

Dolly (*who knows an order when she hears it*) Yes, Mother.

Strowde Die . . . how we hate the word! And we none of us really believe we're going to.

Lady Peckham I believe it.

Strowde Oh, we're ready to surrender what we've done with and don't value . . .

Eleanor The work of our minds lives on.

Strowde By taking thought to? Show me a living faith, and I'll show it you careless of life. Dolly there, in her pride of body . . .

Dolly I say!

Strowde . . . would jump out of that window for sixpence.

Dolly I'll do it for a pound. Oliver's underneath.

Strowde But this world of the mind we've made for ourselves is cumbered with things that we won't let die. Ask Oliver . . . if I yield to temptation and go back to trying to help govern this ungrateful country whether he'll promise to see me decently assassinated when I've done my devil-most?

Dolly (*her head out of the window*) Oliver, will you please see Evan decently assassinated?

Oliver's voice It hasn't been settled yet who's to be let off living . . . but he may choose his lamp-post on the chance.

Strowde You'll be content, Mildred, if a little of you lives on in that child?

Lady Peckham Heaven forbid I should worry her!

Dolly What a disgusting thought!

Serocold Then don't you think it.

Dolly I won't!

And, every bit herself, she sets out down the gallery.

Strowde Dolly, I'll toss you for a pound.

Dolly (*at this gleam of great hope*) Oo! Suppose I lose.

Strowde A month's credit.

Dolly Oo!

But, too fearful of the risk, **Dolly** *disappears.*

Strowde The life of the mind is a prison in which we go melancholy mad. Better turn dangerous . . . and be done away with.

Dolly's *voice is heard from the end of the gallery.*

Dolly Evan.

Strowde Hullo!

Dolly I'll risk it. Heads!

Strowde *takes out a coin and tosses it.*

Mr Kittredge There is, of course, that faculty we call the soul by which we may escape into uncharted regions.

Strowde Heads it is!

Dolly (*her voice is fervent*) Thank God!

Mr Kittredge But the rulers of men seldom seek them. Very naturally!

Joan Why?

Mr Kittredge A confusing place, the world where the soul wanders . . . made of mud and light . . . and the mud sticks and the light dazzles. Lonely . . . yet in it we can keep nothing of our own. For entering we abandon everything but hope . . . and hope is a lure.

Joan Towards what?

Mr Kittredge This is a secret.

Joan They can overhear.

Mr Kittredge . . . well-known, and disbelieved. It's so discouraging. The soul of man is in the making still . . . we are experiments to be tried again and yet again . . . and the light lures us to extinction. Can you rule a country prosperously on such a creed? No . . . have a comfortable Kingdom of Heaven just round the corner . . . or who will take a step towards it?

Strowde Besides, Stephen, you don't want this country governed.

Serocold Truthfully, I think we want it kept amused at the moment . . . till we see what's going to happen next.

The three men begin to move down the gallery. **Susan**, *attentive, has already been standing for a moment or two by the turret door. Some moments ago too,* **Eleanor** *came to the end of her report and her brother's notes on it, and she has been sitting – her face unchanging, but particularly still.*

Strowde So I'm not your man.

Eleanor Evan.

Strowde (*pausing*) Yes.

Eleanor (*a little cryptically*) Are these notes for vulgar reading?

Strowde (*even more so*) My legacy to you.

Mr Kittredge (*casually, to his host*) I don't quite understand why Mr Bellingham hasn't dissolved before this.

Serocold We can't get defeated in the House on any likely issue.

Strowde Prisoned minds, Mr Kittredge . . . and a world of power to be wielded that might stagger the purpose of a Caesar. What the deuce will happen next? For all that I don't much care, I shake in my shoes.

The three men have disappeared.

Lady Peckham What notes, Eleanor?

Eleanor Evan poking fun at my report.

Susan *goes out by the turret door. The three women, without looking, are conscious of her disappearance.*

Lady Peckham That's a strange, still girl. Is she stone-cold inside, or just on the boil?

Joan I see great beauty in her.

Lady Peckham (*her eyebrows up*) Do you!

Joan It'll shine out in time.

Lady Peckham I don't understand Americans. They're so solemn.

Joan, *light of foot, moves slowly down the gallery.*

Eleanor They take things seriously.

Lady Peckham And so devilish gay when they're gay.

Eleanor I don't find them hard to understand.

A moment's silence, now that the two are alone; then **Lady Peckham** *cocks her head with what, unkindly, might be called a grin.*

Lady Peckham We two old harridans, Eleanor!

Eleanor (*mustering enough humour*) Thank you.

Lady Peckham Between us, I expect, we've tasted most of the fat and the lean of life. Well . . . nothing tastes like it.

Eleanor You're worried about Oliver.

Lady Peckham Not a bit.

Eleanor What took him to that meeting? Who encourages him in this foolishness?

Lady Peckham I think he spins it out of his own inside.

Eleanor Well, as long as he behaves himself! . . .

Lady Peckham I hope he'll do more than that.

Eleanor (*with a will-not-be-exasperated sigh*) We're at odds, I'm afraid, Mildred.

Lady Peckham (*plumply*) We always were.

The distant lunch-gong is heard.

Lady Peckham I should get Evan married to Joan Westbury if I were you. That might settle him. Or are you too jealous of her?

Eleanor What an amazing question!

Lady Peckham You're so consistent, Eleanor . . . that's what's the matter with you.

Eleanor There's little I could do . . . in any case.

Lady Peckham Were you ever in love?

Eleanor, *for a second, does not mean to answer. Then – why shouldn't she?*

Eleanor Once.

Lady Peckham What happened?

Eleanor (*after a moment's appropriate emptiness*) Nothing.

Lady Peckham I believe you. (*She doesn't in the least mean this to be brutal; commiserative rather. Then she goes on.*) If you hate Joan, try putting a little poison in her soup . . . and then getting on your knees to ask God to forgive you for it. That'd teach you something.

They have collected their belongings, and make a move now for lunch.

Eleanor A little hard on her!

Lady Peckham Well, considering everybody in this world means considering nobody, you know. . . .

They pass down the gallery.

Scene Four

It is Sunday evening about ten o'clock (summer-time). **Joan** *is sitting alone by the open window; the clear sky still glows a little. She has turned out the light near her, but those farther down the gallery are apparent. After a moment* **Oliver**'s *voice is heard from below.*

Oliver Lady Westbury.

Joan Yes.

Oliver May I come up?

Joan You may. (*When his way of coming up is apparent she calls out.*) Oliver! You'll kill yourself!!

His head and shoulders appear at the window. He stops, a little breathless. This is something of a feat for a one-armed man, though a creeper may be helping him a little.

Oliver That wasn't so bad. Now comes the pull. If you take hold we'll both tumble. Hold your breath and think hard. Now!

With great effort he flings himself over the window-sill into the room, and rolls on the floor. But he picks himself up lightly enough.

Oliver And I'm not drunk, am I?

Joan You shouldn't run such risks.

Oliver I was last night . . . on one half-glass of claret. Nobody noticed. Tonight I've had a bottle of port to my own whack . . . and I'm so sober that it hurts. May I sit and talk to you?

Joan Yes.

He sits on the window seat facing her, not very close.

Oliver Shall I try not to talk about myself?

Joan No, I'd like you to.

But not many people would find her easy to talk to at all, she is so still and so aloof. There is a little silence.

Oliver Why won't Evan take me on?

Joan He hasn't told me.

Oliver They say you're going to marry him.

Joan (*her eyebrows lifting*) Do they? (*Then whimsically.*) Well . . . shall I?

Oliver Don't ask me. I'm in love with you too.

She lets the simple speech find its full value in her ears, then says as simply . . .

Joan Thank you, Oliver.

Oliver (*in a happy, quite childish surprise*) D'you mean it?

Joan Didn't you expect so much as a thank you?

Oliver May I say just once . . . I love you . . . like that? The echoes won't be troublesome.

They have not moved, either of them. She is listening in the stillness to other boys' voices.

Joan I live among echoes, my dear. But you mustn't.

Oliver I won't. (*His voice hardens to a perversely obstinate tone.*) What am I to do, please, if Evan won't take me on?

Joan Is he your only hope?

Oliver (*with deliberation*) He's in my way.

Joan What does that mean?

Oliver Sounds like a plot to blow him sky-high one day as he walks into Downing Street. I think I did make Uncle Stephen believe at dinner that I'd been sworn into at least one secret society . . . for all he pretended not to.

Joan It's Mr Serocold's business, I suppose, to take such things seriously.

Oliver Yes, it is. So why doesn't he? Tell them the truth and they don't believe you!

Joan I will.

Oliver The men with the secrets that count will know each other when the time comes, won't they?

Joan Yes, that sounds more dangerous.

Oliver There'll be nothing doing else.

Joan Why is Evan in your way?

Oliver (*launched on the full youthful enjoyment of a talk about oneself*) I wonder what it is in one that picks out a man or a woman. Evan was picked out for me, you may say. Mother has always been fond of him. My father was fond of him. I remember saying once, when I was eight, that I meant to grow up to be like him.

Joan And you're not fond of many people.

Oliver I hate most people . . . when I come to think of it.

Joan Is that why it hurts you to be sober?

Oliver I shall swear off drink again, though . . . it just doesn't do not to know what a glass of claret's going to cost you.

One half of her disposition towards him is as simple (though by no means the same) as his towards her. But the other half is – in involuntary defence perhaps – coloured by the ironic superiority of forty-something to twenty-something.

Joan But tell me how one soberly hates people. I don't think I know.

Oliver Well, you can't love the mob, surely to goodness! Because that's to be one of them . . . chattering and scolding and snivelling and cheering . . . maudlin drunk, if you like! I learned to be soldier enough to hate a mob. There's discipline in Heaven. If I can't love a thing I must hate it.

Joan How long have you been so unhappy?

Oliver Don't think I'm out after happiness, please.

Joan (*gravely*) Do you ever pray, Oliver?

Oliver (*prompt*) All the time. Whenever I'd a hard job on in the City I'd walk there in the morning praying like fun. If I hadn't prayed my way in at this window I'd have broken my neck. I pray all the time.

Joan How old are you? I forget.

His face takes on a deeper shade than any yet; and all the fantastic flourish goes out of his speech.

Oliver I believe I'm still eighteen.

Joan How's that?

Oliver Years don't count for much, do they . . . against memory, say? Parts of me seem to forget all about the war . . . but there's some part of me doesn't. A shell missed me outside Albert and did for my watch. I could shake it and it would tick for a bit . . . but the spring was gone. I've an idea I don't grow any older now . . . and when I come to die it'll seem an odd out-of-date sort of catastrophe. I'm furious that I'm still alive at all. Perhaps it's that makes me hate people. I used to pray night after night at school that I'd be killed when I got to France.

Joan (*moved, but more deeply by memories*) That was perverse of you . . . to be fighting against our prayers.

Oliver Oh, once I was there I didn't mind saving my skin. But I tell you . . . this is a beast of a world to have left on one's hands.

A little silence; then **Joan** *rallies to the commonplace.*

Joan Well, what are you going to do about it?

Oliver Destroy.

Joan What?

Oliver All I can learn to.

Joan Didn't you see enough destruction?

Oliver A futile sort. My firm bought a lot of shares, and we thought we had a mine in Eastern Galicia . . . so I was sent out two years ago to see. The town was a rubbish heap. Typhus had done well too. But there they were breeding children to build it all up again . . . that being the cheapest way. So if we can't do some better destroying than that who'll ever be able to make a fresh start? Save me from weary people with their No More War. What we want is a real one.

Joan And where's the enemy?

Oliver If I knew where I shouldn't be sitting here helpless. I'm looking for him. But we're tricked so easily . . . on from the time that we're tricked into getting born! This world's all tricks, isn't it? Well, it's something to feel free from the greedy instinct to live.

Joan (*puzzled, kindly, and as curious as it is in her to be*) And what has Evan to teach you?

Oliver I want to find out how it is he has failed.

Joan Has he failed, then?

Oliver (*a trifle savagely*) Yes . . . and you'll have to comfort him for it if you marry him.

Joan (*provokingly, rather*) But wise men like your uncle say that if he'll take office again, now the bunglers have had a chance . . . there's his career still. And he wasn't a failure in office before.

Oliver He'll need more comfort than that, if I'm right about him. Nothing's much easier, is it, than to make that sort of success if you've the appetite for it. Find a few ready-made notions to exploit. But Evan set out to get, past all tricks, to the heart of things . . . didn't he? Don't you know? Don't you love him? Are you weary of the puzzle too?

Joan The very tallest of us ask for comfort sometimes.

Oliver Is it a stone-dead heart of things . . . and dare no one say so when he finds out?

Joan I suppose one never would dare.

Oliver Evan won't take me on because he's afraid of me.

Joan (*the one-time mother in her sharply asserting itself*) Nonsense!

Oliver I can tell he's afraid of me. Why? Because he knows that I know he has failed. And he knows that I hate him for it.

Joan Very wicked nonsense, Oliver!

Oliver (*flinging out harshly*) Oh, do him in with comfort if you like. Trick him. Do your best, dear Evan, and no man can do more in this worst-of-all-possible worlds! If he had any self-respect left in him he'd thank you to hate him rather.

Joan (*with a flash of inspiration*) You're very like him.

Oliver (*struck, though he could not say why*) Am I?

Joan Oh . . . not in any ordinary sense.

Oliver We're all like Mother to look at . . . more or less.

A short silence, while they turn back from this blind alley.

Joan (*lightly enough*) And how is it . . . with all else to be thrown on the rubbish heap . . . that you love me?

Oliver You're out of reach.

Joan (*as if she did indeed, and better than ever he could . . .*) Yes . . . I understand.

Oliver So I'm not jealous of the fellow. But I rather wish I hadn't told you.

Joan Why?

Oliver (*boyhood having its way*) Or that you'd laughed . . . that would set me free again. Please set me free.

Joan Am I to ask Evan to take you on?

Oliver (*obsessed*) Yes . . . for I want to be free of him too. Somehow he's right athwart my understanding of things, though I can't tell why. And I won't take a step that I can't see clear. Then I shan't take many . . . is the answer. I've been told that before.

Joan If you came to understand him you might learn not to hate him.

Oliver Yes, there's that danger!

Joan *surveys him for a moment, then says with evident intent . . .*

Joan Oliver . . . you never laugh now, I've noticed.

Oliver At myself?

Joan Well, that's a simple form of destruction. You might try it to begin with.

He stands up, stung, as she meant he should be.

Oliver Good-night.

Joan I've made you angry.

Oliver (*pride quite forbidding response*) No, I was off on my walk when I saw you at the window.

Joan Every night . . . wet or fine . . . how many miles?

Oliver Seven or eight . . . till I'm too tired to think.

Joan (*more sorrowful for him than she can say, or he could understand*) The night is all one's own, isn't it . . . if only the inconsiderate sun wouldn't rise.

Oliver (*taking refuge in bravado*) Is this how you comfort m e ? There's no need, thank you. I've not failed yet. (*Then, for a last shot, as with charming impudence.*) Good-night, Joan.

Joan But mind your prayers, Oliver. (*He turns, rather amazed.*) For innermost prayers are answered . . . they must be . . . and in mockery sometimes.

Oliver Something in me w a s killed, d'you think?

Joan Not stone-dead, we'll hope.

Oliver No, Joan . . . we won't hope, whatever else we do.

He opens the door into the turret.

Joan Not by the window again?

Oliver Too easy.

Joan (*in the same soft, clear voice that welcomed him*) Good-night, then, my dear.

He goes away.

Scene Five

It is Monday morning, a little after nine. **Sir Leslie Heriot**, *in motoring things, comes striding along as if looking for some-one. He is an ebullient, middle-aged man, pleasant, coarse-grained, and always a little louder than, we'll hope, he means to be. If anything is written quite unmistakably upon him, it is success and an intense enjoyment of it. He glances out of the window; then faces down the gallery again just as* **Strowde***'s voice is heard from the other end.*

Strowde Hullo, Heriot.

Heriot Hullo, Strowde.

Strowde What are you doing here?

Heriot Came to run Stephen up to town. Good morning, Miss Strowde.

Eleanor's voice Good morning, Sir Leslie.

Strowde *appears.* **Eleanor** *must be lagging behind.*

Strowde You must have left early.

Heriot Seven o'clock. I've not been at home . . . week-ending at Eckersley . . . it's sixty miles . . . the road must be better through Basingstoke. How are you?

Strowde I'm alive.

Sir Leslie *takes up an habitual 'I-never-beat-about-the-bush' attitude.*

Heriot Get any talk with Bellingham yesterday?

Strowde He didn't come.

Heriot (*flavourishly*) I knew he wouldn't.

Strowde How's your job nowadays?

Heriot (*who, oddly enough, is really a modest soul*) There's enough to do without making more. But I'm up to the trick of it this time. Let your office fellows pull the cart while you drive.

Strowde That is undoubtedly the whole art of government.

Heriot (*as one who reverences the process*) And take time to think. I used to keep my nose buried in papers eight hours a day. Now I send for the men who write them . . . there's a new lot of quite good young men . . . and size t h e m up instead. (*Turning his head.*) How is my Women's Industry Committee getting on, Miss Strowde?

Eleanor *now appears.*

Eleanor We're making the interim report you asked for.

Heriot (*with entire honesty*) Did I?

Eleanor Though I think it's a pity to mangle the subject.

Heriot Oh no . . . no, no! Be practical . . . that's the great thing. (*He just does not smack* **Strowde** *on the back*.) Does this fellow help you out at all?

Eleanor, *who – how surprising! – has not come to talk to* **Sir Leslie,** *is searching the writing-table.*

Eleanor Surely I did leave my spectacles. . . .

Strowde (*answering Heriot*) Not at all.

Heriot And the great history's finished?

Eleanor No.

Heriot I hear you're coming out into politics.

Eleanor I think not.

Heriot But do . . . it's great fun. No, perhaps you're right. We need intellectual spade-work. . . .

Strowde (*having found the spectacles*) Here they are.

Eleanor Thank you.

Heriot (*magnanimously overriding the neglect of him for a pair of spectacles*) And I take off my hat . . . I do indeed . . . to this steady self-sacrifice of all personal ambition by which public men profit . . . or should profit. (*Then in his never-beat-about-the-bush attitude again.*) Strowde . . . have we got to fight you at the election?

Strowde Who said I was going to stand?

Heriot (*omniscient*) But you are.

Eleanor *has now passed out of sight.*

Strowde I've been asked to.

Heriot I know all about it.

Strowde When is it to be . . . secrets apart?

Heriot (*as colleague to colleague*) I doubt if the old man has started to make up his mind. November . . . February. We could drop the Insurance Bill if the Chinese business would straighten out.

Strowde You think you'll come back?

Heriot Who else can? (*As brother to brother.*) Look here
. . . is it only Bellingham stands in the way?

Strowde Of . . . ?

Heriot . . . your coming back to us?

Strowde (*blandly*) Oh, dear, no.

Heriot What else?

Strowde Why do you want me?

Heriot (*benevolent, warm, but, one fears, patronising*) My
dear fellow . . . am I to flatter you?

Strowde (*a shade subtly*) If you think it advisable.

Heriot Well, I won't. I'll come straight to the point. I
came here this morning to come to the point with you.

Strowde (*as he would encourage a child*) Good.

Heriot *now speaks, as he would tell you, with a due sense of
the subject's importance.*

Heriot It's two years since I told Bellingham how vital I
felt it to be for the party to get you back. I've given him
till now to make it up with you. Well, now I'm ready to
say that sine qua non . . . sine qua non me! . . . We must
find you a seat again, and a seat in the Cabinet, after the
election.

Strowde (*easily*) I've found the seat, Heriot.

Heriot Even if we fight you there?

Strowde Do your damnedest.

Heriot I don't want to.

Strowde *now takes the rudder.*

Strowde Bellingham's getting a bit feeble, is he?

Heriot (*innocently pricking an ear*) D'you hear people say
that?

Strowde If he'll take me at your dictation it'll show the gang, won't it, that you've got a stranglehold on him? And it'll show you that he feels you've got the party behind you.

Heriot (*playfully disapproving*) That's very tortuous.

Strowde Tortuous . . . but not very tortuous.

Heriot (*the statesman again*) Bellingham is a leader to whom I have been consistently loyal . . . and to whom I shall be as consistently loyal as long as he is my leader. Does that imply that I am to sacrifice the interests of the party rather than . . . put pressure on him?

Strowde (*aggravatingly unimpressed*) How soon do you think you'll be strong enough to kick him out?

Heriot (*with true dignity*) Strowde . . . I cannot humour your brutality. I am a realist, I hope . . . but matters of this magnitude do surely demand a certain amenity of mind for their discussion.

Strowde (*all unmoved*) As a detached observer, I've been giving you a couple of years.

Heriot (*nearing exasperation*) If you think this intellectual ruthlessness of yours is a strength, you're wrong . . . it's a weakness. People don't answer to it . . . and political facts most certainly never answer to it.

Strowde (*tart*) What the devil, my dear Heriot, is a p o l i t i c a l fact?

Heriot (*placable*) Now, now, don't let's begin generalising. We're men of affairs. As an under-secretary the old man declares he never knew what you'd say next. No wonder he thinks that in the Cabinet you'll be the death of him.

Strowde I daresay I should be.

Heriot (*ignoring that point*) But I tell him we must consider your essential value. You certainly will find him feebler. But after a year or two of the old hard grind I'm pretty confident you'd find yourself . . . subdued to what you work in.

Strowde And with?

Heriot Or with. The potter's hand! Statesmanship . . . so I phrase it . . . (*And he enjoys phrasing it.*) . . . is the art of dealing with men as they most illogically are, and with the time as it nearly always most unfortunately is. We hope for a better . . . we strive for a better. Never let us cease to proclaim that. But the day's work must be done.

Upon which wise maxim he comes to a full close.

Strowde (*casually*) You're making a fool of yourself over the Trusts.

Heriot (*who is a keen picker-up of good ideas*) D'you think so? Why do you think so?

Strowde Your figures are wrong.

Heriot They're official figures.

Strowde They'll mean nothing two years hence. If the Act makes the business attractive its finance will be swamped . . . and if it doesn't the big companies won't work it . . . then the little ones can't.

Heriot *swallows this, somewhat wryly. But, confound it,* **Strowde** *is worth having to work with.*

Heriot Destructive criticism . . . not to be ignored on that account . . . Salomons said something of the sort to me six months ago. But we are faced with the demand for a Bill.

Strowde It being the business of the legislature to legislate.

Heriot God knows I'd be glad to drop it. But that'd only make room for the emergence of several most awkward questions . . . just as the election's coming on. Well, if nobody works the damned Act at least it can't do any harm. (*And he throws the business where he so safely throws all business, upon the stream of time.*) Where were we?

Strowde (*casually*) Do you mind my sister joining the discussion?

Heriot Not at all (*And glad to re-assert some superiority.*) I never make mysteries.

Strowde (*lifting his voice a trifle*) Eleanor . . . spare us a minute.

Heriot And I'm sure Miss Strowde is the soul of discretion.

Eleanor *appears again.*

Eleanor Yes.

Strowde (*an enigmatic eye on* **Eleanor**) We two have worked in unison for so long.

Heriot, *with a second person – and a woman! – to deal with, becomes very oracular.*

Heriot Well . . . to write history or to make it . . . that is the question.

Eleanor (*drily, finely*) The writing should warn one to be rather more particular in the making, Sir Leslie.

Strowde (*the unkindness pleasantly masked*) The practical question is . . . could Heriot and I between us get rid of Bellingham the sooner? I might put that problem to the old gentleman if he sends for me.

Heriot (*with a gape*) Thank you.

Strowde Adding, of course, that you scouted the very idea when I so much as hinted it . . . as you do.

Heriot I naturally do.

Strowde (*hitting clean*) That's your method. It isn't mine. In some things perhaps I'm even less of a mystery-maker than you. Bellingham's sixty-seven. He has poor health. He has been twice Prime Minister. He ought to be able to measure by now the amount of annoyance he can endure.

And you don't suppose that when you were putting your sine qua non this idea didn't occur to him.

Heriot (*brought to something very like sulkiness*) I can't help his suspicious nature.

Strowde But if we d i d n ' t get rid of him the sooner the intermediate friction would not, on the balance, be profitable to the country. (*Then, venturing rather far in irony*.) And we must think of our country, Heriot.

Heriot Your humour eludes me.

Strowde (*infinitely businesslike and cheerful*) Then there's a further possible question . . . how long would it take me after to get rid of you?

To this, however, **Heriot** *rises, happily, like a man.*

Heriot I bet you a thousand pounds you don't.

Strowde I'll bet you a set of my history in half-calf to the Premiership that I do.

Heriot Let's be serious. Serocold's waiting for me.

Strowde You repeat your offer?

Heriot What's your alternative?

Strowde Shall I sit below the gangway and snipe at you?

Heriot You've been getting your eye in lately, I've noticed.

Strowde The Chinese meeting? You deserved that.

Recovering his vantage. He is, after all, a Minister of State, and Strowde – !

Heriot Excellent speech. Personally, I'd be grateful to you. Fighting keeps me up to the mark . . . and with a timid public opinion it's the man in office who scores. Look at this present opposition . . . sitting like a row of turnips . . .

Strowde (*finely*) Or shall I stick to intellectual spade-work?

Heriot (*who, within his range, be it noted, is anything but a fool*) You won't. You're restless. You'll get back to the House and you won't have enough to do there. You'll grow depressed and dyspeptic and you'll take to making acid interruptions inaudible in the press gallery. You'll find yourself chief of a little group of righteous high-brows in passionate agreement upon abstract principles, without an interest in common and considering themselves insulted if you ask them to vote solid.

Strowde (*with some genuine admiration*) Now here is a wise man, Eleanor . . . a disillusioned man.

Heriot (*genuinely pleased with the compliment*) Don't look at me so sternly, Miss Strowde.

Eleanor It's an effect of the sunlight on my spectacles, Sir Leslie. Please forgive them!

Heriot's *glance goes by chance down the gallery.*

Heriot Who's this?

Strowde Lady Westbury.

Heriot Do I know her?

Strowde You must have known Mark Westbury.

Heriot Oh yes . . . useful fellow . . . Egypt did for him.

So much for Mark. **Strowde** *sticks to his hard jesting.*

Strowde If you really want to ease matters with Bellingham I should tell him of our bet. The prospect of a fight over the inheritance would amuse him. He wouldn't think the worse of you . . . and he'd like me the better for it.

Heriot (*ruefully appreciative*) So he would . . . the old scoundrel!

Joan *appears.*

Joan Good morning.

Sir Leslie *beamingly descends on her.*

Heriot How d'you do, Lady Westbury? I fear you don't remember me . . . Leslie Heriot.

Joan (*with shadowless courtesy*) Yes, indeed. You once gave me tea in your big room in Whitehall after my husband had been waiting for you three hours and a half.

Heriot (*to encourage her*) Strong Indian tea . . . and you hated it.

Joan (*poising the words*) Not the tea, I'm sure.

Heriot The cake, then . . . office cake!

Joan (*not having a mallet and chisel handy*) Perhaps it was the cake.

Having made this success, **Sir Leslie** *turns the light of his assurance on* **Strowde**.

Heriot When are you coming to town, Strowde?

Strowde Wednesday morning.

Heriot Lunch with me.

Strowde All right.

Heriot (*benevolent*) Good-bye, Miss Strowde. Forgive me. You'll thank me. Don't think me a cynic. I respect ideals. But I test them . . . as life tests them.

Strowde (*with a mischievous smile*) My sister really thinks of us both as being about ten years old. I've been a trouble to her, Heriot . . . and her fear is now that I may corrupt your happy faith in life.

Heriot (*infinitely robust*) Try.

Eleanor Nothing would, Sir Leslie, I'm sure.

Heriot (*in bright innocence*) I do feel young . . . and look at the work I get through.

Serocold's *voice is heard from the end of the gallery.*

Serocold Heriot, are you ready?

Heriot Coming.

Serocold I must be at the office by eleven.

But **Strowde** *grapples him with a voice that has, indeed, more than a little steel in it.*

Strowde But if we're to be fellow-conspirators, we must agree on a creed.

Heriot A programme?

Strowde The father and mother of a programme.

Heriot Well?

Strowde (*adding, for reassurance, a touch of humour*) I believe, for instance . . . Heriot, when I've won that bet I'll open Cabinet meetings by having this repeated, all standing . . . I believe that men cease to be fools to become knaves, and that we must govern them by fear and with lies. They will work under threat of starvation. Greed makes them cunning . . .

Serocold's voice Evan . . . I shall be late back.

Strowde Wait a minute! . . . but desire makes them dangerous. If they rightly remembered yesterday, they wouldn't get out of their beds tomorrow. Sleep's the great ally of the rulers of this world . . . for it rounds each day with oblivion.

Heriot *never does quite know when this fellow is serious.*

Heriot That's a creed I should keep to myself.

Strowde That, I know, is the rule. But . . . as between souls of discretion . . . don't you agree?

Heriot Seriously, I do not. And I take these things seriously, Strowde . . . or I shouldn't be where I am. I am a democrat . . . with certain reservations. (*He interrupts himself for a benevolent . . .*) Good-bye, Lady Westbury.

Joan Good-bye.

Heriot *now takes* **Strowde***'s arm and starts down the gallery as a ship might leave a bay, with such swelling sails.*

Heriot I have an almost unbounded faith in the ultimate perfectibility of man. I think that the political, the social, the ethical progress of the centuries are evidence of it. But mind you . . . the freer the democracy the firmer must be the guiding hands. Use force when necessary. And do not expect to find in the masses a grasp of the principles upon which we base our actions. Appeal rather to the heart of the people . . .

The two men disappear. The two women wait, smiles suppressed for a decent thirty seconds.

Eleanor Well?

Joan (*evenly*) I remember Mark saying after that interview . . . Deliver us from clean-shaven young Ministers, with busts of Napoleon on the mantelpiece. And he has grown vulgar.

Eleanor He caricatures himself now. Men of that crude and abounding vitality of mind seldom mature . . . fortunately. When they do they're dangerous. Evan shouldn't poke fun at him so recklessly.

Joan Oh . . . by the time the sting penetrates he's thinking of something else.

Strowde *returns.*

Strowde One can't help liking him.

Eleanor (*very definitely*) I can.

Strowde You prefer people all of a moral piece. Our Heriots are stitchings from the rag-bag. There are sound bits in him. After all, we British have had the cutting-up of some good minds for this last generation or so. He's not one of God's elect. However, he offers to represent u s. The puzzled human elector finds a bit of his favourite stuff in the patchwork, and says . . . Ah, this is my man. Heriot has courage and good health . . . and he's a success.

Eleanor What is his offer worth?

Strowde (*unexpectedly*) It was worth while manœuvring him into making it. The next move is Bellingham's. No hurry for mine.

And this seems, in a flash, to release **Eleanor** *from some inhibition. For she speaks as she has not yet spoken.*

Eleanor Thank you for letting me hear your talk, Evan. I see I can be no more use to you. You're my brother . . . I thought I knew you . . . you've become a stranger to me. I fear there's only one thing I believe in . . . choosing a cause to serve it single-mindedly. When you first took office, after six months you rode open-eyed for a fall. I saw that, if no one else did. I worked at your book with you. Your brains went into it, no doubt. My life went into it. What does it mean to me to feel that if I burned every copy now, you'd hardly shrug your shoulders . . . and to find this task of mine . . . which you've taught me, and thank you . . . this report spattered with your mockeries! I sat up last night crying over it like a child over a copy-book. From today, please, let's pretend to be like-minded no more. Turn in your tracks and be the thing you despise. Does it matter? The curse is on you, it seems, of coming at last to despise whatever you do and are. I'm sorry . . . but I must save myself . . . my soul, if you like . . . from despair.

A silence follows, noticeable, though her voice was never lifted. Then **Strowde** *says, as quietly . . .*

Strowde That's clearly put . . . and quite indisputable.

Eleanor Perhaps I shouldn't have said so much before you, Joan. Perhaps I've been right to.

Strowde I shall now have to advertise . . . Wanted, a political hostess . . .

He pauses, his sentence unfinished. In the silence **Eleanor**, *unhurriedly, but with neither another word nor a look, gets up and goes out by the turret door.*

Joan Upright, downright Eleanor!

Strowde (*as if following out his uninterrupted thought*) Or will you save me a sovereign's worth of agony column, Joan, and take the job?

She does not answer at once, and when she does, it is as if some other woman, far away, were speaking.

Joan No, I can't.

Strowde *looks at her; then refuses the words' meaning.*

Strowde Am I to tell Bellingham and his gang, then, to go to the devil without me? By all means.

Joan That's another matter.

Strowde Do you mean you won't marry me, Joan?

Joan I can't.

Now he must take the meaning, and he does. He allows himself a moment to recover reasonableness.

Strowde How long since you made up your mind to say this? You could have given me some sign. I've been taking things too much for granted.

Joan (*rather helplessly*) I did, too.

Strowde (*keeping control at the cost of a loosening rein*) What has happened? What have I done? What has changed you?

Joan (*dully, almost*) I love you still.

Strowde Don't say that.

Joan (*as if she would get to that far-away woman if she could*) But . . . let me be.

Strowde (*fiercely, even brutally*) So I did! . . .

Joan Like a fool? You leave that unspoken. (*Then pitifully.*) Do I seem to be cheating you now?

Strowde (*recovering reasonableness, kindliness too*) Let's say no more for the moment. I see what's wrong. We mustn't

try to live out the fag-end of a difficult past. We must start
fresh.

Joan (*with a little smile*) When the war was at its worst,
they say you were at your hopefullest. I see why they want
you to work with . . . You'll lose little in losing the last of
me.

He sits close by her, friendly, brotherly; but more.

Strowde I want you.

*She turns and looks at him, eyes to eyes. But her look is
fearful.*

Joan How did you find your way into the dream that my
true life is? I wish you never had. The selfish soul of me
might have died the sooner, left lonely . . . and who'd
have been the wiser then? I could have done my duty to
the end . . . married again, even . . . headed a dinner-table
. . . not yours, though!

*She does her best to make light of the strange trouble; and he
helps her.*

Strowde Why not mine as well as another?

Joan Should I have liked you if I'd never loved you, I
wonder?

Strowde The answer is that you did, you know.

Joan And we couldn't let well alone. But you're free of me
now . . . I set you free. Oh, this has been a jealous devil,
like all barren things.

Strowde Barren?

Joan (*her voice now echoing all the meaning of the dreadful
word*) Ask your heart . . . and your own life ever since . . .
God forgive us! It isn't that one sits idle. I've known how
to be kind . . . I've hated evil . . . when I've suffered loss
I've suffered indeed. But none of it has truly mattered. My
boys . . . yes, a bad blow. And when Eleanor came tip-
toeing with the news from Cairo I let grief have its will of

me . . . I knew I so safely could . . . and I slipped the more easily out of its clutches back into my dream. And we agreed to be glad, you remember, that I could still care for Mark.

Strowde Yes. I said I understood that. I fear I lied to you. I never did.

Joan He was very good to me. So would you be. One must live honourably. But all the while I was half-ashamed to be giving him what I valued so little. And you want what's left!

Strowde My dear, don't despise me for that. I won't lose your love in winning you.

Joan But you would.

Strowde Why? Why ever?

Joan We chose to dream. The empty beauty would vanish at a touch.

He sees defeat. But he tries to outflank it.

Strowde This is merely morbid, Joan.

Joan (*responding readily enough to his common sense. This, truly, is what is so hopeless*) Isn't it? Try beating me. I've laughed at myself. I've prayed . . . these past weeks with your eyes on me . . . for some miracle to give birth in me to anything wholly human that I could bring you. (*With a sudden change of front, though.*) I do think that if I could once go quite obliviously to sleep I might wake up different.

Strowde I didn't know you weren't sleeping well again.

She turns a little desperate for a moment.

Joan Evan, has one to die to sleep? Well, surely then there'll be an end to this terrible constant consciousness of being . . . of purposeless being.

Strowde You're not, in your doctor's sense, ailing, are you, except for this? You've seemed so well and so gay.

Joan He can't make me sleep . . . and he can't keep me still. I'm one of Nature's pranks, I tell him . . . body and mind, quite conscienceless now, quite irresponsible.

He makes now a new and a different effort.

Strowde You'd better marry me, Joan. I'll find you lots to do . . . work you to death by midnight. You shall sleep like a log and wake every morning a different woman. I'll be a perfectly selfish husband, I promise you. Think how a bride will deck my election platform! And you must flatter me, please, with constant affection . . . for my brainwork's too apt to be dry and cruel. And we shall need to go soft a little . . . to be genial. (*But the helpful irony breaks down quite.*) Oh, my dear love! Oh, my dear . . . my dear!

She is helpless to sustain him.

Joan I'd like to make you happy, too. And Oliver told me last night that he loved me.

Strowde (*struck*) Why do you suddenly tell me that?

Joan (*with no further intention*) It's interesting and à propos. He was standing just where you're standing now. Do what you can for the boy. He finds life hard at the moment. Give him a hand.

Strowde (*gravely deferent*) If you say so.

Joan Thank you.

Strowde Give me yours.

With an amused smile she lifts it and looks at it rather disparagingly.

Joan This?

Strowde (*as a friend*) Marry me.

Joan (*taking the privilege offered*) Some other time! Oh, can't we pretend that there'll be some other possible time?

Strowde No other but the time one wastes and comes to want.

With baffling swiftness she has changed.

Joan And the eternity in which we met.

Strowde In which I won you.

Joan Yes, Evan . . . truly, utterly.

Strowde (*violently breaking out*) Don't mock me. There's nothing to separate us . . . and here we stand apart. (*He has not moved her, he has not even recalled her to this their battleground.*) Where are you, Joan . . . where are you?

She shakes her head sadly.

Joan Go to work and forget me.

Strowde (*viciously*) I'd better. Indeed, it has been a barren business . . . you're right.

Joan With everything real made bitter to you?

Strowde Worse, my dear . . . tasteless. And I've sampled much. Would it help to find things to forgive me?

Joan (*with a half-smile*) Oh, I've tried that.

Strowde Well, well . . . let nothing about me be a reproach to you. If I've only cared to believe the unbelievable and attempt the impossible . . . if that only ends in damnable impotence, what wonder! I lose you.

She is, by this, you would say, a little surprised at her own coldness.

Joan Yes, I won't keep you waiting for the miracle.

Strowde What sort of creatures are we to set up as spiritual ladies and gentlemen? Strength's in the mud that we're made of. Housekeeping and my career . . . but I'm not clever enough to get you safely tangled in that. I feel like a boy crossed in his first love affair. When we were out on the hill there yesterday, watching that rainbow, I was shaking standing beside you . . . you were so beautiful.

Joan The first double-rainbow I'd ever seen . . . except one in a book.

Strowde But even that didn't help!

She brings herself back to the world of passing things, but – ironically – it only prompts her to ask . . .

Joan What's the time, Evan?

Strowde Twenty to ten.

Joan I must go and say good-bye to Susan.

He is utterly defeated.

Strowde So our lives can't be made to fit . . . and here's an end. We two are evidently not the centre of a divinely appointed system of things.

Joan But you don't believe it is.

Strowde I've never found worse to say of it! Though if we're to keep some patient pity for our fellow-men, perhaps it's the best faith to hold. What do you mean to do, by the way, if you don't marry me?

Joan (*frank to herself*) I'm done.

Strowde I've energy left. Let's hope that I find nothing new to believe in.

She is by the window, and she draws a long breath as if that might bring her new life; and, in a sense, it seems to.

Joan There's a chill in the air. Summer's over . . . its burden's lifting. I'm deeply unhappy to be failing you . . . but I could start off light-heartedly round the world this morning. Would you follow me if I beckoned you . . . a day's march behind?

Strowde Yes.

Joan No . . . we'll go for a walk down to the lake before lunch . . . and talk politics. I've set you free.

Strowde Have you? That may be beyond your power too.

Joan (*facing him*) But, deep deep down in your heart . . . you never did picture us married and settled, did you?

Strowde No . . . I'll confess it.

Joan Nor I . . . ever. That is what's so strange . . . and so wrong, I suppose. Forgive me.

Strowde (*with a smile*) I shall never forgive you . . . for that would be to lose the very last of you, Joan.

Joan Twelve o'clock?

Strowde Earlier if you like. I've only these letters to see to.

Joan I'll try.

She goes down the gallery, lightly, not happily; rather as if happiness were as nothing to her. He sits to his letters. After a moment he finds himself saying . . .

Strowde Most merciful God . . . who makest thy creatures to suffer without understanding . . .

But he leaves the prayer unfinished and goes on with his letters.

Act Three

Scene One

*At the **Strowdes'** house in Bedford Square. **Evan** works habitually in the front room downstairs. It is lined with books. His big writing-table is between the windows; he sits – and is sitting at the moment – with his back to them. On his left, and facing the door, is a smaller table, its chair backing on to the bookcases.*

*It is a morning in March, and foggy without. **Oliver** comes in, carrying a time-table and some opened letters. He does not speak, and has time to go to the smaller table and put them down, as well as to glance at a few others left there for him, before **Evan** says, habitually, and hardly looking up from his own writing . . .*

Strowde Morning.

Oliver Morning, sir.

Strowde I thought you'd be late in this fog.

Oliver I walked. Will you make up the diary now?

Strowde Yes.

Oliver *deals with diary and letters and time-table with a chief-of-staff air.*

Oliver Unless you motor half the night I don't see that you can speak for Hughes at Neath on the twenty-first and at Dover the next afternoon.

Strowde Cut Dover. Philpot will lose the seat anyhow.

Oliver I'm keeping four free days for emergencies in that fortnight.

Strowde Get me the Bible, will you? I want to verify . . . I think it's First Kings, nineteen. I must go to Nottingham. There's a letter. . .

Oliver Yes . . . for the Saturday. And a solid four at Stockton, Tuesday to polling day . . . will that be right?

Strowde Ask Duddington.

Oliver He has rung up to say he may take the twelve-forty down today, and not wait for us.

Oliver, *with the Bible taken from its place, walks over to* **Strowde** *and at the same time puts a press-cutting on his table.*

Oliver Did you see this?

Strowde (*giving it half a glance*) The *Guardian*?

Oliver Yes. They're all ducking and dodging over the Trust question.

Strowde (*without contempt*) Naturally.

Oliver (*with his chapter found*) What's the quotation?

Strowde Now, O Lord, take away my life, for I am not better than my fathers. Very modern and progressive and disillusioned of Elijah! Why ever should he expect to be?

Oliver Verse four.

Strowde Thank you.

Oliver And these to go back in the History file?

'These' are some manuscripts piled a few inches high on the table. They might be, and are, the chapters of a book.

Strowde Please.

Oliver Clumbermere's coming at t h r e e, you know.

Strowde Yes.

Oliver *has noted the wrong entry on the appointment tablet; he now puts down the lump of manuscript he has taken up, to alter it. And this moment the* **Parlourmaid** *enters.*

Maid Did you ring, sir?

Strowde What time must we leave, Oliver?

Oliver The train's four-fifty.

Strowde Pack my bag for one night, please. No dress clothes. Tea at four-fifteen. Miss Strowde gone out yet?

Maid No, sir. She's expecting Miss Kittredge to call for her at eleven.

Strowde Will you lunch?

Oliver Thank you.

Strowde Mr Gauntlett will lunch.

Maid Yes, sir.

The **Maid** *goes.* **Strowde** *has now finished his writing and leans back.* **Oliver** *stands beside him.*

Strowde I doubt if it'll be such a walk over.

Oliver For you . . . at Stockton?

Strowde The whole election.

Oliver Well . . . you like a good fight.

Strowde (*genially*) You want us whacked. Traitor!

Oliver Not more than enough to hurt.

Strowde If we were, Bellingham'd throw up the leadership.

Oliver Then a year or two's opposition would pay you.

Strowde Personally . . . yes . . . with anything worth opposing. How much longer do you mean to stay with me, Oliver?

Oliver (*guardedly*) That's still for you to say.

The relation between the two is obviously an easy one as long as it relates to the work they are busy about. **Strowde** *himself, his mind on immediate things, has lost much of his brooding* *air. But* **Oliver**, *it would almost seem, has acquired it.*

Strowde We must see that the sweets of office don't quite spoil your old appetite for revolution. (*He hands over the sheets of paper he has been busy on.*) Put this straight . . . it's the speech for Thursday . . . and type that bit of it in triplicate.

Oliver *still has a part of the History manuscript in his hand. He holds it and looks at it as if it were something more than typed paper.*

Oliver Why do you get all this stuff out night after night?

The question and the action draw them beyond business bounds, and their tone to each other changes. **Strowde**'s, *one would say, turns restrainedly affectionate, and* **Oliver** *seems to grow sensitive and very watchful.*

Strowde My derelict past. I've been looking for what I could steal from it. Live stuff . . . almost! You've read it?

Oliver You said I might.

Strowde I wanted you to.

Oliver Who else ever has?

Strowde No one. Yes . . . Eleanor typed those three chapters you're holding. The rest . . . no one.

Oliver (*nodding towards the bookcase where they are*) Why did none of it find a way into the four upstanding volumes?

Strowde (*with a smile for the past*) First it was to be for the first, you know . . . and then for the last.

Oliver And now there's to be no last.

Strowde Do you feel like writing one?

Oliver Whenever a thought was precious to you . . . you hid it away here.

Strowde Whenever it was not current coin . . . I laid it by. A queer task . . . bestowing the love of one's mind. (*He* *fingers the lifeless paper at his side.*) Scraps of me, too unsure for utterance. As if this flimsiness itself could cohere and live! Well, I bequeath it to you, Oliver . . . this much of the failure you were so keen to track down. Burn it. It's just worth destroying.

Oliver, *however, seems to find more in the matter than this.*

Oliver But better inherit a failure, I suppose . . . for there's something to be done with it . . . than a success.

Strowde (*with his kindly smile*) That sounds quite wise. Are you growing patient?

Oliver (*a bitter tang in his voice*) I'm turning coward, perhaps.

Strowde I doubt it. What has happened?

Oliver I'm lonely.

Strowde (*with a head-shake*) Why, of course!

Oliver (*something from deeper down ousting the bitterness*) I meant to live with the dead. I felt I must never forget them. But they're dead to me now. I used to find courage by mustering in the dark that regiment of fellows . . . I've marched miles with them night after night. One crack regiment, I thought, temptation proof, could make an end of the muddle you've made. And you'd be glad enough when the time came. But the time never comes, you told me. Damnable of you!

Strowde (*and he means it*) I'm sorry.

But **Oliver** *has evidently learnt how to indulge in the self-destruction of laughter.*

Oliver Never mind. I'm busy. I'm growing hopeful and helpless and almost good-natured. Don't give me away, though.

Strowde (*merrily*) Have we begun to impress even you . . . the gang of us . . . with our statesmanlike airs? Do you thrill at the sight of the red-leather despatch-box with First

Lord of the Treasury on it and an Urgent slip sticking out? You must take a cold chisel to the lock of it the first time it comes to me.

Oliver *now does put the papers away, and out of his mind too; and tackles the forthcoming subject in lively earnest.*

Oliver But I can't see what's to stop you, Evan, from being thrust to the top of this muddle of minds.

Strowde No . . . quite immodestly . . . nor can I.

Oliver I watch them sizing you up. They don't like you.

Strowde Why should they?

Oliver Why do they trust you, then?

Strowde I'm not altogether one of them . . . and they've lost the habit of trusting each other.

Oliver Heriot thought he was making a smart move when he had you handed the hardest job going . . . this Clumbermere business.

Strowde Do you think he wants me to fail at it?

Oliver *(answering acutely to this test)* No . . . I think he hopes that some sorry moment will give him a chance to wring your hand and say: Well, never mind, old man!

Strowde *(appreciatively)* Yes, I can hear him.

Oliver Mulready wants to quarrel with you.

Strowde I can't oblige Mulready.

Oliver What, not with one little row, and then kiss and be friends . . . instead of flattering him till he feels a perfect fool?

Strowde He is . . . and if he wasn't kept in mind of it he'd become a nuisance.

Oliver You do treat Uncle Stephen as a fellow-creature.

Strowde One's fond of Stephen.

Oliver *now drops the liveliness a little and puts* **Strowde** *on the defensive.*

Oliver But I sit and watch you thresh out a scheme with some man . . . who's honest and capable at least. How is it he doesn't see that you're mocking him?

Strowde (*deprecatory*) No . . . I assure you.

Oliver Every letter I write for you . . . it's like laying a snare.

Strowde (*ironic*) Why . . . am I not theirs very faithfully, their most obedient humble servant? If the schemes will come to nothing in the end, is the mockery mine? What do you expect of me, Oliver?

Oliver Poor devils! Each one of them believes in something. If it's not in what he's doing it's in what he hopes to be . . . even if it's only in what he has failed to be. I suppose he expects you to believe a little in him.

Strowde (*sarcastic*) That's unreasonable. (*But now, in coldest sincerity . . .*) Are you still out to destroy? I'm showing you the sure way. It's to fulfil. The reddest revolutionary is but a part of what he turns against. It's the destiny of a spiritual generation to destroy itself by fulfilling its faith and completing its work . . . and we dignify our passions to this end! Not so pleasant, I grant you, to be doing one's share of the job cold-heartedly and open-eyed. But disbelief's a power . . . and power is satisfying. I lived half my life in the happiness . . . and unhappiness . . . of a vision. One fine day I find that the world I'm living in is nothing like the idea of the world I've been living by. It comes quite casually . . . conversion to disbelief. But you know it's the truth you've found by finding you've always known it . . . known all along that your vision was a vision and no more.

Oliver And you leave happiness and unhappiness behind?

Strowde You cease to suffer . . . you cease to hope. You have no will to be other than you are. You are, therefore, extraordinarily efficient. Be something ruthlessly . . . what else counts? . . . and let life become what it will. Watch me succeed, Oliver. That will teach you how to down me in turn. It's the best service I can do you.

Oliver *finds but one comment.*

Oliver Wouldn't you sooner I killed you now where you sit?

Strowde That would be rash and well-meaning of you . . . and hardly worthwhile.

Oliver (*drawn on now irresistibly*) I came to get what I could from you . . . though you told me to go my own way . . . and I've tried to since. But I've never been able to get free of you, Evan. When I was small you were jolly to me . . . and I liked that. Then I turned against you and wondered why. Odd, how one ignorantly stores up scraps of knowledge about people and things till one can put them together and make out what they mean. Three times, I think, Mother has started to try and tell me about . . . us three. I've managed to stop her . . . for where was the need . . . when, in every sense that counts, I believe I've always known.

Strowde *has nothing to say but . . .*

Strowde Have you? Oh, my dear boy!

Oliver Don't . . . don't. We can't begin to be fond of each other.

Strowde (*half-humbly*) No . . . I could never find any way to begin. But lately . . . I've learnt to be rather fond of you. I hope nothing I ever said seemed to give your mother away.

Oliver (*in a way, the more confident now of the two*) Oh no! Dear Mother and all the other facts of Nature . . . one accepts them and has done with it. There was one fellow at school . . . I never knew of his saying a word . . . but he had some damned story about her inside him, I could see.

So I made a row with him . . . though scrapping wasn't the thing . . . and as near killed him as was decent. One can't be her son for nothing.

Strowde What makes you tell me now that you know?

Oliver I . . . had a feeling you'd like me to.

At this moment the **Maid** *comes in, announcing 'Mr Serocold'. He is close on her heels.*

Serocold Sorry I'm late.

Strowde You'll be later at Number Ten.

Serocold The PM always keeps me waiting. Slack's the word!

Strowde Here's what I'm going to say on Thursday. Oliver'll type you a copy.

Serocold, *with a nod to his nephew, takes the few sheets of paper.*

Serocold You're seeing Clumbermere?

Strowde Three o'clock.

Serocold (*having hit on the passage marked for typing; as he reads*) His people won't like this, will they?

Strowde (*with a pleasant curtness*) They're not meant to.

Serocold (*as he pulls a face*) I'm very sure Bellingham won't.

Strowde He need not, either.

Serocold (*pulling it even longer*) But, my dear fellow, this is a pledge.

Strowde Well . . . I'm nobody. I'm not in the Government . . . I'm not even in the House yet. If I choose to stake my small reputation that the Trust question will have to be squared inside those lines, what does it matter?

Serocold *hands the damned thing back, saying . . .*

Serocold How long will this take you, Oliver?

Oliver Three minutes.

Oliver *goes off with it.*

Serocold (*in deprecatory protest*) Evan . . . you are difficult.

Strowde (*as one skilled in hitting nails on the head*) I've gruelled at this business, my dear Stephen, till I know its necessities . . . and we'll have to come to their heel.

Serocold (*the ever-comforting phrase*) In time.

Strowde And I know Clumbermere. He has got his Bellinghams and Heriots and Stephen Serocolds to deal with too. So I give him a pistol, you see, to put at their heads, and he gives me one to put at yours.

Serocold (*rueful*) Quite so. Set the strong men face to face, and they're back to back before you know where you are.

Strowde Thank you!

Serocold But surely if we must offend our own people we might at least get some support out of Clumbermere's lot for doing so.

Strowde Good Lord . . . we don't want their support! Then Clumbermere would have to start bargaining with us for a great deal more than it's good to give him. He knows that, too.

Serocold But I've to persuade Number Ten.

Strowde (*with finality*) Tell Number Ten that if I'm right it's all right . . . and if I'm wrong they'll be rid of me.

The door opens and **Eleanor** *looks in.*

Eleanor Evan, are you busy?

Strowde Yes . . . come in.

Eleanor Come in, my dear.

This is to **Susan Kittredge**, *who then follows her.* **Eleanor** *shakes hands silently with* **Stephen**.

Strowde Good morning, Miss Susan.

Eleanor Bad news.

It is indeed written on their faces.

Strowde What?

Eleanor Joan's very ill.

Serocold Joan Westbury!

Susan A letter from my grandfather this morning.

Serocold Is she still out there?

Susan Since Christmas.

Eleanor May Evan read it?

Susan Of course.

Susan *has the letter in her hand.* **Strowde** *takes it without a word.*

Serocold What's the matter with her?

Eleanor It's a tumour on the brain.

Serocold Good God!

Susan Grandfather didn't know for a while that she wasn't sleeping at all. Now she's had a doctor from Boston that he says he can trust. (*Then to* **Strowde**, *who is silently intent on the letter.*) I'm afraid it's dreadfully illegible . . . he never types.

Serocold Aren't they operating?

Eleanor They won't. They give her a few weeks.

Serocold When was that written?

Eleanor Ten days ago.

Serocold Does she know?

Eleanor He doesn't say.

Serocold Poor Joan! I suppose they dose her with morphia.

Eleanor Surely!

Serocold I must go.

After all, what can be done, and what more can be said? Glancing at **Strowde**, *he goes out.* **Eleanor** *and* **Susan** *talk on in lower tones.*

Eleanor You've been crying.

Susan (*who has been, indeed*) I do all the usual things, I'm afraid.

Eleanor Never be afraid, my dear, of doing the usual things.

Susan And she's three thousand miles away.

Eleanor What a worry for your grandfather! He's being most kind.

Suddenly **Strowde** *speaks, and they both turn.*

Strowde This is from Countesbury?

Susan Yes.

He goes back to his reading.

Eleanor I thought she was ill in the summer. Why . . . she had planned to go on to Japan, hadn't she, Evan?

Susan Yes. He thinks that the illness . . . her mind . . . they say it makes one very restless.

Serocold *looks in again with the paper that* **Oliver** *had typed in his hand. He says softly, not so softly as to make sympathy mawkish . . .*

Serocold Goodbye, Eleanor. Let me know when you hear again, please.

Eleanor You're dining tomorrow.

Serocold Oh . . . yes. (*To* **Susan**.) Goodbye.

Susan Good-bye.

He disappears. **Strowde**'s *intent stillness – for the letter is long and not easily read – sets up a strain. It is half to relieve it that* **Susan** *says . . .*

Susan I'll write today . . . but it'll miss the mail.

Eleanor To Joan?

Susan I'm sure Grandfather would have cabled if she were . . . worse.

Eleanor She's dying, my dear.

Susan I know . . . though I don't understand it really.

Eleanor That is as it should be.

Susan Why?

Eleanor If we thought often of dying we should soon think of nothing else. Time enough, then, for you.

Susan But . . .

Strowde *has finished the letter, has risen, and with a curt* 'Thank you' *he hands it her back and goes out.* **Eleanor** *comments on the slight strangeness of this . . .*

Eleanor Evan had hoped to marry her, you know.

Susan Yes.

Eleanor The election won't leave him much time to be unhappy.

Susan No.

Eleanor's *businesslike mind will work.*

Eleanor Twenty past ten, is it?

Susan Just.

Eleanor When did you last hear from Joan herself?

Susan Two weeks ago.

Eleanor Was she ill then, when she wrote . . . did she say?

Susan No. But that may have been because . . . we were playing a childish game . . . I did once start to tell you . . . pretending we'd changed places. She has my rooms at home . . . they're in a wing by themselves built out over the garden. So she used to write me . . . such good letters . . . and sign them Susan. I was no use at answering. I've kept them all.

Oliver comes in.

Oliver Morning. Morning, Susan.

Susan Good morning, Oliver.

He picks up the railway guide from his table and turns the leaves. Later he sits and unlocks a drawer for some money. This seems to break the spell that still held **Eleanor** *slightly, and she says to the girl . . .*

Eleanor If you wouldn't mind waiting at the Ministry while I see Mr Pemberton . . . then we could go straight on to Poplar. They'll give us lunch at the factory. I must be back and at Grosvenor Road by two-thirty. I'll get my papers.

Susan Very well.

Eleanor This is shocking news, Oliver.

Oliver Very.

Eleanor *goes.* **Susan** *looks across, with a distinct frown, at the taciturn young man.*

Susan Don't you care?

Oliver Yes. What good will that do?

Susan Some good to you.

Oliver I wasn't thinking of my own moral improvement for the moment.

Susan Must we quarrel . . . even about this?

Oliver (*bitter-sweet*) It's how I show affection for you, Susan.

Susan Thank you. (*But she cannot play up to this sort of thing now, and she bursts out.*) I'd give anything to be with her. Oh . . . how horribly casual you all are! I bring you such news . . . you all say that you loved her . . . you go about your business . . .

Oliver Sentimental Susan!

Susan How is one to learn to like you? I've tried not to seem a sightseer . . . simply curious about everything. I've tried to forget myself among you and find out what I really cared for. I knew how to love her without wasting time about it, thank goodness. (*And then – common sense catching up with emotion.*) Selfish brute . . . that won't save her! You're right.

Eleanor's *voice is heard from the hall, 'Ready, Susan'.*

Susan (*repentant for what she thinks is her harsh unreason*) I'm sorry, Oliver.

Oliver (*armoured and cool*) Why should you like us, my dear Susan?

Susan, *honestly a little hurt, goes without another word.* **Oliver** *goes about his business, whatever it is, with an almost suspicious steadiness. After a moment* **Strowde** *comes back.*

Strowde As it happens the boat doesn't sail till three.

Oliver The eleven-twenty train will do you, then.

Strowde They're keeping me a cabin.

Oliver You've four hundred-odd in current.

Strowde I'll write to Manning for an overdraft. You can cable another five to New York.

Then, with no more emotion than he'd give to the boat or the train or the bank account . . .

Oliver Do you expect to see her alive?

Strowde Hardly. I'll give you a line for Duddington.

Oliver You might just be back for polling.

Strowde If he thinks he can get my photograph and the gramophone records elected, he's welcome to try. Or you'd make an excellent member. Say to Stephen I'm sorry.

By now **Strowde** *is as busy at his table. The two talk while they work.*

Oliver Eleanor's just gone out.

Strowde Yes.

Oliver You won't come back.

Strowde That's always possible.

Oliver To this conspiracy you won't.

Strowde No . . . I don't see yet another welcome from the gang.

Oliver Why ever are you going? What's the use?

Strowde None.

Oliver *gibes.* Why does it – but it does – seem to make the whole thing a bit more bearable?

Oliver I've been wondering what could happen to save you. You a success! Why . . . the first temptation trips you up.

Strowde (*suddenly, straight at him*) You'd go.

Oliver I can't tell. I'd forgotten her lately. Yes, I'd start swimming there.

Strowde Here's the cheque.

Oliver (*as he takes it*) What about your packing?

Strowde Tell them to fill another bag.

Oliver Will you cable you're starting?

Strowde (*after playing with hope for a second*) No.

Oliver I'll be back in ten minutes.

He gets to the door, when his father's voice stops him.

Strowde Oliver. I'm dumb with you . . . but something that I am you must be too. Forgive me the forgetting it.

To just this much **Oliver** *can and will respond, simply and honestly.*

Oliver I'm glad I've found you.

Strowde I claim no rights in you. But I'm glad.

Oliver It's something to go on with.

As he goes, **Strowde** *echoes him as if the words were – they are! – the very last he wanted to feel the meaning of.*

Strowde To go on with!

Scene Two

We see the corner by the window in **Susan**'s *little sitting-room at Countesbury, Massachusetts. It is a white room; and now the snow outside makes it seem whiter still. And the snow brings with it a silence too.* **Joan**, *wrapped in shawls, is tucked into an armchair.* **Mr Kittredge** *is sitting by her. Her eyes are closed, she might be dead. When she speaks she does not open them at first. And she never moves, at most a hand reaches out; while he – for he sits by her long hours like this – has fallen almost motionless too.*

Joan So white! And white now even when I shut my eyes.

Mr Kittredge No pain then?

Joan None since this morning, thank you.

Mr Kittredge We are wise children when we fear the dark.

Joan Yes . . . now that I don't sleep much at night-time, I'm learning how to lose myself in light. What more has dear Susan to say?

Mr Kittredge I had finished the letter.

Joan Stupid of me!

Mr Kittredge Did you doze?

Joan I slipped out through the window . . . into the snow.

Mr Kittredge Why . . . a step or two further would have taken you into your famous London fog that Susan finds so beautiful.

Joan (*a flicker of light in her eyes*) I was in London this morning . . . there was no fog . . . it was full of cheerful noise. And yesterday I was in camp again beyond Khartoum . . . watching the little black babies crawl about the sand. I can remember one that died and didn't want to die . . . most of them, you know, come and go as easily . . . and he fought the air with his fists.

Mr Kittredge If memory's a measure of affection, we have given bits of our hearts to the unlikeliest things.

Joan (*with a smile for him*) Have you ever given your heart . . . all of a piece?

Mr Kittredge (*responsive; fostering the smile's life, as one might blow, ever so gently, upon a spark*) One tries to. It's the taking coming short is the trouble. Study the money market. That's what sends the values down.

Joan Oh, I have let myself be loved . . . most generously. I'm glad that's to my credit.

Mr Kittredge But never given your heart?

Joan One tries to . . . desperately. Probably it's a mistake to try.

Mr Kittredge We can't help trying.

Her thoughts pass like clouds, the light and shade changing in her face.

Joan I wonder if I've been a very wicked woman.

Mr Kittredge Probably not . . . if you wonder.

Joan I'd have been so content to be nothing but a wife and a mother . . . a link in the chain. In our pedigree book at home there's an Edward Marshall, knight, not so far back, that married . . . two little dashes . . . Eliza. Plain, simple Eliza! Who was she? Scandalous mystery . . . no one wanted to remember! But I've always felt tenderly and dutifully towards my great, great, great . . . and then, after all, one loses count . . . Great-grandmother Eliza.

For a moment or two they do not speak. Her face turns to the window, and in the white light seems lifeless, quite.

Joan Such a bright, silent land! Do you love it as we love England? Not yet. It's harder. It doesn't look back yet and seem to love you . . . as England does.

Mr Kittredge It must take more toll of us first, perhaps.

Joan So many generations of the souls and bodies of men to be given to this earth to breed it a soul of its own.

Mr Kittredge (*puzzled a little*) Of their souls too?

Joan It may have mine and welcome. My old world has a kindly soul . . . with a farm and a church and a house with its garden to show for it. I don't think I want to believe, though, that your quiet spirit must pass into the clatter of cities . . . or is that a music to you with a meaning?

Mr Kittredge With no clear meaning. That's why I've fallen silent in these last years . . . while I watch the new generations giving themselves to strange tremendous forces to breed . . . what sort of a monster world.

Joan (*with just one nod of the head*) Yes, I was very scared sailing up the harbour to New York and driving to the station. Those blasphemous towers of Babel weren't a bit like you. But I think you'll come out on top. Yes . . . I have a vision of the sublimer you, conscious, persistent, wise . . . coming out truly on top.

Mr Kittredge Well . . . it may be that a consciousness of purpose is still the greatest power.

Silence falls again. **Joan** *breaks it to a livelier tune. She is happy now, always, when she speaks of her boys.*

Joan Harry, till he was ten, poor infant, had dreadful headaches . . . and he asked me once, Mother, am I good? So I said he was. Then he asked, need he pray for eternal life? For if it's going to hurt like this, he said, I don't see how I could bear it.

Mr Kittredge I wish I'd known Harry.

Joan I wish he'd known you in time. Some of those boys, under the shadow of death, came suddenly to a maturity of mind.

Mr Kittredge This world at least was theirs. What a gift to them!

Joan (*reproachfully*) You're seldom bitter.

Mr Kittredge Too seldom . . . I dread the vapid benevolence of old age.

Joan Better the pain of anger?

Mr Kittredge Life keeps us capable of pain.

Joan So uselessly!

Mr Kittredge Not quite. And I think the rough and cunning God of Nature abets our honest passions of love and hate . . . because they never quite cancel out . . . and he profits on the balance. Even as our worldly virtue thrives upon alien sin . . . let us most humbly remember.

Joan (*her heart bowed*) But barren righteousness there is no god to pardon.

Mr Kittredge None . . . though men have made many.

She looks at him appealingly now.

Joan I have that shamefullest sin to confess . . . a sin of being. I have treasured a secret self . . . oh, an ego, if ever there was one.

Mr Kittredge (*humouring her thought*) A tyrant?

Joan Too aloof and alone for tyranny.

Mr Kittredge Lonely?

Joan Never so human.

Mr Kittredge Dear me! What can be done about it?

Joan (*a strain of torture showing*) It doesn't age, it doesn't suffer . . . and now I've lain awake with it so much I doubt if it ever sleeps. So I have this dread that it's undying.

Mr Kittredge (*with a certain dispersive briskness*) I once knew a promising young man possessed of the same devil. He fell in love, had his heart broken . . . broken into. Ego came out to fight and could never quite get back again.

Joan (*responding with a gleam of merriment*) How vulgar . . . says my secret self, and sniffs. No, I could never flatter it into being a heart-breaker. It was never half so human. May I confess?

Mr Kittredge Will my absolution serve?

Joan Give it me of your wisdom and your kindness if you can. (*And there follows her soul's confession.*) Once, in the sheer place of my self's refuge, I found that I was not alone. I turned back to life for safety. We loved the unattainable in each other, so we said . . . and were content to part. When there was no more need for parting we found that it was true. A faith was born to us . . . a dead faith . . . to my shame. And I left him to bear its burden. The world he worked for had much hope of him . . . and need of him.

Mr Kittredge And he failed it?

Joan He let life go. He worked on . . . lifelessly. Better if we had disbelieved.

Mr Kittredge There's no doing that.

Joan Rash uplifted souls! Too proud to pray to the god of the godlike in us to dull our sense and dim our eyes.

Mr Kittredge I do not believe in any such high god.

Joan (*her mind struggling*) Then why had I no power to bring the faith that kindled to a living birth . . . to set it free . . . that we might serve it? Nor any will to give it being? For I hadn't . . . that was the worst. This sacred self that cannot yield to life . . . what is it worth? Let's only hope the soul's as mortal as the body is.

And now brutal, physical ill takes advantage of the tortured mind.

Mr Kittredge Your head is hurting you again.

Joan (*gasping*) Beginning to. Will you please talk to me very sternly?

Mr Kittredge Take my hand.

Joan Thank you . . . that's comforting.

She grips his hand tightly. He talks to steady her, to give her moral foothold, if he can.

Mr Kittredge We must be patient . . . with headaches and in the winter-time of our souls. The first discovery, do you know, of my imaginative life was to find a story coming to an unhappy end and to hide the book away with its last chapter still unread. But suddenly that small boy thought: No story ever ends. A very moral anecdote. (**Joan** *cannot help another gasp.*) Grip my hand hard . . . and I'll grip yours harder.

Joan Please.

Mr Kittredge My dear, my dear . . . are there to be no honest failures in this world? Is man's salvation from the brute so small a business that we should each expect a rounded share in it? I've written a book or two on ethics . . . unfinished stories in their kind . . . not so bad though. But maybe what I've best learned how to do by that is to sit here so cleverly . . . confound the pain, we've had three weeks of it . . . and hold your hand.

Joan Be stern with me . . . or I can't bear it, I'm afraid.

Mr Kittredge I'm afraid you can. Headache or heartache or a harder thing . . . those that can suffer them must suffer them, it seems. You are the stuff, Joan, that forges well.

There comes into her voice a touch of conquering strength.

Joan I am learning a way, I think, through the dark and clamour of this pain. Will you tell him, please, that as the light grows there's always a moment when he's with me . . . till it grows too dazzling.

Mr Kittredge I'll tell him. Ah . . . the grip's loosening. Not such a long bout.

She comes, almost as suddenly, out of the agony. Taking her hand back, she finds it stained.

Joan Oh . . . I've cut your hand with my ring.

Mr Kittredge (*gallantly*) Good . . . I have shed my blood for you.

Joan (*with a lady's smile for her knight*) Thank you.

Mr Kittredge Keep the head still now. Set your mind free.

Again a silence falls.

Joan (*her eyes closed, and, as it would seem, exhaustedly at ease*) Yesterday you told me that three times in your life you had been near to . . . it was a deserter's phrase . . . falling out from the tyrannous procession of the years!

Mr Kittredge Yes . . . three times . . . no more. Good friends, clean enemies, and hard work have kept me happy mostly.

Joan What held you in place?

Mr Kittredge Inconsequent things. Once, it was the thought of an unfinished book that had been paid for. Once, a night's sleep made all the difference. But once my self-respect did seriously protest against a premature indulgence in the ignorance of death.

Joan Did the troubles pass?

Mr Kittredge No. They were unsolved problems. I face them still.

Joan To be so hustled in our chains down this road we call time. Then to be hustled off it . . . crippled still . . . into an eternity of empty freedom . . . a mocking threat! I've taken every happening so easily . . . and I'm at peace about the past. A little tired now, by this pain, and memory plays tricks . . . with real and unreal. That's most immoral, I'm sure.

Mr Kittredge There is an Eastern prayer . . . for those that would leave life behind . . . begins: From the need to know by name or by form . . . deliver me.

Joan (*with quite a laugh; a child's laugh*) Oh, I like that! Anyway, though, my geese were always swans . . . weren't yours?

Mr Kittredge Are there any fairer swans?

Joan (*as if she prayed*) For all denial of what I had to give . . . forgive me. From the soul's empty freedom . . . deliver me. If death cannot make fruitful may it break and end what life could not break nor use.

Mr Kittredge (*his voice very hushed*) But we must be patient in understanding too. What gospel is it for the flesh that dies to know it serves a greater end than its own? Joy of life is its heritage. But man's soul is of man's making. He stumbles and halts in his chosen ways. In the way of vision . . . we see and find small reason to believe. The way of thought brings power . . . but it is power to bind . . . it is law. Whence comes our newer being and its freedom . . . how has life been gained for the soul? I do not know. What is to come of it? We're conscious mostly yet of the good life's failure. A bitter business!

Joan I've tried to be bitter. So have you. And that's a failure.

Now comes the comfort of his faith. And she listens, as to the absolution she had asked.

Mr Kittredge This I can believe. The generation of the spirit is not as the generation of the flesh . . . for its virtue is diffused like light, generously, unpriced. Doing and suffering and the work of thought must take its toll of us. And all that life corrupts death can destroy. Then we may cease to know. But, freed from self's claim upon it, scattered, dissolved, transformed, that inmost thing we were so impotently may but begin, new-breathed, the better to be. For comfort's sake we lead our busy lives. Who wouldn't want to forget sometimes this strange, new, useless burden of the soul? Left comfortless, we must bear it for a while as bravely as we may. (*He is conscious of a change in her. He looks keenly, for perhaps the great change has begun.*) Joan . . . where are you?

Joan Not so far.

For a passing moment her face is alert.

Mr Kittredge Why . . . what can you hear now that my chattering ceases?

But impalpably it is veiled.

Joan Nothing any more. There's silence now. There's light and silence.

He hardly thinks that she will open her eyes again.

Scene Three

Strowde's *study again.* **Lord Clumbermere** *is sitting waiting; an old gentleman* (*though his birth did not formally*

*confer the title) of an ungainly figure and an originally
insignificant face, which the sheer practice of life has made
characteristic and interesting. He is reading a little leather-
bound pocket-volume. The* **Maid** *opens the door.*

Maid Beg pardon, my lord . . . I wasn't sure that
neither of them had come in.

Lord Clumbermere No.

Maid (*speaking back to the hall*) Will you wait
upstairs, miss?

Susan's voice I can leave this on the desk . . . or I'll write
Mr Strowde a note.

Whereupon the **Maid** *holds the door wide, and* **Lord
Clumbermere** *rises with cumbrous politeness as* **Susan** *comes
in, a cablegram in her hand.*

Susan Here? Excuse me.

She goes to **Oliver**'s *desk and sits there. The* **Maid** *goes.* **Lord
Clumbermere** *sits down again.* **Susan,** *having taken a sheet
of paper, decides not to write. Instead, she puts the cablegram
itself into an envelope, which she addresses. Then, looking up,
she finds* **Lord Clumbermere** *is looking at her.*

Lord Clumbermere (*in his soft, slow way*) You came with
Miss Strowde to see round our Garden City. I showed you
round. My name is Clumbermere.

Susan (*colourlessly*) Yes. I didn't think you'd remember
me.

Lord Clumbermere You're Miss Susan Kittredge. You
come from America.

Susan Yes.

Lord Clumbermere That cablegram's bad news. I'm
sorry.

Oliver *comes in hurriedly, and as if directly from the street.*

Oliver You never got my message, my lord! Your City

office said they could find you . . . I rang up Grosvenor Square as well . . . and you've been here since three.

Lord Clumbermere (*charitably unreproachful*) I have.

Oliver I'm very sorry. The message was that Mr Strowde couldn't keep the appointment with you . . . he is sailing this afternoon on the 'Aquitania'.

Lord Clumbermere Sudden.

Oliver *takes, for the first time, a good look at* **Susan** *and sees in her face . . .*

Oliver Susan . . . what's the matter?

In silence she hands him the envelope.

Oliver She's dead?

Susan Yes.

He says, automatically, as he opens it . . .

Oliver Please excuse me. (*He reads it, and then for all comment . . .*) This has come through quickly. (*Then turning again to the sympathetically attentive old gentleman.*) My uncle thought . . . I've just left him . . . you might like to make some suggestion to avoid bringing your business with Mr Strowde to a standstill.

Lord Clumbermere I know no more than you tell me, of course . . . but if you now want to telephone to Southampton to stop him, there's a line in my office that can be relied on . . . and it's at your service.

Oliver (*with a frown*) Thank you. The boat sailed at three.

Susan (*striking, involuntarily, almost an eager note*) That might mean four.

Oliver (*coldly masking some surprise*) It might.

Lord Clumbermere (*accommodatingly*) Then the Admiralty wireless will do as well. He could land at Cherbourg.

Oliver (*bringing all this to a full stop*) Yes. You'd rather not see my uncle, of course. His point was that . . . whenever Mr Strowde did come back the Government's relations to him might have altered.

Lord Clumbermere *is pleasantly amused at the senatorial tone; but he keeps his secret.*

Lord Clumbermere I catch that point.

Oliver And if you think the business pressing . . . ?

Lord Clumbermere I think we had now better let things happen for a little . . . will you tell your good uncle with my compliments? But say I'm always pleased to talk to a man that has a mind of his own and knows it . . . when they find another.

Oliver I'll say so. And I'm sure Mr Strowde would have wished me to say that he was sorry to leave things in the lurch.

Lord Clumbermere (*expanding a little, now that* **Oliver** *has, apparently, finished patronising him*) Well, you know, from one cause and another . . . accidents and such-like . . . that's always occurring. We just can't help thinking this world won't go on without us . . . the evidence is that it will. A little differently? Perhaps. Any worse? That's more doubtful. (*Then rolling round a smile on* **Susan**.) Not that you should feel this way.

Susan Why not?

Lord Clumbermere (*making it into quite a little song*) You're young. I'm old.

Susan If it's all to make so little difference, why do you work fourteen hours a day, Lord Clumbermere?

Lord Clumbermere (*naughtily*) The newspapers say that of me. I don't do more than six hours' real work.

Susan (*with friendly persistence*) Why do any?

Lord Clumbermere It's a habit I've got into. It passes the time . . . keeps me happy . . . and I don't know what else would.

Susan *now hesitates a moment; but then, keenly . . .*

Susan It isn't my business to ask, I know, but . . . do you want Mr Strowde to come back?

Lord Clumbermere In a friendly sense?

Susan (*putting it very straight*) Do you think he ought to come back?

Lord Clumbermere (*rather like a benevolent old bear whom a rash cub has defied*) Dear young lady, that pistol is not loaded. It is not my business to say.

Susan (*contrite*) I beg your pardon.

Lord Clumbermere *now takes account of the silent* **Oliver**.

Lord Clumbermere Am I keeping you and Miss Kittredge from private conversation?

Oliver No, I think not.

Lord Clumbermere For my next appointment is not till four, and I have only a mile and a quarter to walk to it. This is my day for meeting men on their own ground. If I meet them on mine more than four days a week, I find I grow too obstinate.

Oliver, *wrought as he is today with suppressed emotions and a tortured mind, can really hardly bear this sententious old gentleman.*

Oliver Is that a bad business quality?

Lord Clumbermere It is an unpleasing human quality.

Oliver I thought that the set jaw and the thump on the table were the only sure signs of a strong man.

To this juvenile outrage **Lord Clumbermere** *unexpectedly responds with a pathetic and disarming smile.*

Lord Clumbermere Don't you like me?

Oliver (*shamed*) I'm sorry, sir . . . if that sounded rude.

Lord Clumbermere I judged you didn't like me when you came to bring papers to that Amalgamated Plantations meeting last November year . . . which was the first time I saw you.

Oliver (*recovering superiority*) It must please people amazingly to find out how well you remember them.

Lord Clumbermere (*with meek benevolence*) I hope it does. I mean it to. Will you be out of a job now?

Oliver (*much taken aback*) Well, I've hardly had time to consider. Possibly.

Lord Clumbermere I can offer you one.

Oliver A firm offer?

Lord Clumbermere I make no other kind.

What prouder moment for a young man than when – with studied courtesy – he can refuse an offer!

Oliver No, thank you, my lord. I've tried the City. I am against you, I fear.

Lord Clumbermere Is that so? And what are you for?

Oliver It's not an easy question to answer, you think?

But **Oliver** *is not a pretentious fool; for all that he is sometimes tempted to behave like one.*

Lord Clumbermere I think there's only one way to answer it, Mr Gauntlett . . . and I doubt if you've had time to find that. Miss Kittredge has her eye on this little volume that I carry in my pocket to occupy odd moments. No, it's not a Testament . . . though I carry a Testament sometimes. Nor a Ready Reckoner. Allow me.

He hands it to **Susan** *with a bow.*

Oliver (*who is being won to friendliness*) What is it, Susan?

Susan Everybody's Book of Short Poems.

Lord Clumbermere They're poor poems mostly, I should suppose. It was the Everybody's caught my fancy just about forty years ago, at Bletchley station, when I was travelling in ink.

Oliver Ink for everybody!

Lord Clumbermere That's what I had to make it if I could.

Oliver You did.

Lord Clumbermere (*warming comfortably to reminiscence*) Then bottles, pens, paper, typewriters, rubber, lead mines, and a line of steamships. I have prospered, you may say, by giving people what they want . . . and then a little more of what they want . . . and sometimes, maybe, by persuading them to take rather more than they did want. Are you against that?

Oliver (*with some severity*) What do you want, my lord?

Lord Clumbermere Ah . . . that's the riddle . . . and there's a catch in it. There's always a catch in the riddles life sets us to guess, Mr Gauntlett. I have had to live to find the answer . . . and I don't say I've found it out yet. Now the poem I happened to be reading when Miss Kittredge came in . . . page sixty-two, I have no literary memory, but I retain numbers . . . is entitled, 'I know that my own will come to me'. A helpful thought . . . but an awful thought. I never supposed I wanted lots of money . . . but I've got it. I despise titles . . . I'm a lord. I was bred to the Baptist ministry, and I still think I'm a spiritually minded man. And perhaps if I'd been blessed with three children instead of seven, I might be running a chapel now. You'd say I've sunk my soul . . . not to mention other people's . . . all in money and money's worth. Well, money's a hard master . . . so is success. You think you're all for truth and justice. Right. Come and run my pen factory and find out if that is so.

Oliver *sees that this does need an answer.*

Oliver If I ran your pen factory, I'd be for the pen, the whole pen, and nothing but the pen.

Lord Clumbermere Then you'd be little use to me. If we want a good gold nib, it's religion we must make it with.

Oliver I'm sure that sentiment has been applauded on many a Pleasant Sunday Afternoon.

Lord Clumbermere It has.

Oliver (*making his attack*) But are you a devil, then, my lord, that you want to beat the souls of men into pen nibs?

Lord Clumbermere I hope not. But if I am, Mr Gauntlett, please show me the way out of the pit. For I've tried to uplift my fellows . . . gratis; that was a failure . . . at five per cent; that wasn't quite such a failure . . . but it was all a failure really. Odd now! My last turn-to with Mr Strowde was on this very subject, when we crossed with a party on the 'Caronia' to a conference upon the scientific management of industry in Chicago. (*To* **Susan**.) You're not from Chicago?

Susan (*who is very attracted by* **Lord Clumbermere**, *though much of her mind is elsewhere*). No, I've never been there. I don't know much of America, I fear.

Lord Clumbermere (*with a bow that a duke might envy*) You a r e America . . . you don't need to be too self-conscious. I must have done a hundred miles round the decks coming and going, arguing with him. A fine mind. That's eighteen years ago. I was interested in his future.

Oliver Did you offer him the pen factory?

Lord Clumbermere (*quite unable to resist this*) Why, Mr Gauntlett, I wish to make no comparisons . . . but I offered him the rubber and the steamships. And I will again if he wants a job.

Susan One for you, Oliver.

Oliver (*gallantly*) Yes.

Lord Clumbermere But he said he had enough to think about.

Oliver (*joining battle again*) You don't despise sheer thinking.

Lord Clumbermere Why, no. My factories are run by thought.

Oliver As well as by faith and honour.

Lord Clumbermere *grows a little graver; and he speaks to himself now, as much as to his hearers.*

Lord Clumbermere Yes, I'm greedy of all three. And I get greedier. I sometimes wish I didn't . . . but I do. Why should the immortal part of man be all used up making him safe and comfortable? It's humiliating. And even the demand for simple goodness is greater than the supply. My business swallows a lot . . . it could swallow a lot more.

Oliver (*bitterly*) Then do you wonder there are people that want to blow you and your factories to smithereens?

Lord Clumbermere No, I sympathise. But it isn't practical of them . . . and it wouldn't be popular . . . for where should we all be then? Subtracting evil doesn't leave good . . . not as I was taught to do sums. So I must seek salvation the other way.

Oliver What is that?

Lord Clumbermere *meditatively looks at his watch; he gets up, and as he speaks, recaptures his little volume.*

Lord Clumbermere On page one hundred and twelve . . . thank you, I wasn't forgetting it . . . there is a poem entitled 'It's the little bit extra that counts for God'. A good thought. Righteousness is profit, Mr Gauntlett . . . and before we can have honest profit we must pay our way. I know that is only the creed of a businessman. It's half-past three . . . and I'm a slow walker. (*To* **Susan**.) Good afternoon.

Susan (*thanks in her eyes*) Could you give me a job?

Lord Clumbermere I might.

Susan I may come and ask for one.

Lord Clumbermere Do. My coat's outside. (*He pauses, to add a little shyly.*) I liked to think when I was beginning to do well that my business was, as you might say, the practical side of literature. Great poems must have been written in my ink . . . and treaties have been signed with my pens. So's my hat. (*As he goes out he is saying to* **Oliver**.) Will you tell your uncle then that I think things must be let happen for a little now . . . till we see a chance to interfere again . . .

The door closes on the two of them. But in a moment **Oliver** *returns – to find* **Susan** *very ready for him.*

Susan Oliver, why wouldn't you telephone? I thought he'd stay talking for ever! Don't you mean to send the wireless?

Oliver I don't think so.

Susan Why not? Don't they want him back now?

Oliver *can let himself go at last; and, what's more, he can take it out of* **Susan**.

Oliver Did they ever want him here? They hated him, they were afraid of him, they're thankful to be rid of him and they're furious he's gone! Poor Uncle Stephen . . . I caught him at Downing Street . . . and his temper for once did run out like a line with a fish at the end of it. You should have heard Henry Chartres over the telephone. Stop and see Eleanor's face when I tell her. Then there's Duddington, his election agent . . . he'll be here soon.

Susan (*piercing all this*) But why don't y o u want him back?

Oliver (*scornfully*) He threw away a seat in the Cabinet, did he, just to go and cry at her bedside? But now it's too late he's to dodge back thanking God she didn't wait to die till he was well out on the Atlantic. Don't be so materially minded, my dear, even if you are a sentimentalist.

She is stubborn to her point, spiritedly gentle in her insistence on it. He lashes at her from any vantage he can find.

Susan I didn't say I thought it right his going at all. I hadn't an idea he'd gone.

Oliver What a wife you'll make some day, Susan, for a successful man!

Susan What's the precise point of that, please?

Oliver Spartan but accommodating! Ever ready to indicate the practical ideal.

Susan What's to happen to this world if people won't choose their duty and stick to it though their hearts break?

Oliver Yes, you've the patter quite pat. Good girl . . . trailing with your notebook at Eleanor's heels too . . . giving Clumbermere and Co. marks for their interest in Social Welfare. And she's not been looking so glum lately at the wicked party politicians round the lunch-table.

Susan She's been glad to see him busy again . . . and happy.

Oliver Busy and happy . . . oh, what more is there to be! (*He even takes a turn at what he thinks is a most American phrase.*) And isn't it just too wonderful to have the great men that govern the great British Empire feeding off the very next plate!

Susan (*who has a temper*) Will you send that wireless?

Oliver (*his heart speaking at last*) No . . . let him go . . . he was glad to go.

Susan Do you mean to torture him for a week with the doubt if he'll find her alive?

She pressed her advantage quite legitimately, and **Oliver** *owns up.*

Oliver Ah . . . you have me there. Smart Susan!

Susan Isn't it for him to say now whether he'll come back or not?

Oliver Yes. He won't.

Susan I'm sure he will.

He considers this dispassionately, and with a touch of weariness, for he has been at some strain.

Oliver There's time enough then. If I go down to the Admiralty I can actually talk to him. I'll take you. You can tell him in a hushed voice . . . not too hushed, and it'll be a bit broken by the buzzing . . . that Joan has . . . passed over, is the pretty phrase, isn't it . . . and will he please come back and forget her.

But, now that she has made her point, **Susan** *may have a fling too.*

Susan Oh . . . it's been nothing but an afternoon's delight to you . . . the destruction of his going. Oliver . . . what has maimed you so! I'm sorry . . . I'm very sorry. I forgot your arm.

Oliver Maimed in my mind, you mean?

Susan (*remorsefully*) Yes.

Oliver I daresay.

Susan It's wrong of me to be impatient just because I can't understand you . . . or any of you. But this talk about everything, and nothing said about anything! I think that silly old man was quite right about you, Oliver . . . and you don't know what you want.

Oliver There's a worse mischief with most of us, Susan. What we do want doesn't count. We want money and we want peace . . . and we want our own way. Some of us want things to look beautiful, and some want to be good. And Clumbermere gets rich without knowing why . . . and we statesmen sit puzzling how best to pick his pocket. And you want Evan to come back to the muddle of it all.

Susan (*with strait vision*) He belongs here.

Oliver If he'd come back . . . he or another . . . and make short work of the lifeless lot of us!

Susan Is there such a thing?

Oliver As what?

Susan Short work.

Oliver (*feeling, all the same, that she is getting the better of him*) Clever child!

Susan Why didn't Joan marry him? They'd have had some happiness at least . . . and that would have helped.

Oliver (*a last effort*) Why doesn't life pan out into pretty patterns and happy endings? Why isn't it all made easy for you to understand?

Susan Don't mock at me any more, Oliver.

Oliver I'm sorry. (*Then, knowing it is truth indeed as he says it.*) I only do it because I'm afraid of you.

Susan Nonsense.

He looks at her, half-enviously, a little fearfully.

Oliver You're so alive.

Susan (*fearlessly commonplace*) If she loved him she should have married him.

Oliver *shakes his head.*

Oliver Love isn't all of that sort. Sometimes it brings Judgment Day.

Susan But that's when the dead awake . . . isn't it?

Oliver Yes . . . to find this world's done with.

Susan *is ready enough to believe there are things involved that she doesn't understand. But she means to understand them. After all, with good-will, what can't be understood!* **Oliver**

watches her, questioning himself about her, spokes the wheel of her thought occasionally.

Susan I see that he had to go.

Oliver He didn't stop to argue it.

Susan But he'll come back . . .

Oliver If he does!

Susan W h e n he does . . . different.

Oliver Why?

Susan *does her best to say; knows, as she says it, how flat and inadequate it must sound.*

Susan Loving her so to the last . . . and being cheated . . . is like dying for love. He'll be born again . . . in a way.

Oliver You believe in miracles. You would believe in miracles. Simple Susan!

Susan (*simply indeed*) Of that sort. Don't you?

Oliver No. (*And that ends it.* **Susan** *looks dashed, but recovers as quickly. He gets up saying . . .*) I'll go to the Admiralty now.

Susan I'll wait for Eleanor.

Oliver Then you'll tell her?

Susan (*a smile dawning*) That he's coming back . . . and that she won't know him again?

Oliver (*grimacing for her benefit*) Poor Evan!

Susan Wouldn't you want to be raised from the dead?

Oliver No, indeed.

Susan You'll have to be . . . somehow.

He stops at the door and considers her as she sits there, modest, confident – confident, it would seem, merely in an honest mind and her unclouded youth. Then he says . . .

Oliver Do you wonder I'm afraid of you, Susan?

And goes out.

Rococo

A Farce

1911

Rococo was given four matinée performances at the Court Theatre in February, 1911, then was produced at the Little Theatre, 3 October 1911, under the direction of the author, with the following cast:

Rev. Simon Underwood	Nigel Playfair
Mortimer Uglow	Arnold Lacy
Reginald Uglow	Godfrey Tearle
Mrs Mary Underwood	Carlotta Addison
Miss Carinthia Underwood	Agnes Thomas
Mrs Reginald Uglow	Mary Jerrold

Do you know how ugly the drawing-room of an English vicarage can be? Yes, I am aware of all that there should be about it; the old-world grace and charm of Jane-Austenism. One should sit upon Chippendale and glimpse the grey Norman church-tower through the casement. But what of the pious foundations of a more industrial age, churches built in mid-nineteenth century and rather scamped in the building, dedicated to the Glory of God and the soul's health of some sweating and sweated urban district? The Bishop would have a vicarage added, grumbled the church-donor. Well, then, consider his comfort a little, but to the glory of the **Vicar** *nothing need be done. And nothing was. The architect (this an added labour of but little love to him) would give an ecclesiastical touch to the front porch, a pointed top to the front door, add some stained glass to the staircase window. But a mean house, a stuffy house, and the* **Vicar** *must indeed have fresh air in his soul if mean and stuffy doctrine was not to be generated there.*

The drawing-room would be the best room, and not a bad room in its way, if it weren't that its proportions were vile, as though it felt it wanted to be larger than it was, and if the window and the fireplace and the door didn't seem to be quarrelling as to which should be the most conspicuous. The fireplace wins.

This particular one in this particular drawing-room is of yellow wood, stained and grained. It reaches not quite to the ceiling. It has a West Front air, if looking-glass may stand for windows; it is fretted, moreover, here and there, with little trefoil holes. It bears a full assault of the **Vicar**'s *wife's ideas of how to make the place 'look nice'. There is the clock, of course, which won't keep time; there are the vases which won't hold water; framed photographs, as many as can be crowded*

*on the shelves; in every other crevice knick-knacks. Then, if
you stand, as the* **Vicar** *often stands, at this point of vantage
you are conscious of the wall-paper of amber and blue with a
frieze above it measuring off yard by yard a sort of desert
scene, a mountain, a lake, three palm-trees, two camels; and
again; and again; until by the corner a camel and a palm-tree
are cut out. On the walls there are pictures, of course. Two of
them convey to you in a vague and water-colour sort of way
that an English countryside is pretty. There is 'Christ among
the Doctors', with a presentation brass plate on its frame; there
is 'Simply to Thy Cross I Cling'. And there is an illuminated
testimonial to the* **Vicar***, a mark of affection and esteem from
the flock he ministered to as senior curate.*

*The furniture is either very heavy, stuffed, sprung, and
tapestry-covered, or very light. There are quite a number of
small tables (occasional-tables they are called), which should
have four legs but have only three. There are several chairs,
too, on which it would be unwise to sit down.*

*In the centre of the room, beneath the hanging, pink-shaded,
electric chandelier, is a mahogany monument, a large round
table of the 'pedestal' variety, and on it tower to a climax the
vicarage symbols of gentility and culture. In the centre of this
table, beneath a glass shade, an elaborate reproduction of some
sixteenth-century Pietà (a little High Church, it is thought; but
Art, for some reason, runs that way). It stands on a Chinese
silk mat, sent home by some exiled uncle. It is symmetrically
surrounded by gift books, a photograph album, a tray of
painted Indian figures (very jolly! another gift from the exiled
uncle), and a whale's tooth. The whole affair is draped with a
red embroidered cloth.*

*The window of the room, with so many sorts of curtains and
blinds to it that one would think the* **Vicar** *hatched conspiracies
here by night, admits but a blurring light, which the carpet
(Brussels) reflects, toned to an ugly yellow.*

*You really would not expect such a thing to be happening in
such a place, but this carpet is at the moment the base of an
apparently mortal struggle. The* **Vicar** *is undermost; his*

baldish head, when he tries to raise it, falls back and bumps. Kneeling on him, throttling his collar, is a hefty young man conscientiously out of temper, with scarlet face glowing against carroty hair. His name is **Reginald** *and he is (one regrets to add) the* **Vicar***'s nephew, though it be only by marriage. The* **Vicar***'s wife, fragile and fifty, is making pathetic attempts to pull him off.*

'Have you had enough?' asks **Reginald** *and grips the* **Vicar** *hard. 'Oh, Reginald . . . be good,' is all the* **Vicar***'s wife's appeal.*

Not two yards off a minor battle rages. **Mrs Reginald,** *coming up to reinforce, was intercepted by* **Miss Underwood,** *the* **Vicar***'s sister, on the same errand. The elder lady now has the younger pinned by the elbows and she emphasises this very handsome control of the situation by teeth-rattling shakes.*

'Cat . . . cat . . . cat!' gasps **Mrs Reginald,** *who is plump and flaxen and easily disarranged.* **Miss Underwood** *only shakes her again. 'I'll teach you manners, Miss.' 'Oh, Reginald . . . do drop him,' moans poor* **Mrs Underwood.** *For this is really very bad for the* **Vicar.**

'Stick a pin into him, Mary,' advises her sister-in-law. Whereat **Mrs Reginald** *yelps in her iron grasp, 'Don't you dare . . . it's poisonous,' and then, 'Oh . . . if you weren't an old woman I'd have boxed your ears.' Three violent shakes. 'Would you? Would you? Would you?' 'I haven't got a pin, Carinthia,' says* **Mrs Underwood.** *She has conscientiously searched. 'Pull his hair, then,' commands* **Carinthia.**

At intervals, like a signal gun, **Reginald** *repeats his query: 'Have you had enough?' And the* **Vicar,** *though it is evident that he has, still, with some unsurrendering schooldays' echo answering in his mind, will only gasp, 'Most undignified . . . clergyman of the Church of England . . . your host, sir . . . ashamed of you . . . let me up at once.'*

Mrs Underwood *has failed at the hair; she flaps her hands in despair. 'It's too short, Carinthia,' she moans.*

Mrs Reginald *begins to sob pitifully. It is very painful to be tightly held by the elbows from behind. So* **Miss Underwood,** *with the neatest of twists and pushes, lodges her in a chair, and thus released herself, folds her arms and surveys the situation.* 'Box my ears, would you?' *is her postscript.*

Mrs Reginald Well . . . you boxed Father's.

Miss Underwood Where is your wretched father-in-law?

Her hawk-like eye surveys the room for this unknown in vain.

Reginald (*the proper interval having apparently elapsed*) Have you had enough?

Dignified he cannot look, thus outstretched. The **Vicar,** *therefore, assumes a mixed expression of saintliness and obstinacy, his next best resource. His poor wife moans again. . . .*

Mrs Underwood Oh, p l e a s e, Reginald . . . the floor's so hard for him!

Reginald (*a little anxious to have done with it himself*) Have you had enough?

The Vicar (*quite supine*) Do you consider this conduct becoming a gentleman?

Mrs Underwood And . . . Simon! . . . if the servants have heard . . . they must have heard. What will they think?

No, even this heart-breaking appeal falls flat.

Reginald Say you've had enough and I'll let you up.

The Vicar (*reduced to casuistry*) It's not at all the sort of thing I ought to say.

Mrs Underwood (*so helpless*) Oh . . . I think you might say it, Simon, just for once.

Miss Underwood (*grim with the pride of her own victory*) Say nothing of the sort, Simon!

The **Vicar** *has a burst of exasperation; for, after all, he is on the floor and being knelt on.*

The Vicar Confound it all, then, Carinthia, why don't you
d o something?

Carinthia *casts a tactical eye over* **Reginald**. *The* **Vicar** *adds
in parenthesis . . . a human touch! . . .*

The Vicar Don't kneel there, you young fool, you'll break
my watch!

Miss Underwood Wait till I get my breath.

But this prospect raises in **Mrs Underwood** *a perfect
dithyramb of despair.*

Mrs Underwood Oh, p l e a s e, Carinthia . . . No . . .
don't start a g a i n. Such a scandal! I wonder everything's
not broken. (*So coaxingly to* **Reginald**.) Shall I say it for him?

Mrs Reginald (*fat little bantam, as she smooths her feathers
in the armchair*) You make him say it, Reggie.

But now the servants are on poor **Mrs Underwood**'s *brain.
Almost down to her knees she goes.*

Mrs Underwood They'll be coming up to see what the
noise is. Oh . . . Simon!

It does strike the **Vicar** *that this would occasion considerable
scandal in the parish. There are so few good excuses for being
found lying on the carpet, your nephew kneeling threateningly
on the top of you. So he makes up his mind to it and enunciates
with musical charm; it might be a benediction. . . .*

The Vicar I have had enough.

Reginald (*in some relief*) That's all right.

*He rises from the prostrate church militant; he even helps it
rise. This pleasant family party then look at each other, and,
truth to tell, they are all a little ashamed.*

Mrs Underwood (*walking round the re-erected pillar of
righteousness*) Oh, how dusty you are!

Miss Underwood Yes! (*The normal self uprising.*) Room's
not been swept this morning.

The **Vicar**, *dusted, feels that a reign of moral law can now be resumed. He draws himself up to fully five foot six.*

The Vicar Now, sir, you will please apologise.

Reginald (*looking very muscular*) I shall not.

The **Vicar** *drops the subject.* **Mrs Reginald** *mutters and crows from the armchair.*

Mrs Reginald Ha . . . who began it? Black and blue I am! Miss Underwood can apologise . . . your precious sister can apologise.

Miss Underwood (*crushing if inconsequent*) You're running to fat, Gladys. Where's my embroidery?

Mrs Underwood I put it safe, Carinthia (*She discloses it and then begins to pat and smooth the dishevelled room.*) Among relations too! One expects to quarrel sometimes . . . it can't be helped. But not fighting! Oh, I never did . . . I feel so ashamed!

Miss Underwood (*Britannia-like*) Nonsense, Mary.

Mrs Reginald Nobody touched you, Aunt Mary.

The Vicar (*after his eyes have wandered vaguely round*) Where's your father, Reginald?

Reginald (*quite uninterested. He is straightening his own tie and collar*) I don't know.

In the little silence that follows there comes a voice from under the mahogany monument. It is a voice at once dignified and pained, and the property of **Reginald**'s *father, whose name is* **Mortimer Uglow**. *And it says . . .*

The Voice I am here.

Mrs Underwood (*who may be forgiven nerves*) Oh, how uncanny!

Reginald (*still at his tie*) Well, you can come out, Father, it's quite safe.

The Voice (*most unexpectedly*) I shall not. (*And then more unexpectedly still.*) You can all leave the room.

The Vicar (*who is generally resentful*) Leave the room! Whose room is it, mine or yours? Come out, Mortimer, and don't be a fool.

But there is only silence. Why will not **Mr Uglow** *come out? Must he be ratted for? Then* **Mrs Underwood** *sees why. She points to an object on the floor.*

Mrs Underwood Simon!

The Vicar What is it?

Again, and this time as if to indicate some mystery, **Mrs Underwood** *points. The* **Vicar** *picks up the object, some disjection of the fight he thinks, and waves it mildly.*

The Vicar Well, where does it go? I wonder everything in the room's not been upset!

Mrs Underwood No, Simon, it's not a mat, it's his . . .

She concludes with an undeniable gesture, even a smile. The **Vicar**, *sniffing a little, hands over the trophy.*

Reginald (*as he views it*) Oh, of course.

Mrs Reginald Reggie, am I tidy at the back?

He tidies her at the back – a meticulous matter of hooks and eyes and oh, his fingers are so big. **Mrs Underwood** *has taken a little hand-painted mirror from the mantelpiece, and this and the thing in question she places just without the screen of the falling tablecloth much as a devotee might place an offering at a shrine. But in* **Miss Underwood** *dwells no respect for persons.*

Miss Underwood Now, sir, for Heaven's sake put on your wig and come out.

There emerges a hand that trembles with wrath; it retrieves the offerings; there follow bumpings into the tablecloth as of a head and elbows.

The Vicar I must go and brush myself.

Mrs Underwood Simon, d'you think you could tell the maids that something fell over . . . they are such tattlers. It wouldn't be untrue. (*It wouldn't!*)

The Vicar I should scorn to do so, Mary. If they ask me, I must make the best explanation I can.

The **Vicar** *swims out.* **Mr Mortimer Uglow**, *his wig assumed and hardly awry at all, emerges from beneath the table. He is a vindictive-looking little man.*

Mrs Underwood You're not hurt, Mortimer, are you?

Mr Uglow's *only wound is in the dignity. That he cures by taking the situation oratorically in hand.*

Mr Uglow If we are to continue this family discussion and if Miss Underwood, whom it does not in the least concern, has not the decency to leave the room and if you, Mary, cannot request your sister-in-law to leave it, I must at least demand that she does not speak to m e again.

Whoever else might be impressed, **Miss Underwood** *is not. She does not even glance up from her embroidery.*

Miss Underwood A good thing for you I hadn't my thimble on when I did it.

Mrs Underwood Carinthia, I don't think you should have boxed Mortimer's ears . . . you know him so slightly.

Miss Underwood He called me a Futile Female. I considered it a suitable reply.

The echo of that epigram brings compensation to **Mr Uglow**. *He puffs his chest.*

Mr Uglow Your wife rallied to me, Reginald. I am much obliged to her . . . which is more than can be said of you.

Reginald Well, you can't hit a woman.

Mr Uglow (*bitingly*) And she knows it.

Miss Underwood Pf!

The sound conveys that she would tackle a regiment of men with her umbrella: and she would.

Reginald (*apoplectic, but he has worked down to the waist*) There's a hook gone.

Mrs Reginald I thought so! Lace torn?

Reginald It doesn't show much. But I tackled Uncle Simon the minute he touched Gladys . . . that got my blood up all right. Don't you worry. We won.

This callously sporting summary is too much for **Mrs Underwood**: *she dissolves.*

Mrs Underwood Oh, that such a thing should ever have happened in our house! . . . in my drawing-room!! . . . real blows!!! . . .

Mrs Reginald Don't cry, Aunt Mary . . . it wasn't your fault.

The **Vicar** *returns, his hair and his countenance smoother. He adds his patting consolations to his poor wife's comfort.*

Mrs Underwood And I was kicked on the shin.

Mrs Reginald Say you're sorry, Reggie.

The Vicar My dear Mary . . . don't cry.

Mrs Underwood (*clasping her beloved's arm*) Simon did it . . . Reggie was throttling him black . . . he couldn't help it.

The Vicar I suggest that we show a more or less Christian spirit in letting bygones be bygones and endeavour to resume the discussion at the point where it ceased to be an amicable one. (*His wife, her clasp on his coat, through her drying tears has found more trouble.*) Yes, there is a slight rent . . . never mind.

The family party now settles itself into what may have been more or less the situations from which they were roused to physical combat. **Mr Uglow** *secures a central place. There is silence for a moment.*

Mr Uglow My sister-in-law Jane had no right to bequeath the vase . . . it was not hers to bequeath.

That is the gage of battle. A legacy! What English family has not at some time shattered its mutual regard upon this iron rock? One notices now that all these good folk are in deepest mourning, on which the dust of combat shows up the more distinctly, as indeed it should.

Mrs Underwood Oh, Mortimer, think if you'd been able to come to the funeral and this had all happened then . . . it might have done!

Miss Underwood But it didn't, Mary . . . control yourself.

Mr Uglow My brother George wrote to me on his death-bed . . . (*And then fiercely to the* **Vicar**, *as if this concerned his calling.*) . . . on his death-bed, sir. I have the letter here . . .

The Vicar Yes, we've heard it.

Reginald And you sent them a copy.

Mr Uglow*'s hand always seems to tremble; this time it is with excitement as he has pulled the letter from his pocket-book.*

Mr Uglow Quiet, Reginald! Hear it again and pay attention. (*They settle to a strained boredom.*) 'The Rococo Vase presented to me by the Emperor of Germany' . . . Now there he's wrong. (*The sound of his own reading has uplifted him: he condescends to them.*) They're German Emperors, not Emperors of Germany. But George was an inaccurate fellow. Reggie has the same trick . . . it's in the family. I haven't it.

He is returning to the letter. But the **Vicar** *interposes, lamb-like, ominous though.*

The Vicar I have not suggested on Mary's behalf . . . I

wish you would remember, Mortimer, that the position I take up in this matter I take up purely on my wife's behalf. What have I to gain?

Reginald (*clodhopping*) Well, you're her husband, aren't you? She'll leave things to you. And she's older than you are.

The Vicar Reginald, you are most indelicate. (*And then, really thinking it is true . . .*) I have forborne to demand an apology from you. . . .

Reginald Because you wouldn't get it.

Mrs Underwood (*genuinely and generously accommodating*) Oh, I don't want the vase . . . I don't want anything!

The Vicar (*he is gradually mounting the pulpit*) Don't think of the vase, Mary. Think of the principle involved.

Mrs Underwood And you may die first, Simon. You're not strong, though you look it . . . all the colds you get . . . and nothing's ever the matter with me.

Mr Uglow (*ignored . . . ignored!*) Mary, how much longer am I to wait to read this letter?

The Vicar (*ominously, ironically lamb-like now*) Quite so. Your brother is waiting patiently . . . and politely. Come, come; a Christian and a businesslike spirit!

Mr Uglow's *very breath has been taken to resume the reading of the letter when on him . . . worse, on that tender top-knot of his . . . he finds* **Miss Underwood**'s *hawk-like eye. Its look passes through him, piercing Infinity as she says . . .*

Miss Underwood Why not a skull-cap . . . a sanitary skull-cap?

Mr Uglow (*with a minatory though fearful gasp*) What's that?

The Vicar Nothing, Mortimer.

Reginald Some people look for trouble!

Miss Underwood (*addressing the Infinite still*) And those that it fits can wear it.

The Vicar (*a little fearful himself. He is terrified of his sister, that's the truth. And well he may be*) Let's have the letter, Mortimer.

Miss Underwood Or at least a little gum . . . a little glue . . . a little stickphast for decency's sake.

She swings it to a beautiful rhythm. No, on the whole, **Mr Uglow** *will not join issue.*

Mr Uglow I trust that my dignity requires no vindication. Never mind . . . I say nothing. (*And with a forgiving air he returns at last to the letter.*) 'The Rococo Vase presented to me by the Emperor of Germany' . . . or German Emperor.

The Vicar Agreed. Don't cry, Mary. Well, here's a clean one. (*Benevolently he hands her a handkerchief.*)

Mr Uglow 'On the occasion of my accompanying the mission.'

Miss Underwood Mission!

The word has touched a spot.

The Vicar Not a real mission, Carinthia.

Mr Uglow A perfectly r e a l mission. A mission from the Chamber of Commerce at . . . Don't go on as if the world were made up of low-church parsons and . . . and . . . their sisters!

As a convinced secularist behold him a perfect fighting cock.

Reginald (*bored, but oh, so bored!*) Do get ahead, Father.

Mr Uglow (*with a flourish*) 'Mission et cetera.' Here we are. 'My dear wife must have the enjoyment' . . . (*Again he condescends to them.*) Why he called her his dear wife I don't know. They hated each other like poison. But that was George all over . . . soft . . . never would face the truth. It's a family trait. You show signs of it, Mary.

The Vicar (*soft and low*) He was on his death-bed.

Reginald Get o n . . . Father.

Mr Uglow 'My wife' . . . She wasn't his dear wife. What's the good of pretending it? . . . 'must have the enjoyment of it while she lives. At her death I desire it to be an heirloom for the family.' (*And he makes the last sentence tell, every word.*) There you are!

The Vicar (*lamb-like, ominous, ironic, persistent*) You sit looking at Mary. His sister and yours. Is she a member of the family or not?

Mr Uglow (*cocksure*) Boys before girls . . . men before women. Don't argue that . . . it's the law. Titles and heirlooms . . . all the same thing.

Mrs Underwood (*worm-womanlike, turning ever so little*) Mortimer, it isn't as if we weren't giving you all the family things . . . the miniature and the bust of John Bright and Grandmother's china and the big Shakespeare . . .

Mr Uglow Giving them, Mary, g i v i n g them?

The Vicar Surrendering them willingly, Mortimer. They have ornamented our house for years.

Mrs Reginald It isn't as if you hadn't done pretty well out of Aunt Jane while she was alive!

The Vicar Oh, delicacy, Gladys! And s o m e regard for the truth!

Mrs Reginald (*no nonsense about her*) No, if we're talking business let's talk business. Her fifty pounds a year more than paid you for keeping her, didn't it? Did it or didn't it?

Reginald (*gloomily*) She never ate anything that I could see.

The Vicar She had a delicate appetite. It needed teasing . . . I mean coaxing. Oh, dear, this is most unpleasant!

Reginald Fifty pound a year is nearly a pound a week, you know.

The Vicar What about her clothes . . . what about her little holidays . . . what about the doctor . . . what about her temper to the last? (*He summons the classics to clear this sordid air.*) Oh: De mortuis nil nisi bonum!

Mrs Underwood She was a great trouble with her meals, Reginald.

Mr Uglow (*letting rip*) She was a horrible woman. I disliked her more than any woman I've ever met. She brought George to bankruptcy. When he was trying to arrange with his creditors and she came into the room, her face would sour them . . . I tell you, sour them.

Mrs Reginald (*she sums it up*) Well, Uncle Simon's a clergyman and can put up with unpleasant people. It suited them well enough to have her. You had the room, Aunt Mary, you can't deny that. And anyway she's dead now . . . poor Aunt Jane! (*She throws this conventional verbal bone to Cerberus.*) And what with the things she has left you . . . ! What's to be done with her clothes?

Gladys and **Mrs Underwood** *suddenly face each other like two ladylike ghouls.*

Mrs Underwood Well, you remember the mauve silk . . .

The Vicar Mary, pray allow me. (*Somehow his delicacy is shocked.*) The Poor.

Mrs Reginald (*in violent protest*) Not the mauve silk! Nor her black lace shawl!

Miss Underwood (*shooting it out*) They will make soup.

It makes **Mr Uglow** *jump, physically and mentally too.*

Mr Uglow What!

Miss Underwood The proceeds of their sale will make much-needed soup . . . and blankets. (*Again her gaze* *transfixes that wig and she addresses Eternity*.) No brain under it! . . . No wonder it's loose! No brain.

Mr Uglow *just manages to ignore this.*

Reginald Where is the beastly vase? I don't know that I want to inherit it.

Mr Uglow Yes, may I ask for the second or third time today? . . .

Miss Underwood The third.

Mr Uglow (*he screws a baleful glance at her*) May I ask for the second or third time . . .

Reginald It is the third time, Father.

Mr Uglow (*his own son, too!*) Reginald, you have no tact. May I ask why the vase is not to be seen?

Miss Underwood (*sharply*) It's put away.

Mrs Reginald (*as sharp as she. Never any nonsense about* **Gladys**) Why?

Mr Uglow Gladys . . . ignore that, please. Mary?

Mrs Underwood Yes, Mortimer.

Mr Uglow It has been c h i p p e d.

The Vicar It has not been chipped.

Mr Uglow If it has been chipped . . .

The Vicar I say it has not been chipped.

Mr Uglow If it had been chipped, sir . . . I should have held you responsible! Produce it.

He is indeed very much of a man. A little more and he'll slap his chest. But the **Vicar**, *lamb-like, etc . . . we can now add dangerous. . . .*

The Vicar Oh, no, we must not be ordered to produce it.

Mr Uglow (*trumpet-toned*) Produce it, Simon.

The Vicar Neither must we be shouted at.

Miss Underwood. . . . or bawled at. Bald at! Ha, ha!

And she taps her grey-haired parting with a thimbled finger to emphasise the pun. **Mr Uglow** *rises, too intent on his next impressive stroke even to notice it, or seem to.*

Mr Uglow Simon, if you do not instantly produce the vase I shall refuse to treat this any longer in a friendly way. I shall place the matter in the hands of my solicitors.

This, in any family – is it not the final threat? **Mrs Underwood** *is genuinely shocked.*

Mrs Underwood Oh, Simon!

The Vicar As a matter of principle, Mary. . . .

Reginald (*impartially*) What rot!

Mrs Underwood It was put away, I think, so that the sight of it might not rouse discussion . . . wasn't it, Simon?

Reginald Well, we've had the discussion. Now get it out.

The Vicar (*lamb-like . . . etc.; add obstinate now*) It is my principle not to submit to dictation. If I were asked politely to produce it. . . .

Reginald Ask him politely, Father.

Mr Uglow (*why shouldn't he have principles, too?*) I don't think I can. To ask politely might be an admission of some right of his to detain the property. This matter will go further. I shall commit myself in nothing without legal advice.

Mrs Reginald You get it out, Aunt Mary.

Mrs Underwood (*almost thankful to be helpless in the matter*) I can't. I don't know where it is.

Mr Uglow (*all the instinct for law in him blazing*) You don't . . . ! This is important. He has no right to keep it from you, Mary. I venture to think. . . .

The Vicar Husband and wife are one, Mortimer.

Mr Uglow Not in law. Don't you cram your religion down my throat. Not in law any longer. We've improved all that. The Married Woman's Property Act! I venture to think. . . .

Miss Underwood *has disappeared. Her comment is to slam the door.*

Mrs Underwood I think perhaps Carinthia has gone for it, Mortimer.

Mr Uglow (*the case given him, he asks for costs, as it were*) Then I object . . . I object most strongly to this woman knowing the whereabouts of a vase which you, Mary. . . .

The Vicar (*a little of the mere layman peeping now*) Mortimer, do not refer to my sister as 'this woman'.

Mr Uglow Then treat m y sister with the respect that is due to her, Simon.

They are face to face.

The Vicar I hope I do, Mortimer.

Mr Uglow And will you request Miss Underwood not to return to this room with or without the vase?

The Vicar Why should I?

Mr Uglow What has she to do with a family matter of mine? I make no comment, Mary, upon the way you allow yourself to be ousted from authority in your own house. It is not my place to comment upon it and I make none. I make no reference to the insults . . . the unwomanly insults that have been hurled at me by this Futile Female . . .

Reginald (*a remembered schoolmaster joke. He feels not unlike one as he watches his two elders squared to each other*) 'Apt alliteration's artful aid' . . . what?

Mr Uglow Don't interrupt.

Mrs Reginald You're getting excited again, Father.

Mr Uglow I am not.

Mrs Reginald Father!

There is one sure way to touch **Mr Uglow**. *She takes it. She points to his wig.*

Mr Uglow What? Well . . . where's a glass . . . where's a glass?

He goes to the mantelpiece mirror. His sister follows him.

Mrs Underwood We talked it over this morning, Mortimer, and we agreed that I am of a yielding disposition and I said I should feel much safer if I did not even know where it was while you were in the house.

Mr Uglow (*with very appropriate bitterness*) And I your loving brother!

The Vicar (*not to be outdone by* **Reginald** *in quotations*) 'A little more than kin and less than kind.'

Mr Uglow (*his wig is straight*) How dare you, Simon? A little more than ten minutes ago and I was struck . . . here in your house. How dare you quote poetry at me?

The **Vicar** *feels he must pronounce on this.*

The Vicar I regret that Carinthia has a masterful nature. She is apt to take the law into her own hands. And I fear there is something about you, Mortimer, that invites violence. I can usually tell when she is going to be unruly; there's a peculiar twitching of her hands. If you had not been aggravating us all with your so-called arguments, I should have noticed it in time and . . . taken steps.

Mrs Underwood We're really very sorry, Mortimer. We can always . . . take steps. But . . . dear me! . . . I was never so surprised in my life. You all seemed to go mad at once. It makes me hot now to think of it.

The truth about **Carinthia** *is that she is sometimes thought to be a little off her head. It's a form of genius.*

The Vicar I shall have a headache tomorrow . . . my sermon day.

Mr Uglow *now begins to glow with a sense of coming victory. And he's not bad-natured, give him what he wants.*

Mr Uglow Oh, no, you won't. More frightened than hurt! These things will happen . . . the normal gross-feeding man sees red, you know, sees red. Reggie as a small boy . . . quite uncontrollable!

Reginald Well, I like that! You howled out for help.

The Vicar (*lamb-like and only lamb-like*) I am willing to obliterate the memory.

Mrs Reginald I'm sure I'm black and blue . . . and more torn than I can see.

Mr Uglow But what can you do when a woman forgets herself? I simply stepped aside . . . I happen to value my dignity.

The door opens. **Miss Underwood** *with the vase. She deposits it on the mahogany table. It is two feet in height. It is lavishly blotched with gold and white and red. It has curves and crinkles. Its handles are bossy. My God, it is a vase!!!*

Miss Underwood There it is.

Mr Uglow (*with a victor's dignity*) Thank you, Miss Underwood. (*He puts up gold-rimmed glasses.*) Ah . . . pure Rococo!

Reginald The Vic-Cocoa vase!

Mr Uglow That's not funny, Reginald.

Reginald Well . . . I think it is.

The trophy before him, **Mr Uglow** *mellows.*

Mr Uglow Mary, you've often heard George tell us. The Emperor welcoming 'em . . . fine old fellow . . . speech in German . . . none of them understood it. Then at the end

. . . 'Gentlemen, I raise my glass. Hock . . . hock . . . hock!'

Reginald (*who knows a German accent when he hears it*) A little more spit in it.

Mr Uglow Reginald, you're very vulgar.

Reginald Is that Potsdam?

The monstrosity has coloured views on it, one back, one front.

Mr Uglow Yes . . . home of Friedrich der Grosse! (*He calls it grocer.*) A great nation. We can learn a lot from 'em!

This was before the war. What he says of them now is unprintable.

Reginald Yes. I suppose it's a jolly handsome piece of goods. Cost a lot.

Mr Uglow Royal factory . . . built to imitate Sèvres!

Apparently he would contemplate it for hours. But the **Vicar** *. . . lamb-like, etc.; add insinuating now.*

The Vicar Well, Mortimer, here is the vase. Now where are we?

Mrs Reginald (*really protesting for the first time*) Oh . . . are we going to begin all over again! Why don't you sell it and share up?

Mrs Underwood Gladys, I don't think that would be quite nice.

Mrs Reginald I can't see why not.

Mr Uglow Sell an heirloom . . . it can't be done.

Reginald Oh, yes, it can. You and I together . . . cut off the entail . . . that's what it's called. It'd fetch twenty pounds at Christie's.

Mr Uglow (*the sight of it has exalted him beyond reason*) More . . . more! First-class rococo. I shouldn't dream of it.

Miss Underwood *has resumed her embroidery. She pulls a determined needle as she says* . . .

Miss Underwood I think Mary would have a share in the proceeds, wouldn't she?

Mr Uglow I think not.

The Vicar W h y not, Mortimer?

Mr Uglow (*with fine detachment*) Well, it's a point of law. I'm not quite sure . . . but let's consider it in Equity. (*Not that he knows what on earth he means!*) If I died . . . and Reginald died childless and Mary survived us . . . and it came to her? Then there would be our cousins the Bamfords as next inheritors. Could she by arrangement with them sell and . . . ?

Mrs Underwood I shouldn't like to sell it. It would seem like a slight on George . . . because he went bankrupt perhaps. And Jane always had it in her bedroom.

Miss Underwood (*thimbling the determined needle through*) Most unsuitable for a bedroom.

Mrs Underwood (*anxious to please*) Didn't you suggest, Simon, that I might undertake not to leave it out of the family?

The Vicar (*covering a weak spot*) In private conversation with y o u, Mary.

Mr Uglow (*most high and mighty, oh most!*) I don't accept the suggestion. I don't accept it at all.

The Vicar (*and now taking the legal line in his turn*) Let me point out to you, Mortimer, that there is nothing to prevent Mary's selling the vase for her own exclusive benefit.

Mr Uglow (*his guard down*) Simon!

The Vicar (*satisfied to have touched him*) Once again, I merely insist upon a point of principle.

Mr Uglow (*but now flourishing his verbal sword*) And I insist
. . . let everybody understand it . . . I insist that all
thought of selling an heirloom is given up! Reginald . . .
Gladys, you are letting me be exceedingly upset.

Reginald Well . . . shall I walk off with it? They couldn't
stop me.

*He lifts it up; and this simplest of solutions strikes them all
stupent; except* **Miss Underwood**, *who glances under her
bushy eyebrows.*

Miss Underwood You'll drop it if you're not careful.

Mrs Underwood Oh, Reggie, you couldn't carry that to
the station . . . everyone would stare at you.

The Vicar I hope you would not be guilty of such an
unprincipled act.

Mrs Reginald I won't have it at home, Reg, so I tell you.
One of the servants'd be sure to . . . ! (*She sighs
desperately.*) Why not s e l l the thing?

Mr Uglow Gladys, be silent.

Reginald (*as he puts the vase down, a little nearer the edge of
the table*) It is a weight.

*So they have argued high and argued low and also argued
round about it; they have argued in a full circle. And now
there is a deadly calm.* **Mr Uglow** *breaks it; his voice trembles
a little as does his hand with its signet ring rattling on the
table.*

Mr Uglow Then we are just where we started half an hour
ago . . . are we, Simon?

The Vicar (*lamb-like in excelsis*) Precisely, Mortimer.

Mr Uglow I'm sorry. I'm very sorry. (*He gazes at them
with cool ferocity.*) Now let us all keep our tempers.

The Vicar I hope I shall have no occasion to lose mine.

Mr Uglow Nor I mine.

*He seems not to move a muscle, but in some mysterious way his
wig shifts: a sure sign.*

Mrs Underwood Oh, Mortimer, you're going to get
excited.

Mr Uglow I think not, Mary. I t r u s t not.

Reginald (*proffering real temptation*) Father . . . come away
and write a letter about it.

Mr Uglow (*as his wrath swells*) If I write a letter . . . if my
s o l i c i t o r s have to write a letter . . . there are people
here who will regret this day.

Mrs Underwood (*trembling at the coming storm*) Simon, I'd
much sooner he took it . . . I'd much rather he took
everything Jane left me.

Mr Uglow J a n e d i d n o t l e a v e i t t o y o u, Mary.

Mrs Underwood Oh, Mortimer, she did try to leave it to
me.

Mr Uglow (*running up the scale of indignation*) She may
have tried . . . but she did not succeed . . . because she
could not . . . because she had no right to do so. (*And
reaching the summit.*) I am not in the least excited.

Suddenly **Miss Underwood** *takes a shrewd hand in the
game.*

Miss Underwood Have you been to your lawyer?

Mr Uglow (*swivelling round*) What's that?

Miss Underwood Have you asked your lawyer?

He has not.

Mr Uglow Gladys, I will not answer her. I refuse to
answer the . . . the . . . the female. (*But he has funked the
'futile'.*)

Mrs Reginald (*soothing him*) All right, Father.

Miss Underwood He hasn't because he knows what his lawyer would say. Rot's what his lawyer would say!

Mr Uglow (*calling on the gods to protect this woman from him*) Heaven knows I wish to discuss this calmly!

Reginald Aunt Mary, might I smoke?

Miss Underwood Not in the drawing-room.

Mrs Underwood No . . . not in the drawing-room, please, Reginald.

Mr Uglow You're not to go away, Reginald.

Reginald Oh, well . . . hurry up.

Mr Uglow *looks at the* **Vicar**. *The* **Vicar** *is actually smiling. Can this mean defeat for the house of* **Uglow**? *Never.*

Mr Uglow Do I understand that on your wife's behalf you entirely refuse to own the validity of my brother George's letter . . . where is it? . . . I read you the passage written on his death-bed.

The Vicar (*measured and confident. Victory gleams for him now*) Why did he not mention the vase in his will?

Mr Uglow There were a great many things he did not mention in his will.

The Vicar Was his widow aware of the letter?

Mr Uglow You know she was.

The Vicar Why did she not carry out what you think to have been her husband's intention?

Mr Uglow Because she was a beast of a woman.

Mr Uglow *is getting the worst of it, his temper is slipping.*

Mrs Underwood Mortimer, what language about the newly dead!

The Vicar An heirloom in the family?

Mr Uglow Quite so.

The Vicar On what grounds do you maintain that George's intentions are not carried out when it is left to my wife?

And indeed, **Mr Uglow** *is against the ropes, so to speak.*

Miss Underwood The man hasn't a wig to stand on . . . I mean a leg.

Mr Uglow (*pale with fury, hoarse with it, even pathetic in it*) Don't you speak to me . . . I request you not to speak to me.

Reginald *and* **Gladys** *quite seriously think this is bad for him.*

Reginald Look here, Father, Aunt Mary will undertake not to let it go out of the family. Leave it at that.

Mrs Reginald We don't want the thing, Father . . . the drawing-room's full already.

Mr Uglow (*the pathos in him growing; he might flood the best Brussels with tears at any moment*) It's not the vase. It's no longer the vase. It's the principle.

Mrs Underwood Oh, don't, Mortimer . . . don't be like Simon. That's why I mustn't give in. It'll make it much more difficult if you start thinking of it like that.

Miss Underwood (*pulling and pushing that embroidery needle more grimly than ever*) It's a principle in our family not to be bullied.

Mrs Reginald (*in almost a vulgar tone, really*) If she'd go and mind her own family's business!

The **Vicar** *knows that he has his* **Uglows** *on the run. Suavely he presses the advantage.*

The Vicar I am sorry to repeat myself, Mortimer, but the vase was left to Jane a b s o l u t e l y. It has been s p e c i f-i c a l l y left to Mary. She is under no obligation to keep it in the family.

Mr Uglow (*control breaking*) You'll get it, will you . . . you and your precious female sister?

The Vicar (*quieter and quieter; that superior quietude*) Oh, this is so unpleasant.

Mr Uglow (*control broken*) Never! Never!! . . . not if I beggar myself in law-suits.

Miss Underwood (*a sudden and vicious jab*) Who wants the hideous thing?

Mr Uglow (*broken, all of him. In sheer hysterics. Tears starting from his eyes*) Hideous! You hear her? They'd sell it for what it would fetch. My brother George's rococo vase! An objet d'art et vertu . . . an heirloom . . . a family record of public service! Have you no feelings, Mary?

Mrs Underwood (*dissolved*) Oh, I'm very unhappy.

Again are **Mr Uglow** *and the* **Vicar** *breast to breast.*

The Vicar Don't make your sister cry, sir.

Mr Uglow Make y o u r sister hold her tongue, sir. She has no right in this discussion at all. Am I to be provoked and badgered by a Futile Female?

The **Vicar** *and* **Mr Uglow** *are intent on each other, the others are intent on them. No one notices that* **Miss Underwood**'s *embroidery is very decidedly laid down and that her fingers begin to twitch.*

The Vicar How dare you suppose, Mortimer, that Mary and I would not respect the wishes of the dead?

Mr Uglow It's nothing to do with you, either.

Miss Underwood *has risen from her chair. This* **Gladys** *does notice.*

Mrs Reginald I say . . . Uncle Simon.

The Vicar What is it?

Reginald Look here, Uncle Simon, let Aunt Mary write a letter undertaking . . . There's no need for all this row. . . .

Mrs Underwood I will! I'll undertake anything!

The Vicar (*the Church on its militant dignity now*) Keep calm, Mary. I am being much provoked, too. Keep calm.

Mr Uglow (*stamping it out*) He won't let her . . . he and his sister . . . he won't give way in anything. Why should I be reasonable?

Reginald If she will undertake it, will you . . . ?

Mrs Reginald Oh, Aunt Mary, stop her!

In the precisest manner possible, judging her distance with care, aiming well and true, **Miss Underwood** *has for the second time today, soundly boxed* **Mr Uglow**'s *ear. He yells.*

Mr Uglow I say . . . I'm hurt.

Reginald Look here now . . . not a g a i n!

The Vicar (*he gets flustered. No wonder*) Carinthia! I should have taken steps! It is almost excusable.

Mr Uglow I'm seriously hurt.

Mrs Reginald You ought to be ashamed of yourself.

Miss Underwood Did you feel the thimble?

Mrs Underwood Oh, Carinthia, this is dreadful!

Mr Uglow I wish to preserve my dignity.

He backs out of her reach that he may the better do so.

Miss Underwood Your wig's crooked.

Mrs Reginald (*rousing: though her well-pinched arms have lively recollections of half an hour ago*) Don't you insult my father.

Miss Underwood Shall I put it straight? It'll be off again.

She advances, her eyes gleaming. To do . . . Heaven knows what!

Mr Uglow (*still backing*) Go away.

Reginald (*who really doesn't fancy tackling the lady either*) Why don't you keep her in hand?

Mr Uglow (*backed as far as he can, and in terror*) Simon, you're a cad and your sister's a mad cad. Take her away.

But this the **Vicar** *will not endure. He has been called a cad, and that no English gentleman will stand, and a clergyman is a gentleman, sir. In ringing tones and with his finest gesture you hear him. 'Get out of my house!'* **Mr Uglow** *doubtless could reply more fittingly were it not that* **Miss Underwood** *still approaches. He is feebly forcible merely. 'Don't you order me about,' he quavers. What is he but a fascinated rabbit before the terrible woman? The gentlemanly* **Vicar** *advances – 'Get out before I put you out,' he vociferates – Englishman to the backbone. But that is* **Reginald**'s *waited-for excuse. 'Oh, no, you don't,' he says and bears down on the* **Vicar**. **Mrs Underwood** *yelps in soft but agonised apprehension: 'Oh, Simon, be careful.'* **Mr Uglow** *has his hands up, not indeed in token of surrender – though surrender to the virago poised at him he would – but to shield his precious wig.*

'Mind my head, do,' he yells; he will have it that it is his head. 'Come away from my father,' calls out **Mrs Reginald**, *stoutly, clasping* **Miss Underwood** *from behind round that iron-corseted waist.* **Miss Underwood** *swivels round. 'Don't you touch me, miss,' she snaps. But* **Gladys** *has weight and the two are toppling groundward while* **Reginald**, *one hand on the* **Vicar**, *one grabbing at* **Miss Underwood** *to protect his wife ('Stop it, do!' he shouts), is outbalanced. And the* **Vicar** *making still determinedly for* **Mr Uglow** *and* **Mr Uglow**, *his wig securer, preparing to defy the* **Vicar**, *the mêlée is joined once more. Only* **Mrs Underwood** *is so far safe.*

The fighters breathe hard and sway. They sway against the great mahogany table. The Rococo vase totters; it falls; it is smashed to pieces. By a supreme effort the immediate authors of its destruction – linked together – contrive not to sit down among them. **Mrs Underwood** *is heard to breathe, 'Oh . . . Thank goodness!'*

Vote by Ballot

A Comedy in One Act

1914

Vote by Ballot was presented by the Stage Society for two matinées at the Court Theatre on 16 and 17 December 1917, with the following cast:

Lord Silverwell	Nigel Playfair
Hon. Noel Wychway	Henry Daniell
Lewis Torpenhouse	Campbell Gullan
Maid	Magaret Omar
Mrs Torpenhouse	Mary Jerrold

It is one of those days of spring in England when the English spring is behaving itself. The sun shines while through the open French window into **Mrs Torpenhouse**'s *drawing-room and adds another pattern to the carpet, while little motes that must otherwise inhabit the room unseen seem happy in its beams. It is a pretty room, empty at the moment, for ten minutes ago* **Mrs Torpenhouse**, *with a garden hat on, her hands looking enormous in rough gloves, a basket slung to her arm, went out through that open window. It is* **Mrs Torpenhouse**'s *own particular room and she lives her life in it. But it is called the drawing-room; just as* **Mr Torpenhouse**'s *particular room is called the study. Then there is the dining-room, of course, and there is* **Mrs Torpenhouse**'s *bedroom. It is* **Mr Torpenhouse**'s *bedroom, too, but it is called hers. Then there is his dressing-room. There is a spare room where you can put anybody, and another spare room where you can hardly put anybody. And there are places for the three servants (oh, but they will n o t keep the windows open!) and there is a garden room, and a few odd holes and corners. With that you have an upper middle-class English house (be careful about the 'upper') standing in the suburbs of a country town, run on (say) £500 a year. And* **Mr Torpenhouse**'s *salary, 'all in', is £800, so there is a comfortable margin. Besides, there are the accumulated savings of thirty years, never touched, the interest on them accumulating too.*

It is not quite a typical house, for the **Torpenhouses** *are not exactly typical people and the house reflects them: in particular it reflects her. In the drawing-room, for instance, you will find furniture which could only have been chosen by someone who liked good furniture because it was good. There are no wonderful 'pieces', they are not all of a period; but it seems* *that each chair and table must have been asked to join the others, first for its own sake and then because they would all get on well together. The curtains are such pretty curtains and they look neither too new nor too old. The patterns on them and on the wallpaper and the carpet are modest patterns. There are not too many ornaments about either – some few things bought because she liked them, some kept for old association's sake. Vivid colour the room does lack. Possibly to* **Mrs Torpenhouse** *life itself is an affair of delicate half-tones, of grey and blue and mauve, and white that is not too white. Well, everything is spotlessly, chastely clean and well-polished where polish should be.*

On this spring morning . . . and it is nearly noon . . . while she, with garden hat and gloves and basket is outdoors, the square-faced, saucer-eyed **Parlourmaid,** *stiff in print frock, shows into this drawing-room* **Lord Silverwell**. *He is sixty and his country riding clothes are smart. They are his armour, for beneath a quite harmless pomposity one may discern a slightly apologetic soul. A man, one would say, who has been thrust willy-nilly into importance. Nor when we learn that he is a wealthy manufacturer, a self-made man, a petty prince of commerce, need we revise this judgment. Mostly such folk are left wondering, after the first few years, how on earth they did get rich. In their hearts they are sometimes a little ashamed of it.*

But the **Parlourmaid** *whose bugle eye does not discern the innermost of things, is impressed by the visitor, even a little confused.*

Maid Yes. M r s Torpenhouse is at home, sir . . . (*Her little mouth left gaping, then closes on the bigger morsel.*) my lord.

Lord Silverwell Then I'll wait for Mr Torpenhouse. And tell Mrs Torpenhouse that . . . (*But he swallows it altogether*) is here.

Maid Yes, my lord.

The **Maid** *is going as* **Mrs Torpenhouse** *arrives through the window. The* **Maid** *then does go.*

Mrs Torpenhouse I saw you ride up. Someone took your horse? I was down in the meadow looking for mushrooms.

She removes the enormous glove to give him a pretty, hardly wrinkled hand. Though she is not a tiny woman, she is fragile, and there is about her both expectation and surprise, as if she felt that all the queer things the world did do were simply nothing to the queerer things it might.

Lord Silverwell That's a new maid.

Mrs Torpenhouse Yes.

Lord Silverwell She knew there was a title now, but she didn't know what title . . . and I was too shy to tell her.

Mrs Torpenhouse Lewis is at the Town Hall.

Lord Silverwell So's Noel. I said I'd wait for them both here . . . if I may.

They sit down. She shows him a little, though a very little gentle deference.

Mrs Torpenhouse Lord Silverwell sounds much nicer . . . but Lewis says the town was disappointed.

Lord Silverwell (*enthroned in the bigger chair, his voice takes on, I regret to say, a rather pompous tone*) I thought that well over . . . and as soon as I could speak of my impending . . . elevation I took advice. Cuttleton? D'you think that ought to have been the title? I owe the place much . . . it sounds as democratic as a peerage can.

Mrs Torpenhouse But it's how much the town owes you, Lewis says, they were thinking of. I suppose they'd have liked to stand sort of godfather to you in return.

Lord Silverwell (*it's odd: he can be pompous and shy at the same time*) Wychway of Cuttleton, I should have liked. But to ennoble your own name . . . one has to have done something. My own estate . . . Noel was born there, even though I bought it . . . that's modest and yet dignified . . . I hope. (*He looks at her even a little appealingly.*)

Mrs Torpenhouse Lewis likes it. And have you been to the House of Lords yet?

Lord Silverwell Not for worlds! I . . . I . . . it'll have to be done, though.

Mrs Torpenhouse But they don't wear anything special there, do they? Coronets and things?

Lord Silverwell Only on certain occasions.

Mrs Torpenhouse Have you got yours yet?

Lord Silverwell I've ordered one. It's usual.

Mrs Torpenhouse What's it made of?

Lord Silverwell Silver gilt.

Mrs Torpenhouse (*her eyes twinkling*) Now mind it's kept clean.

Lord Silverwell (*she has him at his ease*) Once a week with the forks and spoons.

Mrs Torpenhouse I'm serious.

Lord Silverwell When did Torpenhouse go to the Town Hall?

Mrs Torpenhouse Lewis has been going and coming all day. (*She seems, naïvely, as she says it, to be liking the sound of her husband's name. It is one gentle way of loving him.*) He's very anxious.

Lord Silverwell We're all anxious.

Mrs Torpenhouse He ate no lunch.

Lord Silverwell Noel ate no lunch. I ate a fair lunch. But I'm very anxious . . . and whichever way it goes now . . . most annoyed.

Mrs Torpenhouse *shakes her head. She almost seems to imply that this isn't genuine annoyance, but what she says is:—*

Mrs Torpenhouse I can't take any real interest in politics, so I just don't pretend.

Lord Silverwell (*a certain well-known sort of vehemence growing on him*) At the very best the majority will have been cut down . . . cut to nothing . . . cut to ribbons.

In the simplest way she tries to recall him . . . to himself.

Mrs Torpenhouse But why should you be nervous of the House of Lords when you've been a r e a l Member of Parliament all these years?

Lord Silverwell (*who conscientiously will not be recalled*) My position over this election is a very awkward one. Did you read the papers this morning?

Mrs Torpenhouse Lewis reads both the papers at breakfast.

He begins to perambulate the room, stiffly, in his riding breeches, for greater emphasis.

Lord Silverwell Of course they're sick about it . . . in spite of that one ballot box and our peculiar hopes on a re-count. It's been a safe seat ever since 1886, the second time I held it for them. I promised them it was a safe seat when they offered me the barony. And now if my own son's to lose it . . . ! What could be more awkward?

'They' seems to be not the public generally, nor even the electors of Cuttleton, but some higher, more mysterious power.

Mrs Torpenhouse Yes . . . I'm afraid I don't understand.

Short of someone who understands better than you do, the most consoling thing is to meet someone who doesn't understand at all. **Lord Silverwell** *is quieted, and, pausing in his walk, contemplates her garden basket with a sad but not unfriendly eye.*

Mrs Torpenhouse One ought to pick them first thing in the morning . . . but I can't get up so early as I could once.

Lord Silverwell (*moodily: perhaps he thinks of mushroom picking as a boy*) We grow them in a cellar.

Mrs Torpenhouse's *face lights up.*

Mrs Torpenhouse There's Lewis putting his stick in the umbrella stand.

But it is **Noel Wychway** *who comes in. The Honourable* **Noel Wychway**, *in full etiquette he is, but only for the past three weeks, and he will always drop that silly, snobbish-sounding prefix when he can.* **Noel** *is thirty or a little more. He is an example of what the good things of life, lavishly given, from good food to good education, can do for any man. They can do much and he shows it. They cannot do more, and he, before all people, knows it. He greets* **Mrs Torpenhouse** *punctiliously, and then, amusedly grim, faces his father, who at sight of him goes grimly glum.*

Noel How d'y do, Mrs Torpenhouse?

Lord Silverwell Well, Noel?

Noel One!

Lord Silverwell A g a i n s t you?

Noel Yes.

Lord Silverwell (*with some solemnity*) I'm damned! Mrs Torpenhouse will excuse me.

Noel It's not your fault, Father . . . and I 'm damned.

Mr Torpenhouse *comes in.* **Lord Silverwell** *pounces on him.*

Lord Silverwell Lewis, can we petition? One can always prove bribery, if one wants to.

Noel No . . . let it be.

Lord Silverwell (*protestant: pathetic*) But it leaves me in such an i m p o s s i b l y awkward position.

Mrs Torpenhouse Will you have tea?

Mr Torpenhouse Yes, Mary.

Lord Silverwell Thank you.

Noel (*as he sits and stretches: a man who knows the worst*) By one vote, mind you! Two hundred and twenty-five in that extra box . . . We were fifteen to the good last night, not fourteen . . . I wish the fool had never found it. One vote!!

Lord Silverwell (*with a sudden snap*) I wish I knew whose vote.

Mrs Torpenhouse And have you really not got in for good and all?

Mr Torpenhouse (*who has hovered near the door*) I'll tell . . . what is her name?

Mrs Torpenhouse Kate.

Mr Torpenhouse . . . to bring tea. I must wash . . . that committee-room table . . .

He disappears. A man past sixty; not handsome, not even distinguished. But there is something in his face, a touch of enthusiasm, which would mark him out from common men. There is a touch of music in his voice, a falling cadence which lets you know that sometimes his thoughts are on far-off things. One understands how a woman would marry him. At this moment the woman who did marry him says—

Mrs Torpenhouse Lewis is v e r y upset.

Lord Silverwell (*with sudden violence*) Braxted let us down. Have you seen his letter?

Noel No . . . confound his letter.

Lord Silverwell Lewis has it. (*Then he gets up again, to resume his perambulating vehemence.*) That shows you the personal attention one ought to pay to a small constituency. I did thirty years ago. I spent a solid three years tackling every man in the place. Then I got careless . . . But that shouldn't have made you careless. No, it's

418   Vote by Ballot

not your fault . . . I daresay Lewis remembers . . . he
should have put you in the way of it.

Noel Dash it . . . I've had three weeks . . . not much
more.

Lord Silverwell One vote! I suspect Braxted. If Braxted
had voted straight . . . and you'd been elected by the
Mayor . . . that would have been bad enough . . . a casting
vote!

Noel Well . . . Braxted came down for the re-count . . .
and he told me . . . not that he need have told me . . . that
out of personal regard for you . . . no kindness to me at all
. . . he deliberately spoiled his voting paper . . . so there.

Lord Silverwell (*with one sweeping gesture rejecting Braxted*)
I don't believe him. He went against you. You read his
letter?

Mrs Torpenhouse (*in her soft voice*) Lewis thinks Mr
Braxted is far too violent to mean anything he says.

*Then comes a paternal-filial scrap. Quite good-natured; the
usual happy family thing.*

Lord Silverwell I never liked your address.

Noel You didn't expect me to copy your address.

Lord Silverwell My address got me in last January.

Noel You got in last January because you'd always got in.

Lord Silverwell I'm not blaming you.

The **Maid** *arrives with tea.*

Mrs Torpenhouse Here's tea . . . we shall all feel better
then.

Lord Silverwell (*forgivingly*) Your meetings were excellent
. . . Lewis assures me.

Mrs Torpenhouse And you never went to one of them?

Lord Silverwell A Peer of the Realm . . . you see . . . (*He has to take breath after it.*) may take no part in an election.

Mrs Torpenhouse Not even to help his own son! That isn't natural, is it?

She begins to administer tea; a priestess of consolation. **Torpenhouse** *comes back. But he is still troubled and the trouble seems deep in him. He takes a chair apart.*

Lord Silverwell Lord Mount-Torby may have been too radical for them.

Noel Nobody else was radical enough.

Lord Silverwell He speaks well. Got that letter of Braxted's, Lewis?

Mr Torpenhouse I tore it up . . . I didn't know you wanted it.

Lord Silverwell There may have been a dozen other men who did as he said he'd do. . . .

Mr Torpenhouse Spoilt his paper on purpose . . . he told us. . . .

Noel (*excusably irritable in defeat under his careless mask*) When he knew we'd lost!

Lord Silverwell If he says so, I daresay he did. With all his faults he's a feeling fellow.

Mrs Torpenhouse (*thankful to hear a soft word*) Oh, y e s.

Lord Silverwell If a dozen voted Tory because you weren't radical enough for 'em . . . silly fools! . . . and hadn't the honesty to tell you so as Braxted told you, still a hundred men calling themselves Tories must have gone for you because you're . . . because you were. . . .

Noel Your son!

Lord Silverwell (*with a vicious snap: he is rapidly evolving some real feelings about this affair*) Well . . . not a smooth-headed carpet-bagger of a Conservative penny-a-lining barrister, whatever else you are! I'm sorry to seem upset, dear Mrs Torpenhouse. . . .

Mrs Torpenhouse Give Lord Silverwell his tea, Lewis.

Lord Silverwell . . . But my position with the party whips is . . . I do assure you . . . a most impossibly awkward one. (*And now we can place the mysterious 'They'.*)

Noel It's no use, Father . . . yes, sugar, please . . . we thought we knew the town and every man's politics in it. Well . . . we didn't. I shan't stand again.

Mrs Torpenhouse (*as she ministers tea to poor* **Noel**) Don't say that.

Lord Silverwell (*with a sudden serious rectitude*) Lewis, I hope all the men at the works voted straight. I don't mean those whose opinions we know. There are Tories and Socialists . . . and I've never attempted to penalise a man for his political opinions. But all those that aren't anything in particular. If I didn't think they'd voted like one man for you, Noel, I . . . I should be very deeply hurt.

Noel You'd have won the seat yourself, Torpenhouse.

Torpenhouse *gives him a quite scared look.*

Mr Torpenhouse No.

Noel Well, you've been a first-rate chairman of committee, and I'm sorry I've let you all down.

Lord Silverwell (*as he stirs his tea*) If Noel won't stand again I really think you'd better, Lewis.

Noel (*in settled relief*) I won't.

Mr Torpenhouse (*with that same almost scared look*) I couldn't.

Mrs Torpenhouse Oh, Lewis!

Lord Silverwell Yes . . . why not?

Mr Torpenhouse I couldn't . . . afford it.

Lord Silverwell Now I know what you can afford and what you can't.

Noel (*encouragingly*) You stand.

Mr Torpenhouse There are reasons why I couldn't.

Mrs Torpenhouse Lewis, I think it'd be nice for you to stand . . . if only one felt sure you wouldn't be elected.

The charming inconsequence of this lets **Torpenhouse** *relax to saying genially . . .*

Mr Torpenhouse My dear Mary, don't talk nonsense.

Mrs Torpenhouse (*she smiles gravely at him*) That may sound silly . . . but it isn't.

Lord Silverwell (*with some decision*) Lewis, our factory has made Cuttleton what it is, and my estate is the biggest in the county . . . no credit to me, of course, but that's so. If I can't any longer sit for the place and Noel really means now to go and work up the South American branch . . .

Noel For a couple of years.

Lord Silverwell (*truly a patron and a peer*) . . . who else should have the seat but you? You're my man of business . . . you're more than that by a long way. Confound it all, if it had been your money instead of mine in the beginning you'd be Lord Something-or-other now, and I should be . . . !! And I strongly suspect Cuttleton knows it too.

Mrs Torpenhouse (*as she glows with gentle pride*) Lewis, when you're asked like that I'm sure you ought to, just to show people that it's true . . . some of it . . . of course, only some. But if it comes to being elected and spending all your time in that draughty, stuffy House of Commons we came to see you in, Sir Alfred . . . there, how one does slip back! . . . well, his health wouldn't stand that. And then of course I should have to interfere.

Torpenhouse *bows his head and his voice seems to come from rather far away.*

Mr Torpenhouse I'm too old. I wish I weren't.

Lord Silverwell We must get the seat back.

Noel Don't be depressed about my losing it, Torpenhouse.

Mr Torpenhouse I wish I could begin my life over again. I'm very unhappy . . . I . . . I . . .

With no more warning he bursts into tears and sits there crying like a child. The rest of them are really alarmed.

Lord Silverwell My dear Lewis!

Noel My dear Torpenhouse . . . for Heaven's sake! It hasn't been your fault.

Mrs Torpenhouse Oh, Lewis, I knew the strain'd be too much for you. He's had nothing to eat today.

Mr Torpenhouse It's not the strain. I'm all right. Let me alone.

He extricates himself from their petting; moves to a chair further apart still; turns away, his shoulders heaving. **Lord Silverwell** *is puzzled and tactful.*

Lord Silverwell Elections . . . very wearing things. We'll talk of something else. Give me some more tea, my dear lady.

Mrs Torpenhouse He's not strong.

Suddenly **Torpenhouse** *turns back. There are unashamed tears on his cheeks; one quite ridiculously smears his nose. But his face is vivid and his eyes and his voice are very steady indeed.*

Mr Torpenhouse Wychway!

Noel Yes.

Mr Torpenhouse No, no . . . your father . . . Lord Silverwell . . . I want to call you by your old name. . . .

Lord Silverwell (*encouragingly, as a nurse to a child*) So you shall.

Mr Torpenhouse I have been a pillar of Liberalism in this town for thirty years . . . haven't I?

Lord Silverwell All honour to you.

Mr Torpenhouse Be sure your sin will find you out.

His voice rings aloud. But then his knees seem to give way and he sits of a heap gaping at them. **Lord Silverwell** *gapes in return.* **Noel** *is puzzled.* **Mrs Torpenhouse** *soothes him . . . what she says is no matter . . . in her soft way.*

Mrs Torpenhouse My dear, you're very excited.

Noel (*trying ironic humour as a tonic*) Well, it has at last . . . but only by one vote.

Emotion seizes **Torpenhouse** *again, but this time rebellious, incoherent.*

Mr Torpenhouse Today? Ah! . . . but until today . . . the day of triumph! Oh, it's very difficult! This is my hour!!

Lord Silverwell My dear old chap, you're not well.

Mrs Torpenhouse Oh, Lewis . . . do sit down.

Mr Torpenhouse Mary, I shall confess all . . . with pride . . . oh, with such pride. Noel . . . you have some right to complain.

Noel Not at all . . . take it easy . . . better by yourself. See you tomorrow.

Mr Torpenhouse No; I mayn't have the courage. Noel . . . you're a good fellow . . . In a sense it never mattered with your father . . . and even now he won't understand. Boys together!

He is standing, waving his arms at them. He looks very queer indeed.

Lord Silverwell Of course we were!

Mrs Torpenhouse (*going to him, her tears starting now*) Oh, . . . Lewis!

Mr Torpenhouse Don't hold me! Don't cry, Mary. It was my vote.

There is a silence: and the two other men look at what he has said (in a sense) as they might at some queer object that had marvellously dropped through the ceiling.

Noel What d'you mean?

Lord Silverwell My dear Lewis . . . what do you mean?

Torpenhouse *is attacking them now. He shakes his fist.*

Mr Torpenhouse I needn't have done it. Couldn't I have spoiled m y paper? The Mayor would have voted you in. No, no!

Lord Silverwell Do you mean you voted the wrong way by mistake yesterday?

Noel (*his eyebrows askew*) I don't think that's what you mean, is it?

Mr Torpenhouse (*erect, heroic*) As a Tory I have never fully approved of the secrecy of the ballot. . . .

Lord Silverwell (*with a wild effort to capture the situation*) Lewis, if you're ill let your wife send for the doctor. If you're not, let's understand what it is you're trying to say . . . and stop talking nonsense.

But **Torpenhouse** *only looks at him now in the kindest way and shakes his head.*

Mr Torpenhouse Wychway, we have been good friends. I have served you faithfully . . . I don't regret that. Noel, I am quite calm now and I think it my duty, as chairman of your committee, to inform you that yesterday I deliberately voted against you.

Lord Silverwell You're not serious.

Mr Torpenhouse My vote was serious.

Noel (*grimly*) It was.

Lord Silverwell (*to the listening earth; and the political heavens as well*) But w h y?

Mr Torpenhouse For conscience's sake.

Lord Silverwell (*with a certain direct dignity; after all he is the man's chief*) Lewis, explain yourself.

Mr Torpenhouse It isn't easy.

Mrs Torpenhouse Lewis, don't you think you'd better go and lie down?

Lord Silverwell (*tartly*) No, I don't think he had.

Torpenhouse *now faces his friend and the situation very squarely.*

Mr Torpenhouse Lord Silverwell . . .

Lord Silverwell Don't call me that. I mean, don't say it in that tone. Hang it, man, you queered the election!

Mr Torpenhouse You probably have never known what a moral difficulty was.

Lord Silverwell Haven't I? Why haven't I, pray?

Mr Torpenhouse Well, you've been so successful. And look at the money you've made. . . .

Lord Silverwell I have made it honestly.

Mr Torpenhouse You see? I said so.

Noel (*cutting in coolly; sharply a little, though*) But what had I done to land you in such a queer dilemma?

Mr Torpenhouse (*with perfect simplicity*) Personally I am so sorry, Noel. . . .

Noel No, believe me, Torpenhouse, personally I'm not very much annoyed . . . though I could easily pretend to be. And politically I'm quite excited.

Mr Torpenhouse Thank you.

Noel You disapproved of my special little brand of

opinion? Well, so did my father. He thought my address horrid. It was lucky he'd lost his vote.

Lord Silverwell Don't joke about this, Noel.

Noel But I think we'd better. (*For an air of extreme discomfort is gradually settling on them all.*) Come on, somebody must explain. You felt, for the party's sake, that you couldn't withdraw from the chairmanship . . . so you paid me out privately. I quite understand.

Mr Torpenhouse (*almost to himself it seems*) Oh . . . but I'm punished.

Lord Silverwell Punished! Noel's punished. Let me tell you, Torpenhouse, that you have behaved dishonourably.

Mrs Torpenhouse (*with proper decorum, if they are to disgrace themselves*) Lewis . . . shall I go?

Mr Torpenhouse (*firmly*) I have. But you don't know how . . . or begin to.

Lord Silverwell Then we'll hear the worst, please.

Mr Torpenhouse (*glowering at him now*) I am a Politician.

Noel So we find. No . . . I beg your pardon. (*Noel's nerves are really a little strained and irony is his only vent for them.*)

Mr Torpenhouse A serious politician. For thirty years I have voted straight. That at least is a comfort.

Lord Silverwell Do you mean to say that all these years you have been voting against m e?

Mr Torpenhouse Yes, of course.

Lord Silverwell And been chairman of my committee!

Mr Torpenhouse Well, as chairman of your committee . . . and your man of business . . . I always got you in. What are you grumbling at?

Lord Silverwell This is unbelievable!

Noel No. Get it all clear, Torpenhouse . . . and you'll feel better.

Mr Torpenhouse Yesterday it was sheer force of habit, Noel, nothing else. I felt so sure you were safe . . . by a hundred or two at least. I never stopped to think. And now, at last, when I'd given up all hope of this damned constituency ever doing the right thing . . . to beat you . . . to have my better nature triumph in spite of itself! And by my own single vote!! Mary, God has been very merciful to me.

Caught in this sudden whirlpool of feeling and thought, he almost breaks down again.

Mrs Torpenhouse Oh, hush, Lewis, don't say things like that.

Lord Silverwell Torpenhouse, this is very serious. I've always known there was a kink in you. You've had strange tastes . . . in books and things like that. But I never thought it was a moral kink.

Noel My dear Father, this needs understanding. Don't lumber us up with injured feelings.

Lord Silverwell Noel, please stop treating me as if I were a fool. If ever you have to look back on thirty years of a friend's deception . . . I'm sorry, it's a harsh word, but I cannot take this lightly.

Mr Torpenhouse (*gently*) My friend, I've never taken it lightly, if that's any satisfaction to you. You see, you haven't a conscience. . . .

Lord Silverwell (*exploding*) I will n o t be talked to like this. No moral difficulties . . . lumbered up with feelings . . . no conscience!

Mr Torpenhouse Yes, but I hadn't finished. A tormenting conscience, like mine.

Lord Silverwell Can you wonder!

Mr Torpenhouse I have wondered all my life why spirits should possess us.

Lord Silverwell (*his eyes inclined to bolt; but he tries the heavily ironic, a leaf from* **Noel**'s *book*) Dare I say: Keep to the point? Dare I hint that perhaps you don't know either what you're talking about? With Noel looking at me? No!

Mr Torpenhouse Why could I give my body and mind to working up the boot trade for you . . . and never my soul at all?

Lord Silverwell I never asked for it. I've never given my soul to the boot trade.

Mr Torpenhouse You have.

Lord Silverwell I have not.

Mr Torpenhouse Why, whatever else has made it? My disinterested business ability! Is that the price of success the god of this world asks?

Lord Silverwell We will not argue that.

Mrs Torpenhouse Dear Lewis, what did you want to give your soul to?

Mr Torpenhouse Dear Mary, I've never discovered. That's why I'm a failure at sixty-three. (*Then to his old friend.*) I made you a Liberal. . . .

Lord Silverwell You did not make me a Liberal. (*It is a relief to him to scrap.*)

Mr Torpenhouse I did. It was wrong of me, but I did it deliberately. For it seemed the only thing you could be.

Lord Silverwell I was always a Liberal. You helped put me into Parliament. I've said so . . . and thanked you, more than once.

Mr Torpenhouse You were a voter. . . .

Lord Silverwell Well, I voted Liberal so . . .

Mr Torpenhouse You voted a n y way. (*And then with sudden extraordinary fire.*) Don't interrupt me when for once in my life I'm saying something serious about m y s e l f.

Lord Silverwell (*in cheerful amazement*) Oh, go on! I'm the culprit here, I suppose.

Mr Torpenhouse I was a Tory. That meant something to me. It was a faith . . . a creed!

Lord Silverwell Then you could have stuck to it.

Mr Torpenhouse I was very fond of you.

Lord Silverwell I should have appreciated your independence of spirit.

Mr Torpenhouse Would you? I wonder. You're such a healthy man, Wychway, and everything agrees with you . . . and you do like people to agree with you too. For Heaven has made you yourself as nearly all of a piece as possible. It takes perfect machinery to do that . . . with our boots, doesn't it? But I'm a cobbled bit of goods. I've always known it. And that has made me an unhappy man all my life.

Mrs Torpenhouse *sits there, forgotten. At this her lips quiver.*

Mrs Torpenhouse Oh, Lewis!

Torpenhouse *has not forgotten her. He turns and says with real chivalry, though whimsy follows close. . . .*

Mr Torpenhouse I reverence my life with you, my dear . . . and thanks to the beauty that's in you . . . it has grown into being a good habit instead of a bad one. But it's a habit, Mary, now.

Mrs Torpenhouse (*simply*) Do you remember saying to me years ago when you'd had bronchitis . . . and before the nurse too . . . that there were things about you I must never want to understand?

Mr Torpenhouse (*quaintly*) Yes . . . before the nurse!

Mrs Torpenhouse And I went away and I cried and cried.

Mr Torpenhouse (*apostrophising himself*) Brute!

Mrs Torpenhouse And then I thought: Well, it's only like having a husband and a visitor in one. And I haven't minded a bit; though I've never dared say so till now . . . when we're all old people . . . except Noel.

Noel (*loving her; who could help it!*) Noel won't tell.

Mr Torpenhouse (*stoutly*) I don't feel old. And sometimes I feel wicked. I'm tempted to go kissing pretty girls. And if it wasn't they'd dislike it . . . for I'm not much to look at . . . I'm not sure I hadn't better kiss one and have done with it.

Mrs Torpenhouse (*ever so mischievously*) You may try, if you'll tell me whether she lets you.

Torpenhouse, *quite master of himself now, jovial actually.* . . .

Mr Torpenhouse Well . . . and what are you thinking of, old Wychway?

Lord Silverwell (*in the spirit of it*) You are! A Tory at heart . . . a true Tory, by Jove!

Mr Torpenhouse Why, we're all wrapped in hypocrisies, fold on fold! So shall I set up now as a libertine country squire? I resign my place with you, of course, Wychway.

Lord Silverwell (*attacked thus in quite a new place*) What?

Mr Torpenhouse Don't you want me to?

Lord Silverwell Must you? I suppose you must. Dear me, this is very vexing.

Noel No, no!

Mr Torpenhouse Thirty years' heartless deception!

Lord Silverwell Well, I must be allowed to feel it.

Mr Torpenhouse That isn't the reason. I want to resign.

Lord Silverwell You w a n t to! No, really I think that is too bad. Just when I've taken the peerage and Noel's going away. Look here: what you have done is unforgivable. But after all politics are only politics, and now, by Jove, instead of asking me to forgive you, you make matters worse by resigning. We can't do without you, and you know it. Put your foot down, Mrs Torpenhouse. Whatever else has happened . . . why cap it by trying to break up the whole system of things like this? (*He finishes breathless, but justified.*)

Mrs Torpenhouse (*with judgment*) Lewis must stop working sometime.

Lord Silverwell I think at least it was for me to object to your remaining.

Mr Torpenhouse (*with meaning . . .*) But I know you won't . . . you see.

Lord Silverwell (*. . . which is utterly missed*) No, I am prepared to face a great deal for your sake. I am stupid enough to be very fond of you, Lewis. . . .

Mr Torpenhouse Bless you.

Lord Silverwell (*piling it on, quite sincerely*) I thought we had been something more than master and . . . agent. I thought we had been friends. If I have been mistaken. . . .

Mr Torpenhouse You've not been mistaken.

Noel (*who mistrusts these competing emotions*) What is it you're prepared to face, Father?

Lord Silverwell (*assuming importance*) Well, I have been thinking as well as one could in these trying circumstances. Must the whole town know of this?

Noel (*agape*) Certainly not.

Lord Silverwell Then ought we to tell each member of the committee . . . in confidence?

Noel That comes to the same thing, doesn't it?

Mr Torpenhouse (*a little shamefaced now*) I don't mind hanging on as chairman for a bit . . . say, till the next election's in sight.

Lord Silverwell No, that seems to me a little immoral.

Noel What's worrying you, Father?

Lord Silverwell For conscience's sake, ought there not to be some sort of public announcement?

Noel (*with the utmost impatience*) What on earth good will that do?

Lord Silverwell (*parental; fine-spirited*) It will be very painful to m e . . . very galling. I may be made to appear almost ridiculous. But it is of Lewis I have been thinking. When in doubt, make a clean breast of things. It seems to me that this is a public matter. So somebody should be told. It may not so much matter who . . . and not the whole truth perhaps. . . .

Mr Torpenhouse (*curtly*) I shall tell nobody else.

Lord Silverwell That might perhaps relieve m y mind, Lewis, but are you sure that on general principles you are not wrong?

Mr Torpenhouse Look here! Is the ballot secret . . . or is it not?

Lord Silverwell That seems to me hardly a subject at the moment . . . either for joke or argument.

Mr Torpenhouse Wychway, you're so trying when you're pompous.

Lord Silverwell I am not pompous.

Mr Torpenhouse I beg your pardon . . . I shouldn't have said it.

Lord Silverwell Nonsense . . . you know you can say what you like to me . . . you always have. But you've no right to tell me I'm pompous.

Mr Torpenhouse Who wants to stand in a white sheet with his real and sham opinions hung round him? Confound it . . . set me the example. Withdraw your poster that Wychway's boots are the best. Advertise what we really think of them.

Lord Silverwell Wychway's boots a r e the best.

Mr Torpenhouse Then why don't you wear 'em?

Lord Silverwell If we must go into details . . . because one of my feet is larger than the other and it would be absurdly extravagant to have a special pattern manufactured. Wychway's boots are the best that can be made in the circumstances for the price, and any sensible man reading the advertisement reads that into it.

Noel I've been wearing 'em at all our meetings . . . on the platform . . . and sticking 'em well out. But I don't like the shape.

Lord Silverwell My dear Noel, we have twenty-four different shapes.

Mr Torpenhouse I've worn them for thirty years. And whenever the spring weather comes they hurt me . . . not at other times.

Mrs Torpenhouse I have tried my best to wear them . . . but you don't make a point of ladies' shoes, do you?

Lord Silverwell No. Women, my dear Mrs Torpenhouse . . . who purchase our class of goods, seem to prefer to pay seven and six or ten and six for a thoroughly showy, shoddy article. We make a few . . . to satisfy our retailers, but I have always given instructions for that line never to be . . . as we say . . . pressed. We are wandering hopelessly from the subject.

Noel There's one supreme happiness I could get out of this situation. Torpenhouse . . . stand at the next election on the other side . . . your right side. By Jove . . . if you will I'll come back and fight you and watch you beat me.

Mr Torpenhouse Noel . . . don't mock me.

Noel I'm serious.

Mr Torpenhouse You're not sixty-three. You've not wasted your life.

Lord Silverwell (*sharply*) In my service?

Mr Torpenhouse (*as sharply . . . throwing it back*) Yes.

Lord Silverwell Torpenhouse, you'd better stop. Noel, we'd better go. You're beginning to say things you'll be sorry for.

Mr Torpenhouse Not till tomorrow . . . when you'll have forgotten them.

Lord Silverwell Thank you. Of all the queer suggestions you have made this afternoon . . . that seems to me quite the queerest. I think I may say without exaggeration . . . I am doing my best not to be pompous . . . that this unhappy business will leave its mark on me.

Mr Torpenhouse What sort of a mark?

Lord Silverwell Had we not better let things rest for the moment? We are all very upset.

Mr Torpenhouse But I want you to understand a little, dear old friend, how the whole thing happened. All it ever meant to you and this sweating little town of yours to have a seat in Parliament and you sitting in it was as far from the statesmanship I'd kneel and pray for as the rag heap on which his poem will be printed is from the soul of the man who sings it. I've watched you in Parliament shout and chatter about this measure and that . . . yes, and I've shouted and chattered outside Parliament too . . . it has been so easy . . . taking our tune from those worthy people who are given the country to govern and kindly give us something to chatter and shout for while they're so busy-bodily doing it. From one decade to another . . . the same old tune . . . different words to it. It really didn't seem to me that it could hurt England at all to have you in Parliament. . . . Honestly, I don't think it ever has. . . .

Lord Silverwell Thank you.

Mr Torpenhouse Oh, if having you and five or six hundred men like you talking there could hurt her . . . well, only by God's mercy could she be saved anyhow! And I owed so much to you, Wychway, in those old days . . . and I do now . . . that I felt I owed it to you first of all just to be silent when they asked you to stand. I dug a pit for myself then. I think if we'd waited a few years the other side might have asked you too.

Lord Silverwell I should have refused.

Mr Torpenhouse Why? We could have kept you unattached. Of course, I meant at first to keep out of the vile business altogether. But that was no use. You wouldn't even try to get on without me. I wondered if I could make you a Tory. But that didn't do. You hadn't the stamina or the style. So I had to help you discover that you were a Liberal. Once I thought I'd declare right against you. . . . Perhaps it would have braced you up and made you take things seriously.

Lord Silverwell Take things seriously!

Mr Torpenhouse What I call seriously. But it was that ticklish Home Rule time. I'd have smashed you politically if I had. You were wobbling badly over it, you know, and it wouldn't bear wobbling over. So of course I couldn't. And my fraud grew and grew . . . and all my salvation when the day came was to fold up my little Tory vote so tight and drop it gently in. Well . . . Newman could find comfort telling beads at a miracle-working altar in Naples. It all seems unreal now . . . as I look back on it.

Lord Silverwell Lewis, I wonder at you . . . you still show a most twisted sense of things . . . I must say it.

Mr Torpenhouse I h a v e a twisted sense of things. I told you so. I am the crooked man . . . whose life's a crooked mile . . . he earns a crooked sixpence . . . and climbs a crooked stile . . . into a straighter world for him, he always hopes.

Lord Silverwell Have you ever done a thing for me . . . have I ever asked you to . . . which was not straight as a die? I wish to be told.

Mr Torpenhouse In one word?

Lord Silverwell Yes or no.

Mr Torpenhouse White or black . . . Liberal, Tory . . . true or false. If only God had made you such a world . . . and given it to you once for all . . . why then perhaps that honest best you've always done would be enough to keep it straight! But under our clothes and in your boots we're queer God's creatures still.

Lord Silverwell Frankly, it all sounds to me mere rubbish. But if that's how you feel . . . why you couldn't abstain from voting, I can't think . . . that would have been bad enough.

Mr Torpenhouse I did one year. I simply couldn't stomach the other man that time.

Lord Silverwell Then if you ever let it be a personal question, the least you could have done was to vote for me. No, Lewis, I take that very badly.

Mr Torpenhouse That year I was tempted to vote for you. You were turning so nicely that year . . . but I knew you'd still go the wrong way at Westminster . . . So I didn't.

Lord Silverwell Turning?

Noel Tory.

Lord Silverwell What on earth do you mean?

Mr Torpenhouse Oh, you've been turned for some years now. It has quieted my conscience a little . . . when I grew sure you would. That's why they've made you a peer . . . and for other reasons. So that it shouldn't be noticed.

Lord Silverwell Are you serious?

Mr Torpenhouse Of course.

Lord Silverwell I have never been so insulted in all my life.

Noel My dear Father!

Lord Silverwell Torpenhouse . . . you will apologise.

Mr Torpenhouse I'm afraid I can't.

Lord Silverwell Then we part.

Mr Torpenhouse I thought we'd better.

Noel That seems a pity, though, doesn't it, if you're really in political agreement for the very first time?

Mr Torpenhouse I doubt if we should find quite that. Mine is hardly the official Tory mind. Why should it be? But he of course. . . .

Lord Silverwell Mrs Torpenhouse . . . Good-bye. As I prefer not to be discussed like this in my own presence, I will remove the temptation.

Mr Torpenhouse We must part as good friends as possible.

Lord Silverwell Whether, my dear fellow, it is worth-while our doing anything but forget all the nonsense we've been talking, I . . . I . . . will consider tomorrow. You're an unaccountable chap, you know. You always were, confound you. Noel, if you've your car here I'll drive home.

Noel I'll walk. I want a walk.

Lord Silverwell See you tomorrow, Lewis . . . see you tomorrow.

Lord Silverwell *goes*.

Noel I'll tuck him in warm. You ought to lie down, you're a bit shaken.

Mr Torpenhouse Just a bit.

Noel We must have you in Parliament. Stand . . .

somewhere else . . . next January. It'd relieve your mind
. . . and if you did get in they'd be the better for having
you, Heaven knows.

Mr Torpenhouse What, join that mob of vulgar
demagogues who now prostitute the name of Tory to the
nation! Thank you.

Noel Yes, after a meeting . . . after a glorious rally to our
great principles I used to feel something like that about my
lot. That's really why I'm not standing again. But then I'm
nothing particular. I'd be one of the mob . . . just as he
was. You wouldn't.

Mr Torpenhouse I shouldn't have been . . . perhaps.

Noel Good-bye, Mrs Torpenhouse.

Mrs Torpenhouse Good-bye.

Noel *goes*.

Mrs Torpenhouse My dear, I felt quite frightened for
you. Are you better?

Mr Torpenhouse Better than I've been for years.

Mrs Torpenhouse Oughtn't you to have done it?

Mr Torpenhouse Done what, Mary?

Mrs Torpenhouse Voted wrong.

Mr Torpenhouse I did not vote wrong.

Mrs Torpenhouse Well . . . right.

Mr Torpenhouse It was a matter for my own conscience.
The ballot is secret.

Mrs Torpenhouse I never thought it was really secret. I
thought that was just pretence . . . like the other things.

Mr Torpenhouse I am prepared to advocate the abolition
of the ballot. It compromises dignity and independence.

Mrs Torpenhouse And that would have saved all this
happening.

Mr Torpenhouse It is, in itself, demoralising.

Mrs Torpenhouse You know . . . I've got a vote.

Mr Torpenhouse Of course . . . for that property at Swindlands. Only for the Borough Council.

Mrs Torpenhouse Oh, not a real one. And I've never used it, for it seemed so silly. Is there a ballot there?

Mr Torpenhouse Yes.

Mrs Torpenhouse Then the next time I shall go over, it'll be such fun. D'you remember years ago when we promised to have no secrets?

Mr Torpenhouse I remember.

Mrs Torpenhouse You kept this from me.

Mr Torpenhouse There are others, Mary.

Mrs Torpenhouse I don't mind. I daresay it has been good for you. I shan't tell you about my ballot . . . ever.

Mr Torpenhouse My dear.

Mrs Torpenhouse Are you really going to leave Lord . . . Mr Wychway?

Mr Torpenhouse If he'll let me.

Mrs Torpenhouse He ought to. I wanted you to ten years ago.

Mr Torpenhouse We've money enough.

Mrs Torpenhouse Have we? Could we do anything with it?

Mr Torpenhouse Would you like to travel?

Mrs Torpenhouse Yes, perhaps.

Mr Torpenhouse I've meant and meant to go to Spain . . . not for a week or two . . . for a year . . . to live there a bit.

Mrs Torpenhouse Why Spain?

Mr Torpenhouse I thought of it when I had to learn Spanish for our South American business. What a waste, otherwise!

Mrs Torpenhouse I don't think I should like Spain. But you go . . . why not?

Mr Torpenhouse What . . . after telling you I wanted to kiss pretty girls?

Mrs Torpenhouse They wouldn't look at you. Yes, it was rather vulgar of you to say that . . . and before Noel. Young men think you mean these things.

Mr Torpenhouse It's not such a journey to Spain . . . and if I didn't like it I could come back. You could have Eleanor to stay with you. Wychway won't let me leave.

Mrs Torpenhouse You could make him.

Mr Torpenhouse I'm rather done up . . . I'll take a book to my room. . . .

Mrs Torpenhouse Yes . . . sleep's what you need . . . I do think.

So **Torpenhouse** *goes to his room to lie down. And he may take that journey to Spain, and in the years that are left him he may do lots of other things. Why not indeed?*